Fundamentals of Early Childhood Education

Melodie A. McCarthy

John P. Houston
UNIVERSITY OF CALIFORNIA

Fundamentals of Early Childhood Education

Winthrop Publishers, Inc.
Cambridge, Massachusetts

Library of Congress Cataloging in Publication Data

McCarthy, Melodie A
   Fundamentals of early childhood education.

   Bibliography: p. 343
   Includes index.
   1. Education, Preschool. 2. Child development.
I. Houston, John P., joint author. II. Title.
LB1140.2.M22   372.21   79-18180
ISBN 0-87626-297-3

Design by Amato Prudente

© 1980 by Winthrop Publishers, Inc.
17 Dunster Street, Cambridge, Massachusetts 02138

Printed in the United States of America

10   9   8   7   6   5   4   3   2   1

to

RUTH *and* JOHN

Contents

Preface

This book is written as a guide to the education of young children in pre-schools, nursery schools, childcare centers, and other early childhood education facilities. While it can help the experienced teacher, the text is principally focused on the new, future, or relatively inexperienced educator.

Our primary aim is to provide a clear, coherent picture of an area that is much more complex than one might at first assume. This complexity begins with the fact that the teacher does not merely work with children, although the children are obviously of primary concern. The teacher must also learn to interact effectively with parents, other teachers, and administrators. In addition, she or he must become familiar with the various theoretical approaches within this field, and should be able to relate these considerations to those of the program and of curriculum development and implementation.

We have tried to introduce the reader to early childhood education on a number of interrelated levels. Specifically, we have addressed historical, theoretical, and practical issues and have tried to bridge the gaps that generally exist among them. Our special intent has been to try to "make sense of" theoretical issues by drawing them into, and relating them to, everyday practical problems within the educational setting. We have tried to present major theoretical positions, including learning theory and Piaget's work, in such a way that their relevance to "real," practical, applied problems can be seen clearly.

It is important to be able to apply these various theoretical approaches in the actual teaching situation. We do this by using hypothetical examples and by drawing upon anecdotes and personal teaching experiences. This text contains many practical suggestions, as well. It contains suggestions for determining program goals and ways of reaching those goals. In addition, references for further study and exploration are provided.

The main thrust of this text is developmental: that is, we feel that everyone involved—the children, teachers, parents, and administrators—

are all growing, learning, and changing. In short, they are all developing. Programs change and develop, too: this is a dynamic area, not a static, unchanging one.

Each early childhood educator is a unique individual with her or his own style and character. Accordingly, particular theories and certain practical hints will be more helpful to some readers than to others. No one theory has all the answers for everyone. Practical suggestions will be helpful to some but not to others. We recommend an eclectic approach in which the reader understands and considers all alternatives, and then chooses the ones that will "work" for her or him.

In short, this book is written to provide the reader with an introductory view of this complex, growing area. We have attempted to be helpful, relevant, and realistic. We have tried to bridge the gap between theory and practice in a clear and simple manner.

Finally, to be consistent with the nonsexist attitude advised in the text, we have tried to use feminine and masculine gender words with about equal frequency. Assuming that a predominance of feminine examples might come as a refreshing change, we have, if anything, leaned toward the use of feminine gender examples and pronouns.

MAM
JPH

Los Angeles, 1979

Acknowledgments

We wish to thank the many schools and individuals that aided us in our efforts to write this book. Specifically, we appreciate the cooperation shown by Montessori School, Long Beach, California; Crestwood Preschool and Kindergarten, Van Nuys, California; Isabel Patterson Child Development Center, Long Beach, California; Country Gardens School, Sherman Oaks, California; and Hill and Dale Preschool, Van Nuys, California. Our photographs were produced by Terry McCarthy, Melodie McCarthy, and Dean Hopgood. Special thanks go to Dorothy Miller of the Bandon Day Care Center, Bandon, Oregon, for her support and helpful criticism.

*Fundamentals
of Early Childhood
Education*

1

The History of Early Childhood Education

Education has an extensive history. There are many good accounts of the slow, sometimes almost agonizing, growth of general educational efforts before the 1800s (see Ariés, 1962; Braun and Edwards, 1972; Durant, 1954). The long development of educational theory and practice stretches from the Greek philosophers, including Socrates, Plato, and Aristotle, through the Roman Empire, into the Middle Ages, the Renaissance, and on to more recent centuries. Many profound changes in educational thinking and practice took place in early times, some of which affect the way we live even today.

However, surprisingly enough, it was not until the beginning of the nineteenth century that the education of very young children, or *early* childhood education as distinct from primary and secondary educational levels, began to be thought of as a distinct form of education. Since it is impossible to provide a full history of educational thought in a single chapter, and because our primary concern is with *early* childhood education, we begin our historical review at that point in time when the concept of a distinct field of early childhood education first began to appear. Readers interested in the long, slow, fascinating progress of general education prior to the 1800s are encouraged to look into the sources cited above.

By looking back into history we can identify the roots of many of the ideas, controversies, and practices that are with us today. We see how actions seem to have lagged behind thought, so that many advanced, progressive ideas expressed during very early periods have yet to be translated into practical use. We are still struggling with many of the ideas and concepts which intrigued early thinkers.

Europe: 1800–1900

Prior to 1800 education typically occupied but a few years of the child's life. Most of this would be at what we would now call the primary or secondary level. Only a small proportion of the population received any advanced education, and these fortunate individuals were usually males from upper class families. Early childhood education, as a distinct form of education, was essentially nonexistent prior to the 1800s. In fact, it was only during the 1800s that people began to think of children as anything more than "small adults," and to recognize that they need and thrive upon special attention and consideration.

Johann Pestalozzi (1746–1827)

The concept of early childhood education was brought into focus as the nineteenth century began, by a man possessed of a unique combination of talent, courage, and devotion. Johann Pestalozzi's work with young children in Switzerland spanned a thirty-year period and through his theorizing, writing, and teaching he became one of the most famous and influential champions of early childhood education in Europe.

In addition to an overall feeling of love, acceptance, and trust, Pestalozzi's approach was marked by five aspects. First, his concern for the care and education of the poor never ended. Most of his students were poor. He felt that education was the key to improving their lives. Second, he believed that children would learn most effectively by *interacting directly with the environment and with each other.* He consistently maintained that a firm knowledge of the physical environment and of personal interactions, based upon close, direct contact with the environment and others, was essential for further progress. For example, he taught geography by having children hike through the countryside with him. He would show them the physical features of the area, noting the hills, valleys, rivers, and so on. Then he would encourage them to construct clay models of what they had seen. Then, and only then, did he show them a map of the area. He believed their capacity to grasp the meaning of the map was enhanced by the physical experience with the environment. One could adopt similar procedures in schools today.

Third, while the children were occupied with their physical exploration of the environment or occupied with other tasks, Pestalozzi felt he had to help develop their spoken language. He was convinced that improved spoken language would aid his later efforts to teach them to read and write. Fourth, his groups were usually age mixed. He believed that the older and/or more advanced children could assist him in his efforts to teach the younger ones. Both young and old would benefit from this process. This is an idea that is receiving a great deal of attention in early childhood education today, and one which we shall discuss in later chapters.

The fifth aspect of Pestalozzi's system that bears mentioning is his emphasis on practical skills. For example, in Pestalozzi's world farming was an extremely valuable skill. He felt that, beginning at a very early age, children could be taught the essentials of farming by actually letting them *do* the necessary tasks, rather than by being told about them. In Pestalozzi's rural village setting, the concept of teaching farming through action to very young children was quite impressive. This aspect of his program emphasized his belief in the value of *practical, applied education.* (Later, Froebel would anticipate the growth of cities and begin to train small motor coordination in an effort to prepare his pupils for work in factories.)

After the village of Stanz was ravaged by Napoleon's forces, Pestalozzi established an orphanage there for young war victims. With the help of a single servant, he cared for, loved, and taught up to eighty children aged 2 to 6 at one time! Most of the orphans were poor, uneducated, underfed, diseased, vermin-infested, and lacked love and affection. For one incredible year he was all things to all these children. He fed, clothed, doctored, loved, taught, and worked with them. He helped them to help themselves and each other. Even his most skeptical critics were forced to acknowledge his success. Unfortunately, the facilities were needed for a hospital; and after only one year of care, the children had to be dispersed.

But Pestalozzi continued his work. He wrote several books and established two large schools (at Burgdorf and at Yverdon) during the next twenty-five years. His efforts became well known. Teachers, rulers, philosophers, skeptics, and followers all came to see his schools and observe his methods. Though immensely successful in his work with children, he was criticized for his lack of administrative skills, particularly as his schools grew in size. Dissension among his teachers caused him unhappiness in his later years, and he eventually gave up his last school. He died shortly thereafter.

Pestalozzi was also criticized because he could not formalize his approach. He could not outline a set of rules for others to follow. Others could not seem to duplicate his success. He himself suffered from his seeming inability to communicate the "secret" of his achievements. But the attributes that made Pestalozzi successful with children may *not* be the kind that can be translated into a pat set of simple rules for others to follow. The man himself, rather than his system, may have been the key to his success. To recreate his efforts one would have to be devoted to the unfortunate of the world, totally unselfish, able to instill trust and love, to teach by doing, and be wholly dedicated to children and childhood. Now that is asking a lot. Pestalozzi himself probably did not realize what an extraordinary person he was. As Ulich (1968) states, "Pestalozzi's example of 'Let the little children come unto me' probably had a greater effect on modern education than all the philosophers ever said or wrote about the task or character of education." His belief in children can be compared in our own day with that of Neill at Summerhill (see Neill, 1960).

It is our hope that the interested student will read some of Pestalozzi's own writings, particularly his description of his work at the Stanz orphanage. The intangible qualities of the man himself, rather than some lists of cut-and-dried procedures, account for his greatness; and some sense of his greatness may be obtained through a reading of his work.

Nevertheless, we can perhaps draw three lessons from Pestalozzi's methods of early childhood education:

1. The fact that someone is a good teacher doesn't necessarily mean that he or she can *explain* that success to others. It may be like expecting an artist to explain why his painting is great.
2. The fact that someone is a good teacher doesn't necessarily mean that others trying to emulate his or her style will be successful. Again, the analogy with the artist fits.
3. The fact that someone is a good teacher doesn't necessarily mean that that teacher will be a good administrator.

Friedrich Wilhelm Froebel (1782–1852)

By opening the first kindergarten, in 1837, Froebel, a German, created a profound change within the emerging field of early childhood education. Like Pestalozzi and so many others before him, Froebel was deeply concerned about children. He rejected the idea that they are merely small adults to be treated as adults are treated, believing that they needed care and protection, in addition to instruction. He was very concerned with their moral development. He saw reformed education as the way to social reform, and he believed social reform was much needed after the destruction and suffering of the Napoleonic wars. Froebel believed that more than anyone else, children suffered from these wars.

Froebel's thinking concerning the education of young children was extremely progressive. For example, he believed, as do many modern psychologists, that a child's early experiences have a profound effect upon the development of an adult personality. He believed that childhood has value in itself, and is not just something we all pass through on the way to adulthood. According to Froebel, children deserve the same rights and respect as adults and must be treated as individuals passing through a unique phase of life. He felt that excessive interference in the child's spontaneous discovery of the world about him could be detrimental. Parents and teachers must be patient and understanding. Froebel understood, as did Pestalozzi, that the emotional quality of a child's life is important, and that the child's emotional life is heavily affected by the quality of parental love. He realized that individual differences in interests and capabilities should be considered in devising a curriculum, and that any educational curriculum had to be related to the child's own experience. Finally, he proposed that *play* is a most important activity for the optimum development of a child. All of these are ideas that still permeate early childhood educational thought.

Froebel was a great admirer of Pestalozzi, and visited his school. But he disliked Pestalozzi's apparent inability to express his teaching methods in clear, reproducible terms. As a result, Froebel developed a much more formal, rigid program within his own kindergartens. He employed specially developed objects, called "gifts," and specific procedures called "occupations" for using that equipment. Although he used many activities that are considered desirable today (e.g., manipulative toys, songs interwoven with activities, fingerplay, crafts) many of them were too difficult or too advanced for most young children. Froebel's expectations seem to have been too high. For example, sewing cards had complex patterns that had to be filled with exact stitching. Fragile, delicate, intricate, and complex activities involving sewing, painting, and weaving must have been frustrating for many youngsters. The procedures were too defined and inflexible. They did not encourage creativity or spontaneity. Little time was provided for "free play."

As a result, it was a simple matter for others to duplicate his methods, particularly his "gifts" and "occupations;" but too often his followers became rigid and inflexible in their application of his procedures. After his death, many became much less experimental and less responsive than Froebel himself probably would have been to new information as it emerged from the growing fields of psychology and education.

As we have seen, it is often difficult, if not impossible, to duplicate another person's way of working with children. The more obvious outward actions may be copied; but the thoughts, feelings, and motivations behind the actions are much more difficult to capture. A superficial duplication of activities can become devoid of meaning or impact: it is a trap which the teacher must avoid. We can learn from others, but there is a limit to how much we can copy successfully.

In spite of these limitations, the reader should realize that Froebel's impact on the field was profound. His progressive thinking still permeates modern conceptions of early childhood education. He stressed moral goals and manipulative exercises. He was a pioneer in attempting to create early childhood programs that were relevant, effective, and enjoyable. His kindergartens spread through Europe and America, and, of course, are still with us today in a form modified by years of research and experience. Many of the toys that are popular today are attributable to Froebel. Indeed, it may well be that he invented more toys for children than existed collectively prior to his time. And as we shall see, the enormously creative task of developing toys was taken up by Montessori.

The United States: 1800–1900

Education during the first half of nineteenth century America left much to be desired. Few schools existed, and those that did were of poor quality. Education for the child of ordinary parents was almost nonexistent. Few children attended schools at all. In the north, many worked in factories. In New England, some two-fifths of the people working in factories by 1833 were between 7 and 16 years of age. In the south, many children worked in the fields. The apprentice system, and its promise of personal advancement, died out. Cities and states rarely tried to educate the "huddled masses."

Common School Reform

However, the second half of the century witnessed a reaction to this poor educational climate. Efforts eventually led to the establishment of publicly supported elementary and secondary schools in many parts of the country. These public schools were made possible through the implementation of a new concept: *property taxes*. By taxing property owners it was possible to develop and expand the number of publicly supported schools.

However, even though the number of educational facilities increased greatly during the second half of the nineteenth century the quality of the educational programs within these facilities left much to be desired (Kneller, 1971). The schools were extremely moralistic and patriotic in character. They emphasized the memorization of specific information. Little attention was given to the capabilities, interests, or happiness of the children. Individual and social development was ignored. Although knowledge of child psychology and information about learning processes were developing, teachers were given no incentive to make use of this information.

Horace Mann (1796–1859) called education the great equalizer of the conditions of men. He and other important reformers believed that education would promote democracy and social harmony by providing equal opportunity for all. But Mann appears to have overestimated the ability of the new educational thrust to solve America's problems and to create equality among men. For example, educational opportunities were not made available equally to all the peoples of the country. In the south few schools were established for the poor, and none for the blacks. The education of blacks in South Carolina and Georgia became *legally* prohibited in 1740. In addition, as a result of Nat Turner's 1831 insurrection, it became illegal in most of the south to teach slaves to read or to write. Discrimination against blacks occurred in the north as well; they were excluded from white schools. Following the *Roberts* v. *City of Boston* case in 1849, the doctrine of "separate but equal" schools became the model throughout much of the country for over a century. Obviously, this is an issue that still exists today.

Many nationalities suffered from discrimination in the field of education. The treatment of Native Americans has always been a national disgrace. Though promised education in numerous treaties, so little was provided that in 1880 few Native Americans could even speak English.

It was during this period that women first began to move into the role of teacher. Prior to this time women had been thought too weak to maintain order in the ungraded, unruly American schools. But the new publicly supported schools allowed for smaller, graded classes which, it was believed, could be handled by women. In addition, women could be paid less than men, and could be discharged more easily if they failed to live up to the strict prevailing moral codes.

In general this period was marked by an upsurge in the number of schools of a rigid nature that emphasized rote memory of content areas.

Progressivism

Partly as a reaction against the rigid inflexibility of the existing system, a movement known as Progressivism began in the last part of the nineteenth century. In John Dewey's philosophy we hear the call for child-centered programs, respect for the child, activities based on the child's interests and capabilities, and flexibility in planning, programs and methods. Dewey (1859–1952) advocated well-trained, supportive, stimulating teachers rather than rigid authoritarians. He was one of the first to emphasize the development of *social skills* and the development of *human relationships* in young children.

Dewey and others represented not only a strong reaction against existing conditions within the field of education, but also a positive involvement in the new and expanding field of child psychology. Teachers in both Europe and America began to realize that a study of child psychology was essential for their success in the field of education. This progressive attitude still exists in many forms today.

American Kindergartens

Early childhood education began in earnest in America in the latter half of the nineteenth century. Froebelian-type kindergartens were widespread by the end of the century. As we have already mentioned, it is here that women began to assume a major role in early childhood education. The first American kindergarten (although German-speaking) was opened in 1855 in Watertown, Wisconsin, by Mrs. Carl Schurz, who had studied in Germany under Froebel himself. During a visit to Boston she met, and apparently influenced, Elizabeth Peabody who subsequently opened a kindergarten of her own in 1860. Peabody became a leading proponent of the kindergarten cause. For many years kindergartens in America were not part of the public school system but were supported by churches and philanthropic organizations. Perhaps unfortunately, most of them were heavily influenced by the followers of Froebel, and were of a rather fixed and inflexible nature.

However, the new American kindergarten teachers quickly threw off some of the Froebelian rigidity, and expanded their roles in the lives of their pupils. They not only spent their mornings teaching (and feeding) children in some of the worst slums in the country, but they also spent their afternoons as what would now be called social workers. They understood the child to be not just a pupil, but a member of a family and a community. If the child was to be helped, the family had to be helped. Early kindergartners (teachers) helped find jobs, medical care, and whatever other services were needed. This is similar to what many intervention programs are trying to achieve today, as we shall discuss in later chapters.

In 1873, due to the efforts of William T. Harris and Susan E. Blow, the first *public* kindergarten was opened in St. Louis, Missouri. Public kindergartens quickly appeared in several areas; but the ratio of children to teachers was greatly increased, and double sessions were introduced. Teachers who had been providing social services were no longer able to do so. In a sense, inadequate public funding, and the resulting increase in teaching loads, worked to the detriment of the teachers, the children, their families, and their communities.

Additional problems arose as kindergartens began to receive public funding. Many of these same problems still exist. For example, a gap existed between the kindergarten experience and the experiences encountered in the rest of the school. Kindergartners and first-grade teachers began to clash with one another. Questions arose as to whether the sole purpose of kindergarten should be to *prepare* the student for the first grade, or whether the first grade should continue the more individualized procedures of the kindergarten. How should the transition be handled? Should the three Rs be taught in kindergarten, or merely "readiness"?

It should be clear to anyone involved in this area that these issues have yet to be resolved to everyone's satisfaction. Be that as it may, the introduction of the kindergarten into the American educational scene represented a significant step forward in the pursuit of adequate early childhood education facilities.

Europe: The Twentieth Century

Maria Montessori

As we move into the twentieth century, we encounter the impressive and influential Dr. Maria Montessori, feminist and first female physician in Italy. After several years as assistant in the psychiatric clinic of the

University of Rome, she was appointed director in 1898 (at age 28) of a state-supported school for defective children. Montessori was heavily influenced by the work of two predecessors: Jean Itard, who tried to educate the now famous Wild Boy of Aveyron; and Edouard Séguin, who worked with mentally deficient children. Itard emphasized the preparation of the senses in the learning process. Sensory training became an important component in the Montessori method. Séguin devised many special materials and specific methods in dealing with the mentally deficient.

Montessori further developed these didactic or instructional materials and methods which proved to be extremely effective in dealing with retarded children. Her didactic materials are similar to some of the manipulative and instructional materials found in modern early childhood educational facilities. Montessori's success helped promote the newly developed idea that the mentally retarded are educable. But she did not believe that the usefulness of her materials and methods was limited to the retarded, and in 1906 she was given the opportunity to prove their effectiveness with normal children.

It was at this time that she organized the first of her Children's Houses in a tenement in Rome. The tenement had been rejuvenated through a rather unusual governmental effort to improve the living conditions of the poor. The idea behind the Children's House was new and striking: the school was to be owned by the tenants, and funded through their rent payments. Children between the ages of 2½ and public school age were eligible. By enrolling their children in the school, parents were freed to work, thereby increasing family income. In addition, damage inflicted upon the newly remodeled buildings by unsupervised children could be reduced. Montessori felt that this communal arrangement, and the centralizing of the "maternal function," was justified by the assistance the mother could provide the family by working. She, like many feminists today, believed a woman can be a good mother as well as a wage earner if she is confident that her children are being well cared for while she works.

Each of the Children's Houses had a directress (teacher), a physician (another innovative idea), and a caretaker. Certain rules were enforced with some regularity, as Montessori felt it was important that the parents be "deserving" of this service. Children had to be brought to the school on time, wearing clean clothes and an apron. Parents were required to cooperate with the school's personnel and attend regularly scheduled conferences with the directress. Parents were also invited to observe and/or participate in the school's activities on an informal basis for the purpose of further understanding their children. For her part, the directress was required to live in the tenement building rather than in some more desirable section of the city. She, too, was required to maintain order, promptness, and cleanliness.

The Children's Houses were educational and not just custodial. Characteristically, Montessori brought to the schools her scientific attitudes, methods, and her didactic materials. The schools soon became famous and stood as examples that have been, and still are being, emulated in many countries.

Montessori lived and worked at a time when people were just becoming aware of health and hygiene procedures that we now take for granted. As a result, infant and child mortality rates were rapidly decreasing. Montessori saw this as an exciting and encouraging trend. But in addition, she felt that the mind as well as the body needed to be cared for and developed. Although child psychology was a new field at that time, many of her methods and materials are consistent with modern theories of how children learn. And although she did not emphasize the emotional development of the child in her methods, one can find in her writings an acute awareness of the child's emotions (see Montessori, 1961, 1962, 1970).

Montessori programs are now to be found over the entire globe. They have been adapted to many different languages and cultures. While some adhere to Montessori's original program, others have modified and expanded her techniques and materials.

In the United States, where Montessori programs are found almost everywhere, an interesting reversal has occurred. Specifically, the original Montessori program was developed to meet the needs of the poor in Roman slums. But in the United States, few Montessori programs deal with low-income clientele. In fact *both* the teachers and the students in American Montessori schools tend to be from middle or high income backgrounds. The American Montessori student tends to be from an upper-income family because most modern Montessori schools are supported by tuition fees. Few low-income families can afford to send their children to a Montessori school. Montessori teachers tend to be from higher income levels because, to become a Montessori teacher, they must pass through an expensive training program. Few Montessori teachers come from poverty backgrounds. So the modern Montessori setting often differs from the original poverty-oriented program. In the modern programs, children from motivated and educated families are taught by teachers with similar backgrounds.

Montessori emphasized the importance of *structure* in the learning environment of her students. Accordingly, the Montessori environment tends to be highly organized on the child's level. Much of the curriculum is composed of work with self-correcting didactic materials. These didactic materials, according to Montessori, must be relatively simple, inherently interesting, and self-correcting. They emphasize the interaction between sensorimotor activity and cognitive development. Thus many of them involve puzzles, stacking blocks, and cards containing numbers

Montessori materials are to be used in certain prescribed ways

and letters which the child arranges in prescribed ways. One example involves "sand letters," or large letters of the alphabet with rough surfaces. By running her hands over these textured letters the child learns the essential movement involved in reproducing the letters. (For a detailed description of the special materials see Montessori, 1914, 1965.)

An essential part of the Montessori program is that these materials be used in *certain prescribed ways only*. In other words, the child is not encouraged to explore the materials and play with them any way she wishes. To the contrary, the goal of the program is to have the child learn to use these materials in the prescribed manner. First, the teacher, whose role is also highly structured, will demonstrate how the materials are to be used. Then she or he watches the children as they try the materials, and notes their progress. If the child uses the materials incorrectly, the teacher does not correct the child, or even discuss the situation with her. The teacher merely has the child put the materials away to be tried again at a later time.

Children work individually, and are not encouraged to engage in social interaction. Emotional development is not stressed or emphasized in the program. Montessori believed that self-esteem would naturally follow as the child became more independent and accomplished. Furthermore, the Montessori materials encourage sensorimotor development, eye-hand coordination, and the development of concepts. Children in Montessori programs are encouraged to learn letters and numbers. Many learn to read.

Although some modern Montessori schools have added little or nothing to the original program, others have introduced a number of variations. While they still use the original materials and procedures, they have added to the overall program. For example, raw materials, such as clay and paint, may be included to encourage more exploration and experimentation than is possible with the original materials. Art, music, and dramatic play may be found in some new Montessori schools.

Other changes have occurred. For instance, some schools now encourage the children to use the materials in new ways, as well as in the original manner. This is intended to encourage exploration and creativity. Teachers' roles have been modified and made less prescribed. Foreign languages are taught in many Montessori schools. And finally, the age range of students has often been extended. The original schools contained 3 and 4 year olds. Now Montessori schools sometimes include children ranging from the age of 2 all the way through junior high school levels.

The Psychoanalytic Influence

Although much less influential than it once was among professional psychologists, the psychoanalytic approach deserves mention here (for a fuller description see Houston et al., 1979). Sigmund Freud, founder of the movement, emphasized the importance of the child's early years in the development of a full-blown, adult personality. Freud was among the first to recognize the importance of very early experiences in determining long-lasting attitudes and patterns of behavior. He believed that every individual passes through several *psychosexual stages* on the way to adulthood. Depending upon how successful one is in passing through each of these phases, and handling the associated crises, one can become a well-adjusted individual, or a neurotic, fixated at an inappropriate, early phase of sexual gratification. Freud's psychosexual stages are outlined in table 1.1.

Freud's work, although basically psychological and not educational, is often taken as important within the field of early childhood education because he had so much to say about the emotional and sexual crises facing youngsters of preschool age. Heavy criticism has been leveled at the Freudian approach because (1) there is little hard experimental evidence to substantiate *any* of Freud's ideas; (2) his ideas were based upon his observations of neurotic adults and not normal individuals; (3) he overemphasized the importance of sex; (4) any piece of behavior can be interpreted as *either* neurotic or normal according to his system; and (5) his approach is sexist (Strouse, 1974).

Eric Erikson, although working in America, is mentioned here because he expanded upon European-born Freudian theory. Basically, he deemphasized the sexual content of the developmental stages while empha-

Table 1.1 *Developmental stages of Erikson and Freud*

Erikson's Psychosocial Stages	Age Range	Freud's Psychosexual Stages
Trust vs. Mistrust Adequate care and genuine affection lead to view of world as safe and dependable. Inadequate care and rejection lead to fear and suspicion.	Birth to 1 year	*Oral Stage* Mouth region provides greatest sensual satisfaction. Unfortunate experiences causing a fixation at this level may lead to greed and possessiveness or verbal aggression.
Autonomy vs. Doubt Opportunities for child to try out skills at own pace and in own way lead to autonomy. Overprotection or lack of support may lead to doubt about ability to control self or environment.	2–3 years	*Anal Stage* Anal and urethral areas provide greatest sensual satisfaction. Unfortunate experiences causing a fixation at this level may lead to messiness, extreme cleanliness, or frugality.
	3–4 years	*Phallic Stage* Genital region provides greatest sensual satisfaction. Unfortunate experiences at this level may lead to inappropriate sex roles.
Initiative vs. Guilt Freedom to engage in activities and patient answering of questions lead to initiative. Restriction of activities and treating questions as a nuisance lead to guilt.	4–5 years	*Oedipal Stage* Parent of opposite sex is taken. as object of sensual satisfaction—which leads to tendency to regard same-sexed parent as a rival. Unfortunate experiences causing a fixation at this level may lead to competitiveness.
Industry vs. Inferiority Making and doing things and being praised for accomplishments lead to industry. Limitation on activities and criticisms lead to inferiority.	6–11 years	*Latency Period* Resolution of Oedipus complex by identifying with parent of same sex and satisfying sensual needs vicariously.
	11–14 years	*Puberty* Integration of sensual tendencies from previous stages into unitary and overriding genital sexuality.
Identity vs. Role Confusion Recognition of continuity and sameness in one's personality, even when in different situations and when reacted to by different individuals, leads to identity. Inability to establish stable traits in perception of self leads to role confusion.	12–18 years	

Adapted from Biehler, R. F. *Psychology Applied to Teaching*, Boston: Houghton Mifflin, 1974.

sizing the *emotional* and *social* crises that each individual must pass through on the way to maturity. His concept of the child's developmental stages is also included in table 1.1.

Although the problems or crises contained within each of Erikson's stages may be important in the life of the child, some have argued that it is an oversimplification to tie each crisis to a specific age bracket.

The McMillans

Like Montessori in Italy, Margaret and Rachael McMillan were British feminists who became involved in early childhood education through an awareness of the appalling condition of the children of the poor as they entered public schools. They, too, felt that something must be done for these children *before* they reached public school age. They formed an "open air nursery school" for children from 1 to 6 years of age.

Many aspects of their school (e.g., an emphasis on cleanliness and health care) were similar to Montessori's. However, the McMillans placed much more emphasis on emotional development and creative activities such as play and art work. They started a program of paid on-the-job training for young girls interested in early childhood education.

Following Rachael's death, Margaret continued to write, teach, and train new teachers. She was also instrumental in getting legislation passed that was beneficial to nursery schools. Her influence, particularly her emphasis upon emotional development, spread internationally.

The United States: Twentieth Century

As this century began in America, two points of view, sometimes referred to as the conservative and progressive approaches, were represented in the field of education. The conservative point of view generally emphasizes authority, rote learning of academic information, and traditional classroom settings. In general, the teacher decides what the group as a whole will study, and how and when that study will occur. The progressive point of view encourages a more democratic setting. Individualized programs of study, freedom of choice, a concern for developing general learning skills, and an emphasis on cognitive and emotional development all characterize this approach.

Nursery Schools Appear

Although kindergartens gained popularity in the late nineteenth century, nursery schools, for children under 5, did not appear until this century in America. So you can see that early childhood education itself can be considered to be in its own infancy. The first nursery school—a Montessori school—was opened in 1915 by Eva McLin. In 1922 Edna Noble White opened a nursery school with a training function. That is, university credit could be obtained through work and study in her school. The purpose was to train young women in child care as it related to careers in teaching and social work and/or as preparation for motherhood.

Abigail Eliot: The Ruggles Street Nursery School

At the time Abigail Eliot, a trained social worker, took over the Ruggles Street Nursery School in 1922, it was loosely affiliated with the Harvard Graduate School of Education. In addition, it received guidance from Dr. Douglas Thom, a child psychiatrist interested in guidance for preschoolers and older children with behavior problems. Eliot was among the first to emphasize the importance of both the teacher/parent and the teacher/child relationships. Her school served as model for many new American nursery schools. She was instrumental in starting several new early childhood education projects, including the Cambridge Nursery School in 1923 which was the first cooperative nursery school, and Pacific Oaks College in 1952.

In 1944 the Ruggles Street School was still in existence, although its name had been changed to the Ruggles Street Nursery Training School of Boston. It was at that time that Eliot expressed her educational philosophy in her *Fundamental Principles* as follows:

1. *Children are persons.*
2. *Education should always be thought of as guidance (teaching) which influences the development of persons (personalities).*
3. *Maturing and learning go hand in hand in the process of development.*
4. *It is important that the personalities be well balanced. Therefore, in guiding children, we should aim to help them develop balancing traits at the same time that we try to supply what they need for self-realization. Some of the balancing traits are:*
   security and growing independence
   self expression and self-control
   awareness of self and social awareness
   growth in freedom and growth in responsibility
   opportunity to create and ability to conform.

The interested reader is encouraged to pursue Abigail Eliot's life and work, for she has been extremely prominent in promoting and developing the nursery school movement in America.

NAEYC

In 1925 Patty Hill called the first formal meeting of twenty-five pioneers in the field of early childhood education in this country. This group represented the beginning of what eventually became the National Association for the Education of Young Children. This professional organization has a distinguished membership and remains an influential force in early childhood education today. It publishes many of the crucial and outstanding publications in the field. Its journal, *Young Children*, stands as an important archive of early childhood education.

Legislation through the Years

During the Depression, emergency legislation under Franklin Roosevelt's Work Projects Administration program gave federal support to nursery schools. As a result, the nursery school movement grew considerably during that era. Abigail Eliot was again involved in these efforts.

During the Second World War, the Lanham Act provided more federal money for the care of children from families involved in the war effort (Evans, 1971). A most impressive effort during this time was the Child Service Center provided by the Kaiser Shipyards in Oregon. Under the direction of James L. Hymes, Jr., this was a specially built, equipped, and staffed child care facility. It provided a round-the-clock, progressive program catering to the needs of child and family in normal and emergency situations. Unfortunately, the end of the war brought with it an end to governmental funding. The growing interest in broadly based early childhood education slowed for a number of years.

But wartime testing programs had indicated that high school graduates had become progressively deficient in an academic sense. The blame was placed on progressive education. As a result, educational practices were under close scrutiny by the early 1950s. A new emphasis on fundamental subject matter (mathematics, sciences, foreign languages) began to develop. A new awareness of, and concern for, strong academic training evolved when Russia surprised the world by orbiting Sputnik, its first satellite. Educational improvement became a national priority in the United States over the next decade.

With this renewed interest came a renewed belief in the importance of educating children at an early age. For example, Benjamin Bloom, a psychologist working at the University of Chicago, said ". . . it is possible to say, that in terms of intelligence measured at age 17, at least 20 percent is developed by age 1, 50 percent by about age 4, 80 percent by about age 8 and 92 percent by age 13" (Goodlad, et al., 1973). Statements such as this underlined the importance of cognitive development, and the crucial aspects of early experience.

And yet, in spite of the obvious importance of early childhood education, most legislation that has benefitted early education has *not* been designed for that purpose specifically. For example, in the 1930s money was provided for early childhood education, not because of a perceived importance of early education, but because the money would provide jobs for teachers. Funding in the 1940s was seen as a way of putting women into the war production effort. In the 1960s money was used to break the poverty cycle. In the 1970s the reason for funding has sometimes been more tied up with "getting people off welfare" than with educating young children. As a result, funding has not been consistent; it has tended to dry up when these sorts of issues are no longer of primary concern. Furthermore, laws governing early childhood education tend to be the result of social welfare legislation and not education legislation. In other words, benefits to early childhood education have often been "fringe benefits," associated with legislation designed for another purpose.

Intervention

Work such as Bloom's offered an explanation for the lack of intellectual development seen in children living in deprived areas. These children had just not been stimulated effectively at an early age. The need for early intervention in the lives of children found in deprived conditions became very apparent. *Intervention* is the general term applied to efforts to break into, and alter, the *poverty cycle*. The poverty cycle refers to the fact that children born into impoverished conditions tend to remain impoverished throughout their lives. We discuss intervention efforts in detail in chapters 7 and 11.

A growing awareness of the conditions of the poor, and of minority groups, stimulated by growing militancy among these groups, led to new legislation. These legislative acts led to funds for projects such as Head Start, Home Start, Follow Through, and various parent and child centers. Although funding for these programs has increased since 1964, recent indications point to a reduction of funding in the near future (see chapter 7 for further discussion).

Mainstreaming

Perhaps one of the most significant ideas to develop within early childhood education is that of *mainstreaming*. Basically, mainstreaming refers to efforts to bring handicapped children into contact with nonhandicapped children and to allow them to develop together. The idea is to avoid, as much as possible, isolating handicapped children and to avoid having them grow up believing they are inferior to nonhandicapped children.

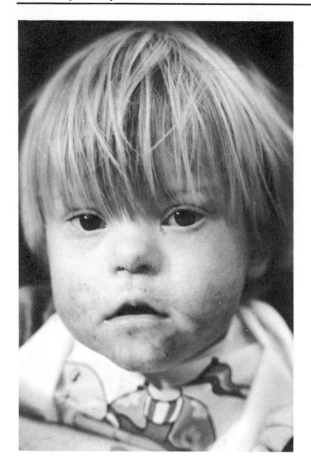

Mainstreaming breaks down unnecessary barriers between handicapped and nonhandicapped children

The handicap can be seen as just one more difference among people rather than some enormously important, frightening, and significant fault. Children can learn that no one can do everything and that a handicap can be looked upon as a difference among people that is no more or no less important than differences among nonhandicapped children. In a sense, we are all handicapped in some ways, or less able to do certain things than other people. Mainstreaming is an effort to break the artificial barriers that can grow between handicapped individuals and nonhandicapped individuals when the handicapped are isolated and treated as "not the same as the rest of us."

Other Developments

Beyond intervention and mainstreaming there are other significant developments in early childhood education which should be mentioned. These include concerns for (1) smaller groups; (2) mixed ages in the classroom;

(3) better teacher/child ratios; (4) more teacher aides; (5) cognitive development; (6) the involvement of parents at home and in school; (7) the development of the whole child; and (8) nonsexist education. Each of these concerns will be discussed in the following chapters.

The Need Grows

Demand for quality child care is again growing. As more and more women, stimulated in part by the Women's Liberation Movement, wish to add alternatives to their traditional roles of wives and mothers, the need for good childcare facilities grows by leaps and bounds. At the present, we are witnessing the development of a great variety of both public and private facilities. In fact, there is such a variety that there is now a problem over which terms to use in referring to the group as a whole. Many in the field resent the terms "nursery" and "preschool" and prefer just "school." We shall discuss some of the alternative forms in chapter 7.

Education today has not solved the problems that have faced mankind throughout history. Many feel education at all levels is still of poor quality, as witnessed by the recent growth of "alternative" schools. More public funding is needed. The underprivileged members of our society still receive less than their share of our resources. We still quarrel over the relative merits of the conservative and progressive points of view. Teachers are still underpaid and forced to live with a "low status" position. Sexism and class structure still hamper equitable educational opportunities. Action continues to lag behind thought and theory. We still have difficulty implementing the programs developed by others. We still struggle to convince others that children need special attention, and that all aspects of the individual's development (cognitive, physical, social, emotional) must be attended to. We debate the "readiness" of children to learn at different ages, and the role and importance of freedom versus control. Religion in education causes difficulties. We have trouble telling one another what it is that we do when we are successful with children. We still have trouble listening, too.

In other words, the problems of the past continue and grow. By perceiving the continuity of problems over time, and by appreciating the struggle that has gone before us, we can perhaps be more ready to face the issues ahead of us.

2

Principles of Learning: Their Nature and Applications

In a sense, the next four chapters represent a continuation of our historical treatment. In these chapters, we look at relatively recent developments within three areas that are of prime concern to the early childhood educator. Specifically, in this chapter we shall discuss the principles of learning and conditioning as they have evolved within the field of psychology over the last half century. In chapter 3 we discuss the structure, function, and development of language. Then, in chapter 4 we shall consider the work of Jean Piaget, and the enormous influence his thinking has had in the area of cognitive development. Finally, chapter 5 addresses the issues of sexism and the feminist movement as they relate to early childhood education.

Our treatment of these topics will be introductory. As we progress, the reader should keep in mind that the literature within each area is enormous. Our discussion attempts to avoid theoretical ambiguities, and will, to an extent, focus upon practical applications and suggestions. For those readers interested in delving into the more theoretical aspects of these areas we shall provide appropriate references.

Having completed our preliminary remarks, we now turn to a consideration of the principles of learning as they have evolved within the field of psychology. Many familiar names are associated with their development and application (e.g., Watson, Pavlov, Hull, Skinner). Many of the known principles were discovered through research involving animals such as rats, pigeons, dogs, and monkeys. But humans have also been studied extensively, and the applicability of the general principles of learning to humans, including very young children, is quite logical and often helpful. We do not intend to imply that the learning theory approach has all the answers. But, taken together with other approaches now gaining recognition in the field, it can be useful to the early childhood educator.

Definition of Learning

What are these principles of learning? As researchers in this area quickly discovered, one must first ask, "What is learning?" Many definitions are available, but we shall use one developed by Gregory Kimble (1961, 1967).

It is essentially the same as those proposed by others (e.g., Logan, 1970). According to Kimble, learning is "a relatively permanent change in behavior potentiality which occurs as a result of reinforced practice." What exactly does this mean? Let us look more closely at this definition.

First, Kimble says that learning refers to a "relatively permanent" change in behavior. He thus excludes *temporary* changes in behavior that we do not consider learned changes. For example, a child sleeps when tired, and eats when hungry. Clearly, these are behavior changes, but they probably do not represent new learning. They are temporary changes due to shifts in motivational states, and do not represent new learning. Kimble also includes the term "practice" in his definition of learning. By including this, he excludes behavior changes due to such factors as aging, disease, or accidents. Such factors can easily result in various permanent changes in behavior potentiality, but they are not considered learned changes. For example, the behavior potentiality of a child who has suffered brain damage in a car accident may be permanently changed, but this is not a practiced change and would not be considered new learning.

You may also have noted that Kimble uses the term "behavior potentiality" rather than simply "behavior." Why does he do this? There is a subtle, but important difference in the two terms. Suppose, for example, you are the teacher of a class of very young children. A new child joins your group, and it's her first day at school. She knows how to run, jump, paint, ride a tricycle, and do a variety of things the other children are doing (she has the behavior potentiality), but you do not know this because she is shy and will only cling to her mother or father. Her capacity to do these things remains latent until she feels confident and comfortable in her new surroundings. The actual learned capacities of many children are not apparent when they first start school, and the rate at which they overtly express their learned behaviors varies from child to child and from situation to situation. A teacher who can establish a feeling of trust and support in class will be shown many "secrets" much more quickly than will a teacher who is harsh and unaccepting.

As you can see, it is important, when studying learning, to distinguish between "learning" and "performance." A child's "performance" is not necessarily a true measure of the child's learning. Learning is invisible, and unless the child is motivated to exhibit such learning, it may never be seen. Therefore, when we try to infer how much learning has occurred by looking at performance, we *must* be aware of the fact that motivation as well as learning determines performance (Houston, 1976). In other words, what you see is not necessarily what the child has learned. For a variety of reasons, a child may hold back.

The last part of the definition of learning that we need to consider is "reinforced practice." Reinforcement is a very important concept for the teacher to understand, and to learn to use. Its implications are tremendous. Its application in the classroom (and in life in general) can be one of the most powerful tools you will ever possess. This is a concept we will be examining throughout this book. We hope you will come to realize its complexities and its enormous possibilities as our discussion progresses. For now, think of reinforcement as *reward*.

Classical Conditioning

Having considered a "word definition" of learning, let us turn to a consideration of some different types of learning that are relevant to early childhood education. Learning occurs in a variety of ways in humans and animals. We begin by considering one of the simplest, but not the least important, forms of learning. *Classical conditioning* is a form of learning which is particularly relevant to our study of young children. (This form of conditioning is also known as *Pavlovian* and as *respondent* conditioning.) As we shall soon demonstrate, classical conditioning is particularly pertinent in establishing a child's emotional responses to people, places, and things.

Pavlov's Experiments

Ivan Pavlov's classical conditioning studies are among the most famous and influential in psychology. We shall describe the basic experiment (Pavlov, 1927) and then discuss implications for learning in the young child.

Prior to conditioning, a dog's salivary ducts would be surgically treated so that the flow of saliva could be measured accurately. The dog would be harnessed as shown in figure 2.1. Then a tuning fork would be sounded. At this point the tone did not cause the dog to salivate. Several seconds later, dry meat powder was moved close to the dog's mouth. The dog would then eat, causing saliva to flow. This procedure would then be repeated many times, the sound of the tuning fork being paired each time with the presentation of the meat powder. After a number of these repetitions, Pavlov found that even when the tone was sounded without any meat powder being presented, the dog would salivate. The salivary response had become classically conditioned to the tone.

At first glance this experiment does not seem particularly relevant to the early childhood education setting. But it demonstrated a phenomenon the importance of which should become obvious as we describe an early experiment by Watson and Rayner (1920).

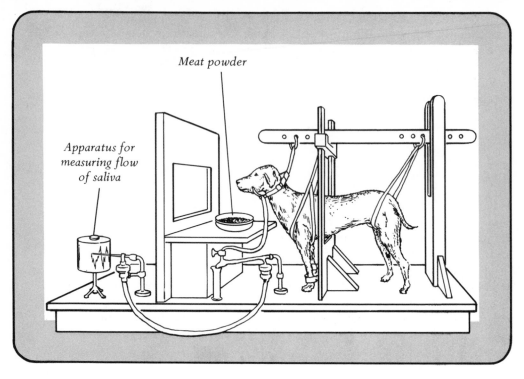

Meat powder

Apparatus for measuring flow of saliva

Figure 2.1 *Pavlov's salivary conditioning apparatus (Adapted from R. M. Yerkes and S. Morgulis, "The Method of Pavlov in Animal Psychology,"* Psychological Bulletin, 6, 1909)

Emotional Conditioning

In the Watson and Rayner study, a young child was classically conditioned to fear a white rat. Prior to the experiment the child had liked and wanted to play with this animal. During the experiment the presentation of the white rat was repeatedly paired with the terrifying noise of a hammer hitting an iron bar. Soon the presentation of the rat alone elicited a fear response in the child. Not only did the child learn to fear the rat, but the fear generalized to a white rabbit, a white dog, and a white fur coat. A negative emotional reaction had been classically conditioned. Incidentally, this cruel form of experimentation is no longer done.

Young children probably undergo many types of emotional classical conditioning. Through classical conditioning, they learn to respond in certain ways to certain stimuli. A series of injections received in a doctor's office can result in a fear response to the doctor's office alone. The presence of a babysitter, paired with parents going out for the evening, can result in tears at the mere sight of the babysitter. But classical conditioning can occur in a positive manner as well. A pleasant first day at school or a pleasant initial interaction with a teacher can elicit a happy response upon subsequent encounters. Can you think of other examples of classical conditioning? What about certain songs that bring back particular feelings from the past?

Four Essential Elements

Let us look at the basic elements involved in every classical conditioning situation. It is important to do this for two reasons. First, only if we know the elements of classical conditioning are we able to judge whether or not a particular piece of behavior occurring in class is classically conditioned behavior. Second, if we deliberately plan to establish or avoid classical conditioning, we must be familiar with the fundamentals of what we are pursuing or avoiding.

The unconditioned stimulus (UCS) is a stimulus that always elicits a particular "natural" or innate response prior to the experiment. In Pavlov's experiment the UCS was the meat powder, while in Watson and Rayner's experiment the UCS was the loud noise.

The unconditioned response (UCR) is the particular response which is always elicited by the UCS. In Pavlov's experiment the UCR was the salivation response to the meat powder, and in Watson and Rayner's experiment the UCR was the child's fear in response to the loud noise.

The conditioned stimulus (CS) is the new, neutral stimulus introduced into the experiment. Initially, this stimulus does not elicit any response. In the first experiment the CS was the tone, while in the second the CS was the white rat.

The conditioned response (CR) is the response to the CS that is learned in the experiment. The salivation in response to the tone (CS) alone, and the fear in response to the rat (CS) alone are conditioned responses.

The UCR is an *innate* response to the UCS, while the CR is a *learned* response to the CS. (For further discussion of these elements the reader is referred to Hulse, Deese, and Egeth, 1975, and Adams, 1976.) For present purposes, it is sufficient to know that if we are to identify a situation as one involving classical conditioning, then we must be able to identify these four essential elements. If we cannot find the four elements, then we are probably not dealing with classical conditioning. For example, suppose you find that one of your children cries almost immediately each time she is brought into a particular room. Is it possible that this is a classically conditioned response? The only way to be sure is to try to analyze the situation in terms of the four elements. Crying would be the conditioned response. The room would be the conditioned stimulus. What might the unconditioned stimulus be, and how might you go about identifying it? Has the child been frightened recently in that or similar rooms? Ask your colleagues, and ask the other children. You may be able to understand the behavior through a little detective work.

Delayed Procedures

There has been a great deal of discussion and experimentation regarding the order in which the CS and UCS should be presented, and the amount of time that should pass between them. Basically, the most effective arrangement for classical conditioning seems to be what is called the delayed procedure. In a delayed procedure, CS presentation occurs before the UCS presentation. The CS remains "on" at least until the UCS is presented. A CS-UCS interval of 0.5 seconds has often been found to be very successful. (For further discussion of these and many other issues in the field of learning, we refer you to Houston, 1976.)

Of What Value Is All This?

What does classical conditioning mean to you as a teacher of young children? How can you utilize this concept in school? Do these basic procedures, developed in psychology laboratories, have useful implications for human relationships outside the laboratory? We feel they do, especially in the area of emotional responses. If a teacher can become aware of how emotional responses, positive and negative, are instilled, there are at least three important benefits. (1) The teacher can learn to avoid situations which might lead to inappropriate, negative emotional responses; (2) the teacher can learn to plan procedures and arrange the environment so that positive, appropriate emotional responses will be assured; (3) given that children have already learned some inappropriate and negative responses, either before coming to the teacher or during those times when the teacher was unable to control the situation, the teacher may be able to understand how such a response was developed, and help the child acquire new and more appropriate responses to the same situation.

Let us begin by providing a few examples of the ways in which positive emotional reactions may be facilitated. A good time to try out your newly acquired knowledge is when you are introducing the child to a new situation, a new activity, or a new person. A little forethought can be most helpful, if not vital, to making the introduction a success. At best these new situations (call them the CS) can be threatening by themselves. But if they are accompanied by *additional* distressing events (call them the UCS) such as a distraught parent, an indifferent, cold, or frazzled teacher, or a loud, noisy, confusing background, then the emotional responses elicited can become classically conditioned to the event in question. Events such as starting school, staying for lunch, going on a field trip, or taking a nap at school can become conditioned stimuli and will tend to elicit whatever emotional reactions were present *when the child was first introduced to them.* If the new activity is introduced in a positive atmosphere, then it will tend to elicit positive feelings in the future. If the introduction occurs in a negative atmosphere, then negative feelings may be classically conditioned.

As we indicated above, these times of introduction are particularly important, for the mere process of meeting the "unknown" can be unsettling. Hence, any additional emotional content thrown into the situation can be important, either reducing the child's anxiety or increasing it. For example, little things such as the difference between the way the classroom looks at naptime (with furniture and toys pushed to the sides, the cots laid out, and the lights turned down low) can make an unprepared child fearful. If not counteracted by a reassuring teacher, and especially if exaggerated by a cold environment or an inattentive teacher, the negative feelings associated with this event can persist and lead to more difficulties in the future. For example, one tense, crying child during naptime can lead to other children becoming "spooked." This, in turn, can lead to more crying, which can prevent anyone's being able to sleep. Tired, irritable children can irritate and unsettle teachers and lead to apprehension on everyone's part concerning the next day's naptime. Once at home the mere thought (CS) of the naptime experience can key off negative feelings (CR) in the child. The child may have nightmares, Mom and Dad may not get enough sleep, and the child may not want to go to school the next day.

In other words, big trouble for everyone involved. And all because a child didn't know how wonderfully magical naptime can be in a soothing environment—with soft music ("who will pick out the record today?"), special stories, a special camping cot, a blanket, pillow, or stuffed animal from home, and teacher there to help with rubbing tummies and tucking in. In other words, be sure that there are plenty of positive feelings when children have to become classically conditioned to new, unsettling events. A key factor is a calm, confident (because you know everything is all right), supportive, happy teacher. The teacher serves as a UCS, and the emotions she or he elicits in the child will become conditioned to the school experience. The clever teacher will be able to see many examples of classically conditioned emotional reactions in the course of everyday work. With practice, a knowledge of the elements of classical conditioning can aid the teacher in maximizing positive experiences.

One can almost feel the positive emotion here . . . and some of it may be classically conditioned

Instrumental Conditioning

Having dealt with the basic principles of classical conditioning and having looked at some potentially useful applications of these principles in the classroom, let us turn to another form of learning that has been labeled *instrumental conditioning.* (A controversy exists as to whether or not classical and instrumental conditioning represent truly different forms of learning. For our purpose, we shall consider them to be, at least on a procedural level, different.)

The Harvard professor B. F. Skinner is a prominent figure in the area of conditioning. In addition to having written many influential books and articles, he is responsible for developing a piece of equipment known as the Skinner box. In its simplest form the Skinner box is an enclosure containing a lever and a food tray. The lever is set up in such a way that when it is pressed a pellet of food drops into the tray (see figure 2.2). A hungry animal, such as a rat, may be placed in the box. Eventually, the animal learns to press the lever regularly to receive the reward (food pellets). This "learning process" is aided by a technique known as *shaping,* which we discuss below. The rat learning to press the lever for food is a simple example of instrumental conditioning. For now, think of instrumental conditioning as learning to do something for reward. Human examples would include a child learning to keep his room tidy

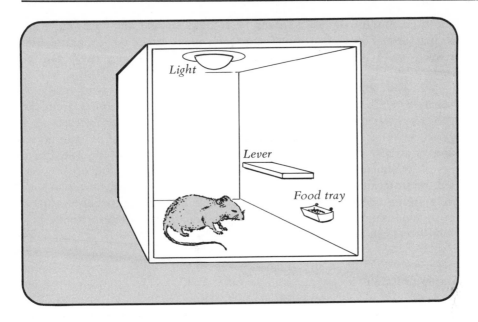

Figure 2.2 *A simple Skinner box*

in return for parental praise or an allowance, a child learning to speak for social rewards, a child learning to hold a pair of scissors for the feelings of self-satisfaction, and so on. Although first investigated among animals in Skinner boxes, instrumental conditioning has proven to be a widespread human phenomenon. Skinner called this *operant conditioning*. Although some psychologists argue that operant and instrumental conditioning are different forms of conditioning (Ellis, 1972), the two will be considered as one in this book.

Positive and Negative Reinforcement

The concept of *reinforcement* is critical in any understanding of instrumental conditioning, for, basically, instrumentally learned responses are reinforced responses. The child will repeat those actions that have, in the past, been reinforced.

There are two kinds of reinforcers. Positive reinforcement is anything that will tend to strengthen a response when it is *given to* the subject after the subject makes the response. For example, if a child makes a first, awkward effort to paste paper onto paper and is reinforced by the teacher saying "Good," then that child may be more likely to experiment further with paper and paste. Of course, different people find different things rewarding. For small children a great many positive reinforcers, both obvious and subtle, can aid learning: attention, toys, presents, parental and teacher praise, hugs and kisses, the chance to do a desired activity, or just a feeling of accomplishment and "growing big." It has been found that satisfying one's own curiosity, congratulating oneself on a job well done, and perhaps even learning itself can be rewarding.

The second kind of reinforcer is the negative reinforcer. A negative reinforcer is something unpleasant that is *taken away* from the subject, or removed from the learning situation, after a certain response is given, in order to strengthen that response. The removal of uncomfortable or painful stimuli such as heat, cold, or noise, can be very satisfying.

Although some psychologists think that learning can occur without reinforcement (Guthrie, 1952), few would deny that rewards have very strong effects on behavior. It is difficult, if not impossible, to think of a situation where learning occurs without a reinforcer. Remember, reinforcers can be very subtle.

Types of Reinforcement

Obviously, the range of objects and events that can be reinforcers is enormous. Anything that is liked is a potential positive reinforcer. But within the preschool setting there are certain classes of rewards or reinforcements that are particularly useful. First, there is the distinction between *intrinsic* and *extrinsic* reward. As we shall see in our discussion of play in chapter 8, there are a great many childhood activities that appear to be reinforcing in and of themselves. An activity is intrinsically rewarding if it is rewarding just to engage in that activity. When children play, they learn an astounding amount about themselves and the world about them. Much of this learning appears to be reinforced intrinsically. Satisfying curiosity, exploring new areas of activity, and manipulating the world around us have all been shown, in the laboratory, to be intrinsically reinforcing activities (Houston, 1976). Many early childhood educators feel that much, if not most, of the preschool learning experience occurs within the context of intrinsically rewarding play activities. Extrinsic rewards, on the other hand, are rewards that "come from the outside." For example, if a child learns to build a block building "just for the fun of it," then the reward is intrinsic. But if he learns to build because he is praised or recognized by the teacher, or because he can show off to the other children, then the reward is extrinsic.

Another distinction that is often discussed within the context of early childhood education is that between *concrete* and *social* rewards. Social rewards are responses from other people that have reinforcing powers (e.g., praise, affection, criticism). Concrete rewards are objects or events other than human responses (e.g., food, toys, prizes). Many researchers now feel that social rewards are much more appropriate in this field than are concrete rewards. For example, although many people still manipulate children by plying them with sweets (which certainly is effective), many feel that this form of manipulation is inappropriate when social rewards are available.

Shaping

As we mentioned above, the rat in the Skinner box "eventually learns" to press the lever regularly to receive food pellets. But if left *entirely* to its own devices, the rat might never learn to press the bar. It might never even *press* the bar; and if it did, it might not associate that act with the delivery of the reward. Thus the experimenter is forced to assist the animal through the use of a procedure called *shaping*. In the shaping process the experimenter, who has control over delivery of the food pellets, rewards closer and closer approximations of the desired behavior. First, he rewards the animal if it faces the lever; then he rewards it only if it approaches the lever; and finally the rat only gets rewarded if it touches and then presses the lever. This procedure can usually be accomplished in a matter of minutes, as opposed to an indeterminate amount of frustrated time if the experimenter would wait for the animal to press the bar itself.

What does all this have to do with life outside the laboratory? These are simple laboratory experiments, utilizing rats not people. Can this possibly be of value to teachers of young children? We would like to argue in the affirmative: shaping may be of great value to the teacher. A few examples may show that this simple learning example contains many of the components of complex human learning situations, and that skill in shaping techniques (along with careful selections of rewards) can be among the most effective teaching techniques available to teachers of young children. This is not to say that learning theory is the answer to all of our problems or that it is better than other proposals. We merely wish to suggest that it can be used in conjunction with other theoretical approaches, and that it is not inconsistent with them.

Shaping and Toilet Training Suppose that you are teaching a group of children (ages 2 to 3½) the basic principles of toilet usage. Some of the older children are already trained, others are not. Your intention, with the aid of the parents, is to bring all of the children to approximately the same level. Toilet training can be a very crucial part of child rearing. If handled calmly, skillfully, and patiently, it can result in a proud and happy child (and a lot less diaper changing behavior for you!). If handled poorly, it can result in a frightened and uptight child, without self-esteem. In addition to maintaining a calm, warm, and supporting attitude (which you can do by reminding yourself that you are going to take it slow, make it fun, and not expect miracles), you might want to concentrate on shaping procedures. That is, you might choose to reward closer and closer approximations to the desired behavior.

Step 1. Assume "being in the bathroom" is the first approximation you wish to reward. At this age many simple things are rewarding. Knowing a little about your children before you dive into this task is a good idea. Having your bathroom walls covered with pictures of toys, animals, houses, trains, fire engines, babies, and so on, can provide a ready form of reinforcement. Being in the bathroom, if it involves looking at and talking about these pictures, can be fun and rewarding. Better still, let the children choose pictures and allow them to help hang them, if they are willing to go into the bathroom in a positive, cheerful fashion. Hopefully, the toilets and sinks will be scaled down to the children's size. If the children are willing to enter the bathroom, you can talk with them about these facilities, noting that they are "just the right size" for them. Being in the bathroom with a friend can be rewarding, particularly if that friend already knows how to use the toilet. Holding hands, hugging, and physical closeness in general can also be rewarding and reassuring.

Step 2. Once the children are willing to enter the bathroom, and to do so freely and without hesitation, you can require that a closer approximation to the final desired behavior be made before reinforcement is provided. Merely being in the bathroom should no longer be rewarded so heavily. Now the child must, for example, talk about using the toilet before reward is presented. Encouraging explanations may supplement the shaping procedure (e.g., "Jimmy has already learned to use the toilet, and soon you will, too—just like you learned to ride your trike and just like you learned to eat with a spoon."). Eventually, you will explain the differences between males and females and let them see it all. You can show them the training pants the older children wear and suggest that they can wear them, too. If the child responds positively to all of this, and talks positively about it, she or he should be rewarded. If the child does not respond positively, reward should be withheld. At the same time, the teacher should be extremely careful to *avoid any type of recrimination.* If the child fails to display the desired attitude, the teacher should remain neutral, and await further responses on the part of the child.

Step 3. Wearing training pants to school can be the next rewarded approximation, even if they are worn *over* diapers. Recognizing the new pants with happy surprise is rewarding. Remarks to the effect that you can see how they're growing and learning, and that you are happy about them and proud of them will be rewarding. But don't overdo it, either. Some children become frightened when an adult seems to place too much importance on this new process.

Step 4. In successive steps, the child might be rewarded for attempting to undress, for sitting on or standing near the toilet, and, finally, for actually using the toilet. Once again the rewards can be praise, hugs, cheers, promises to tell Mom and Dad the good news, special treats or privileges, or whatever your experience indicates will be rewarding.

Step 5. The final stage in the series might be the child's telling the teacher or parent when she has to go to the bathroom, and going when she gets there. Reward, reward!

Of course these steps are only suggestions. Different children will go through the process at different rates, adding or eliminating steps. It is crucial that reward for early steps is phased-out as the child reaches more advanced steps. For example, a child should not be heaped with rewards merely for entering the bathroom. The demands must gradually increase. With experience the teacher will "get the feel of" the appropriate pace. Reinforcement should be concentrated closest to the desired behavior.

Allow for a step backwards and "accidents" now and then. Remain neutral in the event of an accident. Patience and support are always helpful. Let the child know that you understand she is trying and that you understand her task is a difficult one. It is a good idea to discuss toilet training with the children's parents, to establish consistency in the training procedures.

Additional Shaping Examples There are many behaviors that can be acquired through shaping. We shape our children's language, although we are seldom aware of what we are doing. We reward their first utterances with joyful exclamations, and by repeating what they say. The first "Mama" or "Dada" always pulls a lot of attention. But as the child grows, we require refinements in speech before we give reinforcement. As children progress, more complete words, phrases, and finally sentences are required before we reinforce. Few adults will reinforce their 6-year old for saying "Da," even though this sound may have been a major event in the past.

We teach children to eat with a spoon, then a fork, and finally a knife by shaping. We teach them manners in the same way. When you stop to think about it, it becomes clear that we are shaping and being shaped throughout our entire lives. You are being shaped now: the final goal is for you to become an informed, competent, skilled, effective, loving teacher of young children. Your first step (entering college) is rewarded with praise, recognition, self-satisfaction, and so on. Then your efforts are rewarded (we hope) with good grades and additional self-satisfaction. Finally, when employed, you will be reinforced with a first salary and "more important" rewards, such as interacting effectively with other people, and helping children learn and grow (not to mention cleaning up spilled paint and changing dirty diapers. Now those are rewards!).

Three Types of Instrumental Conditioning

There are three types of instrumental conditioning studied by psychologists.

1. *Reward training.* Here, as we have seen, the subject is rewarded for making a particular response, or for displaying a particular behavior. For example, a child may learn to sit quietly when rewarded with the opportunity to listen to a story. She may learn to clean up when praised by a teacher. She may learn to paint for the satisfaction of creating. Physical activities such as riding a tricycle, jumping, hopping, building with blocks, and making puzzles may reward themselves. They may also be reinforced by the teacher or by peer approval. It is clear that reward training is one of the most prevalent forms of conditioning in all of human life.

2. *Avoidance training.* In this situation the subject is punished if she fails to make a particular response. (In general, punishment refers to the delivery of some type of noxious stimulation, such as spanking or scoldings.) In the laboratory psychologists have studied this phenomenon by placing a rat in an apparatus that has two sections separated by a barrier (see figure 2.3). The rat is placed on one side, say the white side, and is given a specified amount of time to jump to the other side, the black side. If the rat fails to clear the barrier by the end of the specified interval, it is shocked. As one might expect, the rat quickly learns to jump to the "safe" black side. If this procedure is repeated a number of times, the rat learns to jump to the safe side *before* the time interval elapses, thus avoiding shock entirely (Mowrer and Lamoreaux, 1946).

Teachers may not want to reward certain behaviors, such as bringing toy guns to school, even though they might be fun for the children

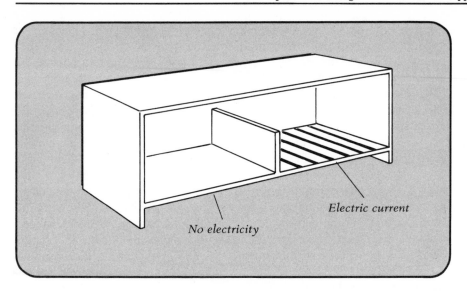

Figure 2.3   *Avoidance training: the basic conditioning apparatus*

In fact, after considerable training, the rat will continue to leap to the black side even if the experimenter disconnects the electricity. Once conditioned, the rat doesn't wait long enough to discover that the danger no longer exists. The experimenter who wishes to break the unnecessary avoidance response must restrain the rat on the white side until it discovers that the situation is no longer dangerous.

There are probably many parallels in the lives of humans, young and old, where similar unfounded fears exist long after the original dangers are gone. For example, a child who has experienced severe punishment from his parents for not washing as soon as his hands become "messy," may compulsively wash his hands for a new teacher even though the teacher may not care about such things. This new teacher may find it difficult to convince the child that he can happily fingerpaint, play with clay, and create things with wet sand. The child doesn't "know" it's safe. You have to show him.

Learned helplessness is an interesting laboratory phenomenon that may be related to the behavior displayed by children that have been subjected to cruel and brutal treatment. If a rat is subjected to repeated shocks on the white side of the apparatus in figure 2.3, and is denied any opportunity to escape from that shock by being harnessed on the white side, then the animal appears to "lose hope" of *ever* escaping. In fact, when the harness is removed and an easy escape is possible, the animal still fails to jump. It cowers on the white side and takes the shocks in a hopeless manner. Unfortunately, many of us have seen children who appear to display similar helpless behavior. They appear lethargic, will not try anything new, and constantly claim that they "can't do it." This pathetic syndrome may have been produced by experiences wherein all attempts to help themselves have been punished. (The interested reader is referred to Maier, 1970, and Strassman, Thaler, and Schein, 1956, for further reading in this area.) Such helpless behavior appears to be very resistant to extinction and can persist for long periods.

3. *Punishment training.* Here the subject is punished for making a particular response. In this situation the desired end is to eliminate a particular response, whereas in reward and avoidance conditioning the goal is to encourage and strengthen a particular response. Punishment training is very common in everyday life, particularly in the world of child rearing. If the subject does something wrong, punishment follows quickly. Children are often spanked or scolded following undesirable behavior. The effects of punishment can be unpredictable. For example, a child humiliated in front of her peers by a teacher may, at least temporarily, terminate the undesirable behavior. However, the child may also form a strong dislike of the teacher. Similarly, a child spanked by her parents for "talking back" to them may stop talking back. In fact, she may stop talking to them at all—especially about things that are important to her. It seems that this type of training procedure may contribute to the "generation gap" we hear so much about.

Children may learn something else from this situation, too. They may discover that parents prefer using force to talking things out, an example that may be followed in their own future relations with others. Finally, for some children who cannot get attention in a more positive fashion, the attention that accompanies punishment may be rewarding and may actually strengthen the undesirable behavior rather than weaken it. (For further information concerning punishment, see Davidoff, 1976; Hall, 1976; Solomon, 1964; Lundin, 1974.)

If given the choice, teachers might be well advised to use reward rather than punishment in influencing behavior. The effects of reward seem to be more permanent, and less subject to unwanted side effects. Unfortunately, such advice is easier to give than to utilize. As we all know, it is simpler to punish unwanted behavior once it occurs than it is to establish the conditions under which desirable behavior will occur in order to reward it. But the fact remains that most psychologists would argue that reward is the better of the two mechanisms.

If a teacher does choose to use punishment techniques, it is essential that the child be provided with the opportunity to acquire an acceptable alternative form of behavior. For example, if a youngster tends to get the teacher's attention by shouting or being disruptive, then it is possible to reduce these behaviors through punishment procedures. The child may be scolded or punished in some other mild manner. But the situation should not be left at this point. Instead, the child should be made aware of alternative, acceptable means of gaining attention, such as raising a hand or speaking softly. And the child should be reinforced for these acceptable alternatives. In other words, the child should not be left dangling. If one mode of behavior is punished and eliminated, it is the teacher's responsibility to provide the child with more socially acceptable means of fulfilling needs.

Continuous and Partial Reinforcement

It is possible to reinforce a subject for every correct response it makes. For example, we may, if we wish, give our rat in the Skinner box a pellet every time it presses the lever. We may praise Sarah every time she asks for, rather than grabs, a toy. This procedure is called *continuous reinforcement*, and it will promote learning. But questions may be raised concerning its effectiveness. First, is it practical, or even possible, in a school setting? Second, does it produce the most lasting type of learning? The answer to both is: probably not.

Let us assume that you and another teacher have a class of children of mixed ages from 2 to 4. You are attempting to promote, through the use of reinforcement, behaviors including toilet use, sharing, verbalizing of needs, cleaning up after activities, dressing and undressing, climbing stairs, fingerpainting, holding bunnies without strangling them, various other large and small muscle activities, not biting each other's fingers, listening to stories, and playing "fire engine" without everyone having to be the driver at the same time. Reward every desirable response? "Impossible!" you say, and you are correct. No one could be in that many places at one time. But you may also be relieved, and not entirely surprised, to learn that continuous reinforcement is also unnecessary. In fact, learning in most situations, in and out of the laboratory, occurs without 100 percent, or continuous, reinforcement.

Partial reinforcement, or a schedule wherein something less than every response is reinforced, is the rule rather than the exception. Many different patterns of reinforcement can be used in learning situations (Ferster and Skinner, 1957; Williams, 1973). For example, we can reward a subject once every five minutes regardless of how many responses it makes; or we can reward every third response, or every tenth response; or we can reinforce responses randomly. Psychologists have worked out the effects of these and many other schedules of partial reinforcement in detail. In general, all partial reinforcement schedules lead to more durable learning than does 100 percent continuous reinforcement.

Unless you are working one to one with a particular subject in a specific learning situation (something which often occurs in the laboratory but seldom outside of it), you will probably find that the most common reinforcement schedule is what is called a variable ratio schedule.

It is an effective pattern in that it produces a lasting effect and a high rate of responding. In this schedule the number of responses the subject must make between reinforcements varies. Sometimes the subject need only respond once to be rewarded, while the next time it may have to respond seven times, the next only four times, and so on. A rat reinforced in this manner will respond at a very high rate, as will humans. This may sound like an odd, inconsistent way to deal with small children; but in reality this is how they are usually rewarded, and they learn a great deal on such a schedule.

As we have suggested, in any given class the teachers are in the process of introducing the children to many new activities. The children are simultaneously learning all sorts of things each day. The teachers cannot possibly reinforce every correct response made by every child. But they can and do reinforce many responses. If they are fairly skillful, they will make the best use of their time by reinforcing key responses for particular children.

For example, new responses might be reinforced more than old responses. A child who spontaneously offers to share a toy for the first time should be reinforced. Older, more well-established responses (e.g., rebuilding a particular block structure) need not, and perhaps should not be reinforced every time. By allocating reinforcement (and time) in this manner, the teacher can "start off" the child's new behavior (sharing) with reward, while allowing the older behavior (building) to become more autonomous and self-sustaining. Of course, reinforcing children with problems can teach other children to have the same problems, so the skilled teacher must reward big and little steps taken by each child and avoid blatant and obvious concentration on "problem" situations.

Stimulus Generalization

Stimulus generalization is a phenomenon that creates as many problems as it solves. It refers to the fact that a response that is conditioned to one stimulus will also be elicited by similar stimuli. This can aid performance tremendously, and eliminate an enormous amount of teaching. For example, if a child learns to eat with one spoon, he will probably be able to eat with any similar spoon without additional teaching. (Can you imagine the effort that would be involved if we had to *teach* the child to use every new design and color of spoon?) If a child learns to make one puzzle, she will probably be able to complete similar puzzles without additional assistance.

However, negative responses can generalize, too. If a child is reinforced (by parental attention and concern) through throwing temper tantrums at home, the child may then exhibit the same behavior in a grandparent's home. If a child obtains a desired toy by grabbing it from another child, she may well do the same thing on seeing a different child with a different toy.

Stimulus generalization is a fact of life. Responses connected to one situation tend to be elicited by similar situations. Sometimes the process aids the teacher, and sometimes it is an enemy. The process of generalization can be countered through discrimination learning, as discussed below.

Discrimination

In a sense, discrimination is the opposite of generalization. In *discrimination learning* the child learns to restrict her response to one stimulus, and to refrain from responding to similar stimuli. Discrimination is brought about by reinforcing responses to certain stimuli and refraining from reinforcing responses to other stimuli. For example, a child who is allowed, or even encouraged, to swear in front of certain adults, will tend to swear in front of all adults (this is stimulus generalization). But, while some adults reinforce swearing, others do not. Thus by being reinforced by some adults, but not by others, the child *discriminates* among the adults, or learns to restrict his swearing responses to certain adults. The tendency to generalize has been reduced.

Obviously, this process of discrimination is essential for effective functioning in the environment. The young child in school must learn many discriminations. For example, she must learn when it is and when it is not an appropriate *time* to run, jump, and make noise. The child must learn *place* discrimination, such as where running and playing can occur (on the playground or in one's yard) and where such responses must be inhibited (in the parking lot or in the street).

The teacher should be aware that the child is attempting to master many of these sorts of discriminations, and that the task is not always easy for the youngster. The teacher can assist by making the necessary distinctions as clear as possible (e.g., "It is *not* okay to throw sand. You may dig in the sand or make things in the sand. But you *may not* throw sand because it might get into someone's eyes. And that hurts!"). As you can see, discrimination is involved in many important "safety rules." In addition, the task of mastering discriminations can be facilitated by prompt, effective reinforcement (e.g., "Very good! You were very quiet during story time today.").

Finally, the teacher must avoid asking too much. When a child, or an animal for that matter, is forced to make a discrimination that is too difficult or too fine, disturbed behavior may result (Maier, 1949). For example, a 4 year old forced to discriminate between the meanings of "idleness" and "laziness" has had her capacity to discriminate clearly exceeded. Although many discriminations that are essential to later learning are formed during the early years, the teacher must be sensitive to the problems that can arise when too much is asked of the very young child. Through experience, a teacher can gain a working knowledge of the types and levels of discrimination that can and cannot be formed by certain age groups and particular individuals.

Extinction

One of the most effective ways of decreasing the strength of a response (behavior) is to cease reinforcing it. This procedure is known as *extinction*. Extinction refers to a decrease in response strength through repeated non-reinforcement. For example, the rat in the Skinner box that has learned to press the lever for food will stop doing so soon after the reward is no longer given. If it had been receiving continuous 100 percent reinforcement for each lever press in the original experiment, the behavior will extinguish quite quickly. It is as though the rat perceives almost immediately that the reward has stopped. If, however, the rat had originally been on a partial reinforcement schedule, the extinction process would take longer.

Of course, extinction can be used very effectively by teachers in the classroom. It is particularly appropriate when used in connection with "behavior problems." For example, children learn very quickly (usually around 4 years of age) that swearing can cause quite a change in the behavior of both the teacher and the other children. Looks of astonishment, confusion, or even anger from the teacher, to say nothing of the gasps and giggles from the other children, can be quite rewarding. A scolding, and the attention it provides, can also be reinforcing. However, if the teacher can stay cool and not react strongly, swearing loses much of its reward value. Much of it will eventually extinguish itself through repeated nonreinforcement.

In fact, if you don't mind children trying out these new and exciting words, you may help them begin to understand what they mean and help them discriminate where and with whom it is "safe" or "unsafe" to use this type of language. If you remain neutral, they will eventually lose interest in using this segment of our language. You may also find that the children will come to think of you as an adult who does not overreact to their testing behavior. They will feel that they can discuss emotion-packed subjects with you. Sex, reproduction, adult relationships, and similar topics of concern will be raised in your presence without anxiety, hesitation, or embarrassment. An adult who will talk instead of scold can be a very valuable experience for a growing child. We will discuss how to talk with children about these and other subjects later in the text.

If one feels that certain problem behaviors are learned and sustained by reinforcement (e.g., by the attention that such behaviors bring), then one might try removing the reinforcement as a first step in changing or eliminating the behavior. For example, Williams (1959) has demonstrated that the temper tantrum behavior of a 21-month-old boy at bedtime was a learned behavior and that it could be extinguished. The parents had inadvertently reinforced the behavior by showing great concern and by staying in the child's room until he fell asleep. Under the guidance of the psychologist, the parents finally put the child on an extinction schedule. That is, at bedtime, they merely said good night and closed the door, allowing the child to cry without any form of social reinforcement. The tantrum behavior gradually extinguished and was completely eliminated by the seventh night (see figure 2.4).

Of course, one must consider that the child with behavior problems may have a genuine need for attention, concern, love, and support that is going unfulfilled. The behavior problem may be a desperate attempt to win the needed support. Thus it is essential, when extinguishing undesirable behaviors, to make a special effort to reinforce some of the positive, desirable responses the child displays (e.g., painting, block building, looking at books, helping clean up, singing with the group). In this manner the need to gain attention through undesirable behaviors will be reduced. The child's self-image and feelings of self-esteem will have a chance to grow and blossom.

Extinction procedures have been effective with many different types of responses. Among others, these include aggressive behavior (Allen et al., 1967), passivity (Johnston et al., 1966), and so-called sex-deviant behavior (Rekers and Lovaas, 1974).

Not all teachers will be interested in using extinction procedures. But for those who are, the key to their successful use is the identification of the reinforcements that are maintaining the behavior. If one of your children repeatedly engages in unwanted behavior, sit down for a moment and try to imagine what might be contributing to maintaining the behavior. What is bothering the child? For example, does the behavior elicit attention, solitude, action, the opportunity to exercise, relief from boredom, relief from having to concentrate, the applause of peers, or your anger? Once you have an idea, try it out. Structure the situation so that your hypothesized reinforcer is not present following the unwanted behavior. Don't be discouraged over initial failures. Life is certainly complicated enough to render the use of extinction procedures less than perfect. (For additional extinction procedures, the reader is referred to Wolpe, 1958.)

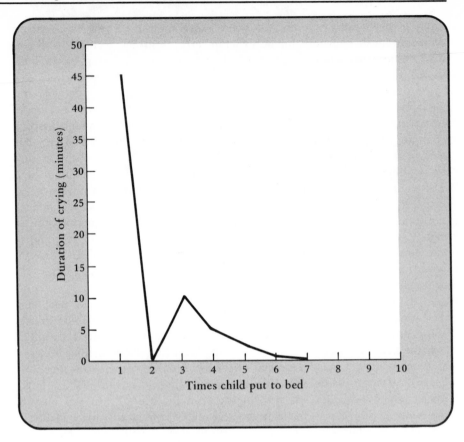

Figure 2.4 *Duration of crying as a function of the number of times a child is put to bed (Adapted from C. D. Williams, "The Elimination of Tantrum Behavior by Extinction Procedures,"* Journal of Abnormal and Social Psychology, *59, 1959)*

It's Not As Easy As It Sounds

On paper, the principles of learning appear to be quite simple and straightforward. But applying them effectively in a complex, rapidly changing preschool situation is another matter entirely. It is just not possible to step into a classroom after having read a chapter such as this, and effectively apply the summarized principles. They will work, but a good deal of experience is necessary before they can be used in a meaningful manner. So, if you do try to apply some of these principles and find that they don't seem to be working, don't be discouraged. With practice, thought, and careful planning, learning principles can be very useful. However, their use is not a skill that can be picked up overnight.

To use conditioning principles, the teacher must be able to make rapid decisions in very complex situations. For example, a teacher attempting to shape a given behavior, such as cooperation, must be able to judge the appropriate amount of improvement that will be required before reinforcement is necessary. This must be done while trying to handle a roomful of wonderfully complicated and fast-moving individuals. It's not easy at first.

Here is an example of the kind of problem the inexperienced conditioner can run into. Suppose a given teacher has decided to try to eliminate the tantrum-like behavior displayed by a 3-year-old girl. The teacher is convinced that the behavior is reinforced by the attention that the child receives each time she flies into a rage. So the teacher begins to extinguish the temper tantrum by withholding reinforcement. This is done by not reacting to the child at all when she flares up. The rest of the staff must be included in this procedure, too. In fact, this simple example requires a good deal of care in planning, discussion, and execution. Suppose extinction progresses fairly well for a while, but then one of the staff members lapses, and responds to the child during a tantrum. This kind of giving-in is understandable. Things may become so hectic that a particular staff member may just not be able to handle it all, and may attempt to quiet the child in an effort to bring some sanity back to the situation. But what is the result of this one instance of giving in? In effect, it amounts to the establishment of a partial reinforcement schedule where the child is reinforced some, but not all, of the time. And as we have already seen, learning acquired under a partial reinforcement schedule is even more lasting, and more durable, than learning which occurs when every response is reinforced. In other words, the entire extinction program may backfire if anyone breaks the solidarity of the new reaction. In fact, if a few people occasionally respond to the tantrums while the others do not, the tantrum behavior may well be stronger than if every tantrum had been reinforced.

Condition with Caution

Katz (1977) suggests that we "condition with caution." She points out that different instances of what appears to be the same behavior may be caused by different factors, and, accordingly, should be handled differently. She gives the example of three different children who all engage in throwing blocks. Their disruptive behaviors all appear to be the same. But Katz points out that one child may be throwing blocks because she has been reinforced for doing so in the past, one may throw blocks because she is emotionally upset, and one may throw blocks simply because no-one has ever told her not to. Although straight extinction or punishment procedures might work in all three cases, Katz points out that each child might best be handled in a unique way. Specifically, she suggests that the first child might best be subjected to some form of behavior modification, the second child might require psychotherapy, and that the third might best be handled by being taught alternative modes of behavior.

The point here is that, because humans are complex, the application of the so-called "simple" principles of conditioning is bound to be complex, too.

Conclusion

In this chapter we have outlined the most basic principles of learning as they have evolved in the laboratory. We have attempted to relate them to issues that arise in the everyday working life of the early childhood educator, and have attempted to provide examples of the ways that they may be of use to the teacher. We have covered emotional classical conditioning, instrumental conditioning, shaping, reinforcement, and extinction, as well as related phenomena and principles.

The study of learning in the laboratory is in its infancy. Thus it is not surprising that our ability to apply the principles of learning is somewhat limited. The reader must recognize that our discussion of learning principles is in no way intended to convey the impression that the learning approach is the correct approach. It is merely one approach among many available. Each teacher must decide just how much of this material should be incorporated into teaching methods. We suggest that an awareness of the principles of learning, taken together with an awareness of alternative approaches, will provide the firmest, broadest base upon which to establish effective teaching methods.

3

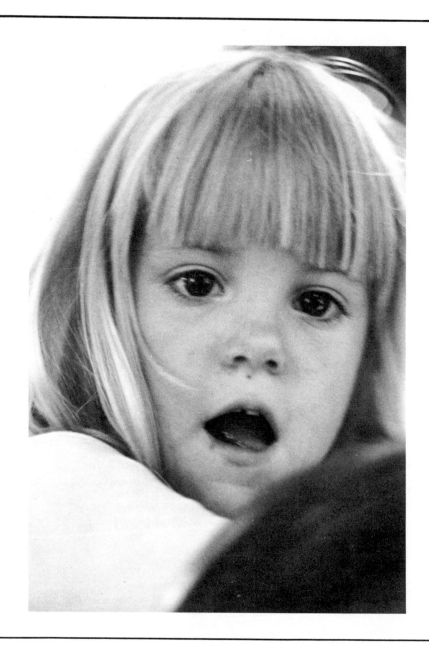

Language
and Language Acquisition

We spent the last chapter outlining some of the rules and generalizations that seem to govern much of the learning accomplished by the child. We tried to emphasize the fact that the learning approach is but *one* way to understand what goes on in early childhood education. It can't provide all, or even most, of the answers. It would be surprising if anyone adopted a strict, exclusive conditioning approach to the understanding of the educational process. A better idea would be to take from the field of learning whatever it is that you feel can be of use, and whatever you can be comfortable with.

We now turn to a consideration of one of the major areas of learning that is encountered by the youngster: that of language learning. In a sense, we are turning from a consideration of the *process* of learning to a consideration of the *content* of learning. What can we say about language, and about the way the rather miraculous process of language acquisition progresses?

An ability to utilize language certainly sets the child apart from other members of the animal kingdom. It is true that many life forms use some type of abbreviated language. For example, birds often use one call to attract a mate, another call to sound a general alarm, and still another to ward off competing members of the same species. Similarly, various investigators have been able to demonstrate that chimpanzees can acquire at least the rudiments of language, provided they are allowed to use a sign language rather than one based on utterances, which would be extremely difficult for them (Premack and Premack, 1975). And many of us have heard of Von Frisch's (1974) famous work with the communication system employed by bees. Workers, returning to the hive, will "tell" where food is located by varying the speed and direction of their "dance." But, in spite of these examples of animal communications (and there are more), language use within the animal kingdom is quite limited. Beyond a few sounds, movements, and gestures the animal kingdom is essentially without language.

Man, on the other hand, talks and writes incessantly, expressing everything from the most basic need to the highest intellectual development through a vast array of complicated language systems. Man seems born to talk, and it is this distinctive quality that contributes to the enormous gap that exists between humanity and the remainder of the animal kingdom.

Obviously, the acquisition of language is one of the most profound events experienced by the child while in the setting of early childhood education. The child may begin the period possessing some language, but acquisition of vocabulary and grammar accelerates during these years. In a sense, the tone and quality of the child's life is set during these years. If language acquisition progresses smoothly and strongly, the child will be at a distinct advantage. Language is a powerful tool. And whether or not that tool is adequately mastered depends, to a great extent, upon what happens during the early childhood years. Thus it behooves us to spend a little time considering what language does for the child, what language is, and how it is acquired.

The Value of Language

What does language do for us? It facilitates communication and thought. In addition, it enables mankind to accumulate information. If you think about it for a moment, you will appreciate that *you* have access to more information and more recorded knowledge than the greatest minds of the past. At the local library is a stockpile of information quite surpassing what was available to Aristotle, Galileo, Newton, and all the rest. Language ensures that knowledge is cumulative. We need not learn and discover everything for ourselves.

Written language provides as great a boost as does spoken language. For example, many primitive peoples around the world developed spoken, but not written languages. Thus, while they held a distinct advantage over animals, they were still limited in their ability to accumulate information, and to pass it on from generation to generation. The transfer of accumulated wisdom had to be done by word of mouth.

Spoken and written language does three things for children. (1) It allows them to communicate. (2) It allows them to store information beyond the capacity of their memory stores. (3) It facilitates their thinking by providing a system of symbols, and rules relating those symbols to one another.

The Structure of Language

Phonemes

Spoken languages are based upon limited numbers of very basic sounds. For example, *all* the language your children use is based on a few dozen basic sounds. The entire English language is based upon approximately forty-five of these basic sounds, and no more. Some languages involve no more than fifteen basic sounds while no language is known to use more than eighty-five elementary sounds. These basic sounds are called *phonemes*. In English, the phonemes correspond roughly to the different ways we pronounce the vowels and consonants of the alphabet. Most phonemes in and of themselves have no meaning; they must be combined with one another to form meaningful units.

The English phonemes include such sounds as the sound of *s* at the beginning of *sap*, the *sh* sound in *short*, and the *e* sound in *bear*. In our analysis of language, we do not go farther than the phoneme. That is, the phoneme is considered to be the basic unit.

Linguists and psycholinguists have described in detail the physical events involved in the production of each of these basic sounds or phonemes. While beyond the scope of this text, we can provide a glimpse of the sort of complicated mouth and tongue movements the young child must master in order to become an accomplished user of language. As examples, consider the *t* sound in *tap*, the *v* sound in *vat*, the *b* sound in *bat*.

As you say *t*, notice that your tongue touches the roof of your mouth. Your lips are open. But when you say *v*, something very different happens. Your top teeth touch your bottom lip. The tip of your tongue no longer touches the roof of your mouth. And when you say *b*, your top and bottom lips touch. Try some other basic sounds, such as *g* in *gun*, and *th* in *the*. In each case, some very distinct and different physical events are responsible for the production of the sound. Obviously, there are many other important aspects of sound production; but these few examples indicate that we can, with some precision, identify the vocal mechanisms responsible for each distinct phoneme. Imagine the task facing the young child about to tackle this complex problem.

Morphemes

In and of themselves, phonemes are meaningless. If a child walks up to you and says *th*, you will more than likely give her a blank look, because we don't normally use isolated phonemes in speech. But we do combine phonemes to form meaningful units, and the smallest meaningful unit in a language is called a *morpheme*. A morpheme is usually composed of two or more phonemes, but not always. A few morphemes, such as the words *a* and *I*, are composed of single phonemes. Many morphemes are words. But not all morphemes are words. Some are prefixes and some are suffixes. Thus, *now*, *jump*, and *cat* are all morphemes (meaningful units composed of two or more phonemes). They also happen to be words. But the suffixes *ity* and *ness* are also morphemes (they have meaning and are composed of two or more phonemes). Similarly, *un* (a prefix) is also a morpheme.

Words may be composed of single morphemes (*now, jump, cat*) or they may be composed of more than one morpheme. In other words, the child may combine morphemes to yield words. *Help* (a morpheme) and *less* (a morpheme) may be combined to form *helpless* (a word composed of two morphemes).

Every language has restrictions upon the ways in which phonemes can be combined and ordered. In other words, the rules of our language do not allow the child to put together just any old phonemes to form a meaningful unit. Certain phoneme combinations are not allowed. For example, when was the last time you ran across an English word beginning with *ws*? Never. *Ws* is not allowed, even though something like *wr* is allowed (*wrote, wry*). Similarly, English words don't begin with *pz*, while *py* is acceptable (*python, pylon*).

Of what significance is all this, you ask? It is the child's familiarity with acceptable and unacceptable combinations that allows her to judge whether or not unfamiliar combinations are true words. For example, consider *hkenite, zinkenite, pjenkenite*. Which of these is a true word? Zinkenite is correct. It is a steel-grey metallic mineral. Possibly you already knew the word, but more than likely you did not. Still, you were able to identify it as the true word, and you probably chose it because you know words don't begin with *hk* or *pj*, while some do begin with *zi*. The *zi* combination is acceptable, and it allowed you to correctly identify a true word when little else in the way of help was available. In the same fashion, the child learns to identify "unacceptable" words by noting the unacceptable combinations they possess.

Grammar

Obviously, language is not limited to morphemes. We do not go about communicating in terms of isolated morphemes alone (although an occasional morpheme such as *stop!* or *yes!* can be extremely effective). We combine morphemes into words, and words into sentences. Just as there are rules governing the combination of phonemes into morphemes, and morphemes into words, there are complex rules governing the ways that we put morphemes and words together to make meaningful sentences. The rules that govern the ordering and positioning of sounds, morphemes, and words in sentences are the rules of grammar.

The ordering of words makes all the difference in the world in terms of the comprehensibility of a sentence. For example, *Janet went outside to the swing,* makes sense only because the words are arranged in a manner prescribed by the rules of grammar. If the rules of grammar are ignored, something incomprehensible as a sentence may result (e.g., *Janet swing the to outside went*).

Phrase Structure

Stimulated by the work of Noam Chomsky (1968), linguists have described the structure of the sentence as prescribed by the rules of grammar, in terms of the various *phrases* the sentence contains. Linguists conceive of a sentence as being structured in terms of phrases. For example, consider the sentences in figure 3.1. As you can see, each of our sentences is usually composed of a *noun phrase* followed by a *verb phrase*. Each of these phrases is then broken down into its own elements. These diagrams represent what is known as the *phrase structure* of the sentences.

Describing sentences in terms of phrase structure assists us in understanding what is and what is not an acceptable English sentence. For example, at the simplest level, the diagrams in figure 3.1 suggest that a verb phrase *follows* a noun phrase. The importance of this can be observed by switching the positions of the noun and verb phrases in figure 3.1. When this is done we have "flew over the town the giant moth," and "ate the button the little boy." Although perhaps comprehensible, neither of these sounds like, or is, an acceptable English sentence.

That the child *ever* masters grammar is impressive, because the rules of grammar are complicated, and not always agreed upon even by natural users of a given language. But the fact that there are rules that govern the positioning of words within sentences cannot be denied. It is these rules of grammar, generally accepted within a given population, that enable humans to communicate with one another.

Surface and Deep Structure

The *deep structure* of a sentence is the meaning behind that sentence, or what it is that the speaker is trying to say. The *surface structure* refers to the actual words used in the sentence by the speaker. There is not always a one-to-one correspondence between deep and surface structure. Obviously, young children often have something in mind but fail to construct an adequate sentence to express that idea. Many young children, in their eagerness to experiment, are almost incomprehensible.

Several different sets of words, or different surface structures, may often be used to express the same underlying deep structure. Thus the child is free to express deep structure in different ways. Even though the surface structures differ, both of the following sentences convey or reflect the same underlying deep structure:

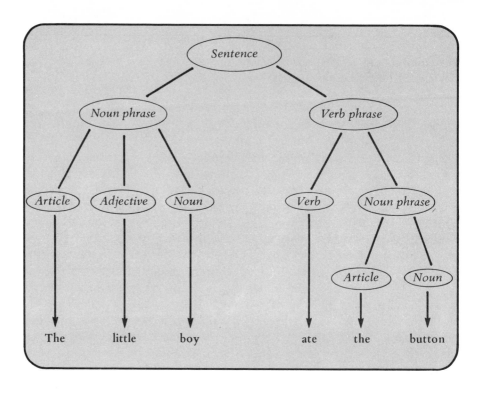

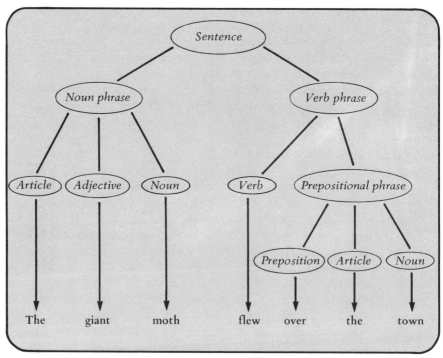

Figure 3.1 *Phrase structure of two English sentences*

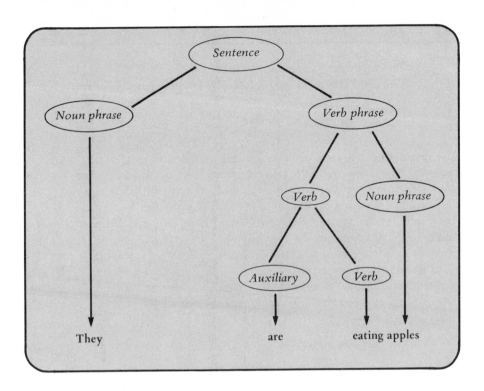

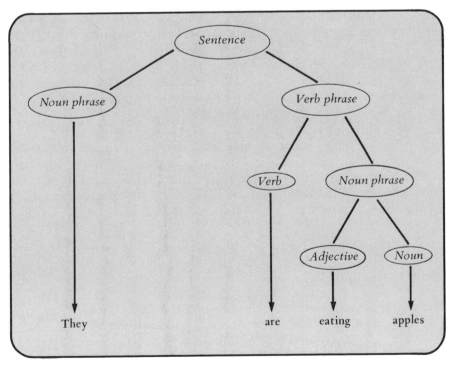

Figure 3.2 *Alternative phrase structure of an ambiguous sentence*

"The thrown toy narrowly missed the child."
"The child was narrowly missed by the thrown toy."

Ambiguous Sentences

The distinction between deep and surface structure is underlined by the fact that the same sentence may express two different meanings. For example, "they are eating apples," could be intended to mean certain individuals are eating apples or that certain apples are suitable for eating. The same surface structure can reflect two different deep structures. Figure 3.2 contains the different phrase structures for this ambiguous sentence. The existence of ambiguous sentences suggests that the rules of grammar are not perfect. The rules of grammar are such that it is possible to generate "acceptable" sentences whose meanings are unclear. Try making up a few ambiguous sentences for yourself.

Grammar Grows and Changes

The reader should also be aware of the fact that the rules of grammar change with time. A language is not stagnant. Rules which were at one time rigidly observed fall into disuse. For example, once textbooks placed a stigma upon prepositions standing at the end of sentences (e.g., What did they do it *for*?). But this rule has been relaxed, particularly in the light of the fact that clumsiness may result when one tries to avoid putting a preposition at the end. For example, which of the following seems clumsy?

"Tell me what it is to which you object?"
"Tell me what you object to."

Putting a preposition at the end of a sentence is no longer looked upon with horror. This change is an example of the dynamic, changing quality of grammar. Most people follow the rules of grammar without really knowing what those rules are. They do it without awareness and on the basis of sound.

The Acquisition of Language

Having taken a look at the structure of language, we now turn to a brief consideration of the progression that language acquisition normally follows. In this section we do *not* theorize about the mechanisms that might account for language development. For now, we merely consider the order in which the elements of language are acquired by the child, saving theoretical considerations for the next section.

Babbling

Within the first few months of life, babies begin to engage in an enormous amount of what appears to be spontaneous *babbling*. Much of this babbling resembles the phonemes and syllables used by the adult population. Apparently babies do not have to be taught how to produce all of the basic sounds of the language. They occur spontaneously. But at this stage the sounds are not organized into meaningful speech; they do not represent true language. Rather, they seem to be spontaneous, often exuberant outbursts of sound. The baby appears to have a fine time trying out its verbal apparatus.

Interestingly enough, all babies, regardless of nationality or living conditions, appear to babble at the same time and in the same manner. The babbling of infants living in different countries is almost impossible to tell apart (Atkinson, MacWhinney, and Stole, 1970; Miller, 1951). Neither the quantity nor the quality of the babbling appears to be heavily affected by the environment. For example, Lenneberg (1967) reports a case in which a deaf child, born to deaf-mute parents, produced babbling which was quite comparable to the babbling of normal children.

In other words, this initial babbling appears to be innate, or predetermined, and it is the same among all children, regardless of their environments. But very quickly, perhaps by 9 months, the baby begins to restrict its sounds to those occurring in the immediate environment. The baby begins to concentrate on the phonemes and syllables that are part of the language she will be acquiring. The other sounds, more appropriate to different languages, begin to drop out. What this suggests is that, as babies, we possess *all* of the sounds required to master *any* language. But as we grow older, we lose the ability to produce many of these sounds until, as adults, it may actually be impossible for us to produce the sounds required in certain additional languages. Anyone who has tried to learn a second language as an adult will understand the difficulties involved in trying to recapture sounds we were all once capable of producing with ease.

Single Words and Holophrastic Speech

After approximately one year of life, the baby begins to acquire a limited vocabulary of true words. The use of these first words represents the beginning of true language. At first these words will not be spoken with complete accuracy. But through time, and with added experience, they approximate more and more closely the speech of adults.

The acquisition of true words begins slowly and then accelerates (see figure 3.3). Although the acquisition of vocabulary begins at a very early age, it need not ever end. Many individuals continue to add to their

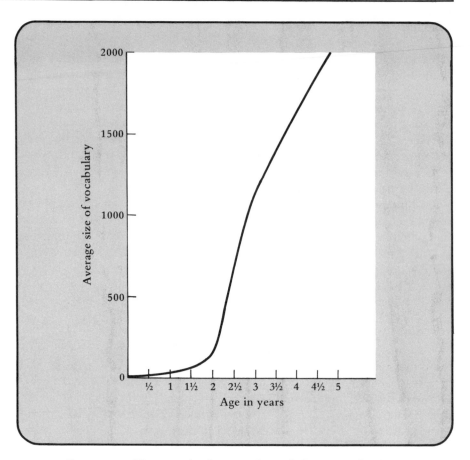

Figure 3.3   *The growth of a typical vocabulary over the first 5 years of life*

vocabulary throughout their lives.   It is probably fair to say that the amount of verbal stimulation one receives (e.g., from T.V., conversation, reading) correlates with one's total vocabulary.

There are different theories about how words and their meanings are acquired.   We shall consider some of these theories shortly.   For now let us concentrate on the fact that children's use of single words is often *holophrastic* (McNeil, 1970).   What this means is that children often use a single word to stand for an entire idea, thought, event, or sentence.   A child's "Mama!" may mean quite a bit more than that single word normally conveys.   By saying "Mama!" the child may mean, "At last! Here comes Mama with the chow!"   When a young child says "Juice!" she may be asking for a drink of a particular liquid, delivered in a particular container, at a particular temperature.   Holophrastic speech underlines the fact that a child's comprehension far exceeds the ability to speak. In dealing with nursery school children, the teacher should be aware of the fact that the child often comprehends more than her speech might imply. The teacher must be able to "read" or "translate" this perfectly natural form of abbreviated speech in order to grasp the child's meaning. Trying to force the child to use more complete grammatical structure just won't work. Holophrastic speech is normal. It appears and disappears without specialized instruction. It should be taken as a sign of normal, healthy language development.

Two-Word Sentences

At about 18 months (the time varies from child to child) babies begin to embark upon the process of acquiring grammar. After a modest vocabularly has been acquired, they begin to put together two words to express an idea. "Baby walk." "Daddy go." "More milk." These are minimal but true sentences. Once the process of putting two words together begins, it progresses at a rapid rate with many two-word combinations appearing daily. (Readers interested in learning more about the different types of two-word sentences used by children are referred to Braine, 1963; and Miller and Ervin, 1964.)

Telegraphic Speech

It is at about this stage that *telegraphic* speech can be identified. In telegraphic speech the child preserves the order of the words he hears in a sentence but leaves out unimportant words. For example, if a mother says, "Here comes Daddy up the stairs," the child might say, "Daddy stairs." The essential, stressed words are maintained in the proper order, while less important words or parts of words such as prepositions, articles, suffixes, and prefixes may be omitted. Again, telegraphic speech should be taken as normal, healthy, and adequate. Special efforts to ensure complete expression of all words in a sentence should be avoided.

Telegraphic speech appears not only when the child is copying or imitating an adult's speech but in the child's own spontaneous speech as well. "Want bed," will do very well to express the idea that the child wishes to go to bed now. In a sense, telegraphic speech may be thought of as an advanced version of holophrastic speech. In both cases complex ideas are expressed in abbreviated fashion, with greater abbreviation appearing in the holophrastic form.

Longer Sentences

Between the ages of 2 and 3 years, children begin to produce longer sentences. The child begins to utilize more complex forms of grammar, and begins to string morphemes together in longer and longer sequences. There are several points concerning this process that should be mentioned:

1. The rate of acquisition is rapid but varied. Although all children add to the length of their utterances in a rapid manner, they do vary considerably. Some children begin earlier and progress more quickly than others (Brown, 1973). Thus, the fact that one child is slower than the others should be no cause for alarm. The developmental rates vary considerably among normal children. Figure 3.4 contains

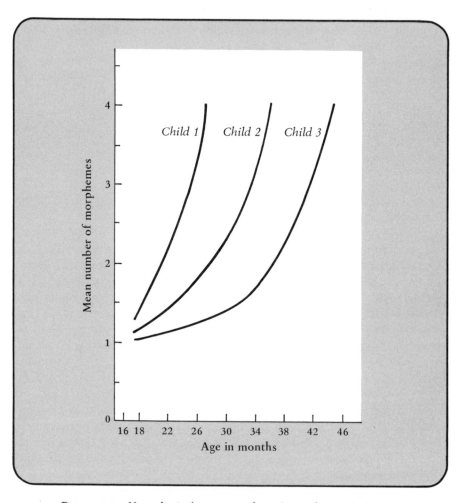

Figure 3.4 *Hypothetical mean number of morphemes in sentences of three children over first 46 months of life*

hypothetical data on three children. As you can see, the children began to expand the length of their sentences at different ages, and some make more rapid progress than others. But all children progress rapidly, building the average length of their sentences from approximately one to four morphemes between the ages of 8 months and 2 years.

2. The order in which grammatical knowledge is acquired seems to be constant from child to child. While children clearly vary in terms of their rates of progress, they all seem to follow the same prescribed order in terms of picking up new grammatical concepts and rules. For example, adding -ing (mak*ing*, go*ing*, see*ing*) tends to appear early in the development of all children. Adding an *s* to pluralize nouns (car*s*, boat*s*) tends to appear a little later. Finally, adding *'s* to indicate possession (Sarah*'s* boat, Stephen*'s* truck) appears only after the two preceding steps have been mastered, regardless of the rate of progress the child is maintaining. Once again, the order in which grammatical knowledge is acquired seems relatively constant even though rates of acquisition do differ.

3. A child's grammar is not exactly the same as adult grammar. (As we shall see in the next chapter, the child's *thinking* may actually be different from the adult's.) Children do not merely mimic exactly what they hear, at least during the early stages. The child may use the same words but put them together differently. It is as though the child is trying out, or testing, hypotheses about the language. It is as though, through experience and feedback, the child alters and changes his first tentative, sometimes unique rules or hypotheses to bring them into agreement with those of the adult world. They revise their own rules of grammar as they learn more about the linguistic environment. The teacher can be most useful by providing feedback and encouragement to the youngster. He must learn through his own experiments with language. Forcing children to learn through drill and rote memorization is probably futile.

Table 3.1 provides some idea of the course of normal language development that a preschool teacher might expect to observe.

Theories of Language Acquisition

Classical Conditioning

There have been a number of different approaches to the understanding of language acquisition. One of the early theories suggested that much of our language is acquired through a process of classical conditioning. For example, the meaning of the word "Mama" may be established through classical conditioning. The sound "Mama" (conditioned stimulus) is

Table 3.1 *Pattern of normal language development*

Age in Months	Physiological Aspects	Sound Aspects	Numerical Size of Vocabulary	Word Type	Sentence Length	Articulation– Appearance of Individual Sounds in Speech *	General Intelligibility
1	Sucking Swallowing	Crying. Small throaty noises					
2		Grunting, sighing, cooing (plays with vowel sounds)					
3	Smiling	Babbling (self-imitation of vowel-like sounds and syllables					
4	Laughs aloud						
5		Squeals, growls. Socialized vocalization					
6	Locates sources of sound						
7–8	Gestures still more meaningful than sounds	Inflection with vocal play to gain attention					

Age	Behavior	No. of words	Part of speech		Intelligibility
9–12	Waves bye-bye; Echolalia (imitation of sounds others make but he does not understand)				
12	First words	1–3	Nouns		1–2 years. Words used may be no more than 25% intelligible to unfamiliar listener. Jargon near 18 months almost 100% unintelligible. Improvement is noticeable between 21 and 24 months.
18	Jargon (much vocalization and imitation of adult speech with few intelligible words. Usually talks to self, animals or toys)	10–20			
2 yrs.	Combines words	100–272	Verbs, nouns	1.7	2–3 yrs. Words about 65% intelligible by 2 yrs; 70–80% intelligible in context by 3. Many individual sounds faulty but total context generally understood. Some incomprehensibility because of faulty sentence structure.
2½ yrs.	Jargon almost gone, more word combinations and phrases. May be nonfluent.			2.4	

Table 3.1 (continued)

Age in Months	Physiological Aspects	Sound Aspects	Numerical Size of Vocabulary	Word Type	Sentence Length	Articulation— Appearance of Individual Sounds in Speech*	General Intelligibility
3 yrs.			600–1000	Nouns, verbs, personal pronouns	3–4	m, n, n, ng, p, f, h, w	3–4 yrs. Speech usually 90–100% intelligible in context. Individual sounds still faulty and some trouble with sentence structure.
3½ yrs.					4	y	
4 yrs.			1100–1600	More pronouns, some adjectives, adverbs, prepositions, conjunctions	4,5,6	k, b, d, g, r	4–5 yrs. Speech is intelligible in context even though some sounds are still faulty
5 yrs.		Quite fluent	1500–2100		4.6–6		5–6 yrs. Good
6 yrs.			2563			t, th, v, l	
7 yrs.						th, z, az, j	

Adapted from Engel, R. C. *Language Motivating Experiences for Young Children,* Sherman Oaks, Ca.: Rose C. Engel, 1976.
* Ages at which 75% of children first utter various types of sound correctly.

repeatedly paired with the mother and her actions (unconditioned stimulus). The baby's responses to the mother's actions (feelings of comfort, well-being, etc.) become classically conditioned to the sound "Mama." Similarly, "hot" (conditioned stimulus) may acquire its meaning through repeated pairings with a certain class of unconditioned stimuli (hot stoves, fires, etc.).

Instrumental Conditioning

Many psychologists also feel that language is acquired through a process of instrumental conditioning (Rachlin, 1976; Skinner, 1957). That is, language is acquired because it is reinforced by parents and others in the child's environment. Each time the young child says, "Dada," she is applauded and rewarded with a show of physical and social affection. Incorrect or undesirable sounds are either left unreinforced or are punished. According to Skinner and his followers, language is acquired just like any other set of responses (e.g., bar pressing, pecking, running, etc.) *All* responses, language responses as well, are assumed to be acquired according to the simple principles of reinforcement, extinction, punishment, discrimination, and generalization, as outlined in chapter 2.

Objections to Conditioning Theory

But objections have been raised concerning the conditioning approach to language acquisition (Cazden, 1972).

1. Many have concluded that language acquisition is much too complicated to be understood adequately in terms of simple stimulus-response conditioning.
2. The use of language has a creative aspect about it that is difficult to explain in conditioning terms. Specifically, the young child uses new, original arrangements of verbal units that she has never before heard or used. Hence, the argument goes, these new combinations could not have been established through a process of reinforcement. The child can generate, or produce unique language patterns; a fact that is difficult to explain in terms of reinforcement principles.
3. Finally, if language were established through reinforcement, it would seem reasonable to expect that children living under widely varying social conditions would acquire language in different ways. But Lenneberg (1969) has presented evidence that suggests that despite widely varying opportunities for social reinforcement, children in all cultures seem to acquire language in a relatively universal, constant pattern. In spite of enormous differences in the amounts and types

of reinforcement, children (even those born to and raised by deaf parents) appear to acquire language in a similar pattern.

Psycholinguistic Theory

These kinds of objections to conditioning theory have led to a new emphasis within the arena of language acquisition theory.

1. Lenneberg's (1969) work has led to an emphasis upon the biological innate aspects of language acquisition. It is now commonly believed that the human is "prewired," and prepared in a biological sense to acquire language. It is as though there is an innate, predetermined quality to our acquisition of language.
2. A second aspect of modern psycholinguistic theory suggests that children learn complex rules of grammar rather than mere strings of words (Chomsky, 1968). It is believed that these acquired rules of grammar can account for the creative, generative quality of our language use which causes difficulty for the conditioning approach. By applying a rule, rather than repeating a string of reinforced words, we can generate new unique utterances.
3. Modern psycholinguistic theory argues that the child forms hypotheses about what is and what is not correct language usage and then proceeds to test these hypotheses in the environment. When one hypothesis proves to be incorrect (it doesn't work for the child), he will revise or replace it, and continue testing until the correct hypothesis (rule) is discovered.

In summary, the psycholinguistic approach offers a promising alternative to the conditioning approach. At the same time, the reader should be aware that *both* approaches may have something to contribute. Reinforcement, as well as innate mechanisms and hypothesis testing may also contribute to our overall acquisition process.

Implications for the Teacher

Taken together, the linguistic and conditioning interpretations of language acquisition suggest several do's and don'ts for the teacher involved in early childhood education:

The teacher should be a good language model.

Reward the use of words and correct grammar. A kind word, a sign of recognition and comprehension, or some social praise will do very well.

But don't over do it. Avoid heavy discussions, or extreme degrees of reward, following any single usage. Allow the child to acquire language through multiple interactions with the linguistic environment.

Expose the child to new verbal materials (e.g., stories, films, even T.V.).

Encourage the child to talk to you, to others (and even to herself). Encourage her to explore, to experiment, and to try out her latest hypotheses concerning the language. Encourage her to interact with the linguistic environment.

Don't worry very much about errors and incorrect speech. They are merely signs that the child is trying out new hypotheses.

Avoid rote memorization and drill. It is neither rewarding nor natural.

By correcting a child, and stating the grammatical rule that has been violated, you may be leaving the child in the dust. The child must learn through experience and interaction, not instruction and lecture.

Sit back and watch the miracle unfold, knowing that we haven't come close to understanding how it is done.

Language and Thought

Words are not absolutely essential for thought. For example, we utilize visual images in our thinking, and emotion probably plays an important part in what we call thinking. But few would deny that words and language form a major component of our thought processes.

An interesting controversy surrounds the role of language in our thought. On the one hand, many have concluded that thought determines the use of language. That is, language is seen as a tool or system with which to express our thoughts, and that our thoughts exist independently of the kinds of language we use to express them. Whorf (1956), on the other hand, has proposed the contrary, and very controversial, notion that language determines thought, rather than thought determining language. As evidence for this, Whorf points out certain ethnographically-based linguistic variations, for example the fact that Eskimos have many different names for various types of snow while we use but a single term. Similarly, certain Philippine Islanders have dozens of names for different types of rice while we speak of no more than a few. Whorf believes that these differences in language actually affect the ways that individuals think about reality. Because they are taught many different labels for snow, Whorf argues, the Eskimos' perception of, and conception of, snow is very different from our own.

But there has been criticism of the Whorfian hypothesis. For example, some have argued that because we don't have labels for many different types of snow does not necessarily mean that we can't conceive

Songs with fingerplays can be fun . . .

of, and don't perceive, different varieties of snow. Certainly young children know the difference between good and bad packing snow, and skiers are very aware of the differences between corn, powder, and packed snow.

This is the old chicken and egg dilemma. Does the existence of many different words for snow lead to a unique conception of snow, or does the cultural necessity of attending to, thinking about, and dealing with, snow lead to the development of a number of convenient, useful names for snow? No-one knows. But the existence of this controversy certainly underlines the close relationship between language and thought.

As we shall see in chapter 4, Piaget takes a position which seems to conflict with Whorf's hypothesis (Piaget and Inhelder, 1969). Piaget acknowledges that language can facilitate rapid and wide-ranging thinking. But he feels that the child's ability to use language is dependent upon the development of more basic forms of thinking that are essentially non-verbal. Piaget believes that the development of cognitive structure stems from the child's own actions, and from the experience and information derived from sensory experience and physical activity.

Finally, Tough (1974) feels that it is an oversimplification to argue that either the Whorfian or the Piagetian position is totally correct. She feels that, "both views are needed to explain how language and thinking support and provoke each other." In other words, language and thinking stimulate one another, and are intertwined in an essentially supportive manner.

. . . and facilitate language learning

Language Differences

Children will differ from their teachers in terms of the language systems (the grammar and pronunciation) they use. For example, some children will have a foreign language as their first language. Similarly, others will speak a form of English that does not conform to Standard English. The various areas of the United States have produced a wide variety of spoken forms of English. New England, the South, the Midwest, and many other areas of the country contain people who speak with "accents." Black English is another remarkably uniform dialect used by many black children throughout the country.

All teachers are faced with the problem of what to do about the various forms of speech found within the classroom. Should the emphasis be on Standard English only, and an attempt made to stamp out regional and ethnic dialects? Or should they be encouraged? Of course, the answers to these questions will depend upon the specific aims of the program and the people involved. But Cazden et al. (1974) have pointed out that the goal of cultural pluralism—many different ethnic groups living together, sharing and borrowing while retaining their ethnic distinctiveness—is a reasonable goal. They feel that the setting of early childhood education provides a perfect opportunity for children to learn about their own cultural identity and to learn about and respect other cultures. To bring about respect for alternative cultures, these authors note that

"Language differences among children and staff—and cultural differences of all kinds—should be welcomed, openly discussed, and used in the curriculum."

But before this free and open acceptance of differences can be realized, Cazden and her associates point out that three myths about language differences must be overcome. First, there is the myth that some languages are better than others. This is simply not true. All languages are complex, highly structured systems of sounds and symbols. Each form of language has the potential to deal with any topic. Second, there is the belief that some dialects represent bad language usage. Again, this is not true. Just because a given dialect does not conform to the dialect that is used to conduct business and governmental affairs does not mean that that dialect is not a good, strong, effective form of language. And third, there is the myth that people who speak a nonstandard dialect are stupid. Language reflects where and with whom one lives, and not how intelligent one is. It's not so much that one has tried and failed to learn Standard English as it is that one may have learned a dialect very well. If we can overcome these prejudices, and accept language differences for what they are—alternative but equally effective forms of language—then we will be on our way to accepting and respecting people who are different from ourselves.

Language Motivating Experiences

Teachers are often in need of suggestions for classroom activities rather than theory. They need specific, practical teaching aids rather than generalizations. Rose Engel's book *Language Motivating Experiences for Young Children* (1968) has proved to be a valuable teaching aid for more than a decade. Engel feels that the basic goals of any preschool language program should include: the development of good listening habits; the building of an adequate vocabulary; the ability to talk with classmates; the ability to contribute to discussions; the development of enough confidence to participate in our culture through the use of language; the ability to relate facts in a meaningful sequential manner.

Her approach is to provide experiences within the classroom that stimulate and encourage verbal development. Her idea is to involve the children by doing rather than sitting and listening. She has carefully constructed some two hundred experiences that range over thirteen major curriculum areas. The activities are broken down into "things to do" and "things to talk about." This division reflects her conviction that children will be more likely to become proficient in language usage if they are allowed to learn while doing something.

Although it is hardly possible to duplicate all of her suggested activities here, table 3.2 includes a number of representative examples.

Table 3.2 *Language motivating experiences*

Experience: TASTING PARTY
Material needed:
Foods contrasting in taste but in same category (if possible), such as cinnamon candies and marshmallows.
Things to do:
1. The child closes his eyes. The teacher drops candy on his tongue. How does it taste?
2. The child closes his eyes. The teacher puts a marshmallow on his tongue. Does this taste the same? How is it different?
3. In response to the teacher's questions the children make verbal comparisons of both tastes. The teacher records these responses and may later read them to the children to recall the experience.
Things to talk about:
1. Children's own new taste experience
2. Names of new foods tasted
3. Words describing flavors and textures
Variations:
1. sweet/sour   seedless grapes/gooseberry
   crunchy/soft   raw celery/cooked celery
   mild/sharp   Swiss cheese squares/sharp Cheddar squares
   sharp/mild   pickle/cucumber
2. Other concepts from each experience may be expected:
   large/small
   rough/smooth
   wet/dry

Experience: GROUPING
Material needed (for each child):
1. Leftover parts from games such as wheels, cars, plastic toys, etc.
2. Shoe box
3. Three small plastic meat trays from butcher shop
Things to do:
1. Sort by color.
2. Sort by living and non-living items.
3. Sort by smooth and rough.
4. Separate into groups of plastic, wood, rubber, etc.
5. Group by weight similarities.
Things to talk about:
1. How items are alike
2. Different ways items are related
3. Material
4. Vocabulary
Variations:
1. Have children exchange their shoe boxes with items.
2. Add different items such as balloons, ribbon strips, plastic pill bottles, etc.
3. Try the same thing with small pictures of animals and groups may be formed of those with tails, without tails; those that swim, walk, fly, crawl; those with fur and those with feathers. There may be some unknowns.

Table 3.2   (continued)

Experience: HEART BEAT
Material needed:
1. Guinea pig
2. Stethoscope: funnel with rubber tubing
Things to do:
1. Child holds the guinea pig and notes the heart beat.
2. Teacher listens to child's heart beat with her ear.
3. Child listens to another child's heart beat with ear.
4. Child listens to the teacher's heart beat with her stethoscope.
5. Child listens to child's heart beat with stethoscope.   Is it easier to hear with or without the stethoscope?
6. Child listens to guinea pig's heart beat.
7. Teacher encourages a child to jump (quickens heart beat) and listen to his own heart with a stethoscope.
8. May lead to dramatic play of doctor's examination.
Things to talk about:
1. Listening
2. Speeds of heart beat in quiet and active periods
3. Name of instrument and its use
Variation:
Child listens to doll with stethoscope.   "What do you hear?"

Experience: TAPE RECORDER
Material needed:
1. Tape recorder
2. Microphone
Things to do:
Record singing and use of rhythm instruments such as with "Jingle Bells."
Things to talk about:
1. Experiences the children may have had with a tape recorder.
2. How do we know whose voice we are hearing on the play-back?
3. Some parts of the recording equipment such as microphone, tape, etc.
Variations:
1. Record a story with children's responses.
2. Record the use of vocabulary as in identifying members of family.
3. Record a speaking "game", such as "Jack in the Box," or nursery rhymes.
4. Use the tape recorder or records with children singing songs.
5. Repeat any of these different songs.
6. For the more mature, record a story and small group may follow along as story is played back.   In recording, give directions when to turn pages.
7. Set up a listening post where children may listen to a tape record with earphones and not disturb others.

Experience: WHIPPED SOAP
Material needed:
1. Soap flakes
2. Water
3. Rotary egg beater
4. Shirt cardboards
5. Coffee grounds

Table 3.2 (*continued*)

Things to do:
1. The children help beat the flakes to whipped cream consistency.
2. The child puts some on a shirt cardboard and uses as finger paint.
3. The child adds coffee grounds and continues to use as finger paint.
4. Clean up.

Things to talk about:
1. Discussion of texture: how does it feel? Is it bumpy? lumpy? rough? smooth? soft?
2. Compare the before and after addition of coffee grounds.
3. Listening to and following directions

Variations:
1. Feeling textured materials: velvet, sandpaper, burlap, satin, net
2. Making collage of textured fabrics

Experience: DRAWING WITH YARN
Material needed:
1. Roving or heavy yarn
2. Starch
3. Crayons, non-roll
4. Shirt cardboards
5. Damp sponges

How to do it:
1. Children dip 8–10 inch lengths of yarn into starch.
2. Wind and drop yarn on the cardboards.
3. Wipe hands on damp sponges.
4. Place in provided area to dry.
5. When dry, they may more easily color one space, as hardened yarn serves to limit the areas.

Things to talk about:
1. Thickness of roving
2. Difference between feel of dry and wet roving
3. Designs or shapes made with roving
4. Colors used
5. Listening to and following directions

Variations:
1. Paint areas delineated by yarn design.
2. Add collage material within areas.
3. "Draw" pictures with yarn.
4. "Draw" pictures with yarn on waxed paper. When dry cut around shape and use in mobile.
5. More difficult is filling in the outlined picture with yarn.

Experience: SPEECH READING GAME
Material needed:
None

Things to do:
1. Play a short game of calling the names of children without voice. Children watch the teacher's face.
2. May be used for dismissing from the table after nutrition.

Table 3.2   (*continued*)

Things to talk about:
1. Helpfulness of looking at a speaker
2. How certain letters are formed and the cue they give
Variation:
Give short instructions for children to follow such as daily activities of home or school.
1. Brush your teeth.
2. Wash your face.
3. Brush your hair, etc.
Particularly valuable:
1. For use with the aurally handicapped.
2. To encourage attention to speech mechanisms.

Experience: APPLESAUCE
Material needed:
1. Hot plate
2. Pyrex covered pot
3. Foley Mill or colander and spoon
4. Apples—one per child
5. Table knives, spoons
6. Sugar
7. Cinnamon or red cinnamon candies
8. Water
How to do it:
1. Children cut apples, tasting in the process.
2. Wash apples and put in pot, add water.
3. Simmer.
4. When tender, cool.
5. Hold Foley Mill as children ladle in cooked apples and turn to separate peel and cores from sauce.
6. Add sugar and cinnamon candies.
7. Eat as part of nutrition.
Things to talk about:
1. Texture, flavor, color of outside and inside of apples
2. Aroma of raw and cooked apples
3. Temperature
4. Changes in volume and color when cooked
5. Sound of bubbling
Variation:
During the fruit season, children may be invited to someone's yard to pick fruit. Bring fruit back to school and wash.   These may be apricots, peaches, or plums. Children remove pits, tasting in the process.   Measure a cup for a cup (fruit and sugar).   Cook, skim, simmer one hour.   Spread on toast or crackers for nutrition.

Adapted from Engel, R. C. *Language Motivating Experiences for Young Children*, Sherman Oaks, Ca.: Rose C. Engel, 1976.

The Next Step

Having spent a little time discussing the nature of language, the value of language, the development of language, the relationship between language and thought, language differences, and motivating exercises, we turn now to a more detailed consideration of the overall cognitive process. Specifically, we turn to a consideration of Jean Piaget's conception of the development of intellectual functioning. We are moving from the specific to the general, or from the concrete to the abstract.

In contrast to the present chapter, where our discussion was primarily of a descriptive nature, we now turn to one of the most influential *theoreticians* within the field of child psychology. Piaget does not limit his interests to language. Language, for him, is just one small part of the overall question of intellectual functioning that concerns him. Piaget wants to understand thinking in its broadest sense, and chooses to attack the problem from a developmental point of view. He wants to know how it is that physical maturation and experience interact to produce what we commonly think of as intelligent people. His conclusions with respect to the development of cognition are pertinent to the task facing the early childhood educator.

4

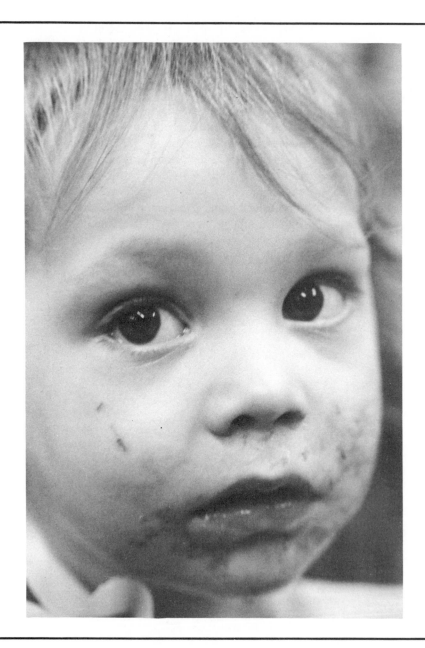

The Influence
of Jean Piaget

The past two decades have witnessed a resurgence of interest in the work of Jean Piaget. This revival has been so intense and so widespread that it has all but taken over the field of developmental psychology. For this reason alone, the teacher should possess at least some familiarity with Piaget's work. Although the work has many critics, few would deny that it has great merit. Working over a span of over fifty years with his wife and two primary colleagues, Alina Szeminska and Bärbel Inhelder, Piaget has developed a body of knowledge and data that both answers and asks questions.

Piaget's work cannot be accepted as final or definitive. It poses at least as many questions as it answers. Once again we recommend an eclectic approach, and suggest that the new student explore Piaget but at the same time listen to the other voices that are relevant to early childhood education. For example, the work of Freud and Erikson, mentioned in chapter 1, is considered essential by many early childhood educators. Choose and utilize what is of value to you.

Jean Piaget was born in Neuchâtel, Switzerland, in 1896. His first great intellectual pursuit was the study of biology. In fact, the publication of one of his first articles stimulated the Geneva Museum to offer him the position of curator of the mollusk collection. But he turned the offer down because he wanted to finish *high school*! He studied extensively in the areas of philosophy, sociology, religion, and psychology (a very new field at the time). He became particularly interested in epistemology, which is that part of philosophy dealing with the study of knowledge, and logic. He received his doctorate in the natural sciences from the University of Neuchâtel in 1918, at the age of 22.

Piaget became convinced that a combination of biological and psychological approaches could be useful in studying the development of knowledge and thought in humans. He was certain that the results of such a study could be expressed in the precise language of logic. In addition, he was convinced that such research had to begin with the study of intellectual development in young children, which is one of the most endearing and convincing characteristics of his work. As a result of his epistemological quest, he and his co-workers have studied children for over half a century. Together they have written over thirty books and published over one hundred articles. Through the years they have at least partially developed a theory of the development of intelligence that is gaining recognition and stimulating further research and study in many countries.

Piaget's work is difficult to study for a number of reasons. First, he writes in French; some of his books and many of his articles have not been translated into English. Second, those writings that have been translated are filled with highly technical, abstract, and confusing terms. The meanings of many of the terms have changed over the years. Third, as mentioned, he felt symbolic logic could provide a precise language for expressing his theory. Unfortunately, unless one has considerable training in symbolic logic, much of his writing is difficult to understand. Fourth, the theory itself has developed and changed over the years. His later works do not always convey the same ideas as his early works.

It would be impossible to capture all of Piaget's complex, often abstract thinking in a single chapter. We will content ourselves with touching upon a few of his most important and basic ideas. In addition we shall try to focus upon some of the implications of Piaget's work for the educator of young children.

An Overview of Piaget's Methods

What Is Piaget Trying to Do?

Piaget is trying to discover how humans acquire knowledge and the ability to think logically. As he sees it, the infant, let us say a baby girl, comes into the world with no real knowledge. She has only a few reflex behaviors (sucking, looking, reaching, grasping, crying). But she does have an inherited potential to learn, and she is motivated to learn. Piaget wants to know how the child moves from this state to that of a complex, logical, knowledgeable adolescent. How does it happen?

How does this child learn about so many objects and people in the world, so many relationships, so many rules and laws, so many behaviors? And equally impressive, how does she acquire an entire language within a few years? How does she learn to read and write? How does she master mathematics, social norms, and games? What are the processes involved in the acquisition of all knowledge? In other words, Piaget is interested in *cognitive development*. Once one grasps the enormity of the task Piaget has set for himself, it is not surprising to learn that even after fifty years of research he still does not have all the answers. On the other hand, those fifty years have not been wasted. Piaget is a recognized pioneer in this field.

What Methods Does Piaget Use?

Given that Piaget's goal is to learn how knowledge develops in humans, how does he go about the task? What method of study does he use? We already know he felt it necessary to focus upon children rather than adults, but how does he go about studying the development of knowledge and thinking?

The Clinical Method Piaget's methods have been criticized as imprecise and arbitrary. But, at the same time, they are also recognized as incredibly sensitive to human responses. These methods may, in the long run, be more valuable than tightly controlled experiments. In the "clinical method" of study, Piaget begins by asking the child a question. Further questioning is then based on the child's answer. Interesting answers are explored. Piaget believes that as much, or more, can be learned about the child's thinking by attending to her *wrong* answers as by analyzing her right ones. The child's answers determine the subsequent questions.

Think about this for a moment: careful questioning and careful listening may be the key to understanding a child's thought. Piaget eventually added the manipulation of material (e.g., clay) to the clinical situation. With this refinement, questions can be centered around the child's answers *and* actions rather than just on the verbal responses. The use of objects is particularly helpful with young children not yet capable of an entirely verbal or abstract level of thought. This clinical method is still being used in Piaget's studies.

Strict Observation At one point in his career, Piaget used another approach. He and his wife studied very intensely the infancies of their own three children, from birth until about 2 years of age. They observed and recorded, in great detail, specific behaviors and the ages at which they appeared. There was some interaction and some manipulation of objects, but very little language or questioning of the children (for the obvious reason that the children were too young). Thus there is *some* overlap between the clinical and observational methods, but the former relies more heavily on questions than does the latter. Piaget's work with his own children led to many of the hypotheses and assertions that form the bulk of his theory (Piaget, 1952, 1954, 1962).

Criticisms and Defense of the Methods

Piaget's methods have been heavily criticized (Ginsburg and Opper, 1969). First, many have found it hard to believe that a comprehensive theory of intellectual development could be based on nothing more than the observation of three infants. According to this view, many children should be studied; and the collected data should be evaluated with modern statistical methods. It has often been suggested that parental bias could color observations of the sort made by the Piagets. Piaget counters this argument by saying that these were preliminary studies. At this early point, he felt statistical testing was premature. He wanted to explore and describe problems to study. Later, statistics could be used.

In spite of the criticism, many of Piaget's observations have been replicated by independent researchers (Décarie, 1965). Few would deny that Piaget is a sensitive observer of children. One may also argue that naturalistic observation has long been a legitimate form of study used by naturalists and biologists in their study of animals. Charles Darwin wrote a "baby biography" of his own child. In a sense, the observational method is a very good one for certain purposes. For example, because Piaget and his wife knew their children so well, they could often determine whether failure to perform a particular task was due to fatigue, lack of interest, sickness, or just lack of ability. This kind of sensitivity can be lost in a formal experiment.

In spite of the fact that it has been used in studying thousands of children at the Jean-Jacques Rousseau Institute of Geneva University (and elsewhere), Piaget's clinical method has also been attacked and criticized. The usual criticisms are that the method is unpredictable and inexact. In addition, some have questioned whether *all* of Piaget's data has been included in the results he publishes, or whether he sorts out that which is interesting or in agreement with what he wants to find.

However, one can argue that his discoveries and insights into the realm of child cognition, gained through the use of this open-ended, child-initiated method, far outweigh the criticism directed toward the procedure. The clinical method is not as rigorous as an experiment, but to the minds of many it has been a fruitful technique. The issue of the accuracy of Piaget's method is still not settled. Cross-cultural replications of some of his work are available (Goodnow and Bethon, 1966; Lovell, 1961). (For opposing views see Braine, 1962; and Fleischman, Gilmore, and Ginsburg, 1966.)

What Has Piaget Concluded?

Given that Piaget has been interested in learning about the development of thinking and knowing in children and that he has used observational and clinical methods, what has he learned?

Stages of Development

Piaget believes that intelligence, knowledge, and the ability to think logically develop from birth through adolescence in a regular, somewhat predictable fashion. For purposes of study and explanation, he has divided this development into four *stages*, with some of the stages being further divided into *substages*. Piaget feels he can describe the kind of knowledge the child is gaining and the quality of the child's thought in each of these stages. Because Piaget only approximated the ages related to these stages and substages, we can conclude that children vary in the rate at which they pass through these stages. The important aspect of the development is that all children go through these stages in the same order. In other words, *all* children acquire skills in the same *order* even though one may be ahead of another at any given age.

Because these stages are so important in Piaget's thinking, and because they can be quite relevant to the task facing the educator, these stages will be discussed in considerable detail in a later section. But for now we turn to a consideration of some additional basic concepts that have evolved in Piaget's work.

Intelligence as Adaptability

Piaget sees intelligence, not as a score on an I.Q. test, but as the ability to utilize what is known and perceived in adapting to the environment. The intelligent act is that which best helps the individual adapt, given the circumstances and the individual's abilities at that particular time (e.g., in response to hunger, the intelligent infant cries, whereas the intelligent adult locates food and eats it). Intelligence is the utilization of what is known in adapting to the environment.

The Interaction of Heredity and Environment

Piaget believes that heredity and environment interact in the development of intellectual activity. The child's physical maturation combines with her experiences to determine intellectual development. If the child's physical maturation is retarded, intellectual development can be retarded regardless of the amount of experiences. Similarly, limiting experience can retard intellectual development.

Cognitive Structures and Schemas

Piaget speaks of a gradual build-up in the child of a hierarchy of *cognitive structures*. Cognitive structures can be thought of as the developing structure and function of the brain and central nervous system. Obviously, we as adults have more complex cognitive structures than do children. We have more thoughts, ideas, images, memories, logical abilities, problem-solving skills, and concepts. Piaget wants to understand how our thinking moved from that of a child to that of an adult. According to Piaget, the development of these structures is a long and somewhat predictable process that begins with perceptions and responses on the reflex level and ends with logical thought processes.

Thus, at birth the child begins with the five senses (touch, taste, smell, sight, and hearing) and a few innate reflex actions (crying, sucking, reaching, grasping, looking). Nothing much is there in terms of cognitive structures. The brain has yet to begin what we normally think of as cognitive or intellectual functioning. The infant perceives the world through its senses and reacts to those perceptions by means of the innate reflexes to ensure survival. If it is hurt, it cries in a reflexive manner. Very little thought is involved. But gradually, through both physical maturation and experience, intellectual life begins to grow, and eventually culminates in the development of logical thinking during adolescence.

Indispensable to the understanding of Piaget's position is the notion that the hierarchical development of intellectual abilities begins on a very *active*, and very *concrete* level. In one sense, during infancy the child's actions *are* its thoughts. If, for example, a child is pounding her rattle against the side of the crib, her thinking at that time is limited to the act of pounding rattle against crib. That is all that is in her head, just that one, momentary experience. She isn't thinking about having done this before, or how much noise it makes, or what her mother or father will think, or what she will do next, or what she just did. She isn't capable of looking at her actions, or talking to herself. She is just pounding, and that is all that she is thinking about.

The next element to be discussed is the concept of *schema*. A schema is a particular kind of basic cognitive structure. It is an overall capacity or potential to perform some particular type or class of action. For example, the child who is pounding the rattle has a pounding schema. The schema is not this particular instance of pounding but the capacity for pounding. She also has a grasping schema, a looking schema, a sucking schema, and so on. This means she has the capacity for grasping, looking at, and sucking on any number of objects in her environment. These schemas (or schemata) are part of the overall developing cognitive structures that make possible the acts of pounding, grasping, looking, sucking, and so on.

Assimilation and Accommodation

According to Piaget's theory, the child can only interact with the world in terms of her existing schemas. When presented with a stimulus in her environment, her existing schemas determine how she can respond to the stimulus. However, the stimulus and her active response to it can subtly modify the schema itself and thereby create a slightly different schema. This, in turn, will create a slightly different response potential.

Piaget suggests that there are two processes involved in the development and modification of schemas. He calls them *assimilation* and *accommodation*. When the child encounters a stimulus—say, a new rattle—she tries to understand it in terms of her existing schemas. She may look at it, reach for it, grasp it, pound with it, and suck on it. If it is not too different from other rattles she has played with, she will understand this new rattle in terms of these existing schemas. This is called assimilation, or the understanding of new experiences in terms of existing schemas. She includes this new experience in with her old experiences, and doesn't have to modify her cognitive activity or her behavior to account for it.

But if the new rattle is slightly different in size and shape from her old, familiar rattle, she must grasp it or suck on it in a slightly different way. She must modify her actions slightly to fit the new, but similar stimulus. This is accommodation. Remember that her actions are closely tied to her thoughts. Because her actions are so closely linked to her cognitive apparatus, any modification in her actions leads to a modification of the cognitive structures. Therefore, accommodation results in slightly modified schemas, or action potentials. She has learned a slightly different way of grasping and sucking on rattles. She slowly comes to understand that this is a slightly different, though similar rattle; and she begins to think of rattles in a slightly different way. All of this is still on a concrete, active level in infancy. She does not have a word, or label, or even a "mental" concept of rattle yet. It is strictly an object she acts on.

Equilibration

According to Piaget, the child constantly attempts to maintain a balance between assimilation and accommodation. That is, the child must maintain a balance between understanding new elements in her environment in terms of what she already knows (in terms of her existing schemas) and modifying her behavior and understanding in terms of her new interactions with new elements. This balance is called *equilibration*. The tendency toward equilibrium is one of the motivating forces in the intellectual development of the child.

When assimilation dominates over accommodation, Piaget says, *play* results. "This is simple play, in which reality is subordinated to assimilation which is distorted, since there is no accommodation" (Piaget, 1962). However, if accommodation dominates and there is no assimilation, *imitation* is the result. *Intelligent adaptation* results when there is equilibrium between assimilation and accommodation.

Through the child's active experiences with her environment, and through these interrelated processes of assimilation and accommodation, the child's schemas and cognitive structures slowly grow and become modified. This results in an increasing ability to process new and old stimuli into ever-growing and expanding schemas in an adaptive manner.

The Moderately Novel Experience

It is not surprising, given the previous information, that Piaget feels that the child learns best from what he calls "moderately novel" experiences. They are those stimuli which are just slightly different from ones previously experienced by the child that will fit into, but slightly modify the child's existing schemas, thereby promoting cognitive growth. In addition, Piaget feels that the "moderately novel" experience stimulates the child's natural curiosity and, therefore, can be considered another motivating factor.

The Development of Symbolic Thinking

While very young, the child cannot think of things she cannot see. She is held by the present. She can't take excursions into the past or the future. Her mind is filled with the "here and now." But gradually, step by step, she acquires the ability to think symbolically. A *symbol* is anything that stands for something else. When the young girl remembers something from the past, she is beginning to think symbolically. She is beginning to use mental symbols to represent objects and events in the past, present, and future. Symbolic thinking represents an enormous step forward in cognitive development.

Interiorization

Gradually, the child's activities become more covert, in the sense that the child can think of doing something without actually doing it. Piaget calls this important step *interiorization*. If our little girl thinks about grabbing a ball without doing it, she is engaged in a symbolic, interiorized act. Instead of thinking by doing, the child can now think with symbols.

Concrete Operations

Once the child has developed some symbolic thinking ability, she can begin to solve problems. But her initial attempts are rather intuitive and illogical. However, in her never-ceasing attempts to adapt to her environment, the child practices interiorized, covert actions. Through experience with interiorized actions she slowly develops what Piaget terms *operations*. These operations can be thought of as logical thinking that has the further characteristic known as reversibility (Ginsburg and Opper, 1969). *Reversibility* is a very interesting and important capacity that takes a surprising amount of time to develop in the child, and means that a procedure can be "undone" or "turned around." If one can add four to three to equal seven, then one can also subtract three from seven to equal four, or four from seven to equal three. Reversibility represents an important step away from purely intuitive problem-solving and a step toward true logical thinking. However, initially the child can only use these operations on things that can be seen and manipulated physically. These, therefore, are called concrete operations and are closely linked with the physical environment.

Formal Operations

Finally, during adolescence, the child (or adolescent) becomes capable of what Piaget terms *formal operations*. At this point operations are *not* bound to the concrete, physical environment. The adolescent is capable of problem solving on a purely abstract or hypothetical level. This is the highest state of intellectual development. It enables the adolescent to think in terms of, "What if . . . ?" and represents the best possible means of adapting to the environment.

Sensorimotor Stage (Birth to 1½ or 2 Years)

Introduction

Having covered a number of concepts and ideas that are basic to Piaget's overall conceptual framework, we now return to his stage analysis of the development of intellectual functioning. We shall discuss each stage, because it is here that Piaget's true gift for careful observation appears, and it is here that the new teacher may gather bits and pieces of information that can be useful in a day-to-day childcare setting. However, the reader must realize that our treatment of the stage analysis is but an introduction.

As we begin our discussion of the stages of intellectual development, be sure to keep in mind that the ages defining their limits are only average ages. Any given child may differ in the rate at which she passes through these stages. The important fact to remember is that children progress through these stages in the same order or sequence. Also, characteristics from early stages will still be seen in later stages.

There are no distinct lines to be drawn here. In describing each stage Piaget generally wishes to describe the preparation for and the attainment of the highest level of intellectual development seen during that stage. In addition, keep in mind that our discussion definitely emphasizes the first two stages, as these cover the area of early childhood education. We include only a brief look at the last two stages for purposes of continuity and overall understanding. A more detailed study is left to the interested reader.

Finally, we should emphasize that the sensorimotor period is one of rapid growth and development. The achievements of the infant during this sensorimotor stage are truly awe-inspiring. Piaget recognizes the importance of the events occurring during this period, and believes that the stage is crucial in the evolving process of intellectual development (Piaget, 1952, 1954). Thus, like other writers such as Freud and Erikson, he is keenly aware of the importance of the very early periods of life, even though his emphasis upon cognitive development is unique. In fact, Piaget considers this period so important that he further divides it into six substages. For our purposes, a discussion of the sensorimotor stage as a whole will suffice. The importance of infancy, and even the prenatal period, is now widely recognized (Ainsworth, 1973; Ainsworth and Bell, 1971; Fantz, 1961; Siqueland and Lippsitt, 1966; Spelt, 1948).

Motivation

As mentioned, the child begins life with a set of sensory mechanisms and motor reflexes. Thus the label sensorimotor. From these beginnings develop the schemas and cognitive structures characteristic of adult life. The child has very little language during most of this early stage. She learns through direct interaction with the environment. Piaget observes that the infant is very active and is motivated by three things: (1) the tendency to practice her reflexes and any other behaviors she has developed and to generalize these responses to a variety of stimuli; (2) curiosity for the "moderately novel" experiences; and (3) the need to maintain equilibrium between the two processes of assimilation and accommodation. All of these may be thought of as intrinsic motivations (see chapters 2 and 8 for discussion of intrinsic and extrinsic motivation in learning and play).

Egocentric Thinking

The child is *egocentric* during this, and much of the following, stage. All that the child perceives, and everything she does, is centered around herself and her needs. Everything is either her or directly related to her. She does not know the world as separate from herself.

One of the most important concepts the child must develop during this stage is that of *object permanence*. This means that the child must learn that objects (toys, clothes, furniture, people, anything) have an existence of their own, independent of the child's subjective state. According to Piaget, the egocentric child sees the world as disconnected pictures or images that appear and disappear. If a young child cannot see a particular object, the object ceases to exist for the child. This is a very literal case of "out of sight, out of mind."

One of Piaget's many observations will serve as an example of the egocentric lack of object permanence (the numbers 0; 7 (28) refer to the daughter's age in years, months, and days):

At 0; 7 (28) Jacqueline tries to grasp a celluloid duck on top of her quilt. She almost catches it, shakes herself, and the duck slides down beside her. It falls very close to her hand but behind a fold in the sheet. Jacqueline's eyes have followed the movement, she has even followed the movement with her outstretched hand. But as soon as the duck has disappeared—nothing more! It does not occur to her to search behind the fold of the sheet, which would be very easy to do (she twists it mechanically without searching at all). . . . I then take the duck from its hiding-place and place it near her hand three times. All three times she tries to grasp it; but when she is about to touch it, I replace it very obviously under the sheet. Jacqueline immediately withdraws her hand and gives up. The second and third times I make her grasp the duck through the sheet and she shakes it for a brief moment but it does not occur to her to raise the cloth. (Piaget, 1954, pp. 36–37)

Eventually, through a good deal of experience with objects disappearing and reappearing, the child learns that hidden objects still exist and can be found. She learns that, in fact, objects exist independently of herself and her own actions. (The interested reader would probably enjoy reading more about this process in Flavell, 1963; in Ginsburg and Opper, 1969; or in Piaget, 1954.)

Reality Concepts

During this stage the child also develops some rudimentary understanding of such factors as space, time, and causality. The child, as always, learns about these things through personal interactions with the environment. For example, if the child wants a toy on the other side of the room but there is a pillow between her and the toy, she eventually learns to go around the pillow or move the pillow as she crawls towards the toy. During this one, simple event, the child gains experience with space, time, and causality. She discovers that the pillow is in front of the toy and that the toy is behind the pillow. She reaches the pillow before she comes to the toy. She arrives at the toy after she leaves the pillow. She also causes the pillow to move out of her way by pushing it with her hand.

Imitation

Imitation appears within the first few months of life. At first, the child can only repeat her own behaviors. Later she can imitate a model but only if the model is repeating one of the child's own behaviors. For example:

> At 0; 3 (5) I noted a differentiation in the sounds of her laughter. I imitated them. She reacted by reproducing them quite clearly, but only when she had already uttered them immediately before. (Piaget, 1962, p. 10)

Piaget explains that at this point the child is still egocentric and does not understand the world apart from herself. Therefore, hearing someone else making a sound she has already made, the child thinks the second sound is her own and she continues to "practice" it. It is only later in this stage, as the child becomes more aware of the environment as separate from herself and, as her skills develop, that she becomes capable of imitating a model's activity. But things move swiftly. By the end of the sensorimotor stage, the child is capable of *deferred imitation*. As Piaget observes:

> At 1; 4 (3) J. had a visit from a little boy of 1; 6, whom she used to see from time to time, and who, in the course of the afternoon got into a terrible temper. He screamed as he tried to get out of a play-pen and pushed it backwards, stamping his feet. J. stood watching him in amazement, never having witnessed such a scene before. The next day, she herself screamed in her play-pen and tried to move it, stamping her foot several times in succession. The imitation of the whole scene was quite striking. Had it been immediate, it would naturally not have involved representation, but coming as it did after an interval of more than twelve hours, it must have involved some representative or pre-representative element. (Piaget, 1962, p. 63)

Here the child reproduces an absent model's actions through memory. This implies that some internalization of action has occurred in the child. Some symbolic "mental" activity is involved. This ability to imitate can be considered a bridge of the gap between sensorimotor and later intelligence.

Other Achievements

The child is busy during the sensorimotor stage, acquiring a wide range of new abilities and adaptive techniques. For instance, she matures physically at a rapid rate. She begins to relate sights to sounds (e.g., she learns that the refrigerator is making that humming sound). Her eye-hand coordination improves. She begins to crawl, then to walk. She develops the ability to recognize certain people (family, friends), and is able to anticipate certain events from a variety of clues (e.g., Daddy is home when the garage door closes). She begins to repeat actions that have interesting consequences (e.g., she pulls the cat's tail again and again). She becomes quite purposeful in her actions. Her egocentricity fades somewhat. She becomes aware of objects as separate from herself. In conjunction, she becomes aware of herself as separate from other objects. And, of course, she begins to speak. All of her experiences, her physical maturation, and her developing language lead the way to new growth in her cognitive processes. She begins to have thoughts that are somewhat more "internal" and "symbolic" in nature. Schemas and cognitive structures have grown, developed, and been modified as a result of the interaction of experience and physical maturation. In general, impressive gains are made during this stage.

The Preoperational Stage: Substage 1—Preconceptual Thinking
(2 to 4 Years)

Introduction

The overall preoperational stage (2–7 years) can be divided into two substages. Hergenhahn (1976) labels them "preconceptual thinking" and "intuitive thought." Interestingly enough, the first substage is the area least studied by Piaget, while the second substage is the area most studied by him.

We shall discuss each substage separately, beginning with preconceptual thinking. During this substage three major, interrelated developments take place: the development of symbolic thought, the acquisition of language, and the appearance of transductive reasoning.

Symbolic Thought

It is during this time that symbolic thought, as described earlier, truly begins to appear. Symbolic thought develops out of the child's earlier ability to imitate things. For example, a child might remember the "monkey at the zoo" through a visual image of the animal, through an internal trace of the sound made by the animal, or through some internalization of the movement made by the animal. In the earlier, sensorimotor stage the child represented things by acting like them. Eventually, this active process becomes more abbreviated, and the imitation becomes more internalized, more "mental." A mental symbol is eventually formed. The mental symbol may be a visual "image," an auditory representation, or an abbreviated form of the remembered movement or action. Some early symbolic thought may be related to language, but not all of it, as the ability to imitate is usually developed at an age when language is minimal.

Before symbolic thought develops, the child can only deal with the here and now. Symbolic thinking enables her to think about the past, the future, and about things that are not immediately present.

Symbolic Play

Symbolic thought is demonstrated in symbolic play, or dramatic play. Here the child can "pretend." She can pretend she is someone she is not. She can pretend she is making a cake in the sandbox. She can pretend a box and a stick are a drum and drumstick. She can eventually "role play." For example, in a game of house, she can play the role of mother, father, baby, or the dog. In play, as we have mentioned, Piaget believes accommodation is subordinate to assimilation.

Piaget feels that symbolic games are important in the child's emotional development as well as in her intellectual development. Young children, because of their size, their lack of certain abilities, and their domination by older children and adults, experience feelings of inadequacy that can lead to frustration and conflict. Through symbolic play, they can dominate and they can win. They can pretend things are what they want and need them to be. As Ginsburg and Opper put it: "In brief, symbolic play, serving a necessary cathartic purpose, is essential for the child's emotional development" (1969). Parenthetically, there are those who disagree with this cathartic view of play (see Ellis, 1973; and chapter 8 has a detailed discussion of various theories of play).

Language

Language develops rapidly during this stage. At first the child experiments with words and has no consistent meanings in mind for them. Then there seems to be a phase during which words have definite meanings but these meanings are very personal in nature. For example, to one child, the word "tricycle" may mean any one of many "wheel toys" that are fun to ride. But for another child the same word may mean, "that toy that Dawn rode over my foot with." Early language, as outlined in chapter 3, may also be holophrastic and telegraphic. To some extent adult language helps the child gain a new perspective on the world. For example, an adult may tell the child that a hammer is a tool just like a screwdriver is a tool. Both belong to the *class* of tools. Information such as this can aid in the formation of a concept. However, adult language is often too difficult for the child of this age to understand. Once again, the child has to do her own experimenting with language in order to understand it. As we saw in chapter 3, the child forms hypotheses concerning language and then tests them. It is evident though that children are well able to learn the vocabulary and grammar of their culture, as they master this task relatively quickly regardless of its complexity.

Transductive Logic

Hergenhahn describes tranductive logic, which also appears in substage 1, as follows:

> During this part of preoperational thinking the child begins rudimentary concept formation. He begins to classify things in certain classes because of their similarity, but makes a number of mistakes because of his concepts; e.g., all men are "Daddy," all women are Mommy," and all toys he sees are "mine." Rather than his logic being either inductive or deductive, it is transductive. An example of transductive reasoning would be "cows are big animals with four legs. That animal is big and has four legs; therefore, it is a cow." (Hergenhahn, 1976, p. 274)

The Preoperational Stage: Substage 2—Intuitive Thought (4 to 7 Years)

Introduction

We now move on to the second of the two substages of the overall preoperational stage. Once again, we must remind the reader that although we will be discussing advances made during this substage, behaviors and modes of thinking from the preceding stage and substage will still be present during this and subsequent stages. For example, we still find imitation, symbolic play, egocentrism, and so on.

As mentioned, this is the area most heavily studied by Piaget and his co-workers. For the purposes of this text we must focus on but a few of the elements and topics Piaget considers to be important. Piaget has been concerned with such diversified topics as symbolic thought, egocentrism, communication, moral judgment, classification, spatial and numerical concepts, mental imagery, general characteristics of thought, a revised clinical method, and equilibration theory. In addition, at the suggestion of Albert Einstein in the early 1940s, Piaget and his co-workers also studied the child's understanding of time, velocity, and movement (Piaget, 1946a, 1946b). Obviously we cannot cover all of this work here. We shall focus upon a few important areas that seem particularly relevant to early childhood education.

Egocentrism in Communication

Although by this time the child has overcome her egocentric point of view in some areas (e.g., her grasp of the object permanence concept), the trait remains in other areas. A prime example of this is in the child's communication. Piaget has observed that a large proportion (possibly 30 percent or more) of the child's speech, especially in the early part of this substage, is egocentric. This egocentrism falls into three categories: repetition, monologue, and collective monologue (Piaget, 1955).

Repetition, as an example of egocentrism, refers to the fact that the child repeats either what she has heard someone else say or what she herself has said. As Piaget describes it, the child does this for, "the joy of repeating for its own sake . . . the pleasure of using words . . . for the sake of playing with them" (Piaget, 1955). Repetition is seen as an example of the assimilating tendency to practice behaviors. Piaget also theorized that it may also involve some wish fulfillment on the part of the child which may be similar to that found in symbolic play.

The *monologue* occurs when the child is alone. Here the child will carry on quite a conversation, but with himself. For example, "Lev sits down at his table alone: 'I want to do that drawing there. . . . I want to draw something I do. I shall need a big piece of paper to do that'" (Piaget, 1955). This is viewed as noncommunicative, egocentric speech.

The *collective monologue* is similar to the monologue except for the fact that it occurs when at least two children are together. Here, even though they are together, the children talk to themselves. None of these types of egocentric speech is communicative. The child is unable to consider the listener's point of view or to transmit information. The child does not even make a real attempt to be sure anyone is listening (Piaget, 1955).

The remainder of the child's speech (70 percent) is *communicative* or *socialized*. In this type speech the child tries to explain something to the listener or tries to influence the listener to do something (Piaget, 1955). The child at least attempts to consider the point of view and needs of the listener. In other words, he tries to determine what it is he will have to say to be of interest to the listener and to transmit something to him. However, this form of communication is still quite limited and imperfect. As Ginsburg and Opper put it,

> *he tells another child certain simple facts, like how to operate a toy. Or he criticizes another child, or asks him questions, or in some other ways interacts with him. While serving a communicative function, such speech nevertheless shows certain deficiencies. The children do not attempt to explain events to one another, they do not speak in terms of causes of events. Also, children do not try to give proof or logical justification for what they have proposed. The reason is that they do not consider the possibility that the listener may have a contrary opinion.* (Ginsburg and Opper, 1969, pp. 88–89)

The child in this stage often uses pronouns (he, she, it, they, and so on) without letting the listener in on who or what it is that the pronoun refers to. The child may omit important features of a story or might get sequences of events confused. These last two faults may sometimes be due to a faulty memory rather than to egocentrism.

Piaget studied *listening* as well as *talking* at this stage of the child's life. Interestingly, listeners at this stage are often sure they understand what other children of the same stage are saying. It doesn't seem to make much difference whether the speaker is clear or not. In fact, the listeners often seem to "free associate," or to imagine what the speaker is talking about. There seems to be a kind of egocentric listening, as well as talking, at this stage (Piaget, 1955).

Classification and Class Inclusion

As mentioned, the child slowly develops the ability to recognize objects in the environment (people, animals, toys, etc.) during the sensorimotor stage. This ability represents a big step forward, but more follows. Eventually, if she is to adapt to the environment successfully, the child must learn to *classify* or *sort* objects into categories. She must realize that many objects are related to one another, and that they may be grouped or classified according to their similarities. It is during this substage (4 to 7 years) that the ability to classify begins to appear. Slowly the child starts to realize that certain groups of things are "toys," certain groups of objects are "food," certain groups of objects are "people," "cars," "houses," "animals," and so on. This emerging ability to classify according to similar properties springs from the child's active interaction with objects in her environment.

Let us begin our discussion of this emerging ability to classify by clarifying what Piaget means by "class" (Piaget and Inhelder, 1964). Imagine a group of objects including two red triangles, two blue triangles, two red circles, and two blue circles. This array contains two dimensions (shape and color) and two examples of each dimension (triangle-circle, blue-red). Piaget describes four characteristics of a class:

1. Classes within a given dimension are mutually exclusive. For example, if we classify according to shape, a given object cannot be in both the triangle class and the circle class.
2. All members of a given class are similar in some important way. All triangles have three connected sides and three angles. All circles are round.
3. Each class may be fully described by listing its members. We can describe the class of triangles by listing all its members: two red triangles and two blue triangles.
4. The defining properties of a class determine what objects are in it. For example, if the class we are defining is that of triangles, we can predict that all objects possessing three connected sides and three angles, regardless of color, will be in that class.

Piaget found that the ability to classify is acquired slowly, and spreads itself over the years. For example, prior to the substage we are now discussing (4 to 7 years), children are incapable of completely accurate classification. Prior to this time, if presented the objects described above, the child might begin by putting like objects together. But she wouldn't be able to complete the task accurately. Sooner or later she would include an incorrect object. For example, if she began to sort out all the triangles, she might include a circle somewhere along the line. Piaget also noticed that very young children may also, at least some of the time, ignore the classification task entirely, and arrange the objects in some imaginary shape such as a tower.

However, by the time children have moved into this substage they seem to be able to arrange objects in true classes. They can accurately sort out all the triangles, or blue objects, and so on. In addition, they may also be able to move a step further and arrange objects in subclasses. For example, they might first divide our eight objects into piles according to shape and then divide those piles according to color.

Alternatively, the child in this substage may first sort the objects by color and then subdivide by shape.

Behavior Versus Understanding

Interestingly, even though the child may be able to group the eight objects according to classes and subclasses, her understanding of the hierarchy she has created is limited. She can do it but doesn't fully understand what she has done. The child does not seem to grasp fully the concept of class inclusion, or the relations among the different levels of the hierarchy.

For example, after sorting the items according to shape and color she may fail to realize that there are more triangles in all than there are either blue or red triangles separately. She may not realize that if the blue triangles are taken away the red triangles will be left. And so on. Understanding lags behind behavior. She does not understand the relationships of the whole to the parts, the parts to the whole, or the parts to the parts. The implications of this for the teaching of mathematics alone are many.

If a child in this substage divides the triangles into red and blue triangles and counts both these new groups, she may understand that there are the same number of red triangles as there are blue triangles (though she may not, as you will see when we discuss numbers in a subsequent section). However, if she is then asked whether there are more triangles or more red triangles, she will probably say they are the same. Piaget explains that once the child has divided the large group into separate smaller groups, the child cannot simultaneously think in terms of the whole group and its separate, smaller parts. She just cannot hold that many different ways of thinking about the situation at the same time.

In the next stage (the stage of concrete operations), the child will be able to understand class inclusion, but only when she can see and manipulate the objects (e.g., the triangles and circles). A fine grasp of the relationships on a purely verbal or mental level will not appear until the fourth—and last—stage (the stage of formal operations). In summary classification abilities are slow to appear and spread themselves over a number of years.

Conservation and Reversibility

Like class inclusion, *conservation* is a concept the child does not have in this stage; but she is working towards it. As Hergenhahn states,

Conservation is defined as the ability to realize that number, length, substance, or area remains constant even though these things may be presented to the child in a number of different ways. For

> example, a child is shown two containers filled to some level with
> some liquid. Next the contents of one container are poured into a
> taller, thinner container. At this stage of development, the child,
> who observed that the first containers contained an equal amount
> of liquid, will now tend to say that the taller container has more
> liquid because the liquid is higher in the container. The child at
> this stage cannot mentally reverse cognitive operations, which
> means he cannot mentally pour the liquid from the tall container
> back into the shorter one and see that the amount of liquid is the
> same in both. (Hergenhahn, 1976, pp. 274–275)

Reversibility refers to a cognitive structure, which, once developed, allows the child to mentally "turn around" a particular procedure or action. It is an essential condition for the child's understanding of the concepts of conservation, seriation, and classification. It is not until the next stage (concrete operations) that reversibility is completely developed, but then only on the concrete level where she can see and manipulate the elements involved. Until then the child seems to center on one characteristic of a given situation while ignoring the others. For instance, the child who said there was more liquid in the taller, thinner container, centered on the attribute of tallness in making his judgment, but totally ignored the other, equally important attribute of thinness. He did not, or more likely could not, coordinate the two dimensions.

Piaget did many experiments that illustrate the child's lack of reversibility during the substage of 4 to 7 years. In one, the child is given two balls of clay which the child agrees are equal. Then either the child or the experimenter takes one of the balls of clay and makes a sausage shape out of it. The child will then say that the amount of clay in the sausage figure is more than the amount of clay in the ball. Asked why, she will say, "Because it is *longer.*" Again, the child ignores the fact that the sausage is also *thinner.* And she is unable to mentally reverse the procedure to see that the sausage can again be made back into an equal ball of clay. If the experimenter or child physically returns the sausage to a ball shape, the child now will again say that the balls of clay are equal. Piaget also feels that giving the child the right answer does not in any way assure an understanding of that answer.

Number Conservation

Piaget is a genius at learning about the thought processes of children by observing what they *don't* know. Through the examples just cited, where the absence of reversibility and the ability to conserve volume were noted, we can probably learn more about where the child's mind is than through an equal number of demonstrations of skills the child does possess.

But Piaget's message doesn't end with volume conservation. Nothing is quite so stunning or important to the educator as Piaget's findings regarding the young child's failure to understand whole numbers. Many children can count to ten or more (or recite parts of the alphabet) by the age of 2 or 3 years. But what meaning do they assign to these numbers? One example will suffice for now, though we shall return to Piaget's work in this area when we discuss the teaching of numbers to children in later chapters.

Consider the following conversation (actually, his clinical method) between Piaget and a child (age 4 years 4 months) as they manipulate a set of vases and a set of flowers. The child

put 13 flowers close together in a row opposite 10 vases rather more spaced out, although he had counted the vases from 1 to 10. Since the rows were the same length, he thought that the flowers and vases were "the same." "Then you can put the flowers into the vases?"—"Yes." He did so, and found he had 3 flowers [left] over. (Piaget, 1965, p. 50)

The three extra flowers were discarded and Piaget continued, to see if the child really understood that the two sets were now equal in number.

The flowers were taken out and bunched together in front of the vases. [That is, they formed a shorter row than did the vases.] "Is there the same number of vases and flowers?"—"No"—"Where are there more?"—"There are more vases."—"If we put the flowers back into the vases, will there be one flower in each vase?"—"Yes"— Why?—"Because there are enough." (The vases were closed up and the flowers were spaced out.)—"And now?"—"There are more flowers." (Piaget, 1965, p. 50)

Even though the child had himself established the one-to-one correspondence (after an initial error), he did not conserve the numerical equivalence when either of the separate rows was made shorter or longer than the other. He focused only on the length of the set of objects in determining the equivalence.

In similar experiments Piaget had a child (age 5 years 3 months) count the objects in two sets. Even though the child came up with the same number for each set, he still maintained that the longer set had more objects than the shorter set. The child seemed to confuse number and spatial relationships.

Piaget's work with number concepts suggests that the instructor can expect the children at this stage to be able to use numbers in certain ways but not in others, and that the capacity to fully understand number concepts requires a great deal of experience with them.

For example, it is clear that the children do learn to count at an early age. This counting process has meaning for the child and can be very useful. They can count pieces of candy to be eaten. They can count the number of chairs at a table. These are valuable abilities. However, performing *operations* on numbers requires a great deal more understanding than does counting. For instance, before she can understand the logic involved in adding, subtracting, and multiplying the child must know that a whole is equal to the sum of its parts. Piaget points out that the preoperational child cannot yet grasp this concept; she cannot yet think of the whole and the parts at the same time.

Furthermore, to be able to understand operations on numbers the child must understand that two objects remain the same two objects no matter how far apart they are placed. Piaget indicates that this understanding is not automatic, and requires time and experience.

The child may also be able to match objects in a one-to-one relationship. However, the ability to match, while it has its obvious uses, does not necessarily imply that the child understands the logical implications of the one-to-one relationship. That is, the child may not realize that the two sets she has matched are equivalent in number regardless of their spatial arrangement.

In other words Piaget's work shows us that the child needs a great deal of experience in dealing with numbers of objects before she will be able to fully understand what they are and how to use them correctly. Counting and matching are good and serve certain purposes well. But the child needs to work with objects in a concrete manner before she can understand the full logical implications of numbers. We discuss ways in which the teacher can provide meaningful experiences with numbers in chapters 8 and 9.

It is not until the stage of concrete operations (ages 7 to 11 or 12 years) that the child fully understands one-to-one relationships and can conserve numbers. And even then it is only on a *concrete* level, where the child can see and manipulate the objects in the number situation. According to Piaget, adolescence must be reached before a child can master conservation on a purely abstract level. The implications of these findings are earthshaking considering how children are taught and tested in mathematics in most schools today.

Intuitive Thought

At this point it should be obvious why this substage (4 to 7 years) has been called one of intuitive thought. The child has but a partial grasp of essential concepts and her understanding of her environment is limited.

In solving problems she makes guesses which are not entirely wrong (she deserves partial credit). She simply does not have a total picture of things, and cannot yet solve problems in a completely logical fashion. For example, she may be able to understand (at least in the human population) that all mothers are females, but she may not be able to comprehend that a mother can also be a sister. She may be able to walk home from school, but she may not be able to tell you the route she follows. She may be able to understand a story that is told to her, but may not be able to repeat it accurately. Even though she may know that there are more yellow balls than red balls in a given group, she may not know that there are more balls altogether than there are yellow balls or red balls.

Incidentally, young children often have trouble verbalizing things they want you as their teacher to understand. "Show me" is a very helpful phrase if you can give them the time and patience to physically explain things to you. They'll love you for it.

While displaying wonderful gains at this stage, the child cannot, and should not, be expected to function in a completely logical fashion, even in the simplest situations. A fully grown logical ability has not appeared; and teachers, parents, and other caretakers who expect their children to perform tasks beyond their ability are headed for trouble. A child pushed beyond her or his capacities can become frustrated, hostile, morose, and unhappy. Parents often want their children to be the best, and push them too hard without realizing the undeniable limitations on a child's abilities. Children need acceptance and support for exactly what they are at any given time in their development. They will learn, but it takes time, patience, and hard work which is what their "play" often is. At this point testing and grading children for correct answers only may be inappropriate, as their logical thinking and problem-solving abilities are only partially formed. Intuitive, and "wrong" answers are appropriate at this point in their development. However, testing in a low-pressure, noncompetitive situation, for the purpose of learning where the child stands in terms of cognitive development, may be desirable. But testing instruments, procedures, and results should be studied carefully.

The Stage of Concrete Operations (7 to 11 or 12 Years)

It is during this stage that the child finally develops the ability to do some of the things many people expect her to do in the previous stage. She develops the ability to reverse operations. She masters an understanding of conservation, classification, seriation, and many other numerical, social, and scientific concepts. However, thought processes at this time must deal with real, observable events that the child can see and manipulate physically. The child can solve rather complex problems, but these problems must be of a concrete nature. Abstract problems are still beyond the child's capabilities. For example, recall the experiment with the one-to-one correspondence between the flowers and the vases. During the present stage, the child would be able to give and understand all the correct answers if, and only if, she could see and manipulate the flowers and vases or see someone else do it. She could not imagine the situation and solve the problems.

The Stage of Formal Operations (11 or 12 to 14 or 15 Years)

During this final stage the development of the ability to think abstractly and logically is completed. The child can finally think through hypothetical situations, and can solve problems on a purely symbolic, mental level, without reference to concrete details. By the end of this stage, according to Piaget, thinking is as logical as it will ever be, and can be used to solve at least some of the seemingly endless problems and puzzles that confront us throughout our lives.

Implications of Piaget's Work for the Educator

If one accepts Piaget's conception of the intellectual development of the child (not everyone does), then the implications for education are quite extensive. We shall review a number of the more important implications as outlined by Ginsburg and Opper (1969).

Childhood Versus Adult Thought

One must recognize that the thought processes of a child are very different from those of an adult. It is not simply that children are smaller people than we are, differing from us in terms of the amount of thinking they do. They actually differ in terms of the type or kind of thinking they do. They differ in terms of the quality of their thought, and not just the quantity of it. The child, especially the very young child, has her own perspective on the world. She has her own subjective, illogical, intuitive, egocentric understanding of reality; the teacher can only bring the child to a more adult point of view little by little, and only as fast as the child is ready to go.

The teacher can certainly promote a child's optimal development, but this is contingent upon an understanding of where *each* child in the class stands in terms of development and performance level. If the teacher fails to become acquainted with every child and each one's way of perceiving reality, an individual child's capacities may well be under- or overestimated. The teacher must pay attention to each child's responses, both right and wrong, and must avoid thinking of all children within an age group as identical.

One of the most difficult things for a new teacher to do is to get inside the child's mind, to discover just how limited and how talented each little person is, and to avoid overestimating or underestimating the child's developing skills. Both overestimation and underestimation can lead to frustration and boredom.

Interaction with the Environment

According to Piaget, children need to interact physically and actively with their environment. They need to touch, feel, taste, see, smell, hear, and manipulate in order to learn. Verbal lessons alone will not bring understanding. We cannot just tell a child something and expect understanding. The teacher must help the child experience what is being discussed and let the child manipulate it, too. Rather than direct teaching, the teacher must provide an appropriate, interesting, safe environment

Interacting with a water-fountain can be as stimulating and as helpful as exploring more elaborate playground equipment.

and allow the children the freedom of movement and choice within that environment that is so necessary for learning to occur.

The child's understanding of reality develops directly from her own interaction with the environment. Piaget has shown in a number of experiments, and at a number of times during the child's development, that verbally correcting wrong answers (and even demonstrating such corrections) will not result in the child's acceptance or understanding of the correct answers in many cases. The child's thought processes are not sufficiently developed to allow her to comprehend explanations or demonstrations of corrected answers. The child must eventually find out for herself by interacting with the environment. One can only guide the child, not instruct her, through moderately novel experiences, to the point of eventual understanding. The child's questions should be answered, of course, and can be a key to what the child is ready to learn about. Don't overwhelm her, however. The teacher must be sure to use only the concepts and language that the child already understands. Essentially, any "explanations" should be on an action-related, concrete level for young children. For optimal learning, then, the teacher must know each child and allow and encourage each to interact with an environment that has been designed with their various needs in mind.

Use Moderately Novel Stimuli

The teacher should keep in mind that children learn best from moderately novel experiences or those that are only slightly different from their previous experiences. To provide such experiences, the teacher must know the children well, must know what will be moderately novel to each of them, and must be sensitive to what might "turn them on." What is moderately novel to one child may well be boring or unsettling to another.

We must recognize that children vary in their rate of development. Thus for any given group of children, the teacher must provide a variety of activities or stimuli to meet their various levels of development (see chapters 8 and 9). Surprisingly, it is easier to do this than to try to keep all children doing the same thing at the same time. Individual children should choose their own activities and should be encouraged to explore these activities in their own way and at their own speed. The teacher should stay aware of each child's progress in various areas. The children should not all be expected to do the same thing. Piaget feels that self-regulation on the part of the child is essential for efficient learning to occur. Many schools now are adopting this "learn by discovery" method. According to Piaget, group instruction, especially on a verbal level with young children, bores some, confuses others, and results in little true learning.

Piaget feels the child must be allowed to interact directly with the environment . . . and the next Picasso should not be told how to apply paint

Let Them Talk

Children need to talk to one another. Verbal and physical communication helps them organize their thought and aids them in expressing their ideas in a communicative rather than egocentric fashion. They learn to listen to each other and to understand that the other person's point of view is different from their own. They should be allowed, according to Piaget, to argue and debate. Such social interaction promotes logical thinking.

Piagetian Programs

Recent years have witnessed an upsurge in the number of early childhood education programs which attempt to incorporate the work of Piaget. Some of these programs emphasize only certain aspects of Piaget's theory, while others base their efforts on Piaget's work exclusively.

103

And, because Piaget's theory is so open to interpretation, it should not be surprising to learn that different programs have different ideas about what constitutes a Piagetian program.

Many schools adopt the Piagetian idea that children learn through discovery, and attempt to allow for this in a general way. Others try to follow Piaget in much greater detail. For example, Kamii and DeVries (1976, 1977) have developed teaching principles and methods that reflect Piaget's thinking in both the cognitive and the socioeconomic realms. Similarly, Weikart and his associates have developed a "cognitively oriented curriculum" that draws heavily upon Piagetian thinking (Weikart et al., 1971). Although both of these efforts are based upon Piaget's theory, they do sometimes disagree in the terms of their interpretations and implementations of that theory.

5

Sexism
in Education

Sexism is, undeniably, an emotional and political issue in the world today. It is one of particular relevance to the field of early childhood education, and cannot be ignored here. In our discussion we shall provide some background information; point out how sexism exists in education; and offer some practical suggestions which may be helpful to the new early childhood educator. We shall also outline some recent encouraging changes and provide some general ideas which might help promote non-sexist education.

But our concern with sexism is not limited to this chapter. The theme runs through the book. Because sexist attitudes have so permeated our lives, we feel it is essential to at least mention or acknowledge sexist influences in discussing such areas as parenting, family life, educational goals, program planning and evaluation, the selection and use of materials and equipment, and staff relations.

Our position is that sexism places unnecessary restraints on *all* of us. A male who only does "boys' things," misses a lot of very pleasant and rewarding activities. A female who only does "girls' things," is equally restricted. Sexist attitudes cheat everyone, female and male alike. Sexism can lead to unnecessary feelings of frustration, anxiety, guilt, anger, bitterness, and disappointment. Both children and adults suffer.

Many readers will already be familiar with these issues, but, by focusing upon very specific instances of restrictive sexist attitudes we hope to highlight the kind of limitations imposed upon human life by them. The fight against sexism requires a constant effort, even on the part of the most well-intentioned individual. The problem requires us to question many of the traditional norms and values of our society; and this process of questioning, learning, growing, and changing is essential and healthy.

What Is Sexism?

Sexism refers to the belief that there are fundamental, innate differences between the abilities and capacities of females and males. Furthermore, the sexist attitude encompasses the idea that the activities of each sex should be limited to those that are "appropriate." Obviously, there are differences between the sexes. But the sexist position maintains that there are many important differences above and beyond the obvious physiological differences, even though the validity of these additional differences has never been established scientifically. For example, the belief that men are *innately* aggressive while women are *innately* gentle and submissive has not been proven conclusively. In fact, some cross-cultural studies suggest no innate differences with respect to aggression (Mead, 1969; Chafetz, 1974). Although males may sometimes appear to be more aggressive than females, this tendency may be learned rather than innate.

The problem is that males and females have been so thoroughly trained to be different from one another, and to believe they are different, that it is almost impossible to distinguish between trained differences and innate differences, even though they may exist. It is the educator's task to break down these beliefs and to avoid inculcating attitudes that eventually limit what we feel we can and cannot do with our lives.

Different but Equal

There are other aspects to sexism. For example, some people believe that the sexes are different but equal. They feel that women and men are equal, but are "suited" to perform different functions in life. For example, they may feel that raising children and housekeeping are just as important as providing financial support for the family. However, they may also feel that, because of her equal but different nature, the woman is better suited for the former, while the man is best suited for the latter—always. This attitude is just as limiting as any other form of sexism. It, too, means we can't all try everything; we must limit ourselves to what is supposedly "best" for us.

Different and Unequal

Most sexist attitudes, however, are based on the fundamental belief that females and males are not only different, but that females are inferior to males. According to this position, the female role in our society is of less value, particularly in a monetary sense. In this case, sex discrimination works towards "different and unequal."

This belief in the inferiority of women is held by females as well as males. For example, in a recent study by Goldberg (1974), college women were asked to judge professionally-written articles. All read the *same* articles, but half the women were told the author was male while the other half was told the author was female. After reading each article, the women rated it in terms of how profound, valuable, and persuasive it was. They also rated the authors in terms of competence and style.

On every dimension the "male" author was rated better than the "female" author. This was even true in the traditionally "female" areas of art, history, and dietetics. In fact, the experimenters had switched the authors' names: the so-called "male" articles had been written by a woman. (See also Honig and Carterette, 1978.)

Sexism Limits Choice

Regardless of whether one defines sexism as a belief that men and women are different and equal or different but unequal, our concern is that when children are trained according to traditional sex role stereotypes, the result is discrimination on the basis of sex. Whether the discrimination is conscious or unconscious, it limits choice. Children are trained to fit one role to the exclusion of the other. They are demeaned if they want to do anything "inappropriate" to their sex role. Originality and creativity are thwarted and diminished. These sexist practices and attitudes are unnecessary, and should be changed.

In general, the traditional expectations in our society are quite straightforward. Females will be wives and mothers. Males will be husbands, fathers, and breadwinners. Other alternatives are not offered to either sex. No crossovers are allowed. Children "naturally" will grow up to be just like their mother and father. These expectations are based upon a value system that states that traditional forms of marriage and family life are the goals of all members of society. Those who do not conform to this pattern are labeled, among other things, failures, losers, misfits, and deviants. Being different can be expensive in a number of ways. By not conforming, one can lose support, love, and approval. One may suffer social ostracism. Status, power, position, responsibility, and money may be withheld. On the other hand, conforming to these standard patterns of behavior is also expensive. By conforming, one limits one's available options, and guarantees that new, creative lifestyles will remain unexplored.

There are some indications that things are changing. For example, while people are still getting married, they are also divorcing at a record rate—approximately one out of three marriages in the U.S.A. ends in divorce (and in California, one out of two). This suggests that, while pressure to marry remains, increasing numbers of people are unhappy in traditional roles and are opting for alternatives.

Furthermore, more and more couples are living together without being married. People are experimenting. Many have suggested that the nuclear family, as we have known it, is no longer a viable model for everyone (Chafetz, 1974; Farrell, 1975). In addition, we now hear of some couples (married or not) who are at least experimenting with some shared roles or with role reversals. Here the woman takes on some of the financial burden while the man shares in the housekeeping and child care responsibilities in a more involved way than has been traditionally acceptable. Changes in our society's value system are overdue. These changes can fruitfully begin in the setting of early childhood education.

Finally, recent statistics suggest that the role of parent is not one that everyone enjoys. It has been estimated (Holmes, 1977) that six out of every thousand children in this country are abused by their parents. This is most likely a conservative estimate. One wonders if some of these parents were pressured into marriage and family life, when other alternatives might have been much more appropriate for them.

The early childhood educator has a unique opportunity, perhaps even the responsibility, of encouraging children to develop their talents, abilities, and interests, regardless of their sex. You can and will be a powerful force in their lives. Your stand with respect to these issues can have a significant impact on the future of our culture.

We now turn to some of the elements and pressures within our society that tend to force us all into stereotyped sex roles. Many of these are in a state of flux. Many of them are changing, slowly. But the early childhood educator should be aware of all of them, and of the impact that can be made on the very young child.

Sexism and the Law

Before we examine the forms of sexism that children face on a daily basis, let's examine its roots in our society and in our legal system. Although the fight for equal rights for both men and women has been very apparent in the last decade, the struggle is not a new one. Part of the problem begins with our system of laws. Sexism can be traced right back to our Constitution. The Constitution of the United States (like the British Common Law that influenced it) is based upon a belief in female inferiority, as ordained by God and nature. This basic instrument of our legal system was written by and for white men. Women were not mentioned at all. Black men were described as three-fifths of a man, and did not originally qualify as "citizens."

Although the Fifth and Fourteenth Amendments were supposedly designed to stop discrimination of any kind and to guarantee "equal protection of the law to all," the courts (dominated throughout history by males) have generally seen these as inapplicable to women, even in fairly recent times (Kanowitz, 1969). Juries have been either exclusively male or male dominated through the years. Although Justice Douglas ruled in 1940 that it was "illegal though not unconstitutional" to exclude women in federal juries, we were reminded as recently as 1970 that "to the present day, the United States Supreme Court has not ruled it unconstitutional for women to be excluded from a jury" (Shulder, 1970). In addition, the legislative branches at all levels (federal, state, county, and municipal) have always been, and still are, male dominated. The vast majority of lawyers have always been males.

Caroline Bird describes the legal status of American married women just a few generations ago:

Legally speaking, they died on their wedding day . . . Under the common law doctrine of "femme couverte," a married woman was "covered" or veiled by the name and authority of her husband. She could not own property in her own right or sign a contract. She could not sue or testify against her husband any more than she could sue or be made to testify against herself. He had a right to her property earned or inherited. He supposedly "represented" her at the polls, and he could even be made responsible for criminal acts committed by her in his presence.

Under the common law, a husband came close to owning the body of his wife. He had the right to "restrain her, by domestic chastisement." If she left him, she lost the right to her children. He could—and sometimes still can—legally require her to submit to sexual relations against her will and reside at a place of his choosing. (Bird, 1972, pp. 16–17).

Married men have been subject to parallel laws. While implying their superiority over women, these laws state that the male is legally and financially responsible for his wife and children.

Until recently, American history books have ignored women's history, just as they have ignored black and other minority history. However, recent writers have begun to recognize that women reformers of the early 1800s were very active in the human rights issues of labor and abolition. In 1848 the Women's Rights Movement officially began at Seneca Falls, New York. Protests were lodged against the common law view of married women, the denial of their right to vote, unfair employment practices, a double standard of morals for men and women, and men's overall tyranny. The 1848 "Declaration of Rights and Sentiments" presented this picture of man's conduct towards women:

He has endeavored, in every way he could, to destroy her confidence in her own powers, to lessen her self-respect, and to make her willing to lead an abject and dependent life. (Brown and Seitz, 1970)

Not until 1920 did women win the right to vote—their only explicitly guaranteed legal "right" (Chafetz, 1974). The other areas of protest at Seneca Falls are still at issue. Under many laws at various judicial levels, women are still viewed as inferior, as dependent, as incapable of responsibility, and as second-class citizens. Unfortunately, women have never united and used their voting power to change the laws; and men have not been particularly willing to help.

There seemed to have been some progress made during the first forty years of this century. "The cultural heroine of young women in the era between the two World Wars became the ambitious career woman, as demonstrated by the popular movies of the era" (Chafetz, 1947). "Happily, proudly, adventurously, attractively career women," were depicted in many of the popular women's magazines (Friedan, 1963). Women's condition with respect to education, employment, and overall activity level seemed to reach a peak during the Second World War, when millions of women worked for the war effort. Many of them stated a desire to continue working after the war (Trey, 1972). But during the years following the war women were once again put in an inferior place, with no legal recourse. Millions of women were fired from their jobs and replaced by returning male veterans. Simultaneously, the marriage and birth rates "boomed." The image and status of women returned to that of the housewife and mother. Recently, the labels of sex object and consumer have also been added.

The 1960s heralded a few legal victories. Among them were the Equal Pay Act of 1963, prohibiting discrimination in pay on the basis of sex, and Title VII of the Civil Rights Act of 1964, prohibiting employment discrimination on the basis of race, color, religion, national origin, or sex (Bird, 1972). But enforcement of these new laws has been minimal until the past few years, partly because there are so many state and local laws to the contrary. In 1972 the Equal Rights Amendment was finally passed by both congressional houses. This amendment, "makes virtually all laws that arbitrarily differentiate between the genders unconstitutional" (Chafetz, 1974). But, as this is written, the amendment still awaits ratification by a requisite two-thirds of the states.

Sexism in the English Language

Just as our legal system has a great effect on our behavior, so too, does our language. Language affects our perceptions, our thinking, and our understanding of the world around us. Unfortunately, our language is permeated by sexist elements. As the young child encounters and absorbs these elements there is a subtle internalization of sexist attitudes. The early childhood educator should be aware of these features, and should try to counteract them.

Like many other languages, ours contains many gender-linked

words. In fact, it is difficult to speak and write in a gender-free manner, as we quickly discovered in writing this book. For example, when we speak of a person, we must use that person's name, or a gender-linked pronoun (she or he). Although *they* is gender-free, we do not have a gender-free, singular pronoun. We are forced to use *she* or *he,* or to avoid the singular altogether. Traditionally, the pronoun *he* is used to refer to any singular where the gender has not been specifically stated. For this reason, many more male pronouns are spoken, read, and heard than female pronouns. *He* stands for both genders. In this book we have tried to use he and she about equally.

Many generic or general terms that refer to both (or neither) males and females are actually masculine-gender words. For example: mankind, mailman, chairman, man, man-made (manufactured), manhunt, manhole, forefathers, brotherhood, man-hours, manhandle, and man-slaughter. To young children, who often understand and use words in a very literal sense, those words may mean the male gender only. Again, the implication may be that men are more important than women. Even the words *women, human,* and *female* have masculine bases.

In addition, dictionaries often define words in a manner that reflects traditional, sex-role stereotypes. For instance, manly has been defined as "having qualities becoming to a man; manlike; esp., brave; resolute; noble," (Webster, 1951). The synonym given is "male." *Womanly,* on the other hand, is defined in the same dictionary as, "possessed of qualities characteristic of women, as gentleness, compassion, modesty; feminine." Its synonym is "female." In the same book, the antonym for "male" is "female."

There is another feature of our language that is demeaning to females. Although this is not often a concern in the early educational setting, young children are exposed at home, in the streets, on television, and in movies to the fact of women being referred to in derogatory terms. Examples include bitch, whore, chick, broad, old maid, and girl (referring to a woman). Clearly, there are more. Does a man get the same feeling when called a *stud,* or *bachelor* as a woman does when she is termed a *whore,* or a *spinster?* These words reflect societal values, and a double code of morals for men and women. Early exposure to these elements can begin to influence attitudes in young children about women and men.

Table 5.1 contains some alternative forms of speech that can do much to eliminate sexism in our everyday language. We might be well advised to change our language, and to alter the forms of language used in the books we read to children. Children need to know that women as well as men can be mailpersons, chairpersons, and firefighters, and that they can be brave, aggressive, noble, dominant. They also need to know that men, too, can be tender, passive, forgiving, and fearful. They need to know that all persons can try, and do, and be, all things.

Table 5.1 *Alternatives to sexist language*

Sexist	Better or nonsexist
man	person human being people women and men
manpower man-made	human energy manufactured made by men and women
forefathers or fathers	precursors ancestors forepersons
brotherhood	amity unity community the community of people
Miss Mrs. Mrs. Jack Jones	Ms. Ms. Mary Jones Mary Jones
airman, fireman, etc.	airperson, fireperson, salesperson
chairman	chairperson
lady girl (as synonym for adult female) the little woman the weaker sex little old lady	woman person individual
authoress, aviatrix, heiress	author, aviator, heir (don't need an "ess" ending)
lady lawyer, lady doctor	lawyer, doctor
man and his world	people and their world
mankind	humankind
the farmer and his wife	the farmers, the farming couple
Ted Johnson and his wife	Mary and Ted Johnson (or reverse) or Mary Jones and Ted Johnson (or reverse)

Sexist	Better or nonsexist
mailman	mail person, mail carrier
chick, broad, babe	woman, person
"Mrs. Mary Kyle, wife of Earl Kyle and editor-publisher of the *Twin Cities Courier*"	"Ms. Mary Kyle (or Mary Kyle), editor-publisher of the *Twin Cities Courier*"
spinster, old maid	woman or unmarried woman
directed by the wife of Mao-Tse tung	directed by Chiang Ching, wife of Mao-Tse tung
DFL ladies	DFL women (ladies is value-laden)
manhood	personhood
proving his manliness	proving his humanness
women's lib women's libbers libbers	women's liberation, feminist movement women's liberationists, feminists women in the women's movement
dame	woman, person, individual (or her name)
gal	woman, person, indiviudal (or her name)
the lovely, vivacious Mrs. Gandhi	Ms. Gandhi
Doris Lessing is an excellent British woman novelist	Doris Lessing is an excellent British novelist
Amelia Earhart did what few people —men or women—could do	Amelia Earhart did what few people could do
Everybody did his work	Everybody did his/her (or her/his) work Everybody did their work (Equality outweighs grammar)
The student . . . he	The student . . . he/she (or she/he)

Adapted from *The Emma Willard Task Force on Education: Sexism in Education*, Minneapolis: The Emma Willard Task Force on Education, 1971.

Prenatal Sexism

Sexist attitudes are at work even before a child is born. Expectant parents debate the color of the nursery. Pink, blue, or yellow? Friends and relatives experience a similar dilemma regarding gifts. Few parents will dress a baby boy in pink without a twinge of uneasiness.

Parents, friends, and relatives often have a preference with respect to the sex of an unborn child. The two most common questions immediately following the birth of a child are, "Is it normal?" and, "Is it a boy or a girl?" Inherent in such preferences is the assumption that the parents' expectation for boys and girls are different, and that girls and boys will be treated differently. Females and males are expected to do different things. Girls will be trained in "domestic" affairs, while boys will be trained to be "breadwinners." The system is ready for the infant, and is keyed to its gender.

Sexist Child Care: The Self-Fulfilling Prophecy

Over the years society has decided that certain characteristics are necessary in order for the genders to be successful in their traditional roles. To fit the prescribed mold (i.e., breadwinner) in this competitive, capitalistic society, the male has needed to be strong, assertive, dominant, highly motivated, rational, unemotional. Females, on the other hand, need a different and complementary set of characteristics. To fill the bill as wife, mother, and moral supporter, tradition has prescribed that the woman be passive, dependent, intuitive rather than rational, and, of course, willing to accept herself as "the weaker sex."

Some would argue that these differences are innate. But it seems reasonable to assume that many, if not most, of the differences between male and female are unconsciously instilled. So-called masculine and feminine traits are present to some degree in every human being. However, society differentially sanctions certain characteristics and forbids others on the basis of sex. In other words, society trains male and female genders to be more distinct than they need be. Society promotes these stereotypes through its religious, social, childrearing, educational, employment, legal, and linguistic systems.

In fact, we don't actually know the extent to which males and females are similar or different. That there is still a great deal of overlap between the two, despite all the training, argues for similarities of the sexes. (For discussion of different sex role stereotypes in other societies, see Mead's studies, 1969, of three highly different tribes.)

Merton (1957) discusses one interesting aspect of sex stereotyping, the "self-fulfilling prophecy." The statement is made that "The female is the weaker sex." Assuming this to be true, parents, teachers, and other caretakers do not encourage, train, or even allow girls to develop their muscles in active pursuits. They are not rewarded for playing contact sports, climbing, wrestling, or engaging in building or construction games. In fact, they are often dressed neatly and told to "act like a lady and don't get dirty." Boys, on the other hand, are quite thoroughly trained physically. It doesn't take too many years before girls *are* the weaker sex. The prophecy is then fulfilled. From this point on girls are further eliminated from such "boys' games" as baseball, basketball, and football because they are by this time not only weaker but seemingly less coordinated.

Another self-fulfilling prophecy begins with the belief and statement that "Boys don't cry." This belief and its concomitant behavioral restrictions set the stage for the belief that men are rational and unemotional while women are irrational and emotional. Little boys as young as 2 are often not allowed to cry or to express their emotions. Girls, on the other hand, are encouraged to understand and express feelings. In fact, many girls learn to use crying as a manipulative behavior, first with their fathers and later with boyfriends and husbands. Thus the prophecies are fulfilled.

Sexism in Children's Books

We now turn to a consideration of the sexist attitudes inherent in many of the books we read to our children. Without being aware of it, we provide our children with sexist models almost everytime we open up a colorful, funny, or exciting new children's book. The early childhood educator should be aware of these subtle, often unnoticed influences, and guard against them.

After an investigation of children's books available in libraries and bookstores, one researcher states that, "an almost incredible conspiracy of conditioning prevails." Look over a few books yourself. You will find nearly everywhere "the notion of male superiority and female inferiority, male rights and female duties" (Fisher, 1974). Fisher points out that although females represent 51 percent of the U.S. population, their representation in picture books varies between 20 and 30 percent. "There are five times as many males in titles as females, four times as many boys, men, or male animals pictured as there were females."

Not only the quantity, but the quality of female representation is sexist. The following passage characterizes Fisher's discoveries concerning females in young children's books:

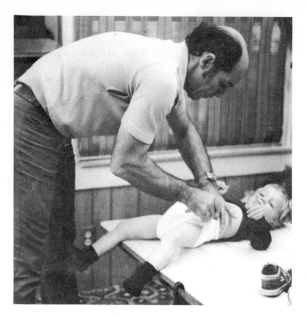

Male early childhood educators can help break down sex stereotypes

What they do is highly limited; more to the point is the sheer unreality of what they do not do. They do not drive cars. Though children see their mothers driving all the time, not a single description or picture of a woman driver could I find. In the world today women are executives, jockies, stockbrokers, taxi drivers, steelworkers; in pictures these are nonexistent . . . Little girls in picture books tend to be passive, though sometimes manipulative. They walk, read or dream. They seldom ride bicycles; if they do, it is seated behind a boy as in Dr. Seuss's One Fish, Two Fish, Red Fish, Blue Fish *. . . Though there have been women doctors in this country for over one hundred years, and pediatrics is one of their preferred specialties, there was not a single woman doctor to be found. Women are nurses, librarians, teachers, but the principal is always male. They have emotions; they get angry; they disagree; they smile; they approve; they want to please. What they do not do is act. Boys do; girls are—a highly artificial and unsatisfactory dichotomy.* (Fisher, pp. 119–120)

Fisher did know of one book that depicted working mothers (*Mommies at Work,* by Eve Merriam). But she couldn't find it in stock in any of the bookstores she visited. And even this book has short-comings:

However, while commendable—there are mommies who split atoms, build bridges, direct T.V. shows, who are dancers, teachers, writers

. . . and can serve as good models

and doctors—it is also highly apologetic. The end, "all mommies
loving best of all *to be your very own mommy and coming home
to you," gives it away. We don't feel the need to say about Daddy
that he loves his children more than his work. Couldn't Mommy
matter-of-factly like working and baby, too, as I'm sure many
do?* (Fisher, p. 120)

Fisher points out that one of the most influential books is also one
of the worst offenders. According to her, the more populous males in
Richard Scarry's *Best Word Book Ever:*

*really do get to do everything. Toys, for example, are defined by
showing thirteen male animals playing with exciting toys—a
tricycle, blocks, castle, scooter, rocking horse, as well as the traditional toy soldiers and electric trains. Two female animals play
with a tea set and a doll! Many pages had only males as protag-
onists, but the one page which showed only women was . . .
what else? In the Kitchen. The most infuriating page was entitled
'Things We Do.' Males in Scarry's book world dig, build, break,
push, pull, and do fifteen other active things, including eating.
The only two things females do are watch and sit . . . No wonder
both boys and girls identify with the boys' role in life.*
(Fisher, pp. 121–122)

Fisher also points out that in books about blacks, females are
even less in evidence. Furthermore, fantasy books, such as those of

Dr. Seuss and those of Maurice Sendak (e.g., *Where the Wild Things Are*) are primarily about males. It seems that about the only place in which females fare better than males throughout history is that of folktales. Many of these involve themes of wish-fulfillment, comeuppance, and the vindication of the underdog. In folktales women are often smarter than men and often utilize trickery. Fisher theorizes:

> *The folktales reflect a preindustrial culture where, though women may not have had equality, they did play vital functioning roles. They were not consumers or sexual objects, justified only by mother-hood, as today's world all too often defines them. They were producers who functioned in agriculture and home industries such as spinning and weaving, who worked side by side with their men. Evidently the folktales survive because they have certain psychological validities.* (Fisher, p. 118)

Young males, as well as young females, suffer from sexist influences in books. Wouldn't it be more reasonable if boys did not always have to be tough, aggressive, adventurous, and superior? Boys should be able to sit, to cry, to cook, to sew, and to dance when the spirit moves them. It would be nice if all boys and girls could also see excellent books like *William's Doll* which shows a boy's natural, healthy interest in dolls. He wants a doll he can feed and cuddle and take care of. If doll play is such good preparation for parenthood for females, why not for males? And why shouldn't girls enjoy trains as in *A Train For Jane*?

Nonsexist books should be readily available

In the years since Ms. Fisher made her investigation, nonsexist books have been increasing. *Young Children*, the bimonthly NAEYC Journal, has a section on new children's books in each issue. *Ms.* magazine also frequently reviews new children's books.

Sexism and Television

Although there are now a few programs and advertisements that are deliberately nonsexist, television comprises one of our major sources of sexist attitudes, models, and behaviors. The average American child is exposed to this daily.

Young children, unaware of the commercial motivation behind advertisements, certainly must obtain a rather peculiar view of people and their needs. Housewives are depicted as spending all their time worrying about which product will make their shiny floors shinier, their whites whiter, their colors brighter, their coffee richer, and their cakes lighter. The females in these commercials are dedicated to winning the love and approval of other family members, all of whom seem to lead more active, exciting, and carefree lives.

Single women are often seen as wanting to be glamorous, sexy, cool, and attractive. They want to be noticed by men. This entails clean breath, perfect hair, no odor anywhere, the latest styles, a great deal of makeup, hairsprays, perfume, protein in their shampoo, iron in the diet, an elegant, sporty, or "intellectual" car, and a tennis outfit.

Single men, also being transformed into sex objects and outrageous consumers of the glamor industries, are now encouraged to have the dry look, to know what they like in wine, to keep up with the latest styles, to shave closely, to use aftershave lotion, to hold a tolerant attitude towards liberated women, to own a pocket computer, and to have dandruff-free hair. All this, a tennis racket, a sailboat, and the latest sportscar will no doubt make him a success in his career, and a hit with the "ladies."

These images no longer apply just to whites either. These are requirements that cross the lines of race, color, and creed. Blacks, who never even appeared in commercials before, are now subject to the same doubts about their mouthwash, the same need for cleaner, brighter laundry, and the same insecurity about the acceptability of their overall bodily condition.

These advertisements may well increase personal anxieties because they imply that there is always a need for further improvement, and because they imply that to *become* a real woman or a real man, an enormous amount of money and effort is required. No one is acceptable, let alone attractive, as they really are. An egocentric point of view, an obsession with keeping up appearances, is encouraged.

Beyond advertising, general television programming (with a few exceptions) reflects the traditional, sexist point of view. Males dominate females. Males are active, females passive. Males do, females watch (and are impressed). Men appear in a great variety of roles. Women are domestic, supportive, and achieve their identity through men. Women need a husband, a house, and a family for fulfillment. Nothing more, nothing less, nothing else. These themes appear repeatedly in adult series (new and repeats), in movies, and in children's programs.

In 1974, Bergman wrote an article criticizing *Sesame Street*. The contention was that male characters (human or puppets) are seen far more often than females, and that females are seen in traditionally stereo-typed roles. Girls were often passive, and only vaguely involved in scenes about the more active, interesting boys. Women were almost always mothers and housewives—often nagging ones at that.

On the positive side, *Sesame Street* does contain a few sequences that have good nonsexist themes. The men on the show are warm, nurturant, and understanding people. However. the ratio of males to females (humans, puppets, and announcer voices) remains well below the level of equal representation. On a given show one may find five times as many males as females. It seems young females still have to identify with little males to put some adventure and fun in their lives.

Then, of course, there is the matter of television violence. Males prove their strength and establish their masculinity by fighting and killing. Violence is depicted as a very common problem-solving technique. By the time a child becomes a teenager she or he typically has witnessed thousands of murders on television.

As teachers you cannot control what children watch (unless there is television within your school's program). But you can be aware that this is a strong force in their lives. You can discuss some of their favorite shows with them. You can begin to make them aware of the *unreal* quality of television programming. Children can learn to discriminate between "real life" and the "weird world" of T.V., but they need some help and guidance in forming this discrimination. Furthermore, you can discuss television programming with parents, and help them become aware of the sexism (and the violence) inherent in so much of it. They may then decide for themselves if they wish to limit their children's television viewing, or at least temper its effects with discussions and comments.

Sexism and Toys

Obviously, the play situation affects the child's physical, cognitive, emo-tional, and social development. While playing, children form self-concepts and learn about other children and adults. As we have mentioned, many early childhood educators feel the play situation is vitally important in the preschool experience. A close look at traditional, seemingly harmless play equipment and activities reveals a surprising amount of sexist content, similar in many ways to the sexist elements we have already discussed in connection with literature and television.

The advertising and packaging of toys and play equipment often reflect sexist attitudes. Generally, in most advertisements (in catalogs, in magazines, on television) and on the toy packages themselves, boys are shown far more often than girls. In addition, boys are shown in more active and problem-solving roles, while girls are shown in more passive, dependent, and supportive roles. Girls are often shown watching boys do or make something. Females then admire or use what the males have made.

Manufactured toys represent an important element of the play situation that is particularly susceptible to sexist divisions. Toys are often broken down into two categories: boys' toys and girls' toys. The former tend to be more varied, more interesting, and more expensive. The selection for boys includes complex train sets, books, cars, trucks, tractors, bikes, rockets, "action" dolls (often violence-oriented), guns, models, chemistry sets, erector sets, blocks, and equipment for a variety of team sports. Their costumes include doctor (never nurse), astronaut, policeman, superman, Indian chief, cowboy, football player, and more.

Girls' toys, on the other hand, are directed toward domestic chores, child care, and crafts. They include sets of dishes, cooking utensils, toy ovens and dishwashers, toy vacuum cleaners, mops, brooms, craft kits, possibly tinkertoys, and, of course, dolls. Dolls are perhaps the biggest moneymakers in the billions-of-dollars-a-year toy industry. Dolls presumably prepare young girls for their roles as mothers. Interestingly enough, boys do not receive similar practice in the father role. However, fashion dolls are an even hotter sales item than the more traditional baby dolls. These dolls have clothes and accessories for a variety of situations, and the constant emphasis is on *appearance*. Does she have the suitable wardrobe? Is her hair properly groomed? Will she attract males?

In addition to baby dolls and fashion dolls, female toys also include make-up kits, perfume, nail polish, and jewelry. These items and the play that develops around them add to the young female's growing awareness that, to be acceptable, she must be cute, clean, well-groomed, and pretty. In preparation for her adult role, she is constantly reminded that her natural features could use a little improvement . . . a little lipstick here, a little eye shadow there. One wonders when toy electric shavers for that "unsightly" hair will appear, and when toy feminine hygiene sprays will crowd the shelves. These kinds of toys can lead to self-doubt. How attractive can one really feel if one is constantly reminded that one is so far from painted, sprayed perfection? How will this imperfect female ever win that superior male and be allowed to fulfill her destiny as wife and mother?

Little girls can enjoy firetrucks as much as little boys do, and little boys can enjoy dolls

Parental and educational support of the toy industry feeds the young female's growing insecurity. The child's involvement with these toys is later replaced by involvement with the (also enormous) adult fashion and glamor industries.

The costumes that are available for young females reflect traditional attitudes about appropriate roles for women. They include the princess, the baton twirler, the nurse (never doctor), the bride, the squaw, the ballerina, and the mother (complete with apron, baby doll, broom, and make-up kit). It is not that these are inappropriate roles for girls to imitate. Rather, it's that, until recently, they have been the *only* roles available to them in play and in real life.

The fact that boys have been given more interesting and varied toys contributes to the overall belief that males are superior to females. If boys received the most interesting and most expensive toys, they must be better and more valuable than girls. For some this is changing, but we still have a long way to go.

Sexism and Play

In the first two years of life, children of both sexes are generally allowed to play together and to play with the same kinds of toys. At this early age, it is generally acceptable for boys to play with an occasional doll or stuffed animal, and it is acceptable for a girl to play with blocks, or an occasional toy truck or car.

However, by the time they are 2 to 3 years of age, girls and boys begin to play separately as sanctioned by parents, teachers, and other caretakers. Boys play "boys' games," and girls play "girls' games." By this time they are being given sex-typed toys. In fact, they are *expected* to play differently by their families, friends, and teachers. By the age of 3 Sammy may actually be *forbidden* to play with dolls, toy ovens, or cooking sets. And, of course, there is always the attitude, "Whatever would Lilly want an electric train for?"

Very early in life, at home and in school, children are segregated according to gender for a variety of activities. Females are encouraged to cook, paint, dance, and play in the "doll corner." Boys aren't encouraged to engage in these rewarding activities. They are invited to play with blocks, trucks, cars, and trains, to engage in woodworking, and to learn team ball games. These are activities denied to girls.

When both male and female supervisors are present, the males often lead and oversee the boys' activities, while the females supervise the girls'. Incidentally, the female supervisors are often expected to be responsibile for traditional female chores such as changing wet diapers or cleaning up snacks, while males set up chairs and equipment. Such jobs should be shared in a nonsexist environment.

It is not surprising that some females reject their passive, dull, and inferior roles and become tomboys. As if to say, "We don't blame you," society allows the young female to be a tomboy for a number of years . . . but not forever. Generally by the onset of puberty she has been put in her inferior place.

On the other side of the coin, boys who show an interest in inferior female activities are labeled sissies and are immediately pressured to shape up. They are not allowed a grace period. Boys quickly learn that to be masculine, they should never be caught acting like a girl. "The fear of femininity is only a first step in the race to build masculinity. The second step is an easy corollary: boys must take on what girls are allegedly afraid to do—actions such as killing" (Farrell, 1975). Boys see these attitudes and actions in books, on television, and in movies (if not in real life); and they practice them in their play. The male's fear of appearing feminine can be quite debilitating and destructive through the years (Nichols, 1975).

The recent trend toward repeal of homosexual rights ordinances across the country has revealed a strong antihomosexual attitude within the general population. This backlash may well make any sexual or behavioral crossovers, or any interest in the activities of the opposite sex, appear even more threatening and dangerous, even when homosexuality is not involved.

Sexism and Self-Concept

Introduction

So far, we have defined sexism and have devoted a section to each of several major elements in our society that contributes to and maintains prevailing sexist attitudes (i.e., the law, language, prenatal attitudes, childrearing practices, books, television, toys, and play situations). In this section we will discuss the impact of all this on the young child's self-concept. In the face of this enormous pressure to conform, how does the child fare? What does the child think of herself or himself?

Obviously the answers to these questions are difficult, for there are as many different ways of adjusting to the sexist pressures as there are people in the world. But there are some general patterns that may be usefully discussed.

Clearly, the early childhood educator is interested in providing each child with a good, strong, positive self-concept. One's self-concept, however, can be positive or negative, realistic or unrealistic. It can be dynamic, flexible and changing; or it can be fairly stable. It refers to how valued and loved one sees oneself to be, and how intelligent, competent, and skillful one sees oneself to be. More often than not, it is probably a mixture of positive and negative attitudes about oneself.

Our particular concern here is with how the self-concept relates to sexism. Young females may either accept or reject the prevailing conception of what it means to be female. Similarly, a young male may either accept or reject society's conception of what a male ought to be. None of these four positions is perfect. Each leads to some difficulties, and each provides some form of support for the individuals in their search for strength, peace of mind, and fulfillment. We shall comment on each of the four positions.

Accepting Male

Positive Aspects The young male who accepts and conforms to tradi-tional sex-stereotyped attitudes and behaviors will have a relatively easy time maintaining a positive self-concept. He is allowed to participate in interesting, active, and highly-valued activities. He is given the more fascinating, expensive toys and play equipment. He knows quite early that he will have many career choices because he has seen an enormous number of male models in a variety of jobs. In subtle, as well as obvious ways, he becomes aware that being born male was a stroke of luck. Somehow, he is considered to be better than anyone that happens to be born female.

Negative Aspects All is not roses, however. For one thing, his father is often at work, and does not always interact with him as much as he would like. At times, he has trouble knowing how to be "masculine," because his father is not there as a model, though his mother is. He has to figure it out for himself. One way he can be sure he is being masculine is to be sure he never does anything that is considered to be a female activity—even if he wants to. This pressure can cause anxiety and fear. He doesn't want to be called a sissy. He must be tough, physical, and active. He must reject girls ("You can't play . . . you're only a girl!"), even if he likes them. He must never play with girls' toys, especially dolls, or show any interest in cooking, sewing, or artistic endeavors. He must never show his emotions and never cry. Obviously, he is cut off from a large segment of life's pleasures.

Although his self-concept is aided by the fact that he is considered to be the superior sex, it is a strain to have to achieve and to prove oneself constantly. For many boys this role means rejecting their own sisters, even though they may have been close friends and companions at an earlier age. This forced rejection of girls as a child may sometimes present problems in adult life, when the male is suddenly supposed to fall in love, marry, and live with one of them. He may prefer men, and have trouble interacting with women.

As life continues, this male may well have to support a family. He will be subject to stress in the economic marketplace, when the load could very easily be spread across male and female, to the benefit of both. He will be as trapped as the stereotyped female, slaving over the hot stove at home, with children to deal with by herself. Neither sex will be given any real choice in the matter.

Rejecting Male

Positive Aspects For the boy who rejects the traditional sex-role stereotype, there are unique benefits and problems. On the positive side, this individual opens up a wide range of rewarding activities that are not available to the boy that accepts the stereotype. He can love, squeeze, feed, and dress dolls; he can practice being a father like William in *William's Doll*. He can express his emotions; he can cry and hug a friend. He can be a "chicken." He may learn to relate to women in a more complete fashion. He will certainly be more able to care for himself, having learned to sew, cook, care for children, and clean house. And he feels free to express himself artistically.

Negative Aspects This child's self-concept may suffer (unless he is very strong) because he may well be called a sissy for liking and doing things such as cooking, dancing, painting, and playing with dolls. He may be ridiculed and labeled a traitor. He may be rejected by other boys, and prevented from participating in their activities. Adults will ridicule him, too. Even his parents may be critical. Later in life he may be labeled, again inaccurately, as abnormal or homosexual.

Accepting Female

Positive Aspects There are some benefits associated with accepting the stereotyped female role. Certainly the girl will avoid a lot of abuse, and will generally be accepted by society. Emotions may be freely expressed; and the rewards inherent in the roles of wife and mother cannot be ignored, if one has *freely* chosen these roles.

Negative Aspects But the negative aspects would seem to outweigh the positive. The girl who accepts and conforms to her traditional sex-role stereotype is in for a great deal of trouble in maintaining a positive, strong, healthy self-concept. She has to accept that she is inferior to all males. Given that the average female learns to walk, read, and write before and better than the average male, this is not an easy pill to swallow. All of these skills are highly valued in our society. Still, she is inferior. She constantly hears, "You can't do that. You're only a girl."

To gain approval she must be cute, polite, clean, helpful, quiet, and passive. She must be interested in dolls, sewing, cooking, crafts, and her appearance. She must rein in her energies, and doubt her ability to do just about anything that boys can do. She will become "the weaker sex" as quickly as possible.

As she moves on to elementary and secondary schools, she will remain in less active and more supportive roles. She may learn to hide academic ability. She may try to appear dumber than the male. If she decides to go to college and/or work before she marries, she will be encouraged (by her counselors and others) to go into traditional low-status, low-pay female occupations such as teaching, nursing, social work, and secretarial work (Bull, 1974). She will accept these limited horizons, knowing in her heart of hearts that she isn't capable of anything better. She will be waiting, hoping for Prince Charming to appear. Once married, self-deprecation and male ego-building will be necessary. Her role as wife and mother has been likened to that of an unpaid slave.

Rejecting Female

Positive Aspects The girl who refuses to conform to her assigned role opens up for herself an enormous range of otherwise forbidden activities. She can participate in the full spectrum of prohibited activities that we have been discussing. Clearly, the freedoms involved in this position are what the Women's Equality Movement is all about. She can throw off the yoke of inferiority.

Negative Aspects But the female who refuses to conform to her assigned role may also have trouble developing a strong, positive self-concept. The road will be difficult. First of all, she will have to be very persistent if she is to be allowed to play with boys' toys and join in boys' activities. Many of the important people around her will be critical.

At an early age, she may be allowed to be a tomboy, temporarily. But as she reaches puberty, the pressure to conform will be great. If she continues to rebel, she, too, may be considered abnormal. Although she has had few models in her life, she may decide she wishes to pursue a career. To do this she may have to overcome the advice of her counselors and discrimination in college entrance requirements. If she surmounts these obstacles, she will then have to fight discrimination in employment practices. She will lose out on jobs and promotions because many of the better positions are filled through conversations between men.

Then, too, she may have trouble finding a male strong enough to accept her as an equal and independent person, a man who will help with the dishes without being acknowledged as a saint for doing so. If she marries, she will have two jobs—one paid (her career) and one unpaid (housewife and mother). If she doesn't, she will be considered abnormal. And most of her successes will be attributed to her "man-like" qualities.

Conclusion

Clearly, these four descriptions are oversimplifications. But they do suggest certain conclusions that cannot be ignored. Specifically, they suggest that we *all* suffer from traditional sexist attitudes, regardless of our sex or our choice with respect to conformity. None of the four examples represents an ideal situation. Although difficult to implement, the solution seems obvious: do away with sexist attitudes and practices. If there were no pressure to be one thing or another and we were all free to pursue our own unique, idiosyncratic impulses, then peace of mind and a sense of fulfillment, rather than frustration, bitterness, and/or anxiety, would be commonplace. By encouraging all children to engage in all activities, the early childhood educator can do much to remedy the situation.

Sexism and Parents

Introduction

In chapter 10 we discuss the overall challenge for the teacher of establishing a partnership with parents. For now, we will restrict our attention to the problem of dealing with sexism in parents. To be sure, not all parents are sexist, but some of them are. Many of the male parents you meet will be breadwinners, bosses, and disciplinarians, while many of the mothers will be dependent housekeepers. In other words, many parents lead sexist lives.

Some of them will be content. They may even have discussed the sexist quality of their lives, and decided, for any number of reasons, that they do not want to change. For example, they may feel that it is important that at least one parent stay home with their children and that, as long as the male already has a high-paying job, the female might just as well be the one to stay home. But some parents have fallen into the sexist pattern simply because they have been told by our society that that is the correct one. Many of these parents may be unhappy with their limiting sexist roles, and would well benefit from a change. But change is difficult to bring about. For one thing, the nonsexist position may contradict everything they have been taught. It may contradict their way of life. Being confronted for the first time by the nonsexist position can be intimidating because it implies criticism of the way one has been living. It implies that one has been wrong, stupid, or silly in one's lifestyle. It implies that children must be taught a new and better way—a way the parents may find strange and unacceptable. If confronted, sexist parents can become angry, frustrated, aggressive, fearful, insecure, and confused. In other words, working with such parents can present one of the most difficult challenges of all to the teacher. Severe problems can result if the parents are mistreated in any way. The teacher does not want to create conflicts between the school and the parent or between individual parents. The teacher must find ways to work with parents as partners in exploring all new areas. *Avoid meddling at all costs.*

It is more than likely that the early childhood educator will be faced with a vast array of parental opinions concerning sexist issues. Some parents will be aware, others will not. Some parents will be sympathetic, others will not. Individuals within a family may differ with respect to these issues. Some may want to change, while others will not. And no doubt everyone will vary in terms of what they think should be done to solve these problems.

What Can Be Done?

Given that the situation is a tangled and heavily emotional one, what can teachers do to help? First of all, they can do themselves a favor by recognizing the difficulty of the task. Changing any value is difficult. It takes time, patience, work, encouragement, and understanding. Change may be impossible in many cases. This is not to suggest that the teacher should not try. However, realistic expectations may avoid disappointment and frustration. People do not change easily, even when they want to.

If you work to create a cooperative atmosphere, you may be able to assist others in an effort to promote nonsexist thinking and practices. One approach may be to try to point out to those who favor sex stereotypes that she or he is being hurt or deprived by sexist attitudes, and that she or he would benefit by nonsexist attitudes. In order to do this, communication is needed. There are several techniques for establishing lines of communication; and the most successful are a result of working with and not against the parents.

Consciousness-raising Sessions Such sessions may be organized for parents and teachers who are interested in discussing sexism as it pertains to themselves and to their children. These can be held either at the school or at someone's home. It has been suggested that the initial meetings be all female or all male. This encourages everyone to speak freely, and prevents the males from dominating the conversations. This male tendency to dominate and the female's tendency to submit to male domination must be discussed in both groups before they are joined.

Each person should be given the opportunity to express what she or he feels with respect to sexism and how it affects the lives of their family members. In this manner, individuals will see that they all share many feelings and that they can work within the realm of a supportive, understanding group to make changes. Together the group can explore new and creative ways to deal with their mutual problems.

If necessary, a group leader may be designated to keep the group on the right track and to see that no-one is left out of discussions. This role can be rotated each week among the members to give everyone the leadership experience and the growing sense of confidence that can accompany it. If you run into difficulties, you might call one of the local offices of women's groups such as NOW, either to seek advice or to engage a group leader.

The Subtle Method The consciousness-raising session is all well and good for sympathetic parents. But what does one do about parents and/or staff who are either antagonistic or disinterested? In these situations you might have to use less direct, more subtle methods. For example, parent or staff meetings can be arranged where the announced topic of discussion will not be intimidating. Some examples include: The Child's Role in the Family, Children's Books, The Family and the School, Toys and Equipment for Children, Family Roles, The Parent and the School, Parent Participation, The Nuclear Family, Alternative Lifestyles, and Creativity at Home and at School. Within such discussion sessions, sexist issues can be talked about without labeling them as such and without their dominating the entire discussion. You can introduce nonsexist thoughts for general discussion. An emphasis should be placed upon the value of encouraging each child to develop to the fullest extent and upon the disadvantages of frustrating such development.

Parent Conferences and Casual Talks These are two occasions when a teacher can acquire a feel for the parents' stand on sexism. Rather than frightening them, you want to support them and work with them as partners. You need to gain each other's confidence, trust, and respect before you even begin to discuss alternatives to their lifestyles and child-rearing practices. In general, you will discover that parents respect their children's teachers. Many of them want to believe that the teachers can and will help them with their children. They will tend to consider your advice.

Remember that many of these parents are very young and want help in raising their children. Some *need* help. Just take it slow and easy.

Parent Visits and Participation Parents can be invited to your class and to participate in field trips (undoubtedly, you will need extra drivers anyway). By arranging your class carefully and by choosing your field trips carefully, you can expose the parents, as well as the children, to both sexes operating in nontraditional roles. You can even encourage the parents to engage in nontraditional roles. For example, male parents can be encouraged, in a matter-of-fact way, to assist in such activities as setting up snacks, aiding children who need help, or stirring the batter for a birthday cake. There are many nonsexist activities that parents can be induced to try, without intimidation. Female visitors can be encouraged to help children in the woodworking areas, in ball games, and in the block-building area. You might ask a parent to read one of your nonsexist storybooks to the children without mentioning its nonsexist qualities. By participating in a nonsexist atmosphere, wherein the children are encouraged in *all* areas of endeavor, the parents may see the advantages of such an orientation. On the other hand, if you are too blatant, the parent may go to the extreme of withdrawing the child from the school. As usual, you must know your audience, plan carefully, and be as supportive as possible.

Sexism and Models

The Importance of Models

Children often copy what they see. In fact, they learn many of their skills, much of their language, some of their attitudes, and many of their behaviors by copying other people, or *modeling*. If a child loves or respects someone, then that child will emulate the model's behavior. Obviously, modeling is extremely important in determining what a child will do and believe, and is crucial in all aspects of the early education experience.

Children are constantly bombarded with models, and some of the most important ones are father, mother, and teacher. Many models have sexist attitudes, however. Children are quick to internalize the sexist phrases they hear coming from their important models. "Boys are doctors, girls are nurses." "That's woman's work." "Father is the boss." "Dancing is for sissies." By the time the child is 2 or 3 years old, an enormous number of these model-related sexist beliefs have been internalized. Many of these internalized beliefs will eventually inhibit or frustrate the child. Many of them will limit the child's potential growth.

The Teacher as a Model

Given that models are so important, it would seem that control of the type of model to which the child is exposed would be of great importance. You can't regulate all the models that children see; however, in your role as teacher, you do have a great opportunity to present a number of good, positive, nonsexist models. The most important of these models is you.

You must decide what type of model you will be. If you are female, do you want to show the children that women can, after all, play with trucks, build things, throw and catch a ball, lift heavy objects, fix broken toys, engage in sports, and solve problems? Do you want to show that women aren't limited to cooking, putting on Band-Aids, changing wet diapers, and fixing snacks? If you are male, would you like to show children that men do not always play roughly with little boys and that they can be sought for understanding and emotional contact? Would you like them to see that men can change dirty diapers and scramble eggs as well as women? If you are a male, will you boss your female co-teachers? If you are a female co-teacher, will you allow a male to boss you?

Just as it may not do much good to give toy dishes to a boy whose father thinks cooking is woman's work, so there's not much point in a female teacher telling children that girls are as strong as boys when she expects a male colleague to open doors for her. In other words, you have to practice what you preach. Remember that young children, not yet on a verbal or abstract thinking level, understand what they *see* much better than what they are told. Actions speak louder than words.

Additional Nonsexist Models

In addition to being a nonsexist model yourself, you have the opportunity to present a variety of nonsexist models to the children. For example, by looking over the parents and by looking around the community you can discover a variety of people with jobs and skills that are nontraditional. You will find female mail carriers, photographers, police officers, construction workers, doctors, lawyers, and auto mechanics. Male nurses, typists, bank tellers, cooks, and seamstresses can be found. Many of these people will be willing to visit your class. They can demonstrate some of their skills and talk about their work. Others may agree to have you and your children visit them on their ground.

Photographs of these visiting and visited people can be hung in your classroom. The children can paint pictures of what they saw. Dramatic play can incorporate the nonsexist occupations. For example, after visiting a construction site where females are construction workers, block building by both girls and boys can easily dramatize further the fact that men aren't the only ones that can build. A visit by a female doctor or male nurse can be followed by a game of doctor and nurse with both boys and girls playing both nurses and doctors. A visit from a man who can spend time cooking with the children will stimulate all sorts of games and activities later.

With older children, group discussions of what has been seen and what has been felt can be helpful. These discussions can and usually do bring out attitudes about the equality and/or inequality of the sexes. Discussions such as these typically provide an estimate of how successful or unsuccessful your efforts have been.

Another fine way of exposing children to a variety of models is to hang pictures of men and women in nontraditional and traditional roles about the classroom. The children may make the pictures themselves after one of the previously discussed visits or field trips. These pictures can either be talked about as they are hung, or discussion may be delayed until the children notice them on their own. It is important that the models you introduce are multiracial as well as nonsexist. You want to be sure the children understand that *everyone* can try *everything*.

Needless to say, good models can also be presented to the children through play, toys, equipment, language, books, films, field trips, and your own interactions with others. As future teachers you must consider carefully what kind of a model you want to be. No-one can be a perfect model, but anyone can be a good one.

Suggestions for Nonsexist Education

We close this chapter with a list of activities and actions that can assist the new instructor in establishing a nonsexist setting for early childhood education. We believe that this setting provides a unique, and perhaps never-to-be-repeated opportunity to instill nonsexist beliefs in the very young. It is at this age that many relatively unchangeable attitudes are formed. As such, the early childhood years represent a golden opportunity.

Some of the sexist influences in the lives of your children are beyond your control. Others are not. In this section we concern ourselves with practical suggestions for limiting sexist influences in the early childhood educational setting. As you become familiar with your particular teaching situations, and with the individuals involved, you will no doubt develop practical ideas of your own. In this light, the following suggestions represent starting points.

1. Be a model of nonsexist attitudes and actions. Treat yourself and others as equal, be they children, adults, fellow teachers, visitors, males or females. Do not let others treat you as more or less than an equal. Male and female teachers should share equally in all aspects of the educational experience.
2. Encourage *all* children to participate in *all* activities. Do not allow "boys' games" and "girls' games." Reward all efforts to try something new with approval and enthusiasm.
3. Encourage *all* children to play with *all* toys and equipment. Let them know it's fine if girls get messy, play with trucks, or build with blocks. Encourage boys to cook, paint, and play with dolls. Read or tell stories that reinforce these activities (e.g., *William's Doll*, *A Train for Jane*).
4. Be sure there are a number of nonsexist children's books in the room. If you have interesting but sexist books, read them by replacing the name of the main character with the name of one of the children (female or male) in your class.
5. Emphasize and reward physical development and skills for girls as well as boys. Encourage parents to dress girls as well as boys in appropriate clothes: comfortable, suitable for dirty activities, and easy for children to put on and take off themselves. If necessary, explain to parents that their children will be at a disadvantage if they

are prohibited from some activities because of a concern for their clothes.

6. Hang pictures of males and females engaged in traditional and non-traditional activities. Be sure you have an equal balance. After all, you don't want females to believe they can't be homemakers and mothers. You merely want them to know they have alternatives.

7. As mentioned, field trips and class visitors can show the children that males and females are capable of all sorts of traditional and non-traditional activities. Follow up activities relating to these roles will bring home to the children the fact that they, too, can look forward to a wide range of choices. If a little girl sees a woman doctor, and then plays at being a doctor, the possibility of being a doctor at some future time will seem closer and more likely to her.

8. Try to use nonsexist language as much as possible. Encourage other teachers and parents to do so. Children model language.

9. Let all children know that it's good to express emotion. Boys can cry if they are sad or hurt. Put a photo up that says so. Girls can aggress if someone treats them unfairly or as an inferior. Give them phrases to use such as, "I don't like that!" or, "Don't do that to me!" Help them talk about disturbing events. Help them understand what they are feeling and why. Provide them with appropriate language. For example, you can tell a child, "You were angry when Michael hit you. Tell Michael, 'I don't like it when you hit me! Don't hit me anymore!'" This helps both of them understand and verbalize what they are doing and feeling. They learn the consequences of their actions. It doesn't hurt to add that it makes you angry, too, when children hit each other.

10. Encourage a positive self-image in boys and girls without reference to gender. The efforts of each child should be supported. The accomplishments of each child should be acknowledged and rewarded.

11. Let the children know that, at least in this school, boys do not have to be tougher than girls. They do not have to prove their masculinity constantly.

12. Girls should be taught to be assertive, rather than passive. They should be encouraged to express their desires, their ideas, and their needs. Boys should not dominate in group situations. The strength of girls should be openly recognized and rewarded. Girls, too, can learn when it is and when it is not appropriate to use that strength.

13. Girls should not be made to feel that they must remain clean and pretty to gain approval. It is fairly common for teachers to comment on the appearance of a girl when she arrives at school. "What a lovely dress!" "What a pretty bow!" Inadvertently, this teaches the young female that gaining her teacher's initial approval in the morning hinges on her own appearance. Being neat and pretty guarantees it. This can lead to unnecessary preoccupation with her appearance, if not

outright worry. Children should feel valuable as people, not as clotheshorses.

Morning greetings might better center around other topics. For example, one can say, "Susie, you seem very happy and energetic today. I'll bet you're ready to have a good time," or, "Jimmy, you still look very sleepy today. Would you like to sit in the big comfy chair, and look at some books for a while?" Children shouldn't be made to feel anxious about their self-images, especially at this tender age. The females in your class may already be subjected to such comments and pressures by relatives and friends. They don't need more from their teachers.

14. Staff and parent meetings can occasionally be "consciousness-raising sessions" where more suggestions for nonsexist education may develop. If you know that those who will be attending are nonsexist in their beliefs, these meetings can be arranged easily. But if you know that sexism is a difficult subject for those who will be attending, then less intimidating meetings can be arranged. At these meetings, sexism issues can be introduced gradually and without undue concern.

15. The children should be provided with materials that stimulate imaginative, open-ended, nonsexist play. For example, the costume, dramatic play, and housekeeping areas should contain a large number of outfits. Both sexes should be encouraged to use all of the material. Workshirts, stethoscopes, firefighter hats, hardhats, dolls, dishes, cooking utensils, and ironing boards are appropriate for both boys and girls. Block accessories should also show a variety of roles for both sexes. Nonsexist practices expand rather than limit play and thinking.

If you have trouble purchasing such nonsexist items, you can make them. Cut out pictures of a variety of people figures and back them with cardboard or wood for block accessories. Wonderful, interesting puzzles can be made the same way if you also have a jigsaw available to you.

16. The children can learn a great deal about the world by discussing their own family situation, and the families of other children with the teacher. These group discussions usually reveal that some children live in one-parent homes, that some live in extended family situations, and that some are cared for by babysitters. Such discussions often demonstrate that some of the caretakers are males, thus showing that child care is not just woman's work. The varied occupations of the parents are sometimes revealed, too.

These discussions let the children see that people live in a variety of home circumstances, that many children are cared for by males as well as by females, that mothers work and earn money, and that the traditional nuclear family unit is but one of many acceptable home situations.

Such discussions can be stimulated, or followed up, by reading stories about families, by painting pictures of families, by making clay or playdough families, by dramatic play or puppet games about families, and by child-dictated stories about families. Pictures and stories made by the children along with family photos can be made into family books or albums.

17. You can encourage your school and your children's parents to boycott toys and other products that are advertised or marketed in a sexist manner. If package labels are sexist and you still want your children to have the toys, tear off the labels or take the toys out of the packages before giving them to the children.

You can also use your consumer power (individually or collectively) by writing to toy manufacturers that are sexist in their products or their advertising. Many companies are becoming aware of these problems and are responding, but many are not. Make a point of buying products from manufacturers who have changed their attitudes. Buy from companies which specialize in nonsexist toys.

18. If possible, develop a collection of resource books at your school to be used by teachers and parents. Select books that will raise their awareness of sexism in our society and that suggest ways of counteracting it.

6

Facets of Development and the Whole Child

In chapter 4 we focused upon cognitive development, and, in particular, Piaget's thinking about the development of intelligent activity. Clearly, cognitive development is a crucial concern. But just as clearly, it is not the *only* concern of the preschool educator. Obviously, there is much more to the whole child than a developing set of cognitive mechanisms. If we are to understand and help the child grow and flourish, we cannot restrict our attention to cognitive development. We must consider the other important dimensions of development, namely, the child's *physical*, *social*, and *emotional* development. It is to these concerns that we now turn, because no treatment of child development would be adequate without them.

The plan of this chapter is simple. First, we shall focus upon each of these dimensions separately. But it is an oversimplification to consider any of these dimensions in isolation from the others. When a child learns, grows, and matures, she most often moves forward within all these dimensions simultaneously. For example, successful toilet training does not represent an emotional development alone, or cognitive development alone, or any other single dimension of development. It is a complex event, containing important elements of cognitive, social, emotional and physical development at the same time. Therefore, the latter half of this chapter looks at the fact that development is multidimensional. Specifically, we discuss separation, security blankets, beginning the day, toilet training, and mixed groups. We try to show that each of these complex concerns involves multidimensional development.

Notwithstanding this, our treatment of the various facets of development in the first sections of the chapter can be useful. Only by focusing on each dimension separately can we begin to appreciate the intricacy of their intertwined paths.

The Beginning Preschooler

Given that you will be concerned with the development of children over a span of years, it is a good idea to focus for a moment upon the beginning preschooler. Just where does the 2 year old, or perhaps even the toddler, stand with respect to the overall developmental process? What is the starting point for the sequence of years which will concern you?

Toddlers and 2 year olds are extremely vulnerable, complex, highly motivated individuals. When they enter nursery school they are on the brink of a great adventure. They bring with them an enormous capacity to learn, and, in spite of their limited abilities, represent individuals to be treated with dignity and care.

Although many of these new preschoolers can walk, a child may be carried in by the mother or father, often wrapped in a security blanket and clutching *the* stuffed animal or doll of his young life. Obstructions (e.g., stairs, elevated surfaces) are often, of necessity, negotiated in a crawling fashion. Preschoolers can usually run, too, but not well. Too much speed, combined with little control and/or an unexpected obstacle, can result in a fall. (You will soon come to realize that falls are a natural part of growing up. They are often more surprising or frightening than dangerous. You need not panic or overreact to them. Check the child's physical condition and help her resume the interrupted play.)

Having so much to learn, these new preschoolers need a safe, helpful environment. They have enormous energy, partially developed skills, and never-ending curiosity. They are unable, for the most part, to express themselves verbally. Their world is filled with, and alternates between, delight and frustration. They are capable of unrealistic courage and susceptible to debilitating fear. They want to control, but often can't. They are capable, proud, and independent explorers one minute, and cuddly, tearful, exhausted babies the next. They *have* developed and *have* learned many things, but they are just beginning.

In Piaget's terms, these children are moving from the sensorimotor stage into the preoperational stage of intellectual (cognitive) development. They will show characteristics of both stages. According to Piaget, the actions of the younger children in the group *are* their thoughts, while the older members of the group are just beginning to engage in symbolic thought and play.

Piaget feels the children at this level of development are motivated by three factors: (1) they want and need to repeat and practice all behaviors and actions (especially if they are rewarding); (2) they have an unrelenting curiosity for moderately novel stimuli; (3) they are also motivated by the need for equilibration. If you recall, this is the need for balance between the processes of assimilation and accommodation. Piaget also points out that these children are egocentric in their thinking. Teachers should be aware of these aspects of the children and gauge their actions accordingly. According to Piaget, it is important to allow the children to "learn by discovery" . . . theirs, not yours. Don't push, or help them too much. Provide moderately novel stimuli. Let them do it their own way as much as possible (this encourages creativity and independence). Let them repeat the simplest acts as often as they desire. Let them interact and talk freely with themselves, with you, and with the other children. Don't expect them to share or to be very social at all. Keep in mind that, according to Piaget, intelligence is not an IQ score, but the ability of the individual to adapt successfully to the environment using the available personal and environmental resources.

Parenthetically, it should be noted that toddlers and 2 year olds are usually involved in at least partially separated programs. Two factors contribute to this separation:

1. In some states, licensing requirements that govern educational facilities classify children under 2 as infants. This usually means that the child/teacher ratio (the number of children an adult can legally take care of at one time) is much lower than for the older children. The reasoning here is that if there were a fire or some other emergency, the older children could be walked or guided to safety. Not so the toddlers: they may have to be carried, and one teacher can only carry just so many. One teacher for every four toddlers is required in some states, while one teacher for every twelve children, aged 2 to about 5, is necessary. In many cases, this lower ratio for toddlers is met by having their parents stay at school and participate in the program.

2. This parent participation also can lead to a toddler program that is at least partially separated from the 2 year olds. Here the teacher has not only to plan and supervise the toddlers' activities, but the parents' activities as well. These programs require teachers who are not only skilled in dealing with extremely young children, but who are also skilled in dealing with groups of adults and their children.

In summary, the newest preschoolers have already come a long way along the developmental road—but they are just beginning. They need respect, care, and attention. Your ability to guide, support, and encourage their development can have a significant impact upon their lives. With this in mind we now turn to the dimensions of development.

Physical Growth and Motor Development

Introduction

When children begin in preschool, their small size and lack of motor coordination can be a source of frustration. Nearly everyone is bigger, stronger, and more capable. Parents, teachers, siblings, and other children can, and do, dominate their lives. They have not yet become proficient in running, climbing, or jumping. They fall, pinch their fingers, scrape their arms, and bruise their knees.

"Owies," "booboos," and Band-Aids are common. These young children will often be more than willing to show you several scratches, scabs, and Band-Aids, and will enjoy telling you about how it all happened. "I fell down" is a very common phrase in these groups.

What can be done to encourage the smooth development of necessary motor skills of these youngsters? There are a number of factors that contribute to physical growth and motor development, including heredity, the suitability of the physical environment, nutrition, health care, and practice.

Heredity and Motor Development

There isn't anything the educator can do to change the child's genetic makeup. But the teacher can be *aware* of any genetic problems that exist and can act accordingly. The parents will probably inform you of any known problems and will expose you to any special procedures that are necessary—the fact, for example, that their child wears corrective shoes and should not be allowed to run barefoot. Similarly, another child may be dichromatic, or color-blind. An awareness on the part of the teacher of the type of color-blindness (e.g., red/green, blue/yellow) can smooth the child's eventual adjustment to the difference between herself and the other children.

Sometimes parents are unaware of genetic defects (e.g., poor vision, poor hearing, mental retardation) when the children are so young. The teacher, while scrupulously avoiding unnecessary concern or alarm, should be alert to such possibilities. Discussing any suspected problems with your director or school nurse may be an advisable first step, to avoid panicking parents unnecessarily. A caretaker should not simply advise a parent without being thoroughly familiar with, and trained in the use of, appropriate screening devices. (See Mowbray and Salisbury, 1975, for the detection of visual and auditory defects.)

The Physical Environment

Preschool children need an environment that is safe and, if at all possible, scaled to their size. Tables, chairs, and easels should be low. The children should be able to sit with their feet on the floor, to help develop correct posture. Stairs should be but a few inches high. Tricycles and wheel toys should be small. What good is a tricycle if you can't reach the pedals, much less the ground? Cups should be small (and plastic). Otherwise, two hands are required, which is not what children need to learn. Pitchers should be small so they can learn to pour their own juice. For safety and ease of use toilets should be small, or at least modified by a smaller seat and steps.

Scaling down the physical world makes it a little easier for the children to practice necessary skills. If children can acquire coordinated skills using small objects, they will be just that much further along when they grow enough to be able to use the full-sized objects. They will have had a head start. A small world is less intimidating, as well, and can be an exciting environment for children otherwise trapped in an oversized adult world.

Nutrition and Health Care

Your influence over the children's nutrition and health care will vary depending upon the type of facility. Private schools often have a nutritionist/cook who plans and prepares snacks and lunches. Sometimes the children bring their own. Head Start and other poverty programs usually provide regular meals, as well as some health and dental care and other social services. (Head Start is discussed in detail in chapter 7.)

You may have the opportunity to discuss the menu with your school's cook. Given that the cook is amenable to suggestions, you can mention dishes that you have found appeal to this age group. You can also discuss nutrition with the children, on a level appropriate to their age. It's a simple matter to let children know that certain foods will "make them grow big." You also need to be aware of allergies, and see that certain foods are not served to the wrong children. Encourage, but don't force them to try new foods. Careful attention to color, texture, small portions, and enthusiastic modelling can help many youngsters enjoy and explore new foods. Mealtime can provide a wonderful opportunity for a great deal of social, sensory, and emotional activity. Engel (1968) presents some good cooking ideas that you can incorporate into your efforts.

The teacher can have some influence over the child's health care. For instance, you can see that sick children are not allowed to infect other children. Be sure that wet and soiled diapers are changed quickly to avoid rashes and chills in cold weather. Take care of those runny noses. Encourage children to wash after toileting and before eating. See that your room is clean and sanitary. Discuss brushing teeth and other health habits with the children. Point out possible health problems to parents (rashes, open sores, hearing and sight deficiencies). If you suspect a serious problem, discuss it with your director or school nurse first.

Your attention to matters of health is important, for most schools have no more than a single nurse or someone trained in first-aid. It wouldn't hurt to learn a little first-aid yourself. Something as simple as (1) *stop the bleeding*, (2) *check the breathing*, (3) *keep the victim lying down and warm* can save a life. These procedures are easy to remember and cover some of the absolute essentials. (The Fire Department in your

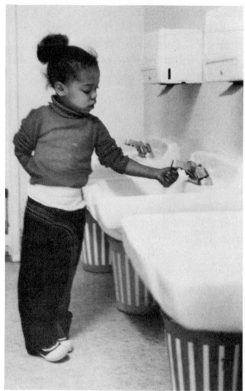

Learning to wash after toileting is important . . . and faucets can be intriguing

area may be able to send someone to your school to demonstrate to the staff some of the essentials of emergency first aid.)

Many schools require a release form from parents before they are legally authorized to take a child to the hospital in case of emergency. Be sure you have this form if you are the person who accompanies the child to the hospital.

Another important health factor you should keep in mind is that most children of this age need occasional periods of rest. If they stay full-day, you will, of course, provide a nap (rest) time for them. In addition, you should provide a variety of quiet times and places intermingled with their active times. Avoid overstimulation. Reading or telling them stories, listening to quiet music, or playing whispering games can provide occasional rest and relief for them (and for you). A soft pillow area in the book corner, a cot in a quiet place, or a big, soft chair can provide escapes for tired, weary little children, who are happily worn-out from all the fun.

Practice and Motor Development

Perhaps the greatest influence you can have upon the child's physical and motor development has to do with the opportunities for *practice* and *exercise* that you provide. Both large and small muscles need to be exercised, and their actions need to be coordinated. Large muscles (arms, legs, neck, shoulders, back, and stomach) can be stimulated by the usual athletic activities such as running, jumping, hopping, pushing, pulling, lifting, climbing, pedaling, steering, throwing, catching, batting, and kicking (preferably not each other). Dancing is very good, too. And remember, both females and males need to be encouraged in all these activities. Small muscle development (hands, fingers, feet, toes, eyes) can be assisted by painting, cutting, pasting, blockbuilding, and puzzles, and by manipulating toys, clay, water, and sand (with hands and feet). Stirring, pouring, and kneading, as in cooking, can be beneficial and fun. Dressing, feeding, and bathing dolls can assist both boys and girls in developing fine motor skills. "Fingerplays" with songs are fun, as are puppets. The pages of a book should be turned by a child, not by the teacher, whenever possible. Simple picture books, containing familiar objects such as bikes, balls, babies, and animals are best at this age.

Tasks such as handling their own buttons, zippers, and shoelaces should be encouraged and rewarded but not demanded, because they are difficult. Don't always put on and take off children's clothing for them. Let them try. You can also encourage them to help you set up and clean up snacks, and to put away toys. As Montessori pointed out many years ago, learning to take care of themselves and their own personal needs can be very useful to children, and helps to build their self-confidence. All these little, gradual accomplishments lead to a positive self-image. Praise them if they succeed. Do nothing if they fail. Don't ask or expect too much. (More about these concerns appears in chapters 8 and 9.)

The principle of *shaping* can be useful in helping the very young children learn to feed themselves. If you recall, shaping refers to a process wherein we reinforce closer and closer approximations of the behavior we desire. At first, reward little ones if they manage to deposit food in their mouths at all (with "Good," or a smile). Don't worry how they get it there. Ignore failures. Then, gradually, require closer and closer approximations to the desired behavior (eating properly with a spoon or fork) before you reward. Begin to withhold social reward unless they at least attempt to use a spoon. You should still allow finger feeding, but remain passive when they do use their fingers instead of their spoon.

Of course, children will learn to use eating utensils without your turning to shaping procedures, but the skill is a complicated, difficult one, and can be facilitated through simple conditioning procedures. Other

Although naptime may not be be on the agenda, the teacher must be flexible at times

rudimentary skills, such as pouring their own beverages and drinking from a cup without spilling, can be facilitated through shaping techniques. Scoldings and punishments are inappropriate and often counterproductive.

The physical development of the child is often described as following two patterns or principles. The first, the *cephalochordal principle*, refers to the fact that the child's growth proceeds from "head to tail." The head, brain, and eyes developed in the embryo before the trunk and limbs. The head of the young child is disproportionately large. The lower body takes time to catch up. The second principle of growth is called the *proximodistal law*. This rule states that development proceeds from the center of the body outward. That is, the head and trunk develop before the arms and legs. The arms and legs, in turn, develop before the fingers and toes.

Because of these growth progressions, the children may have relatively good control over their head, arms, and legs, but relatively poor control over their fingers, hands, toes, and feet. In other words, their bodies are developing unevenly. Their *fine motor* control is not as well established as it will be later. As a result, the children can run, but only awkwardly. Children may make wonderful, sweeping strokes with a paint brush (because their arms are well developed), but be unable to do much fine work (because their fingers are not yet coordinated).

The practical implications of all this are that children need room and big spaces in which to operate. They need large pieces of paper on which to paint and color (the smaller the child, the larger the piece of paper). They need room to move, as they are still using large muscles to do what they will do later with their small muscles. Later they will be able to engage in fine motor activity. But, for now, the creative urge and the need to move must be expressed in a *big* way.

Socialization

Goals

Socialization refers to the processes by which people learn to be acceptable, contributing members of their own society and culture. Any given society is normally composed of a number of different cultures. For example, there are, within the U.S.A.'s competitive, capitalistic society, Hopi and Zuni Indians, Mexican-Americans, and Japanese cultures. Relative to other elements of our society, these cultures discourage competition and encourage cooperation, sharing, and group orientation (Mussen, Conger, and Kagan, 1974). In other words, our society is not a simple, easily defined structure.

Because our society is very complex, it is impossible to devise

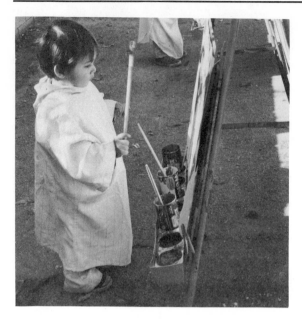

The smaller the child the more space needed . . .

a concrete set of rules and generalizations for promoting social development. The social values you choose to instill in the children you teach will depend upon your own values, your school's values, the parents' values, and the values of the specific culture from which the child comes. Before you take a position with a school, it might be wise to discover the prevailing values within that work setting. They may be in sharp conflict with your own. Once employed, teachers must familiarize themselves with all of the various cultures that are included within that school's clientele. This helps the teacher understand the children's needs and the needs of the parents. If the teachers don't understand the child's cultural heritage, then they can't promote pride in that heritage, or do very much to help the children understand other cultures. If the teachers are well-prepared, they can show their children that people vary, and that variety is interesting and good. The poorly prepared, or thoughtless teacher can promote prejudice, sometimes without even knowing it.

Given that we understand that socialization goals will vary depending on the people involved, are there any goals that seem *general* enough to be applicable to most early educational settings? Perhaps there are. Table 6.1 contains goals that seem appropriate for most cultures within our society.

Obviously, the attainment of these goals involves a long, complex, often difficult process. These are goals to work *toward*, not goals that should be achieved immediately. We must not expect too much from the children at this early stage.

and the larger the paper

The First Steps

The process of socialization is just beginning when the child enters school. Most often the children have had relatively few interactions with strangers, and almost none with groups of strangers. Most of their interactions have been with parents, siblings, pediatricians, relatives, and a few neighbors. Thus the instructor enters the picture on the ground floor.

It is a common error on the part of parents and teachers to expect children of any age to begin to play and share immediately with the other children at school. Sometimes these tiny, new students are pressured to begin complex social activities before they know anything at all about the teachers and the other children. They are often rushed into social activity before they have had a chance to become familiar with and comfortable with the school environment.

Even in the case of older children,.this is an unfair demand. They need time to learn the routines, and to feel relaxed in the school setting. They will be interested; but, as Piaget points out, they should be introduced through small, moderately novel steps. Parents and teachers can smooth the adjustment. The children should be treated in an easygoing, undemanding way. They should be shown, without overpowering them, the toys, equipment, and activities that are available. Keep a sharp eye on whether or not the child is "blanking out" because of overstimulation. Walk through the school slowly. Let them stop and watch anytime, and for as long as they wish. Introduce them to a *few* children. Care should

Table 6.1 *Socialization Goals*

1. To help children get to know the other children, the teachers and other staff members, visitors, and the other children's parents. This should be done at the children's individual speeds. Do not overwhelm them.

2. To help the children fulfill their dependency needs. *Slowly*, the children should be molded to become independent, autonomous individuals with positive, healthy, self-concepts.

3. To provide equal opportunities to both males and females and to encourage all of them to develop all of their interests, talents, and skills together. There should be no "girls' activities" or "boys' activities" exclusively.

4. To encourage the full range of physical and cognitive skills. Cooperative as well as competitive skills should be stressed.

5. To foster effective communication skills.

6. To help the children *become* responsible for their own actions. They should learn that they will have to deal with the consequences of their own actions.

7. To encourage politeness and a regard for the rights of others. Such things may best be learned in a casual, natural way and should not be overly stressed. Teachers can be effective models here.

8. To assist the children in an easy-going manner and to help them learn the daily routines of their class and of the school.

9. To ensure that children learn that people are similar and different in many ways. They should be exposed to models and experiences that demonstrate cultural differences. Tolerance and acceptance are important goals.

10. To encourage the children to take pride in the language, customs, and traditions of their own cultures and society. However, a blind belief in the total goodness of society is to be avoided.

be taken not to overwhelm them or to make unrealistic demands of them.

Months of patience may be required before some of the children become truly relaxed. The first and most important step is to make them comfortable and happy. Complex social interactions need not occur immediately. They will make friends and learn to interact with the other children soon enough.

Sharing is an area wherein excessive demands are often placed upon new students. Everything we know suggests that this early period in their development is *not* the time to expect sharing. In Piaget's terms, these youngest children are egocentric. They are focused on themselves and their own interests and needs. At this point they are not only unable to satisfy the needs of other children through sharing; they are totally unaware of the needs of other children. They are just barely aware of the existence of the other children. They need to get to know and like some of the other children. Slowly, they will learn about the other person's point of view. But initially they need to concentrate on satisfying their own needs. They first need to be made secure and comfortable in this new environment, and that should be the main focus of parents and teachers of these young students.

Three Stages of Socialization in Play

Just as children go through stages of intellectual development, they also appear to pass through three general phases of social development in their play. (We might as easily call these work situations, as much of what we call play is hard, interesting work for them.) We shall look at each stage and some of the practical implications inherent in each of them. (A more detailed discussion of play is contained in chapter 8.)

Stage 1: Independent Play In this stage the children remain egocentric. Although they have a grasp of object permanence, and know that people and things exist apart from themselves, they still focus upon their own needs and interests. For the most part, they play and work alone. They

Solitary play is an early phase in social development

function in the world of and by themselves. This phase is perfectly normal. Attempts to counteract it should not be instituted. For example, the children should not be pressured to function in small groups, or to share. Teachers should arrange the environment to minimize conflict and to maximize opportunities for *solitary play*.

A variety of easily accessible choices should be established. Areas within a given room should be arranged for different activities. Given that the children will all be wanting to do different things at different times, the teachers would be wise to set up different areas containing playdough, simple puzzles, manipulative toys, blocks and accessories, puppets, books, housekeeping materials and costumes, and the like. In the yard, teachers can provide different areas for wheel toys, water, sand, animals, and painting to supplement the usual array of playground equipment.

In addition to different areas, for many activities, the teachers must be sure to establish an appropriate number of individual places within each area and individual supplies for each place. Such arrangements avoid the necessity of sharing, and avoid all children wanting to do something that is only set up for one child to do. For example, if you have a playdough table, be sure to provide several individual places. These should be defined by the obvious placement of chairs and placemats. Each place should include its own playdough and accessories such as cookie cutters, small rolling pins, and children's scissors. The teachers can then point out that only one child can work at one spot. No sharing is necessary. Coincidentally, this situation provides the children with one of their first real experiences with the one-to-one correspondence concept (*one* child for *one* place). Piaget would argue that this early behavioral experience with a very basic mathematical concept can help pave the way for later understanding and learning. The child is learning mathematics by "doing" mathematics. (We discuss mathematics in more detail in chapter 9.)

You will need to limit certain kinds of activities to just a few children. For example, you might find it best to set up no more than two paint easels at one time. With a place on either side of an easel, this limits the activity to four children at one time. Given that you will want to help each child by putting on and taking off aprons, encouraging and rewarding their efforts, printing names (and sometimes titles) on each masterpiece and hanging them up to dry, and cleaning up painted hands, faces, and the inevitable spilled paint, four (or less) kids at one time will more than keep you busy. At this age, some children will finish a picture with only a stroke or two, while others will become engrossed in one or more paintings for quite a while. Avoid letting other children paint on a previous child's picture, and don't put up more easels than you are willing (and able) to supervise at one time.

If you think it is too difficult for individual children to wait for their turn to paint, you can interest them in another activity and assure them that they will have their turn soon. Be sure to keep this promise though, so that the children will learn to trust you when you say these things. Even if they have become engrossed in another activity, you should still make the offer, and leave the choice to the child.

Set up only the activities that there are enough adults (teachers, aides, parents, volunteers, and so on) to supervise well. For example, if there is only one teacher and several inexperienced parents for a toddler group, you might want to set up easels or fingerpainting, but not both. These are terrific, but demanding activities. Focus the adults on specific activities. Avoid having all adults trying to help in all activities. Position yourself where you can keep an overall lookout. Weather and facilities permitting, many of the messy or watery activities can be handled and cleaned up more easily in the yard than in the room. Paper or plastic on the floor can aid such activities indoors.

Because the young children are egocentric, individual help, support, and approval should be given whenever possible. Allow the children to "do their own thing" and function individually. Never require children to draw, paint, or model in a particular way. Such rigid requirements can stunt their creativity and inhibit their confidence in themselves. Eventually, when they are ready, they will begin to interact with other children and begin to function in groups.

Even though you do all you can to provide a variety of choices and to avoid conflict, conflict is inevitable (and not necessarily bad). When the children take things away from one another, there are several things the teacher can do to avoid having them learn inappropriate social techniques. For example, distraction and a short explanation are sometimes useful. If you see Melissa take a toy away from John, much to John's dismay, you can say, "John doesn't like it when you take toys away from him, and neither do I. Let's try to find another toy for you to play with, Melissa." If she accepts the alternative toy, you can leave them to their play. If Melissa continues to seek the original toy, you can tell John to say, "No!" or, "I'm playing with it," depending on his verbal capabilities. Melissa might accept John's statement. In addition, John will have learned a little about being assertive without being assaultive. If Melissa still persists, you can suggest that her turn will be next, and help her find further alternative toys. Physical removal from the scene of conflict to a different area sometimes helps the child forget the unavailable toy. She may be able to develop a new interest in a new environment. Physical or harsh punishments are not acceptable or helpful techniques. The idea is to begin to plant the seeds of sharing, and to help the child understand that alternative modes of interacting, as well as alternative activities, are available.

If all else fails, and you find yourself at a loss, summon another teacher, or take the child to another teacher. At this point you can explain, "Melissa wants the toy John is playing with. We don't know what to do. Maybe you can help us." The other teacher may be able to suggest a better solution or distract the child another way. Many teachers make it a point to help one another in difficult situations. Such a pre-arranged agreement can be particularly helpful if you are having a bad day or if a child seems to be getting to you. Obviously, you don't want to take advantage of the other teachers by calling on them when it is not really warranted. But this technique is a useful one and can serve as a safety valve for your emotions.

Stage 2: Associative or Parallel Play   Clearly, the child does not go on playing in an independent fashion forever. Gradually, and in an on-and-off manner, they begin to adopt a mode of play referred to as associative or parallel play. This occurs when two or more children play *near* each other but continue to carry on their individual pursuits. They associate with each other, but do not yet engage in cooperative play. They are aware of one another, but they don't interact. You might say they play by themselves, together.

Associative play indicates that the children are becoming interested in and aware of others. This movement outward represents an important, positive step in the process of social development. But it doesn't occur all at once. It's a gradual process. Accordingly, the teacher should not have unrealistic expectations or make unrealistic demands. The children will still engage in a great deal of independent play. For the most part, they will still be incapable of sharing or coordinating their play with

In parallel play, children play near *one another but not with* one another

their newly-found friends. They may want to sit next to their friend, or do what their friend is doing, but, beyond this, their play will still be independent.

Given that socialization is an educational goal, associative play should be recognized, supported, and rewarded. You can comment on how nice it is that the children are becoming friends. You can allow them to sit with each other when appropriate. You can comment on how well they are doing their activities together. You can mention these new friendships to their parents. Many parents, upon learning that their child has a genuine friend for the first time, will want to give these children the opportunity to visit with one another outside of the school setting. These visits should be encouraged if, *and only if,* both children respond positively to the suggestion. Don't push it.

Stage 3: Cooperative and Group Play Slowly, the children begin to coordinate their play with the play of others. For example, one child may play the father role, while the other child plays the mother or baby role. They begin to become aware of the other person's needs. They begin to learn how to share. They begin to learn the give-and-take techniques that are so vital in social life. They begin to build things together, play games together, and "cook dinner" together in the sandbox. They begin to role-play in various "pretend" games. They sing and dance together, some of the time. Friendships and alliances are formed and dissolve. At times group activities begin to take on a more homogeneous quality.

Piaget would argue that the children are just beginning to develop the requisite cognitive structures necessary for such play. Hence the process cannot be rushed. On the other hand, conditioning theory would argue that aid and assistance can be provided by the teacher. By rewarding appropriate, emerging behavior, and by serving as a clear, simple model, the teacher can do much to enhance the development process. Through a combination of developmental processes and the patience and guidance of the teacher, the children will come to realize others possess needs just like their own. They will slowly discover that if they share with others, then others will be more likely to share with them. They will eventually learn that they like each other better and have a more enjoyable time when both are willing to share and cooperate in their activities.

You may have noticed that we have avoided reference to even approximate ages in relationship to the three stages of socialization in play. This is because children vary greatly in the rate at which they go through these stages. Some progress much more rapidly than others. Therefore your class will, more than likely, contain examples of all three levels. Furthermore, there is a great deal of overlap in the stages. In other words, even after children are completely capable of cooperative play, they will still enjoy independent and associative play. (In fact, as

In cooperative play, two or more children interact with one another as they play. . . .

adults we still enjoy all three forms of play.) But the *order* in which these three forms develop appears to be constant, despite different individual rates. The principle of constant order and variable rate is one we have discussed many times in connection with Piaget's work.

Communication

Obviously, the ability to communicate has a great deal to do with the overall process of socialization. As mentioned in chapter 3, language acquisition begins with babbling, and then moves on to the use of single words. When normal toddlers and 2 year olds enter school, they may have a vocabulary containing as few as six words or as many as 250 (Jenkins and Shacter, 1975). In other words, children, even at this early age, vary in terms of the size of their verbal repertoire. But most of them display holophrastic speech which, you recall, refers to the situation where a single word refers to an entire thought. For example, the spoken word, "Mine" may mean "this toy is mine." "Up" may mean "Pick me up and hold me, quickly."

    Telegraphic speech also begins to appear during this level of development. In telegraphic speech, many of the minor or non-essential words of a sentence will be left out. For example, "Me go" may mean "I want to go to the store, too." "Baby cry" may mean "The baby is crying."

During this stage, children's language is fairly limited, but they are beginning to experiment, to test hypotheses concerning language use, and to try out sentences.

What Will Help? As mentioned in chapter 3, modern linguistic theory argues that there is an innate, predetermined quality to language development. If this is true, then why bother to encourage and mold language development at all? According to this position, it will all be accomplished in due time anyway. On the other hand, other theoretical approaches, such as the conditioning approach, argue that much of our language usage is determined by conditioning and is influenced by experience. The truth probably lies somewhere between these extremes. Given that we are becoming aware of some of the factors important in language development, it does seem that there are a few things the instructor can do to facilitate language usage.

Reward Correct Usage Whenever possible, the teacher can reward, with a word or a smile, efforts to use language. As the children move from single words to two word sentences and finally to longer sentences, reward the correct forms and remain neutral toward their errors. Don't demand correct usage, but reinforce it when it occurs naturally. Be a good model for them by speaking clearly and simply. Through imitation, hypothesis testing, and confirmation in the form of reward, they will hit upon correct usages. At this point, correcting their errors may discourage them from further attempts at verbalization.

Encourage language use, and involve them in it. Reading, singing, and playing records all involve them in the process. By giving them plenty of "fodder," and a good deal of experience, it may be possible to reduce much of the early noncommunicative speech and listening that Piaget has outlined.

Provide Useful Words and Phrases Linguistic theory emphasizes that language acquisition involves hypothesis testing and not rote memorization. The child tries out different forms of language and discovers which ones work. Linguists argue that you cannot force language upon a child. But you can help them by providing hypotheses for them to test. So many times they are ready to speak to another child but are at a loss as to what to say. It is at this point that the teacher can be helpful.

You can help them by giving them some key words and phrases, once they start showing an interest in interacting with other children. For example, if you see one child trying to join another child, but without success, you might go to them and say something like, "Jimmy, if you want to play with Lisa, tell her so. Say 'I want to play, Lisa.'" This may get the ball rolling. But if Lisa just stares at Jimmy, you might say, "Lisa, if you want Jimmy to play with you, say, 'Okay, Jimmy.'" If she says, "Okay," they have taken a step toward effective communication. You can then reward them by saying, "I like the way you both used your words."

If, however, Lisa shouts, "No!" you can say to Jimmy, "I don't think Lisa is ready to play with anyone right now. You can ask her again later. Why don't you play right over there. Then you can see each other. When Lisa is ready, she can say, 'I want to play.'"

This simple interaction does several things. It introduces them to a form of communication that they might try out later on. It recognizes the opinions of both children. It does not force the children to do something they don't want to do. It sets the stage for later experimental communication. It lets the second child know the first child is interested in playing with her. It gives her a choice, but allows her time to think it over. It softens the rejection, and maximizes the chances for a later, positive interaction.

Obviously, the approach will vary depending upon the situation. But in each situation, give simple, effective words or phrases; recognize the rights and emotions of both children; point them toward future, if not immediate, interactions; and reward any effort they make.

The technique of providing words can be useful in many situations. For example, conflict situations, so common yet so difficult for children to handle on anything but a physical level, can often be improved by the introduction of key words and phrases. For example, if one child is hit by another and comes crying to you, you might ask, "Lizzy, did you like it when Josh hit you?" She will undoubtedly answer in the negative. Then say, "Tell Josh you don't like it when he hits you. Tell him he shouldn't do it again. Go up and tell him, 'I don't like that! Don't hit me anymore!'" After she does so, you might say to Josh, "Listen to Lizzy. It hurts when you hit her. She doesn't like it. Can you tell her, 'I won't hit you anymore, Lizzy?' If Lizzy did something you didn't like, maybe you should tell her what it was, instead of hitting her," and so on.

This example should give you a feel for the general approach. Encourage verbal expression of thoughts, feelings, needs, and so forth. Offer the children a way of using words, rather than them grabbing, hitting, biting, and crying. Provide a simple, working vocabulary for them to try out. They soon begin to pick up on key phrases, particularly those that are useful in defending themselves. "No!" "Don't hit me!" and "I don't like that!" will soon occur spontaneously, and will often be shouted vehemently at the offender. We suggest you reward this assertive language usage (by females and males). You might also encourage the offending child to "Listen to Jeremy's words . . . he's trying to tell you something."

The child that is being grabbed, pinched, or shoved is not the only child that needs words. The offending child can also benefit if you provide some words to express his or her position. For example, Josh may have struck Lizzy because she took his shovel. (It is often impossible to find out exactly what happened.) When Lizzy shouts, "Don't hit me! I don't like that!" Josh may feel a rightful sense of injustice. He will probably say, "She took my shovel!" At this point, it is time to help Josh tell Lizzy that he doesn't like it when she takes his shovel.

Obviously, we are not just talking about bland, logical communication here. Strong emotions are being communicated. (This is an example of the intertwined quality of the developmental process.) The children are learning about their own rights and the rights of others as they learn language. Language learning does not, and as far as we are concerned, should not occur in a vacuum. Learning to use language by testing its power in real life situations can lead to enormous gains in a short period of time. Again, they are learning by doing.

The last step in this episode is to advise Lizzy of possible ways of expressing her original need for a shovel. Tell her she can say the following kinds of things to Josh. "I need a shovel. Can I use yours?" "You can use my spoon, if I can use your shovel." "Can I use your shovel after you?" Then point out to Lizzy that if Josh says no, she doesn't have to hit him. She can ask the teacher to help her find another shovel.

It's not surprising that the transition from actions to words is sometimes difficult. As Piaget points out, it takes quite a while for children to realize that the other individual has feelings and needs. Some toddlers and 2 year olds are not even to this point yet. And, even as adults, we often have trouble verbalizing our own needs and feelings. But with practice and help from their teachers, the children do begin to learn successful communication skills that are so essential for socialization. Learning is particularly successful when the children find out that their new language elements work, or obtain results. It's rewarding to them. You will, in fact, begin to hear the child sing out and echo the exact words and phrases you have given. You provide the elements of a linguistic hypothesis, and they are more than ready to test that hypothesis. If the testing results in some rewards, they will be more likely to use these words and phrases again in their progress toward socialization.

Incomprehensible Speech Remember that children vary greatly in their overall verbal abilities. It is not unusual to find children whose speech you cannot understand, at least at times. They may be babbling, or they may be trying out hypotheses but don't have the right ones yet. Their speech doesn't work. While natural and rather common, this can be extremely frustrating for both of you. In these situations, it often helps to say, "Show me." Using this expression (and often relying upon nearby children), it is often possible to determine the speaker's intent.

Being something of a detective can be rewarding when one works with a group of children who are not yet fully communicative. If you do manage to discover what it is that the child is trying to say, *restate* it for her as simply as possible. Once again, you can provide the words, and hope the child will try them out in the future.

Children very often understand much more than they can verbalize. Thus, it is to their advantage to have a teacher who is willing to be sensitive to their need for labels and linguistic elements, and who is willing to provide them in an appropriate context and in a usable form. On the other hand, don't be too surprised if you find children who can verbalize almost any thought or feeling, and who can partake quite skillfully in just about any activity available at an early age. As we have said, children do vary greatly. Just enjoy, enjoy . . .

Emotional Development

What Are Emotions?

Psychologists define emotions as strong, relatively uncontrollable feelings that often affect our behavior. Emotions are either positive or negative. (Can you think of a neutral emotion?) Emotions have powerful effects upon our behavior, and upon our sense of well-being. Because they are so important in human life, it is not surprising that the emotional development of the child is seen as an important factor within the field of early childhood education.

Emotions do not spring forth fully developed in the young child. They evolve and develop. They can be affected strongly by experience. Experiences and events occurring within the early educational setting can influence the child's emotional development.

Building Self-confidence

One area of particular concern has to do with the child's evolving sense of self-confidence. The emphasis is upon fostering emotions that will lead to a positive self-evaluation. We want to encourage and stimulate emotions which will lead to trust and independence rather than apprehension and dependence. We want them to become (or remain) happy and confident and to hold a strong, positive opinion of themselves. How do we go about obtaining such a goal?

The first thing to realize is that there is no one, magical formula that is universally accepted. What may work for one child may not work for another. In addition, children may vary enormously in terms of what they need. Finally, teachers themselves vary in terms of style and in terms of what they can and cannot accomplish. You will no doubt find ways that work for you and methods that are consistent with your own style. In spite of these complexities, there are some general points that can be made in connection with building self-confidence.

Step 1: Building Trust Teachers must first become acquainted with their children and must give the children the opportunity to become acquainted with them. Get down on their level physically and interact with them, face-to-face. Don't make them look up to you. It can be a physical strain and intimidating. A distant teacher will be of little help.

If you are friendly, cheerful, and calm, as opposed to stern, grumpy, or nervous, the children will be relaxed with you. Then, if you provide them with a variety of interesting activities, without exceeding their capabilities, you will become a source of interest and pleasure to them. If you are warm and encouraging, and support their efforts, they will think of you as someone who *believes* in their ability to learn new things. If you are a source of comfort and affection, they will understand that they can come to you when they need someone. If you are honest with them, they will think of you as a source of information. Love and trust will grow between you. Once trust has been established, almost anything can be accomplished, anything endured.

Step 2: Trust Leads to Dependence As the children come to love and trust you, they will develop a certain brand of dependence that we feel is beneficial, helpful, and, if handled skillfully, temporary. They will come to depend on you as someone who believes in them, and their capabilities. They will count on you, and your unqualified support. They will look to you for encouragement when they want to try something new. They will expect recognition and approval if they succeed, and support and more encouragement if they do not. They believe in your *unconditional* love and assistance. They will expect, without any uncertainty, that you will hold them and comfort them when they are hurt, discouraged, affectionate, or simply exhausted. (Sometimes they will even try to console *you*, if they feel you need it.) In general, they come to know that you, their teacher, cares about them, and believes in them through thick or thin.

This growing, mutual relationship can build the child's self-confidence (and yours). If you believe in them, they tend to believe in themselves. If you care about them, the implication is that they are worth caring about. If *you* love them, they *must* be valuable and lovable. Even the self-doubters cannot entirely ignore someone who believes in them, who helps them succeed, who is excited by their successes, and who is not the least discouraged by any of their failures.

Step 3: Dependence Leads to Independence As the children experience the fact that they can depend on you, and as their self-confidence becomes stable, it sometimes seems that it is their very dependence on you that forms the basis for a new, almost surprising air of independence. By becoming dependent upon you, they unwittingly allow you to be the primary controller of many powerful reinforcers (e.g., a word of praise from you is very important to them). And because you reward their efforts in a wide variety of activities that involve small steps towards independence, you encourage the very behaviors that make them less dependent upon you. You reward not just their movement towards you, but their steps *away* from you as well. Gradually, as they become more confident and competent, they find more and more of their rewards coming from other people, and in the form of a sense of self-satisfaction.

Graded Step Reinforcement: Guaranteed Success One technique that is particularly helpful in building self-confidence and a sense of competence involves the arrangement of reinforcement schedules such that *success is guaranteed*. Basically, the technique involves the reinforcement of very small steps toward a full-blown response pattern. In other words, we are talking about a variety of shaping. Don't ask too much of the child all at once. Guarantee successess on the small, preliminary steps which actually make up the more complex level of behavior toward which you are moving the child. This same technique has been used by Seligman (1977) in treating depressed and "helpless" adults. This technique is particularly useful with young children who are convinced they can't do anything, or have learned to be helpless. For example, sooner or later almost every teacher encounters a child who is convinced she can't do anything. No matter what the activity, no matter how tempting, the child will say, "I can't." (There seems to be a fear of failing— already.) So, you merely show these children that they *can* . . . in little steps.

Suppose Adam says, "I can't paint." The overall task is over-whelming, intimidating. The teacher can help in this case by showing Adam he can, after all, accomplish all the individual steps that make up the act of painting. Engage him in a follow-the-leader type of game. Say, "I'll bet you can hold a paint brush just like this," as you wrap his little fingers around the brush just like yours. Once he holds the brush, say, "That's *right*, Adam." Then say, "And I *know* you can dunk it right into the red paint, like this." Dip your brush in the paint, and wait for him to do it. When he does, say something like, "See, Adam, you've already done two of the steps that are part of painting! I knew you could do it!" (A hug, or other physical sign of affection can help here.) "Now I know that you can blob some paint on this piece of paper, like this." Smear some paint on the paper, keeping it very simple so that your effort will not exceed his. The child will probably follow suit, at which point you say, "See, Adam, we both made paintings." Stand back and admire the paintings and say something like, "I knew you could do it, Adam. Let's write our names on our pictures and hang them up in our room right now (print his name for him). Then we can take them home later. Wait till we show your Mom (Dad)."

Obviously, most children will enter freely into painting and will not require this form of graded reinforcement. But all of us, children included, feel somewhat inept in some areas, and the technique of graded reinforcement can be useful in overcoming the rough spots. It's similar to congratulating oneself in following the successive steps of a new cooking recipe. The overall task may be intimidating, but the individual steps can be handled easily. The results are often very satisfying.

Little, step-by-step successes like this can expose the children to their own unknown talents. Guaranteed success should be a part of many of the activities you plan for your children. And individual attention can be most helpful in building their little egos (female and male). They need the experience of success at this age because so much of their life is frustrating.

Parenthetically, it helps, too, if you are able to remain passive in the face of spilled paint, dirty clothes, wet diapers, and other minor disasters that can make some children very anxious. You might even spill things yourself once in a while. This will make the more fearful children feel more human. It will show them that everyone spills things occasionally and that it doesn't matter to you.

Thus it is that by allowing the children to be dependent on you, you have paved the way for their ultimate independence. The process can be very satisfying to both you and them. Without the initial experience of being close and dependent, the children may find it more difficult to achieve eventual independence.

Discrimination Learning Obviously, we do not mean to imply that all behaviors should be rewarded in our efforts to establish self-confidence. For example, safety rules and the rights of others must be considered. The children must learn to discriminate between acceptable and unacceptable forms of behavior. Certain behaviors, such as fighting and other disruptive activities, generally must be discouraged.

The trick (goal) is to convince the child that you do not object to him as a person, but merely to some of his specific actions. "I love you, but I don't like what you just did." Carl Rogers (1961), the father of client-centered therapy, argues this point strongly. For individuals to become confident and fulfilled, they must experience *unconditional love.* "No matter what you do, I still love you, even though some of your behavior is bound to cause you and others trouble."

Although framed in the context of adult psychotherapy, Roger's point is applicable to children, too. When they do something that is inappropriate, do not attack them as persons ("Bad boy!") Do not threaten their sense of self-esteem ("You never do anything right, you idiot!") Just point out that that particular behavior causes too much trouble for everyone, or results in someone being hurt. Make sure they understand the distinction between your feelings for them and your feelings about their behavior ("Hitting is not okay.") Within this framework, children can easily discriminate among acceptable and unacceptable behaviors.

Of course, you will develop your own ways of encouraging healthy emotional development. Teaching can be a very creative experience. You will discover techniques that work for you, given your particular children and your particular situations. Your methods will vary from child to child, from group to group, and from situation to situation.

Aggression

Aggression as Learned Behavior Aggression can be viewed in many ways. For example, we have already seen in chapter 2, that some aggressive behavior may be learned behavior. That is, the child may learn or acquire aggressive behaviors because those behaviors have paid off, or been reinforced, in the past. According to this view, it is the teachers' task to structure the situation such that aggressive modes of relating to the environment are not sustained by reinforcement. The teacher must be willing to withhold reinforcement, to utilize mild punishment, and to reward alternative, socially acceptable modes of behavior. For example, if a child tends to use force to obtain access to the block area, the teacher must short circuit the system by preventing this behavior from being successful. In addition, the teacher must provide an alternative method of obtaining the same goal, such as asking for a turn in the block area.

Aggression as Modeled Behavior Another view of aggression holds that much of it is behavior which is modeled, or, in a sense, copied from others. For example, there is currently a controversy raging over whether or not children become more aggressive if they watch aggressive television programs. Whatever the upshot of that controversy, it seems clear that the preschool teacher should do everything she or he can to provide appropriate nonaggressive models. If the teacher behaves in an aggressive manner, then the child may well model her behavior after that aggressive model.

Aggression as Innate Some feel aggression is an innate, inherited method of coping with the environment (Maccoby and Jacklin, 1974). For example, a well-known hypothesis in psychology is that frustration sometimes leads to aggression. According to this view, we can become aggressive if we are blocked from motive satisfaction (Hilgard, Atkinson, and Atkinson, 1975). Aggression can take several forms. It can be *direct,* or aimed at the frustrating obstacle, such as when a child attacks another frustrating child. Or it can be *displaced,* such as when a husband (or wife), frustrated at work, takes it out on the kids at home.

Clearly, we cannot allow these aggressive urges to be expressed directly and physically. What can the teacher do? We have already seen that the learning interpretation of aggression suggests that we extinguish aggressive behavior and encourage alternative forms of behavior such as sharing, finding alternative activities, and learning alternative methods of coping. We have also seen that, by providing nonaggressive models, we can eliminate a good deal of aggressive behavior. But what does the innate view of aggression recommend? Whether or not one agrees with this interpretation, the innate view of aggression argues that unexpressed

The flying trowel may be effective . . . but wouldn't words be better?

aggressive impulses can become bottled up and can continue to upset the child. One solution which has been suggested is to find alternative objects upon which the aggressive impulses may be legitimately vented. According to this view we should accept the fact that children will at times feel aggressive. Don't try to hide the fact; find acceptable outlets for them.

For example, we cannot allow children to punch or bite one another, even when they are extremely frustrated. But we can recognize their feelings and let them flail away at a punching bag or punch hanging pillows. They can't hit one another, but, according to this view, they can give a glob of clay or playdough a good smack. Pounding Sarah over the head with a shovel is to be discouraged, but pounding the sand, and pounding pegs with a hammer can be sanctioned. Tearing up old newspapers (to be used later for papier maché), can be relaxing, and fun. Marching and stomping on the playground can be good, too, as is just plain running. In other words, acceptable outlets for minor irritations abound in the educational setting, according to this view.

Probably all three views of aggression (learned, modeled, innate) hold some validity. In any given instance, the alert teacher must consider all three.

Emotional Expression   Emotional expression and experience can be encouraged in many ways in the preschool situation. Music and dancing, for example, can soothe the soul (along with improving coordination and developing muscles). Piaget pointed out that many dramatic play situations, where the child can be the winner for a change, will be helpful in reducing frustration and alleviating anxiety. Cuddling dolls and soft, stuffed animals are soothing and beneficial outlets for anxious or unhappy feelings. Just allowing a frazzled child to sit on your lap for a short while can have a wonderful healing and renewing effect.

Painting and other artistic activities provide children with the opportunity to express themselves in an active but relaxing way. They need time and freedom in these efforts. A child may create several rather involved and complex pictures in a row. All sorts of both positive and negative emotions may be projected into, and expressed by, the paintings. In addition to expressing their emotions, the children can learn a great deal about paint, color, and paintbrushes in a single session (e.g., how they look, feel, smell, taste, and mix together).

Some children will become absorbed and creative, painting first the paper, then their hands, arms, and faces. They will mix colors and invent their own collage techniques by adding bits of paper, leaves, and sand.

As they paint, some children will talk to you in a free-flowing, unselfconscious way. The depth of their emotional involvement will become clear as they express a variety of feelings and fantasies, and discuss past events that have impressed them in one way or another. One child described seeing the movie *Snow White* the night before. As she talked, she painted. Apparently the movie had upset and frightened her, particularly the parts involving the witch and the poisoned apple. As she related the events, her forehead furrowed with concern. It seemed as though painting helped her express and work through her fears. It certainly helped the teacher know what was bothering her. She covered the paper several times, each time with a different color. Painting seemed to help talking, and vice versa. This free expression allowed the teacher to reassure her that it was nothing more than a make-believe story and that witches are not real. Judging from her final picture alone, one would never imagine the amount of thought and emotion that went into it. But a sensitive teacher, and the child, knew. And the teacher was able to mention some of the child's lingering feelings about the movie to her mother. Of course, it is not advisable to force children to talk about what they are creating; but if they do so spontaneously, you may gain some valuable insights into the child's emotional and cognitive status.

When children are having trouble expressing feelings, the teacher can also help them by recognizing their needs. She or he can help them express their emotions in an acceptable way.

Childhood Fears and Anxieties

Many, although not all, children display what we can term childhood fears and anxieties. We are referring to unwarranted fears that may develop as the child learns about the world around her before she can clearly distinguish between what is real and what is not real. For example, many children are afraid of monsters, spooks, the dark, and so on. As the child learns so much, so quickly, about the world, there are bound to be times when fantasy events, and fictional characters, are interpreted as being part of reality by the child. If the child views a television program containing assorted monsters, and no one helps her understand that these are fictitious figures, she may well assume they are real. Plainly stated, the child needs help in discriminating reality from the rich products of human imagination. Based upon what they know, the children's conclusions regarding these fearful events and figures are certainly reasonable. They simply do not, without our help, have the necessary information to judge whether or not a given monster is real or not.

Adults tend to be made anxious by abstract elements such as uncertainty about the future, or the discrepancy between what they value and what they do. Young children, on the other hand, tend to be made anxious by more concrete objects and events such as storms, monsters, the dark, and large animals. The teacher's task is to reduce these concrete anxieties.

There are two helpful suggestions for the reduction of these fears.

First, provide the child with information that will allow her to understand the fictional quality of the feared object or event. For example, assure her repeatedly that there are no monsters at all, anywhere, and that monsters are just things we make up for fun. Point out that monsters on T.V. are merely people dressed up in costumes much like the costumes in the school's drama center. Have other children, who know about monsters, explain the situation to the fearful ones.

Second, whenever possible, show the child that her fears are unfounded. If she is afraid of dogs, bring in a puppy and allow her to become accustomed to it. Then show her a small, friendly adult dog. This is similar to a process known as *systematic desensitization* in psychology. The least feared object in a hierarchy of objects (i.e., the cuddly puppy) is first exposed. The child's fear of this object is gradually extinguished through exposure. Then an object which is a little more frightening (i.e., the friendly adult dog) might be introduced, and so on.

If the child is afraid of monsters, expose her to some rubber Halloween masks. Let her handle them and put them on herself before you put them on. Fears can be gradually extinguished by introducing, in a step-wise fashion, stimuli that produce the fear. Begin with the least fearful stimulus and move toward the more fearful stimuli. Do not move to the next most fearful stimulus until the preceding one no longer elicits a fear reaction of any kind.

In general, childhood fears are lessened as the child receives more information about what is and what is not real.

Greeting the Child

Introduction

Having looked at the various dimensions of development, including cognitive, emotional, social and physical development, we are now ready to move on to a consideration of several factors which appear to involve all of the dimensions of development simultaneously. In other words, we will now deal with the rich complexity that represents the child as a whole. By looking at morning greetings, security blankets, separation, training, and mixed groups, we will see that the child seldom, if ever, develops along one of these dimensions without the others being involved as well.

Be Prepared Most authorities emphasize the fact that the moment the child arrives at school in the morning is the critical moment of the entire day. If all goes well, the day may progress smoothly. If the greeting and initial moments of the day are unsatisfactory, then the day, or at least part of it, can be a struggle. Many problems can be avoided if the teacher will plan ahead and give the problem some thought.

There are a number of daily preparations that are useful. For example, it is a good idea to have prepared your room and yard before the children arrive. If activities are set up ahead of time, the children can get down to them without frustrating delays. It's a good idea to arrive early enough so that you will have a moment or two to relax, say hello to the other teachers, and discuss the plans for the day with your co-teacher. If you are ready, you improve your chances for a successful day. But if you are unprepared and running around like the famed chicken with its head cut off, confusion and chaos will prevail. You will not be able to give the children the attention they may need in bridging the gap between home and school. You may miss important "messages" from the children or parent. You may feel (and look) frazzled and unable to cope. Neither children nor parents will have much confidence in you. Children may become anxious, and some of them may begin to cry (just what you don't need at that point). Impatience and frustration will grow as the children wait for you to get the activities set up. Some may want to help, which in your state, would be worse than no help at all. You may end up rejecting their good intentions. We're sure the picture is clear. Arriving a few minutes early, well-rested, is worth it.

Sometimes "bad days" begin through no fault of your own (e.g., flat tires, personal emergencies). In such instances, you just do the best you can and hope everyone recognizes that this situation is an infrequent exception. A bit of volunteered help from another teacher or parent can save the day. But if help is not available, you can facilitate calm by substituting simple, easily supervised activities for more complex, demanding ones. These bad days often seem to get better as time passes (perhaps because they have nowhere to go but up).

Individual Differences Children vary enormously in terms of what they need when they first arrive at school in the morning. If you have arrived early enough to prepare and relax, you will be on top of the situation and will be sensitive to the children's needs. Everyone, including yourself, will have confidence in you. You will be prepared to size up the condition of the children as each one enters school.

For example, some children arrive at school ready for action. All they need is a quick greeting and hug from you, a quick goodbye and hug from their parent, and they're off and running. They quickly and independently decide upon an activity. They are not at all needy at this point, except perhaps to be left alone.

Other children are carried in half asleep by their parents. These children need a quiet hello, and perhaps a gentle kiss on the cheek or a soft touch. They need a chance to sit quietly with the parent. They need to wake up a little, and like to look around before they move. If too many demands are placed on them at this point, they may become grumpy and irritable. If the parent has to leave, the child can be held for a while by one of the teachers, or put in a soft, quiet place (e.g., a comfortable chair in the book area). Some schools that have young children arriving very early provide cots and a quiet, supervised room where they can sleep a bit more, if they need to.

Shy children (and sometimes new children) need a warm, friendly, confident, but not overwhelming greeting. They don't need to sleep, but they do need a chance to go slowly, to look around, and to find an activity that is comfortable. Too much volume in your greeting can put them into a state of shock or panic. You can overcome their shyness later. Don't overpower them at first.

Still other children come to school with something *very important* to tell you. It's helpful (sometimes wonderful) if you can take the time to listen to their story. "We got a new puppy!", "Grampa Joe died", "Mommy's in the hospital"—each of these events requires a different response. Very often these morning messages can help you improve the day. For example, you might read a book about puppies, rather than another book you had planned to read. You might then invite the first youngster to tell the group about the new puppy. Everyone will no doubt want to join in with stories about their pets. This can also be followed up with painting pictures or child-dictated stories about pets.

In the latter cases, you will want to be sympathetic but reassuring. In addition, you may want to contact the families to find out how the child has been, and is, reacting to the new development. Be supportive of the families, too. You can also exchange suggestions, let the families know you are prepared to help, and arrange to keep in touch.

Sometimes children are brought to school when they are ill. Congestion, coughs, rashes, and so forth should be discussed with the parents. Sometimes a fever may be detected during a morning hug. If the child has a fever or any other condition that may be contagious, it falls upon the teacher to inform the parents, as nicely as possible, that the child might be contagious and should be kept out of school for the day. If available, the school nurse or director can be consulted. Having their child turned away may put a burden on the parents, especially working parents. You should be as sympathetic and helpful as possible, but firm. It can be helpful to inform the parents that their child is routinely protected from contagious diseases in the same manner.

Avoiding Sexist Greetings When you greet the children, it is desirable to comment on the *child* rather than the child's *clothing* (except to say that the clothes are appropriate for an active day at school). Do not say things like, "Oh, how pretty!" when girls enter wearing frilly dresses and patent leather shoes. These will inhibit their participation in many activities, and a teacher's (often unintentional) exclamations of delight only serve to reinforce the wearing of such inappropriate clothing. The girls may then want to wear this sort of clothing to please you!

Some security objects . . .

It is also undesirable, in our opinion, to instill the attitude that little girls should always be pretty and clean, sugar and spice and everything nice. The teacher should not make the children overly concerned about their appearances in general (chapter 5 pinpointed the involvement of these attitudes in sexist ideas and sex discrimination). To the contrary, you should try to encourage whatever it takes to ensure the fullest and most complete participation and development of every child, male and female. Try, as diplomatically as possible, to convince the parents that inappropriate clothing inhibits participation and places their child at a disadvantage.

Again, as the children arrive, try to say something nice about *them* ("I remember the painting you did yesterday") rather than about their appearance.

The Security Blanket

Like Linus in the Peanuts cartoons, many young children have security items (blankets, dolls, stuffed animals, articles of clothing, toys, and so on). If your school does not have an inflexible rule with respect to these items, you may have to decide whether or not to allow them in your group.

There are several reasons why many teachers and administrators do not allow security objects:

1. It is difficult enough to keep track of all the other possessions and items of clothing without adding more. Shoes, jackets, sweaters, socks, hats, mittens, scarves, boots, and other *necessary* items are often lost during the course of a busy day at school. The loss of these items is upsetting to parents. It's not a lot of fun for the teachers either: they must search for them in vain, and then acknowledge that they are lost or were accidentally taken home by another child. This is a difficult situation whether the families are poor and cannot afford to replace lost items or relatively well-off and buy all their children's clothes at Saks Fifth Avenue.

2. If the teacher allows one child to bring a security item from home, then other children tend to want to bring *nonsecurity* items as well. Many children will bring a variety of toys, books, records, and other objects from home. They are often unable to share these delicious items with other children, causing conflicts. If they do share them, the objects can be broken or lost.

3. Many teachers and administrators feel that security objects are unnecessary for the child's sense of well-being. They believe them to be concessions made by permissive parents who spoil and baby their child. It is their position that by this age such things are unneeded and unhealthy.

While we would agree that security objects are sometimes difficult to control, and that they stimulate the children to bring other non-security items to school, we feel that they are not necessarily silly, unneeded, or unnecessary. There are a number of counter-arguments that suggest security items should be at least tolerated, if not welcomed.

. . . are built-in

The most obvious reason for allowing security items in school is obvious from the label for them . . . security. If these items help some children feel safe, secure, and comfortable in a situation that can be difficult, frustrating, exhausting, lonely, or even a little scary, why shouldn't they have them? Security items often bridge the gap between home and away from home. Their feel and their smell can be classically conditioned to the feelings of happiness, safety, and love that they experience at home. In a sense, they allow the child to feel closer to home and to parents who are often missed during the day. Security blankets make difficult times easier. Restful naps, otherwise impossible, can be facilitated by a blanket from home. The beloved item can make a crying child stop crying. Should we also take away the security photographs we adults have of our families, on our desks and office walls?

The problems that these items can cause are not insurmountable. Most schools have some individual space for each child's possessions, such as "cubbies," shelves, or lockers. Children keep extra clothes and school projects in these spaces. When a little girl comes in with a security item, it is not difficult to say something like, "Let's put your blanket in your cubby with your extra clothes. Then, when you want it, you'll know right where it is, and it won't get lost." If she can't give it up right away, suggest that she put it in the cubby when done with it. If she forgets (which often happens) and you find it lying somewhere, tell her you are putting it away, so it won't get lost or dirty.

As a further aid in controlling the number of items brought to school, a clear distinction can be made between security objects and other items. Parents can be informed that unnecessary toys are discouraged, as they are often lost or broken. Certain days can be set aside for "show and tell." (Be careful, though, that these do not turn into "bring and brag" sessions.) If certain children insist upon bringing something, they can be instructed to show the item to the other children, and then to put it in their cubby. If loss or breakage occurs, it can be pointed out that this is why it is a good idea to keep special toys at home.

In general, children seem ready and able to accept the distinction between security and nonsecurity items. They seem able to understand that Jeannie's blanket and Jason's cloth puppet are "special" soft things that make them feel better if they are sad, tired, or lonely. They seem to accept the fact that the security items are relaxers, and not toys. They have seen their effects many times. The other children are often very sympathetic to these needs. Sometimes they will be able to tell stories about other children with similar security objects—or themselves at an earlier age: "Teacher, remember when I used to have a blanket? I'm big now and don't use it anymore." In fact, an occasional child, in a display of empathy, will bring another crying child her own blanket. The other children often enjoy participating in a search for lost security items.

If you are sympathetic, the children will learn sympathy from you. A child with a security item should not be ridiculed. Rather, she should be accepted and tolerated . . . made secure.

Finally, it is wise to keep in mind that, sooner or later, the security object and the need for it fall by the wayside. Few students enter college clutching their blankets or teddy bears. It may take longer for some children, but they all eventually lose the need for their special objects. The inconvenience of having security items at school seems a small price to pay for the powerful calming effect they have upon children. We know of no long term, detrimental effects associated with the use of security items.

Separation

Separation and Anxieties Separation can be difficult for a child of any age, and for the child's parents (Schwartz and Wynn, 1971). It can be particularly difficult for toddlers and 2 year olds. The parents may be anxious about whether they are doing the right thing by enrolling their child in school at such a young age. They often need to be reassured, and informed that their reasons for enrolling the child are good, and legitimate. The parents may also worry about the school they have chosen and about *your* capacity to be good for their child. Your initial words and your initial confident and friendly interactions with their child can go a long way toward reducing their apprehension. If possible, you can encourage them to visit your class and the rest of the school. In this way, they can gain first-hand knowledge concerning the situation. They need help in developing their trust in you, in the school, and in their own decisions.

This may be the first major separation experienced by the parent and child. Your confidence will instill confidence in both of them. If you are unsure, they will be uneasy. The situation may sometimes be complicated by the fact that past separations have been traumatic. In these cases, apprehension and anxiety are often quite strong.

Gradual Separation: Shaping It is in everyone's interest to handle separation in the best way possible. Parent/teacher cooperation is a must in most cases. Together, you and the parents will have to decide on the best procedures for individual children.

In many cases, a process of *gradual separation* can be extremely valuable. This process can be looked at as an example of shaping, as described in chapter 2. In other words, you reward closer and closer approximations to a full-blown separation. Little-by-little, the parent and child will be separated, and rewarded for each successive step.

The first step is to discuss the overall process with the parent or caretaker, but not the child. Inform them that you want to make each step of this gradual separation process as pleasant and rewarding an experience as possible. Parents must be encouraged to take each step as naturally and confidently as possible, and complimented when they do so. You will both want to show the child that everything is perfectly normal and as it should be, as you move through the steps together. Parents, where properly introduced to the concept, can become good behavior modifiers too.

In the next step, the parent visits the class with the child. If, upon arrival, the child spots an area of interest and goes to it, both you and the parent should reward her for this tiny step toward separation (e.g., tell her you are happy she has already found something she likes at school). If the child does not specifically ask for the parent to stay with her, invite the parent, in a tone audible to the child, to "Sit right here where you can see Ruthie wherever she goes." If the child asks

When handled properly, separation can be a simple matter

for the parent, encourage the parent to join her and to reward what she does. Reward, in this case, can be simple parental approval.

If the child does not move toward a particular activity, encourage her to explore (with or without the parent), and to see all of the alternative activities. It is helpful at this stage if the parent can find a toy or activity the child has liked in the past, or a new one the parent thinks she will like. Join them when you can; be friendly, supportive, interested, but not overpowering. Let the child become acquainted with you a little at a time. If the child is too hesitant to engage in any of the activities, just let her sit on her parent's safe, secure lap, and watch. These feelings of safety and security will be classically conditioned to the school environment. Let the child and the parent relax, and move (or not move) at their own, natural pace.

Generally, it is advisable to encourage the parent to spend the entire first session with the child. In this way as few negative feelings and as many positive feelings as possible can be associated with (or conditioned to) the school situation. Typically, a session for the youngest children will be between two and three hours, unless the parents have full-day obligations. In any case, whatever the age, it may be advisable to cut the first day short. In this manner, the child won't be exhausted or overwhelmed when she leaves, and will have pleasant memories of her first day at school. We want her first day to be interesting and happy, not exhausting. First impressions are just as important for children as they are for adults. Considering the number of years this child will be attending school, it seems reasonable to go to a little extra effort to start her off on the right foot.

On the second day, the child will probably be able to engage in some activities without the constant accompaniment of the parent. In addition you will have established some rapport with her. At this point she is ready for the next step. While she is busy and happy, the parent should tell her, in a matter-of-fact manner, that she or he (the parent) is going to the school's kitchen for a quick cup of coffee, to the bathroom, to the school office to pay a bill, or on some other in-school errand. It helps if the child has already seen the office or kitchen so that she will know vaguely what and where it is. Have the parent tell the child that she or he will be back in a few minutes. The parent can give the child a hug and tell her to ask her teacher if she needs anything. The parent should then *go*.

If the parent has done this in a confident, matter-of-fact manner, the child will probably accept it as normal, too. If you see any signs of shakiness in the child, you can probably distract and relax her by going to her and taking an interest in what she has been doing. By being calm and confident, you can show her that everything is all right.

This first separation should be a short one. The parent should return in a calm, happy manner and should reward the child by saying something like, "Hi, I'm back. Did you have a nice time while I was gone? What have you been doing?" This small incident, if all goes well, tells the child several things: (1) things are all right if her parent leaves the yard or room; (2) she can have a perfectly good time at school without the parent; (3) if she needs anything while the parent is gone, she can ask her teacher; (4) when the parent promises to return, she or he *does* return. This faith in the return of the parent becomes very important later, when the periods of separation increase in length. The child must learn that the parent always returns.

It is helpful to try another short separation or two that day, and then to have the parent stay until the end of the day's session. These little separations give both the child and the parent confidence that they can handle being separated in this way. Each successive separation may be a bit longer, but each should be followed by the usual show of affection and interest in what the child has been doing.

During the next session, have the parent begin by spending half an hour or so with the child. When everyone seems comfortable, have the parent confidently tell the child something like, "I can see you are having fun again today. While you are playing here, I need to go to the store to get us some groceries for our lunch. I'll be right back. What do you think about grilled cheese sandwiches and maybe some ice cream for dessert? I won't be gone long." A hug and a quick exit are appropriate at this point.

In this step the parent actually leaves the school, but for a short time and for an appealing reason. If appropriate, some parents may wish to make the separation even more enticing by promising the child a surprise (e.g., a pack of gum)—but avoid too much bribery.

If all goes well and the child is appropriately rewarded, she will probably be able to let the parent go home for a while during the next school session. The parent can explain that she or he needs to get some work done, while the child plays, and that she or he will be back after storytime, when school is almost over, or when the other mommies and daddies come. The parent must return at the time promised, or even before. The child should *not* be one of the last children picked up. After this step, the parent can probably leave and return "when the other parents do."

Vary Your Procedures Naturally, this procedure will vary from child to child. Children develop at different rates along the important dimensions. Sometimes only some of these steps will be necessary. Sometimes extra ones will be required. If a child becomes upset by the mere suggestion that the parent is going to leave, several things can be done. For example, the parent can tell the child that she or he is still going to go but that she or he will wait for a little until the child is ready. This tells the child that the parent is going to go eventually, but it also acknowledges the importance of the child's feelings.

It may also be possible, when the child balks, for the teacher to say something like, "Mommy won't be gone long. Let's go feed the rabbit some carrots until she gets back. I will stay with you. Then Mommy can take care of her business quickly. Give Mommy a quick kiss, and I'll race you over to the rabbits. Let's go!"

If the child appears extremely apprehensive, she can be given the choice of staying with the class or going with her parent. "It won't be as much fun as playing with the boats in the water, but you can come along with me if you want to." This nullifies any feeling of rejection the child may have, gives her an unexpected choice in the matter, and postpones the separation if she's just not ready for it. If the parent takes the child along, the trip should be as short and unexciting as possible. The duller the trip, the more likely the child will be to choose the school next time around.

Some children are prepared to be left at school the first day, and are perfectly comfortable all day. They seem more interested in the new environment than in their parent. Parents and teachers should be alert to signals from the child that say she is ready for the parent to leave. You can counteract parents' possible feelings of rejection by complimenting them on having raised such a self-confident child! At this point the parent should give a hug, and go, before the child picks up any feelings that might make her uneasy. She may change her mind if the parent hesitates too long.

You will find that some children are accustomed to being left with other people and have no fear of being with strangers. Their attitude seems to be one of total confidence in their parents. They seem to say, "Why should I worry . . . I'm only a kid. I'll just have fun like kids are supposed to do."

When Gradual Separation Is Impossible Many working parents just can't take the time to go through the gradual separation process. Others may have a baby at home, or a sick relative. Some parents may have medical problems themselves. And then there are also parents who are so nervous or insecure that they are unable to assist in this process, believing they will only make things worse. All of these parents bring the child in, hand him to you, and leave. The reactions of these children can range from total happiness to total despair.

It is not beyond the realm of possibility that some of these children will cry almost continually for the next two weeks! In such cases, all you can do is be patient, understanding, loving (if the child will allow you to come near), and as creative as possible in trying possible diversions for the child. Eventually, you will win. How long can any child resist the lure of fingerpaints, fire trucks, chocolate pudding, rabbits, swings, waterplay, puzzles, dolls, and *you*? How long can a child cry and repeat over and over, "I want my Mommy. I want my Mommy." Even though it seems endless, the child himself will eventually tire of the complaint.

Many teachers will admit that a crying, whining child can be an unnerving, irritating experience. At times they wonder if the behavior isn't deliberately designed to drive them up the wall. On the other hand, when the child eventually stops crying and begins to show an interest in anything, the sense of relief and accomplishment can be one of the teacher's most satisfying experiences. So, we take the bad with the good . . . as does the child. Such a child can easily become one of your favorite, and most loyal students.

Thus even though these abruptly separated children often pass through a difficult period of adjustment, they, too, can eventually benefit from the school experience and can become indistinguishable from gradually separated children.

Home Visits by Teachers   If the teacher and parents feel it might avoid later problems, they may want to arrange a short visit by the teacher to the child's home. In this way the child meets her future teacher on her own home ground. She can show you her room and her toys. You can share a snack in surroundings that are familiar and comfortable for her. Thus, by the time she arrives at school, the two of you will be at least partially acquainted. The home visit provides a convenient topic of conversation once she enters school. You will have experienced her home environment first-hand and have had a chance to talk with one or both of her parents.

Consider the Parent   The final point we wish to make is that separation can be difficult and unsettling for the parents, particularly for the one most involved in caring for the child. The parents should be given the chance, however brief, to express their feelings. They may feel anxious, lonely, rejected, or vaguely uneasy. The teacher can assure them that these feelings are quite normal for someone who has spent the last few years of their life almost totally involved with a child. Now, suddenly, they find themselves without that child several hours each day the child is in school.

Encourage them to think of the positive aspects of this new-found freedom. Remind them that they finally have that much needed break during the day. They can do something for themselves, be it going back to school, to work, or to a neglected hobby. If they just want to collapse and relax, they should do that. They deserve it. (Parents are discussed more fully in chapter 10.)

Further Thoughts on Toilet Training

Before ending this chapter, we would like to add a few additional comments on the subject of toilet training. Toilet training represents a prime example of the ways in which cognitive, emotional, social, and physical development are intertwined. In chapter 2 we looked at toilet training in terms of shaping procedures. Shaping, or the reinforcement of closer and closer approximations to the desired behavior, works well with many children. But, of course, you may discover other methods that are more effective for you.

Children vary in terms of how much toilet training they need. In fact, some children don't seem to need very much training at all. They have observed other children and their parents. One day they are "ready" and begin using the toilet themselves, with little or no assistance. From that time on, they have few accidents. Some children are trained before they enter school. Others will be helped and motivated by their friends. Some observers recommend that training be delayed until the child shows an interest in learning these things.

Whatever your methods and whatever the child's disposition, there are a few suggestions you might want to consider. First of all, it is very important to remember that children cannot be trained until they have physically matured to the point where control over the sphincter muscles is possible. Thus overall development is dependent upon physical maturation. Before this point, elimination is automatic as soon as the bladder or bowels are full. Demanding that children control elimination before they are physically capable of doing so is unrealistic, unfair, and can cause emotional problems for the child. Most 2 year olds will be physically able to control these muscles. However, you may encounter children whose parents tried to train them before they were physically able to comply, and who may be distressed as a result. In general, older children can be trained faster than younger ones (Papalia and Olds, 1975).

Second, be aware that toilet training can be difficult. Don't rush it. Become well-acquainted with the children, and let them build trust in you. Remain as casual and matter-of-fact as possible when you are in the bathroom with them. In most nursery schools, girls and boys use the same bathrooms. This can be a good, healthy learning experience. Answer their questions about the differences between boys and girls, and how they use the toilet. Use the correct names for the male and female anatomy. A boy has a penis, just like his father. A girl has a vagina, just like her mother. Interest in and questions about sex may appear at this time. Questions should be answered in an accurate, straightforward manner. The children should be given the correct information they seek. Sidestepping the issue can be upsetting for the child. On the other hand, you need not go beyond the range of their questions.

Answer their questions, but don't overwhelm them. If you are comfortable and relaxed, they will be too.

You can also teach them the terms "urinate" and "bowel movement." However, it may be wise to become familiar, as quickly as possible, with the words they are accustomed to using. Then if a child says, "I have to wee," or, "I have to make," you will be alert to their need. While you're training them, they may be more relaxed if you use their labels along with these new terms. Accidents should be accepted calmly and without reprimand. It is helpful to assure the children that soon they will learn to do this just as they have learned to do so many other things. Giving them examples of their previous accomplishments helps them feel confident and encouraged. There is, after all, so much to be learned when you're only two . . .

Unfortunately, toileting may become associated with parental or teacher attitudes about "bad" and "good." A parent might tell a child to, "Be a good boy today," when what is really meant is, "Don't wet your pants today." If this sort of thing is done repeatedly, the child can learn that a lack of control is *bad*. According to Freudian thinking, this attitude may then generalize to other situations: the child may react to pressure to be good (controlled) by being overly controlled (rigid) in a variety of situations. They may be unable to engage freely in a variety of healthy, rewarding activities, and will judge other children who are not in control as bad. Some children will rebel against toileting and either refuse to become toilet trained at all, or refuse to let go of the urine or feces (thus exercising some control over the parents' or teachers' feelings).

Toilet training is an area of potential growth and learning. But, if handled poorly, it can be a potential problem area. Plan ahead, take it slowly, and invite parent cooperation. And keep in mind that toilet training involves development along a number of important dimensions.

Mixed Age Groups

Many early childhood educators believe that the overall, interwoven developmental process can be facilitated by mixing children of different ages within the same preschool setting. Some schools do this on a permanent basis while others do it on a part-time basis. At the very least, it is a good idea to allow the children to visit the other age groups.

Both young and old can benefit from age mixing. For example, the younger ones are given the opportunity to see how they, themselves, will be growing and developing within a very short period of time. They can learn from the older children too. Of course, the teacher must be sure that the older children are aware of differences between themselves and the little ones; in this way they won't expect too much from or overwhelm the younger children. Obviously the older children should not tease the younger ones, or call them babies.

The older children can benefit by exposure to the younger children in several ways. First, the older child's self-esteem can be strengthened if the teacher will quietly point out how much that child has grown and developed in comparison to the younger children. Second, the older children will gain by teaching the younger children. Specifically, teaching younger children helps clarify the thinking of the older children and shows them how much they have advanced. Third, the older children will be admired by the younger ones: "Joey can tie his own shoes— he's 5. I can't—I'm only 3."

The use of mixed age groups is being explored heavily in Britain at the present time. They seem to be ideal settings in which to encourage multidimensional development.

7

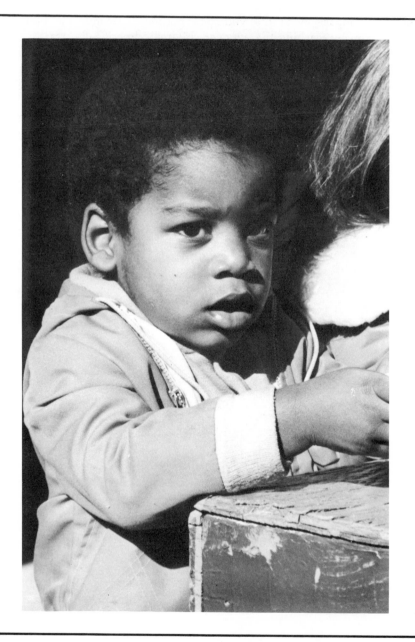

Programs
and Their Evaluation

When we use the term program in this chapter, we refer to the general framework, or overall point of view, that a school adopts in deciding what should and should not be done with the children in its care. The term curriculum refers to the specifics of the program, or to the tactics used in pursuing the overall program strategy. In this chapter we discuss the wide variety of programs and program dimensions currently used in early childhood education, as well as their evaluation. In the next two chapters the more specific issues of curriculum are addressed.

Programs often, but not always, reflect a commitment to one or more theories, such as Piaget's theory of cognitive development, learning theory, or the ideas of Dr. Montessori. These theories, in turn, may determine the type of curriculum employed in the school.

Programs determine the ages of the children to be included, funding, clientele, student/teacher ratios, staff qualifications, student activities, and the amount and kinds of parent participation. The program (along with the budget) can determine the kinds of equipment and supplies used in the school, the ways in which they are used, and the general school environment.

Programs have goals. Depending upon the program, these goals may include such things as the building of self-esteem, the development of the "whole child," the promotion of verbal skills, intervention in home life, and the development of pride in cultural heritage.

To varying degrees, programs undergo some form of evaluation. The evaluation mechanisms are designed to determine whether the goals of the program are being reached and to discover what changes may be appropriate. In the case of experimental programs, evaluation techniques are used, in part, to determine whether or not the program is worth pursuing. We shall return to the issue of evaluation after we discuss the nature of programs and program dimensions.

Matching Yourself with a Program

Parents are not the only ones who should consider alternative programs seriously. The teacher, experienced or inexperienced, should do the same. You may already be teaching, or know where you will be working after your studies. But many readers will be students who have not yet come to this difficult crossroad. Even those of you who are currently employed or are certain of your immediate future may want to, or may be forced to, change in the near future. Whatever your current situation, in fact, a serious look at available alternatives may help you prepare for the future. By considering the full spectrum of available programs, you may discover that there are situations available that are more interesting, exacting, and challenging than you had imagined. On the other hand, a review of available programs may reaffirm your current choices.

For those of you who have not yet completed your formal education, *now* is the time to begin thinking about and working towards your future employment. Don't wait until your schooling is complete. Don't wait until you have that diploma in hand before you try to discover where you might fit in. You may end up taking something you don't really want or, worse yet, finding there are no openings. Even though early childhood education is a growing area and the need for quality childcare is burgeoning, the competition for each and every new job is also growing. Unemployment is high among teachers these days, and good jobs are more difficult to find.

The first step in the process of finding eventual employment or changing positions is to discover what is available. There are not just two or three or even twenty different programs. Almost every program in every school differs in some important ways from every other. The style and quality of any school is determined by a unique combination of factors; it is your task to discover which of the many ways that programs can differ is important to you, and then find a school that best fits your needs. Remember, no school will be your perfect choice. You will have to be flexible and pick the best possible position from what is available. To further complicate the situation, schools themselves often change, at least in subtle ways, from year to year. And groups within the same program will vary to some extent. So you see the process of sorting out differences among programs is not an easy one. As we shall see, there are some important dimensions to keep in mind, but the combinations of these dimensions vary enormously from school to school.

People Make Programs

One of the most basic dimensions along which schools can vary has to do with the motivation of the people involved in the programs. Most of the people in the field of early childhood education are highly motivated and capable of providing quality childcare. Certainly most of your instructors, and those involved in programs related to your college or university, are of high standing. However, on those rare occasions when a poor quality program is discovered, the problem often lies with the people running it. As an extreme example, one might find a school whose program looks good on paper, but whose effectiveness is reduced by a management overly concerned with profit, or by administrators and teachers who are ineffective.

In other words, one of the first important differences among schools that you might want to consider has to do with the effectiveness of the people involved. Regardless of the theoretical underpinnings of the program, are the people motivated and effective? Regardless of exactly what they are trying to do, can they do it? The question of the capacity of the people to act in an effective manner is a general one, going far beyond the sorts of program differences discussed in the next section; but it is an important one. No matter what the formal program claims, it is, in the last analysis, people that make it a success or failure. Before you accept employment you should observe, firsthand, how effective the people involved are.

We now turn to a consideration of some of the other important differences among schools and school programs. These range all the way from rather concrete differences, such as geographical location, to differences of an abstract, theoretical nature. They should all play a part when you consider employment.

Selecting a Program

Climate

Early childhood education programs can be affected heavily by climate. Although this is not one of the loftier dimensions on which to make your choice, it is nevertheless important. Even though a formal statement of a school's program may not mention climate, it will certainly be influenced by the weather. For example, climate can determine the types of outdoor experiences that are available. The newly trained instructor would do well to realize that not only personal life style, but teaching conditions as well, can be affected by climate. Of course, human beings are wonderfully adaptive, and can find satisfaction and pleasure in dealing with almost any climate. But for some of us, weather conditions are important. Think carefully about what the climate can mean to you and the school program. For example, do you thrive in the cold and the snow as found in most of the midwest and northeastern parts of this country? Some love the cold weather, while others are not prepared to deal with snowsuits, boots, and mittens on a daily basis—to say nothing of shoveling snow and driving in it. Do you love looking for lost hats? Some do, some don't. On the other hand, would you thrive in a desert climate, or would you wilt? Some people prefer dry, hot weather and will seek it out, while others will not. What about the hot and humid deep south? Would you prefer the cool, rainy northwest? Does heavy rain make you feel peaceful and cozy, or gloomy and depressed?

In other words, as long as you are considering as many aspects of the situation as you can, you may as well think about the weather. A teaching position might be ideal under some circumstances and difficult under others. On the other hand, you still will want to be as flexible as possible so as not to eliminate too many choices just because you'd prefer to be tanned year round.

Clientele

What kind of people do you want to work with? There are programs for every class and economic bracket, for immigrants and non-white cultures, for large cities, for small rural situations. Would you prefer an Indian reservation or a commune? Do you want to deal with people living in a poverty area? What about prison inmates and their families? The choices are unlimited.

To some extent, your selection of a geographical location can influence the type of student and parent population found in the schools there, although not completely. Some schools have a fairly homogeneous clientele determined by socioeconomic factors in the area. For example,

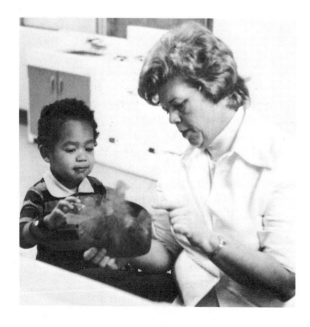

When all is said and done, good programs are made by good teachers

programs in ghetto areas most often deal with people who live in constant poverty. Other programs, often found in the more expensive private schools, cater to the so-called upper middle class—who have their own sets of pleasures and problems. Some programs emphasize the importance of having a heterogeneous population—a mixture of backgrounds and cultures. Still other programs are designed to "mainstream" children with physical or emotional handicaps into the general population. (Mainstreaming, in fact, is a topic of considerable importance at the present time.) Other programs include or specialize in gifted children. Bilingual programs, such as those for Mexican-American children, are a possibility if you speak a second language. In other words, programs differ in terms of the clientele they are designed to serve, and the instructor should be aware of these differences in seeking employment.

Licensing

State licensing is, ideally, supposed to ensure that all schools meet certain standards of health, safety, programming, staff requirements, building codes, teacher/child ratios, and so on. Unfortunately, licensing laws vary enormously from one state to another, and even within a given state. Thus, at present, licensing does not guarantee high-quality conditions.

Cohen and Zigler (1978) argue that consistent federal standards should be developed because state laws:

> typically concern themselves with the physical safety of children (e.g., does the center have enough protection against fire; are the care givers free of communicable diseases?). Other crucial criteria of day care quality, such as the child/staff ratio and the competency of the care givers, tend to be neglected or are beyond the scope of many state licensing laws. (p. 26)

In other words, depending upon location, state licensing may or may not ensure quality care. When applying for a position, the prospective teacher can learn something about the prospective school by examining the strength of the prevailing state licensing laws.

Funding

Parent Fees It is important to consider the source of funds behind any given program because the funding agency or source usually has a tremendous impact upon the nature and operation of the program. There are a number of ways that a program can be funded or sponsored. Most obvious is the income a school can receive from parents in the form of fees. Although parent fees constitute a major portion of preschool financing, they are not the only source of monies.

Government Funding Many programs are at least partially funded by federal, state, and/or municipal governments. The Department of Health, Education and Welfare normally handles federal funding, while state departments of education administer state funding. Local funding is usually the responsibility of local school boards. Head Start and Follow Through Projects are federally funded by the Administration for Children, Youth, and Families which is part of the Department of Health, Education and Welfare. Kindergartens are often funded, at least partially, by state governments and/or city school programs. Day Care Centers often receive government funding, too.

To receive government funds, the program must normally meet standards set forth by the agency involved. Thus the funding agency often imposes regulations concerning teacher/child ratios, curriculum guidelines, the inclusion of minority students and handicapped children, teacher qualifications, salaries, and health and safety standards.

However, identical governmental funding does not guarantee that two programs will bear much resemblance to one another. One may be nothing more than a glorified group baby-sitting organization while another, receiving the same funding, may be a full-fledged educational program. As we have mentioned, the ultimate nature of the program depends upon the people involved in it . . . you, the staff, the administration, and the clientele.

Research projects often receive governmental funding. For example, many intervention studies, in addition to the well-known Head Start or Follow Through efforts, have been and are being funded by governmental agencies. These experimental efforts include infant and home-based programs that we will discuss later in this chapter. Many college and university-based research projects and schools are at least partially funded ' by government agencies. Again, they must normally meet government regulations of various sorts—in addition to college and university research regulations.

Multiple Funding Multiple funding is quite common. Some directors seem to have a laudable talent when it comes to utilizing a variety of funding possibilities. For example, because many of the parents in the school's vicinity are poor, unemployed, or in job training programs, a given school or the parents may qualify for a variety of federal aid programs. At the same time, the school may qualify for some state funding. United Way may provide additional funds. The school may charge fees based on the parents' ability to pay. Where community spirit is high, parents and civic groups may develop fund-raising projects for the school. The city may provide a part-time maintenance man, as well as snacks and lunches for the children. Local merchants and civic groups often volunteer time and supplies. Retirees with time on their hands can find satisfaction in working with the children and staff in a variety of capacities.

Programs and directors such as these meet a variety of needs in a variety of ways. There is always room for creativity and innovation in all facets of early childhood education, including funding. As you explore different programs, be sure to inquire about financial support, and the program requirements that must be met to qualify for that support. Try to meet the individuals who control the budget and the search for funding. By knowing about the financial underpinnings of a program, you can learn a great deal about what teaching in that facility will entail.

Child/Teacher Ratios

One of the most important factors for the parent or teacher to consider in selecting a program is the ratio of children to teachers. In other words, how many children of a given age is a teacher responsible for? The importance of this consideration cannot be overemphasized. Ratios are usually determined by state licensing regulations, and by those who fund or sponsor the program. For example, schools in California that receive federal funding must conform, not only to the State of California Health Department's requirements, but also to the requirement of the Department of Health, Education and Welfare agency from which they receive aid— probably the Administration for Children, Youth, and Families. In addition, when receiving federal funds, the school must also include within its ratios a certain percentage of minorities, nonminorities, and handicapped children.

These ratios are based on safety and child development factors. The thinking, as far as safety is concerned, goes something like this. If there were a fire, tornado, or earthquake, how many children could one teacher escort (or carry) to safety? A teacher in charge of a kinder-garten group may be able to lead twenty to thirty 5 year olds to safety, as children of this age are aware of the danger and can follow directions. But what about 2 year olds? These children may not be able to follow the teacher's directions quickly enough. They might panic, cry, or run in several directions at the sound of the fire alarm. And how many infants can one teacher carry quickly from a burning or collapsing building? California says four, and even that may be wishful thinking. Licensing laws in other parts of the country differ on this issue. Older children can be trained through fire drills, safety discussions, visits to fire departments, and visits by firemen. But younger children would have trouble understanding the significance of these measures. In other words, safety precautions demand that younger groups have lower student/teacher ratios.

Developmental as well as safety factors are involved in the determination of ratio regulations. Generally, the amount of individual care needed at different ages is considered. In addition, the amount of group activity that is possible is weighed in the decision process.

Although infants sleep more than older children, they also need a great deal more personalized attention. They must be fed, changed, cuddled, rocked, and carried from place to place. They need to be talked to and watched very carefully. The infant needs a close, affectionate relationship with the caregiver that is similar to the traditional mother-and-child relationship. Deprived of this, children may not develop as well as they should.

Toddlers and two's also need a great deal of individual attention. Many are mobile but unsteady. They fall often and have a way of "getting into everything." They are often a danger to themselves and each other even in the safest of environments. While they may *want* to do everything for themselves, they still need help with buttons, zippers, and shoestrings. This age group also needs affection and individual instruction. Aggression, self-esteem, and questions must be handled on a fairly personalized basis. Group instructions and group activities should be kept to a minimum.

As the children progress from 3 through 5, the teacher can handle progressively larger groups more effectively, at least in some areas. These children are becoming more capable and more self-sufficient. They can take care of many of their own personal needs. However, they are highly active, curious, and boisterous. They can move farther and faster than their younger counterparts. They are full of questions and are testing their physical skills. They still need individual attention but it should be tempered by a consideration for their need for independence.

Although these children are older and seem to need less care, it is still desirable to keep child/teacher ratios as low as possible. Although these older children are becoming more capable of some group activities, it is not reasonable to expect all members of a group this age to do everything together and at the same time. In general, then, the lower the child/teacher ratio the better, particularly with younger children.

There is another question related to the ratio issue: is it better to have a single teacher with a smaller group or two teachers with a larger group? There are a number of good arguments for the position that the two teachers with more children is better. For example, in an emergency, one teacher can stay with the group while the other takes care of the injured child or goes for help. Furthermore, when there are two adults available, one can introduce and supervise a given activity with those children who are interested in it while the other teacher supervises and works with those who are not. Also, one teacher can handle lunch or snacks while the other cares for the children.

Clearly, it is expensive to have a low child/teacher ratio. Most programs meet minimum licensing or funding requirements. Some even exceed these standards. However, we must once again alert the reader to problems that may arise in this area. The cases that follow are exceptional, but they do underline the differences that can exist between the ideal program and reality. Some schools will always find ways to bend the rules a little. For example, adults who are not always with a group will occasionally be counted as being with that group full-time. Some schools will count their director in the ratio, but directors are normally called away for so many reasons that their presence with a group cannot be depended upon. In one case, parents and teachers were promised a ratio of not more than seven or eight 2 year olds for each of the two teachers and the director—not a very low ratio even with the director there. In reality, however, the ratio was often two teachers to twenty or even twenty-four 2 year olds—a situation which displeased the parents and distressed at least one of the teachers to the point of resigning. Again, this is an exceptional case, but it is worth mentioning.

Sometimes those who must cook, or who are specialists with other duties, are often counted as full time in the ratios. For example, a teacher who was also a speech therapist was counted as a full-time teacher for a particular group. However, several hours of each week she conducted speech therapy sessions in another part of the school, with no substitute provided in her original group. Obviously, this is less than honest, yet schools certainly engage in such practices. Occasionally teachers will report being pressured to remain silent concerning such practices. It is sad to think that these kinds of things still occur. But they do, and you need to watch for them.

In a lighter vein, the student/teacher ratio can have important implications for you in terms of job satisfaction. Do you prefer to work with large groups or are you best on a one-to-one basis? Depending upon where you shine, you may want to seek out a program with a higher or lower ratio.

Physical Space

Educational programs are housed in a variety of facilities. Although some are fortunate to be in a structure planned and built especially for the purpose, most programs use space that has been converted and altered to suit their needs. Some are located in classrooms provided by a public school system. Others are in space allocated by churches, YMCAs, and other community groups. Many are found in residential homes that have been modified to meet the requirements of a particular program. There are even some housed in commercial space, including facilities normally used by retail outlets.

Although licensed facilities must all provide a minimum amount of space per child, schools vary tremendously in terms of how much space they allocate above and beyond this minimum. The nature of the program or the philosophy of the school often determines how much space is needed. In addition, location and use of the raw square footage is affected by school philosophy. Schools vary in terms of the emphasis they place on space and its use. Some indoor spatial arrangements seem open and roomy, while others approach a sense of overcrowding. Some are cozy, others are cold and remote. Some are dull and dark, some light and bright. Some seem to invite the children to interrupt each other's activities, while others are designed to ensure that human traffic patterns will avoid areas of work and play. Some space arrangements force children into constant group interactions, others provide smaller, private areas for quiet, solitary, restful activities. Some allow flexibility in the organization and use of space and equipment, others simply can't be rearranged very much.

Outdoor spaces vary enormously, too. Some of these include large, well-designed yards consisting of grass, dirt, and paved areas. Some have trees and shrubbery—even vegetable or flower gardens. Some have hilly as well as flat areas. Other playgrounds are rather stark, bare, and small. Some facilities depend on nearby public playgrounds or parks for many of their outdoor activities. Obviously, the nature of the physical environment is strongly affected by the kinds and amount of funding available; but the reverse is also true, and a school's program can often influence the nature of the spaces around it.

Staff Requirements

Programs vary widely in terms of the requirements and standards their staff members must fulfill. Some are much more rigorous, demanding a substantial list of credentials, while others are not. Clearly, the kind of people you will be working with depends heavily upon program requirements. This is an area that may be more complex than you may have expected, and it is one that you must investigate and consider carefully.

The most obvious considerations have to do with age, education, and experience. In some states the requirements are only that a teacher must be of a certain minimum age (usually 18 or 21) and have no record of child-related criminal offenses. That is pretty much the bottom line. And there are programs that have no further requirements except that the employers like the applicant.

However, most programs require that teachers have at least a few units credit in early childhood education or that they will enroll in classes during their employment. Some programs require specialized training. In general, recent years have seen a trend toward the hiring of teachers with more education and more experience. This is true for several reasons. First, more and more are choosing this as their career field. Accordingly, schools have more experienced and educated applicants from which to choose. Second, since unemployment among teachers is so high, many basically qualified people are going on in their education before looking for work. The competition is growing. Third, many former housewives, with formal educations, are choosing to enter the field.

There is also a growing awareness among employers that liking children and being able to cope with them on a daily basis is simply not enough to qualify an individual for a teaching position. The demand for quality programs and informed teachers is growing, and owners and directors of early educational facilities are becoming aware of these needs. Many programs now require their teachers to hold a degree, to be certified on a state or federal level, or both. And experience is becoming more and more valuable, too. The more experience you have, the better your chances.

In summary, while programs vary in terms of the credentials they demand of their employees, there still are programs with minimal requirements. The trend is toward a tighter and more competitive employment situation. While this may cause concern on the part of the prospective employee, it is, in the long run, very good for the field of early childhood education. This will be discussed further in chapter 11.

Schedules

Programs vary in the ways that they schedule their days. Depending upon what type of schedule is involved, your work experience can also vary considerably, so it pays to think about what particular types of schedules mean before you accept employment. You will want to decide whether or not you want to be flexible in terms of the hours you work. You will have to make a decision about part-time versus full-time employment.

Many programs involve busy, active mornings, with things slowing down a bit in the afternoon when a good portion of the children's time is taken up by naps. In many of these cases an educational program is pursued in the morning, with the remainder of the day taking on a primarily custodial quality. Some programs devote more time to the educational aspects than others.

Some programs include what is usually called extended daycare. This refers to the fact that the school offers at least custodial care for children who arrive very early or stay very late. Some of these children may be transported to other public school programs for part of the day. In long day programs, you may wish to work the hours during which the educational part of the program occurs. Or you may wish to accept the challenge of the extended hours early in the morning or late in the day. Schools offering this extended service may be open from 7 AM to 7 PM or longer. Extended daycare tries to meet the needs of parents who work long days or odd hours.

Most programs require teachers to be present for a number of hours each week in addition to the time spent with the children. Some of these hours are spent with parents or in staff meetings, while others involve curriculum planning and preparation. It is a good idea to determine ahead of time the extent of these additional hours, and whether they are paid or "volunteered." Many administrators still expect teachers to put in unpaid hours—an expectation which can lead to conflicts, if not resolved before you take up your position.

In-service Training

An area which people often overlook before accepting a position, but which soon takes on a great deal of importance, is the provision (or lack of it) for in-service training for teachers. Some programs include this, others feel it less necessary. Does the school provide resource materials, movies, lectures, and classes for the staff? Do you have the opportunity to visit other schools to observe and learn from a variety of programs?

Many teachers find that once they begin teaching they realize how

Extended daycare can lead to extended naptime

much they *don't* know, and how much they still want and need to learn. For example, you may learn something about gifted children somewhere through your long years in school. But the training will have been cursory. Then suddenly you find that you have a gifted child in your group. Your interest is naturally aroused, and you want to know how to encourage the child and to allay boredom. If your school has provisions for your need to learn, you will be in fine shape. If it does not, you will have to do the research on your own. There are other concerns that you may want to learn more about. For example, you may have second thoughts about how and when to discipline your students. Or you may, for the first time, have a hyperactive child in your group.

The question is whether or not you have to research these issues yourself, on your own time, and at your own expense. Does the school's program provide time for, and assistance in, your study efforts? In general, does the program value and even demand a staff that wants to learn? Does it reward teachers who make efforts to grow and improve themselves? Or does it frustrate and discourage staff efforts of this sort, lowering morale?

Philosophy, Goals, and Values

One of the most important ways that programs vary has to do with the school's overall philosophy concerning childrearing. Just what is it that the school values and wants to instil in the children? What are the goals of the program?

It is almost unnecessary to say that you should know the values and philosophy behind a particular program before you agree to work in it. It is probably fair to say that unless you find a program whose basic philosophy, goals, and values are fairly consistent with your own, you may end up being at least partially dissatisfied. You will be setting yourself up for conflicts and problems that could easily make your life miserable.

You should consider a number of questions. For example, do you favor one point of view over another? Or do you prefer an eclectic approach? Do you feel reinforcement theory has the answers? What about Piaget? What about religion? Are you concerned with the "whole child," or do you feel that some areas should be emphasized over others . . . say, the cognitive over the emotional or social aspects? Do you feel children should determine what goes on in a program, or do you favor a teacher-initiated program? Do you feel the 3Rs belong in the preschool or just "readiness" activities? Should children be free to move about and talk with each other spontaneously, or should they sit quietly and attend to their work? Can you tolerate a high noise level and a certain amount of chaos? Should children learn by discovery? Should play be emphasized? Should a program involve strict respect for authority? Do you favor competition over cooperation? Do you feel children should learn about many races and cultures in a tolerant and appreciative way? Do you feel sexism in education is a problem? Some of these issues may be more important to you than others. On some issues you may have a firm position, on others you may be tolerant or without strong feeling.

In any case you will want to try to find a program that is compatible with your feelings, whatever they may be. You will have to do some investigating. There are a number of sources of information available. You can talk with your college instructors and your fellow students. Obviously, they will have ideas and information that can be of value. You can write to a variety of agencies that support early childhood education programs. One of the best methods of learning about programs is to visit and observe facilities in your area whenever possible. Discuss the programs carefully with the owners, directors, and teachers. Ask them what their positions are with respect to issues that are of concern to you. Observe the programs in action and determine how the programs' stated goals are actually translated into behavior. Volunteer to work in a program for a few days to get an inside point of view.

You may make several unexpected discoveries in your search. First, after observing and participating as a volunteer or aide in various programs, you may find that your own position may be changing with respect to some of your values and goals. For instance, you may have believed that the development of academic skills should be the main focus of a program. However, after working in several groups, you may decide that, at least for many children, emotional development is equally important. You may change your position with respect to the relative importance of social and physical development as well. In other words, your visits to existing programs may be a learning experience for you and may help you clarify exactly what is and what is not important to you.

You may find that there are often differences between what a program says it is and what it actually seems to be. For example, a so-called Montessori program may actually be a highly modified form of what Dr. Montessori had in mind. It may place much more of an emphasis on the creative arts, dramatic play, and group activities than is found in the original Montessori method.

Programs are often modified when those in charge are sensitive to the individual needs of children. In other words, some programs are more flexible than others. Some can adapt to the particular children in the school at a given moment, while others remain rigid, trying to force the children into a defined mold.

You will also discover that there are no perfect programs—but there are some very good ones. You will have to train yourself to be observant and to interpret what is actually occurring within each program.

Something as simple as the placement of decorative material, either at or above the children's eye-level, can give information about the nature of a particular program

Age Ranges and Groups

Programs vary in terms of the ages of the children they attempt to serve and in the ways that they mix or separate these age groups. The teaching experience can be heavily affected by this aspect of the school's program. Until recently preschools concentrated mainly on 3 and 4 year olds, while kindergartens served the 5 year olds. Now, however, early childhood education has branched out. Infants through 8 year olds are now included. In fact, some programs are trying to enroll parents in prenatal programs. Although first through third graders generally attend public schools and are thereby separated from the younger children, developmental factors unite them. For example, Piaget's work has shown that, like the late preschoolers, the early elementary school students are in the pre-operational stage of thought.

It is important to consider well ahead of time which age groups you prefer working with so that you can arrange your own educational program accordingly. Not only is the teaching of infants quite different from teaching kindergarten or early elementary school children, but, in addition, the kinds of credentials needed for each may vary. Your role in the teaching process will vary considerably from younger to older students.

You may also want to consider the various ways that these age groupings can be arranged. You may prefer a group in which the students are generally the same age. This has been the more traditional way of teaching. However, you may discover that a program that mixes children of different ages in "family groupings" has many advantages and potentials you might wish to explore.

Some teachers feel that they work most effectively with children of a certain age. Others find that each age group has an appeal of its own (and an associated set of unique problems). While some teachers prefer the quieter, cuter younger children, others will gravitate toward the older children because they can do more, can communicate more easily, and can take care of many of their own needs . . . and they are out of diapers! It is useful to discover which ages are best-suited for you. However, remember that although you may *think* you prefer a certain age group, experience may change your mind. Be open to a variety of possibilities in your search for a program. Try to observe a variety of ages and age groupings—and participate where you can. In a sense, experience is the best teacher when it comes to this issue and to all the other issues involved in selecting a program. Do some leg work and gain as much firsthand experience (as a volunteer if possible) as you can. Teachers, like young children, can learn by discovery.

Parent Participation

This is a subject that is discussed in depth in chapter 10. Here we need only say that schools vary in the degree to which they invite and seek parent participation and in the ways in which parents participate. The trend is toward as much parent participation as possible. Parent involvement in intervention programs is now being viewed as an essential component if the gains made in such programs are to be sustained.

Kinds of Programs

Having looked at a number of important dimensions that are relevant to the process of discriminating between programs, we now turn to a brief consideration of some of the most easily recognizable types of programs. Each type can vary along most of the aforementioned dimensions, and most of them can receive funds from the several sources discussed earlier.

Church Sponsorship   Many child centers are housed within the facilities of churches or church-run schools. Sometimes the facilities are merely rented on a business basis, and the church exerts no influence over the program. Sometimes the church donates the use of the facility and still remains apart from the program. In these instances, the program is up to the people who have organized it, and it is independent of the church.

However, churches often establish and run daycare or preschool programs of their own. In these cases, religious instruction may be part of the program. More than likely, instructors will want to avoid any program that involves elements that conflict with their own religious views.

Parent Co-ops Sometimes parents develop and administer childcare programs of their own. This is often done in areas where good facilities of some other sort are not available. In these cases the parents fund, control, and participate directly in the programs. Although they may all be very concerned, they may also have very definite and conflicting opinions, and varying amounts of training in or exposure to early childhood education. They often hire a trained and experienced teacher to guide them, and to help deal with their differences.

Private Schools Proprietary schools, or private schools run as businesses, are numerous in certain areas of the country, particularly in large cities. Generally, they are licensed by the state, and must meet city and county health, safety, fire, and building codes as well. They usually charge tuition, thereby excluding poor families from their benefits.

These schools may be owned by an individual or a group of individuals. Sometimes the owners are involved in the actual direction of the programs, but sometimes they hire others to do the job. In these schools it is important for the teacher to know who owns and controls the facility. The teacher should know who is in charge of the program and budget and should be aware of the chain of authority from the teacher up through the administrators and owners. As we shall see in chapter 11, it is important to know who has the final say in areas where problems may arise between teachers, parents, and administrators. Parenthetically, the teacher should be aware of the authority relationships in *any* preschool setting, not just in the private school situation.

Privately owned schools can be good or bad, as is true of the other varieties. Many of them are excellent. But they are susceptible to certain unique difficulties. For example, profit is, more or less, the prime incentive behind the private school. Someone is trying to make a legitimate living through the school. But it is not an easy business in which to earn substantial profits—particularly if the school is small. It is expensive to run a school, yet many parents simply cannot, or will not, pay fees high enough to cover expenses. Rent, mortgage payments, utilities, insurance, salaries, equipment, supplies, taxes, wages, unemployment and social security payments, cleaning services, general upkeep, and the high cost of food often leave little left over for the individuals trying to earn their living in this manner. In other words, it is a tight squeeze. The worry and pressure of trying to make ends meet can sometimes affect the quality of the program.

Some owners are completely dedicated to the welfare of the children, parents, and staff of their schools. Others are not. Some put as much money back into the schools as they can. Others do not. Sometimes profit is of little concern, and sometimes it is paramount.

The quality of these schools can vary enormously. Occasionally parents and prospective teachers will not get a true picture of the program through their first encounter with it. Some owners and directors will say all the right things when people visit and observe their programs. They will be aware of what a good program involves, and will present theirs in that form even though the picture may not be completely accurate. It may take a while for the teacher or parent to learn the truth. (Of course, this tendency to distort is not limited to the owners of these sorts of schools.)

Some schools only allow visits or observations on designated days. Beware of this tendency, for it is tempting to stage a good impression, to put on a good show. Further investigation may reveal higher child/teacher ratios than promised, poorly supplied classrooms, snacks and lunches that are economical but nutritionally inadequate, unacceptable disciplinary measures, small consideration for child development goals, low teacher morale, and so on.

A good clue to the nature of the program lies in the openness of the facility. How available is the staff at any time? Are parents encouraged to visit and participate in the program *at any time*? The good program should be open, with nothing to hide. In extreme cases, owners or directors have been known to require that they be present when parents visit the school in order to smooth over or control internal problems.

Some individuals or corporations have attempted to franchise early educational facilities much in the same way that fast foods are franchised. They buy or build facilities and package a program in a high potential area. While some of these efforts have been successful, many are finding that, unlike hamburgers and tacos, early childhood education programs are too complex to standardize and control in this manner. Quite simply, there are too many things to consider and too many variables to deal with. Packaging is often neither feasible nor profitable. From the teacher's point of view moreover, it should be noted that one is forced to deal with a corporation in these situations, with all that that entails. We do not intend to give the impression that most privately owned programs have these problems, nor that all non-private schools are without these problems. Many private schools are reputable and resourceful, finding ways to supplement low income by utilizing community resources. Some involve parents, and solicit aid from other community members (senior citizens, students, volunteers) in the upkeep and staffing of their facility. As in any program, the quality ultimately depends on those involved in it.

College and University-Based Programs Many colleges and universities now have early childhood education programs on their campuses. Generally, these programs serve several purposes and meet a variety of needs. Many of the children in these programs are those of students and university staff. Besides meeting these needs, such programs provide teacher training for students and a setting for research carried on by professors and students in the areas of child development, psychology, and education. Very often parent participation in these programs is greatly encouraged. The ratio of children to adults is usually very low, providing many opportunities for individual attention. In some cases, there are so many adults in these programs that the usual ratio problem is reversed—too many chiefs and not enough Indians. But generally, university-based programs are staffed by highly-qualified personnel and are among the better programs available.

Public School Prekindergarten In some areas of the country successful efforts to bring the preschool experience into the public school system have been mounted. For example, many children in the Midwest begin their education, not in churches or private preschools, but in publicly financed prekindergarten classes.

Conclusion

A number of different kinds of programs have been mentioned in this text already. We discussed some aspects of the Montessori programs in chapter 1. In chapter 4 we considered the essentials of Piagetian programs. In this chapter, we touched upon church-sponsored schools, parent co-ops, private schools, college and university programs, and prekindergartens. We have also seen that multiple funding of these programs does occur.

While it is possible to highlight differences among these and other programs, it is good to keep in mind that these programs are not totally different; there is a good deal of overlap among them. In fact, if one were to visit several programs, without advance information about their administrative natures, one might well have trouble identifying them. Furthermore, two schools adhering to the same program principles may vary considerably. A Montessori program may be traditional or modified; and either of these may be of high or low quality. No-one can say that all Piagetian, or all church-sponsored programs, are good or bad. One must visit, observe, and participate in a program before it can be evaluated effectively. Speak with the involved people to determine the strengths and weaknesses of the program.

No program is perfect. Constant change and growth are vital. The name, or label, applied to a particular program is not as important as finding a specific program that suits *your* needs and interests, and promises to grow with *you*.

Intervention Programs

We now turn to one of the most important and influential forms of early education for children, the intervention program. Clearly, the intervention program represents a distinct kind of preschool experience and as such might easily have been included in the preceding section. But, because the intervention effort is so important, and because it really cuts across more traditional distinctions among types of programs such as those already discussed, we consider it here on its own. Whether or not to work within an intervention program is an issue that faces all teachers. We are paying special attention to intervention efforts because we feel the problem is special.

The Problem: Intergenerational Poverty Cycles

There are many different kinds of intervention programs, but they all share one basic premise; they are designed to break what has come to be known as the *intergenerational poverty cycle.* Quite simply, this phrase refers to the fact that children who grow up in poverty remain there, and their children remain there, too.

It is instructive to consider the nature and some of the causes of the unfortunate, repetitive, enduring quality of poverty. This is a highly complex problem, and any brief summary of it (such as this) can easily sound oversimplified. You must realize that each individual who suffers from the intergeneration poverty cycle comes from a unique set of circumstances.

There are many factors involved in this terrible cyclical phenomenon. For example, there can be no doubt that racial discrimination has been, and still is, one of the main causes of cyclical poverty. One need not search very far to find people who are more than willing to admit that they hate, and look down upon, all sorts of minorities. In fact, many are still proud of their racial prejudices.

It is difficult enough for an advantaged white American to succeed in our highly competitive society. But when one is a member of a minority, and painfully aware that one does not, and will never have access to the mechanisms of essential education and career preparation, then the necessary motivation to compete and to succeed is diminished. Hopelessness, despair, high unemployment, bitterness, and a certain degree of self-hatred often characterize the minority position. It is into this atmosphere that the children of poverty are born. From the earliest age they see little success, nor even the hope of success. They are not told that they can succeed, or improve their condition. Their parents have few essential skills to pass on to them.

Recent advances in civil rights have often led to a cruel dilemma. The parents of poor minority children can see that some of the barriers of the past are weakening. They see growing numbers of minority group members in positions of authority and power. Yet they know that the chances of their children succeeding are still very slim. They are torn between wanting to encourage their children and wanting to protect them from later disappointment. The hopes of minority parents can be raised only to be dashed at a later point in time. Some see recent changes as nothing more than tokenism, serving as a veneer to cover continuing poverty, unemployment, and discrimination. New and deeper bitterness results.

Because the white middle class has been dominant in our society, white middle class values have been used to evaluate *everyone* in the school systems—as they enter, as they progress, and as they leave. The tests that are used to evaluate *all* children are based upon the standards, customs, and experiences of this dominant group. Educators are finally becoming aware that this has been unfair, and that children who have been brought up in minority cultures, and in non-white, non-middle class environments, have been judged "deficient" because the prevailing tests have not reflected what they know, only what they do not know. If white middle class children were tested with items that reflected the customs and experiences of a minority culture, or any culture different from their own, they might appear to be deficient, too.

There is no doubt that the minority child learns a great deal, experiences a great deal, and is stimulated a great deal during his or her childhood. It is just that *what* they learn is not appropriate for success in a white middle class school setting or a white middle class adult world. For example, a ghetto child may have little idea of life outside the ghetto; she may not be familiar with farms, gardens, restaurants, air travel, and the like. And yet it is these sorts of things that are talked about in white middle class schools. The ghetto child, on the other hand, may know a great deal about food stamps, social workers, and welfare programs—but who ever talks about these things? Where is the opportunity for the ghetto child to demonstrate her substantial knowledge? The smell of flowers may be a topic of conversation in school but the equally varied smells of the ghetto are never mentioned. The food served in the educational institution is usually the food of the white middle class, not that of the ghetto. Clearly then, discussions about food will leave the poverty child at a disadvantage. Although the poverty child may not be familiar with the sounds of expensive recording equipment, she may know a great deal about the sounds of rats at night—but who ever asks about these sounds?

Poverty children suffer in our schools because the very *language* they use may be different from middle-class English. Their first language may be a foreign language, or a form of spoken English that differs from middle class spoken English. For example, compare the speech of a black ghetto youth and a middle class white youth. More than likely, neither child speaks entirely "correctly." Neither will say, "I'm going to . . ." The white child will say, "I'm gonna . . ." while the black child will say something like, "Ahmo. . . ." Or if the black child hears the white youth ask "Jeetyet?" he may be confused by this common middle class distortion of "Did you eat yet?" In other words, the language used in many of our schools is of white middle class form. Because this class dominates, the poverty child is disadvantaged. Sometimes the rule systems in black and white English differ so sharply that an educational caretaker may have trouble decoding black English without having had specific training in the rules used by these individuals (Anastasiow and Hanes, 1976; Harrison and Trabasso, 1976).

These and similar factors tend to make the poverty child *feel* inferior and discouraged in school. Educators are now beginning to realize that the schools must relate to children and their experiences in a more effective manner. And they must help the children feel good about themselves.

The poverty cycle is maintained by many factors. For example, a lack of money lessens the chances of good prenatal, medical, and dental care. The stress of poverty often leads to a tense home environment. Marriages suffer. Life is lived on a basic survival level, and rarely rises beyond it.

As we can see from Maslow's visualisation of his theory of self-actualization in figure 7.1 (Maslow, 1970), the "higher" needs such as self-actualization, the desire to know, and the need to create cannot be pursued until the more "basic" needs, such as the need for biological satisfaction, safety, love, and belongingness are satisfied.

In other words, when the family has to worry about food, shelter, and safety constantly, and often lives in fear, then there is little time or energy left over for more elevated goals. Parents are not free to concern themselves with middle class educational goals. They are unable to think about whether or not their children are learning colors and shapes, and whether or not they can manipulate crayons and scissors. They are too busy with survival-related needs to be concerned with trying to keep up with less deprived families. Poverty and discrimination tend to make feelings of high self-esteem rather foreign to all members of the family.

Low income families can barely afford food, let alone books, toys, and all the other expensive trappings of our modern educational methods.

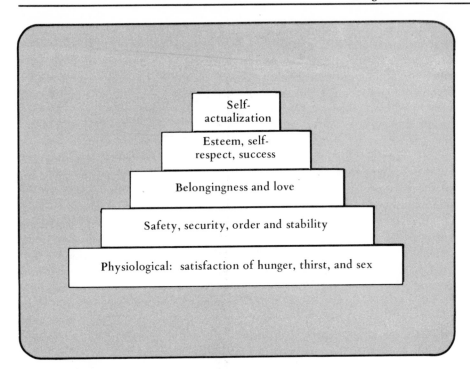

*Figure 7.1 Maslow's pyramid of human motives. All
human beings have a hierarchy of needs, with lower needs
at the bottom and higher ones at the top. We are all
motivated to move towards self-actualization; but higher needs
can only become controlling factors when lower needs have
been at least partially satisfied*

Even the few books that their children do see may reflect a life that is
foreign to them. Many middle class childrens' experiences depend upon
extensive travel. The low income family often finds transportation to
and from work to be an almost insurmountable problem.

The unfortunate upshot of discrimination and poverty is that
when low income children begin public school at 5 or 6 they are already
lacking in emotional and social experiences that contribute to cognitive
development as defined by the white middle class. Sometimes they have
nutritional deficiencies as well, and have had little or no medical and
dental care. To top it all off, many of them must go to school *hungry*.

Intervention As a Solution?

Given that poverty seems to perpetuate itself, and that children of deprived
parents appear to remain deprived, what can be done? One possible
solution to this complex and difficult question has been the development

of what are known as *intervention programs*. This is a very general term that has been applied to many different programs. But all of these have one common attribute: they are all designed to change the child so that she or he will be different from, rather than the same as, the parents. Low income parents can see the value of this approach, can understand how it may help break the poverty cycle, and can themselves help their children attain the goals of intervention. In fact, the parents can benefit from these efforts, too.

Traditionally, preschool education has attempted to socialize the child in a manner which will perpetuate the values, beliefs, and behaviors of the parents. In other words, traditional preschool programs have attempted to make children like their parents. But in the case of the deprived child, this is not a reasonable goal: it would be poverty that would be perpetuated. As we have seen, a sense of frustration, hopelessness, and defeat is often passed on from low income parent to low income child. Hence, the child often becomes trapped in the same difficult position occupied by the parent. But in an intervention program an effort is made to change the values, beliefs, expectations, and behaviors of the child at a very early age. The hope is that, because of the change, the child will be more able to cope with prevailing cultural demands, and will avoid cycling back into the parents' unfortunate situation. Intervention programs are designed to break into the poverty cycle at an early age, before it is too late to alter the child's life pattern so that she or he will be more likely to experience success and fulfillment in our society.

Whether or not these efforts will be successful in the long run remains to be seen. There have been efforts to evaluate the effectiveness of these programs, as we shall see in an upcoming section. But many of the programs remain too new and too innovative for us to evaluate them clearly at the present time.

Head Start

Although it is far from the only ongoing intervention program, Head Start is perhaps the most well known (Zigler, 1978). We have chosen to discuss it in some detail, as it constitutes a prime example of the intervention approach.

The Birth of Head Start   At present the Head Start label refers to a vast array of federally funded activities. But the origins of this network of activities were quite humble. Head Start was stimulated by a developing awareness that the early years of childhood are critical in the perpetuation of the poverty cycle. In 1964 the federal government brought together a panel of child development experts, and asked them to come up with a program which would enable low income children to break out of the poverty cycle. Project Head Start began as a modest summer school program in 1965. It was designed to encourage learning patterns, emotions, skills and attitudes among deprived children which might protect them against a lifelong pattern of poverty.

Originally controlled by the Office of Economic Opportunity, Head Start has since been shifted to the Department of Health, Education and Welfare. Although Head Start has been slowly expanded to, for the most part, year-long programs, this may soon change. Recent trends in this country seem to be undermining the future funding of Head Start. According to Kelber, the fiscal 1980 budget proposed by President Carter includes, "$700 million for the Head Start Program, a reduction after inflation of $20 million that means serving the needs of 20,000 fewer children!" (Kelber, 1979, p. 98). We hope this trend will be reversed in the near future.

A Comprehensive Program From the very beginning Head Start people knew that a comprehensive program would be needed if any real and lasting gains were to be made in breaking the poverty cycle. They knew that the program would have to reach into every aspect of the child's life. It would not be enough to limit the effort to what occurred within the actual school setting, as is often the case in more traditional, non-intervention programs. Accordingly, Head Start has always included many services not normally found in the preschool experience. Traditional educational components, although important, were thought to be but one of many crucial aspects of the Head Start experience. The program had to meet the individual needs of the child, not only within the school itself, but within the context of the home and the community as well. The program had to be flexible, and able to react to unique circumstances. It could not be a program in which authoritarian decrees set the tone in all centers across the country; the parents, the children, and the particular circumstances surrounding each effort would have to be considered.

As a result of these insights, individual Head Start programs vary greatly across the country. But behind each program one can find a commitment to the following general, comprehensive elements:

1. *Education:* Obviously, traditional educational experiences cannot be ignored in any Head Start program. As in all quality early childhood education programs, Head Start helps the child develop cognitively, emotionally, socially, and physically. The attainment of a positive self-concept is a major goal. An effort is made to provide *varied* learning experiences in the hope that these will bring the deprived child up to the level of the non-deprived child when it is time to enter elementary school.

Low child/teacher ratios are considered to be essential if the deprived child is to catch up with the non-deprived youngster. Head Start staff members are often given special training in helping the handicapped children who make up approximately 10 percent of the students in the program. In areas where bilingualism is prevalent, teachers must know the second language, and must be familiar with the culture that they serve. **2.** *Health:* Many children from poverty areas never see doctors or dentists, let alone professionals able to help them with their psychological or emotional problems. An important goal of Head Start is the early identification of *any* health problem. Therefore, each child is given a complete medical and dental examination. Required treatments, such as immunizations and dental work, are provided.

Because many of these children come to school hungry, each child receives a minimum of one hot meal, and a snack each day under the supervision of a trained nutritionist. This nutritionist also plans a program for parents, teaching them how to buy and prepare well-balanced meals, and how to obtain food stamps and other needed assistance.

Every Head Start program must also provide the services of a mental health professional. This individual helps the staff and parents be aware of the special needs and problems of the children, and encourages the emotional and social development of the students.

3. *Social services:* Parents of Head Start children see many of their children's needs going unfulfilled, and do not know how and where to seek help. The Head Start social services coordinator is there to help parents locate community agencies that can help meet some of these needs. The coordinator also assists the parents in obtaining the services offered by the agencies. For instance, the coordinator might accompany parents to an agency and help them fill out the required forms. This can be a great help, especially if the parents are not fluent in English and/or are intimidated by forms and bureaucratic procedures. Particular children may be entitled to a wide variety of services, including those provided by the Veterans Administration, Medicaid, and the food stamp program. But low income parents are sometimes unaware of these opportunities, and the Head Start staff can provide needed guidance and advice.

4. *Parental involvement:* Research findings are beginning to confirm what many educators have always felt to be true—that parents are the most important influence on the child's development. And this includes the father as well as the mother (Lamb, 1976). Accordingly, parental involvement in Head Start is heavily encouraged at all levels including participation in the classroom activities, in workshops, and in policy decisions. Through participation the parents can form a clearer picture of the process of child development, and can learn to work more effectively with their own children at home. Home Start, an offshoot of Head Start, has demonstrated that parental involvement in the child's development is invaluable.

Parental attitudes toward schools may be improved as they learn to deal with the preschool arrangement, and as they discover that people will listen to them and will act upon the basis of their opinions.

5. *Career development and training:* Although not as heavily stressed as it once was, the comprehensive Head Start program includes appropriate staff training. The object of this training is to improve the skills of the staff, and to advance them toward their own career goals. For example, many staff members enroll in classes that provide them with training that is required if they are to receive a Child Development Associate credential. The importance of this credential will be discussed in the next chapter.

A Diverse Approach Although all Head Start efforts conform to the foregoing emphases, individual programs vary a great deal. The mere fact that parental participation is encouraged leads to diversity. The exact nature of the program is not laid down by some central authority; it is the result of an interaction among parents, staff, and the Head Start guidelines. Head Start intends to aid and assist low income families. Since the conditions of poverty vary, in both kind and degree, Head Start efforts must, of necessity, be diverse. Since Head Start is experimental, changes occur from time to time. The approach is not static and rigidly defined; everyone is learning and exploring as time passes. But, in each case, the emphasis is upon a comprehensive effort to break the poverty cycle by intervening, with the help of the parents, in all aspects of the early years of childhood. The effort is to create change, rather than consistency, between one generation and the next.

Head Start has led to, and been influenced by, a number of experimental efforts and outgrowths. For example, Head Start began as a center-based program for children a year before they were to enter public school. But now, many efforts include home-based programs, community programs, or some combination of home, center, and community activities. Project Follow Through was developed to help Head Start children move into elementary school in a smooth and effective manner. Follow Through was also designed to help elementary school teachers find ways of meeting the needs of incoming Head Start children. Home Start, a three-year demonstration that ended in 1975, provided services for parents and children in the home rather than in a preschool center. Many Head Start programs are now including the home-based approach as part of their service to the community.

Program and research efforts other than Head Start are also using home programs. Many infant, and even prenatal, programs are now being conducted within the home setting. Finally, special programs for groups such as Native Americans and migrant workers have been developed. In other words, Head Start is, and has stimulated, a growing, changing, innovative approach to early childhood education.

Program Evaluation

The Need for Evaluation

Evaluation refers to our concern over whether or not our programs actually are attaining their stated goals. If we are willing to invest time and energy in the development and execution of complex programs, such as those we have been discussing, then the effectiveness of those programs should be evaluated. If a program looks good but does not produce the desired results, then it should be changed or abandoned. Similarly, programs that seem, on paper, to be lacking may well turn out to be the effective ones in the long run. In other words, we can't depend upon "gut-level" feelings, or our subjective reactions, when it comes to judging the value of a program. We can't view an outgoing class and conclude, with any certainty, that that class did or did not benefit from our program. They might just as well have become what they are without ever having been introduced to our program. We need carefully designed, and carefully controlled, experimental studies if we are to be accurate in our evaluative efforts. There is no substitute for a rigorous experimental approach to the problem of evaluation. Unfortunately, as we shall see, it is not a simple matter to establish tightly controlled experimental procedures outside an artificial laboratory setting. Trying to establish a valid experimental paradigm within any existing preschool situation presents many knotty problems that are just beginning to be unravelled.

Positive Results

On the other hand, the situation is far from hopeless. There have been many recent attempts to evaluate preschool programs in as rigorous a manner as possible. We may be witnessing the beginning of an era of growing precision in the area of preschool evaluation. Many of the on-going evaluative efforts involve intervention programs, but the problem of evaluation is relevant to *all* preschool programs and not just those that attempt to break the poverty cycle.

Encouraging positive results are reported by Lazar et al. (1977). They, as well as many others, have been concerned with the *long range* effects of intervention programs. Clearly, short-term gains are common in these programs, but there has been great concern over whether or not these effects last, or persist once the student moves on into the elementary school level. Summarizing the results of fourteen longitudinal studies of low income children, these authors conclude:

1. *Infant and preschool services improve the ability of low income children to meet the minimal requirements of the schools they*

enter. *This effect can be manifested in either a reduced probability of being assigned to special education classes or a reduced probability of being held back in grade. Either reduction constitutes a substantial cost reduction for the school system.*
2. *Low income adolescents who received early education rate their competence in school higher than comparable adolescents who did not have preschool education.*
3. *As measured by the Stanford-Binet and the WISC tests, preschool programs produce a significant increase in the intellectual functioning of low income children at least during the crucial years of the primary grades in school.*

Findings such as these are certainly encouraging, and they are not isolated results. For example, Levenstein (1977), Schaefer and Aaronson (1977), and Lally and Honig (1977) all report positive long-term effects following participation in home-based programs. Similarly, Nimnicht, Arango, and Cheever (1977) and Biber (1977) outline what they feel to be effective center-based programs.

In general, the kinds of positive, long-term results that have been reported with preschool programs (particularly intervention programs) include:

1. Elevated IQ scores that persist through at least the first year of elementary school.
2. Fewer children being held back in grade.
3. Fewer children requiring special classes.
4. More children displaying positive self-concepts.
5. More parents appreciating the program and seeing themselves as integral, helpful participants in the program.
6. More beneficial involvement of the parents with the children.

In other words, many preschool educators feel the programs have been, and are, effective and well worth the cost and effort.

Research Issues

While these sorts of results are encouraging, it is instructive to explore some of the methodological difficulties involved in evaluating any preschool program. We discuss these issues, not because we feel evaluation is hopeless or impossible, but because an understanding of difficulties involved in mounting an evaluative effort may help stimulate more and more effective research efforts in the future. A discussion of these issues will also aid the readers in their attempts to understand, and criticize, published research.

Measurement The first problem we face in trying to evaluate the impact of a program has to do with the fact that we need good, valid measures of what it is that we are interested in (Bronfenbrenner, 1974). If the goals of our program include social, cognitive, physical and emotional development, then we need valid tests of social, cognitive, physical, and emotional elements. We can't just look at the child and conclude, "Yes, Billy certainly has developed socially, cognitively, physically, and emotionally." Such a procedure is open to enormous error and distortion. Unfortunately, we do not always have good measures or tests of these critical dimensions. Some are more easily measured than others.

For example, it is a relatively simple matter to obtain IQ scores and to compare the scores of participating and non-participating children. Based upon IQ scores, some investigators (although not all) are willing to draw conclusions about the impact of the preschool experience upon cognitive functioning. That is all well and good—but what about the other critical dimensions of the preschool experience such as social and emotional development? It is not so simple a matter to measure these rather elusive dimensions. Reliable, valid measures of these dimensions are, according to some, sorely lacking. Difficult questions need to be answered. For example, how much development is enough? In what terms or units do we express social and emotional growth? How would we measure self-esteem? How can we assign numbers to levels of self-respect? What is an emotion, which emotions are critical, and how do we measure any of them? These are troublesome questions, to say the least.

There is a tendency to want to engage in intuitive evaluation. For example, we may note that Sharon cried a great deal when she first came to school. She did not want to try anything new; she would say "I can't," and run away. But after nine months, she enjoyed coming to school. She was cheerful, happy, and eager to explore. She took pride in her ability. She appeared to have developed socially and emotionally. The problem here is that our subjective feelings about her progress do not constitute a valid measure of development. First, if someone else had observed the changes she went through, they might come to quite different conclusions. For example, they might say they observed little or no change, or that she had become defensive and pretended to be happy while concealing her tension. Second, we have to wonder about how her change relates to the change displayed by other children. Did she change more or less than the group average? What is the group average? Third, we have to wonder about whether our program had anything at all to do with the changes we observed.

Might not Sharon have shown the same development, or even more, if she had never been exposed to the school at all?

Social growth is not much easier to measure. How can we express the developing level of social interaction displayed by a group? There are many techniques we might use, but each one is open to error and must be carefully controlled. For instance, we could count the number of aggressive acts occurring in September and compare that number with the number of hostile acts appearing in June. Or we could keep track of the number of instances of parallel play that occur within the group. But these are dubious measures, fraught with ambiguity, and lacking in rigor. In other words, measuring social development is a difficult and tricky issue.

How about physical development? Here at least there are some relatively simply tests that can be used to evaluate motor development. And there are averages or norms available with which we can compare our students' performances. But practical issues often arise with respect to these tests. For example, are the school's teachers qualified to administer and evaluate these tests? Can the school afford the time and expense involved in administering them?

Furthermore, it is difficult to evaluate health and nutritional goals, and it is difficult to evaluate the impact of a given program upon handicapped children. In other words, there are a number of dimensions that we would like to measure, but good solid indices of these dimensions simply are not available at the present time.

Many programs that do try to evaluate their programs concentrate on cognitive development, or intellectual functioning. This is rather unfortunate, for a number of reasons, as Bronfenbrenner (1975) has noted. First, cognitive growth is but one goal of the overall program, and yet it is often used to determine the value of the entire program. Second, the tests used to measure cognitive development, particularly in young and culturally varied children, are often difficult to administer and often suspected of being inaccurate. Third, even if the tests were valid and even if cognitive development correlated with social, emotional, and physical development, we would still be left with the problem of trying to decide *how much* growth is the correct, or appropriate, amount.

Psychologists usually identify four qualities of a good test. Specifically, they argue that a test must be *objective, reliable, valid,* and *standardized*. The meanings of these four terms are outlined in table 7.1. Familiarity with these four essential elements can be useful to preschool teachers, not only in their reading, but "on the floor" as well. If someone comes to you with the results of a given test, arguing that they are meaningful, check to see if they meet these four essential criteria.

Experimental Design In the preceding section we noted that the field of early childhood education is faced with a series of problems in terms

Table 7.1   *The four essential ingredients of a good test*

Objectivity

A good test must be objective. This means that the same score must be obtainable by two different testers. If two different people administer the same test on the same child, and come up with the same score, then that is evidence for the objectivity of that test. If two people test a singer for her ability to hit a high C, and one concludes that she can, while the other concludes that she cannot, then that test is not objective.

Reliability

To be reliable, a test must produce the same score for the same individual on two different occasions. For example, if a child scores 125 on an intelligence test on one day and 83 on the same test on another day, then that test is not reliable. Reliability is difficult to establish, but measurement psychologists have devised several techniques for assessing test reliability.

Validity

To be valid a test must measure what it is supposed to measure. This is a most important, and most difficult, quality to establish. If we try to measure intelligence by measuring foot-length, we have an objective and a reliable measure— but it is not valid. Validity is usually assessed by seeing if a test will *predict* behavior. Thus, if persons who score high on a proposed test of creativity actually do creative things in their lives, then we say that test may be valid.

Standardization

Suppose we have a proposed test of anxiety. An individual scores 14 out of a possible 60 on this test. Does a score of 14 mean the individual is highly anxious or not very anxious at all? We don't know until we standardize the test. What this means is that we need to administer the test to a large number of individuals. Once we have their scores, we can compare our individual's score with them. It might turn out that most people score above 20 on the test, in which case the score of 14 might imply low anxiety. On the other hand, most people might score below 10, in which case 14 would indicate high anxiety.

of measurement. Objective, valid, reliable, standardized tests of cognitive, emotional, social, and physical development are few and far between. But there remains an additional problem of evaluation that may be at least as fundamental as the question of measurement—that of appropriate experimental design.

Before we outline the nature of a good, acceptable experiment, it should be noted that early childhood education is not heavily oriented toward experimentation. It is, after all, a service field. Generally speaking, preschool teachers are not exposed to the principles of rigorous experimentation. They have not been asked to design experiments, to collect data, to analyze results, or to interpret findings. They are not trained in the use of statistics. Exposure to the testing procedures used with young children is minimal. We do not mean to imply that all teachers should become accomplished researchers. There is enough to absorb in the process of becoming an accomplished teacher. However, some exposure to the issues and problems facing researchers can help teachers appreciate the complexity of what it is that they are trying to accomplish in the classroom.

A good evaluative effort involves an attempt to assess the impact of a given program upon the social, cognitive, emotional, and physical development of the child. To accomplish this goal, one would, ideally, establish an experimental design which involves at least two groups, the *experimental group* and the *control group*. The experimental group participates in the program while the control group does not. Following participation or non-participation, the two groups are compared on a number of dimensions using a number of tests (which we hope are good tests). We attempt to assess the development of the two groups. If the experimental group scores, or performs, above the control group, then we say we have some evidence for the effectiveness of our program. If, on the other hand, the control group is equal to, or better than, the experimental group, then we have no evidence at all for the effectiveness of our program.

Matched groups. Before we begin our experiment, we must match the experimental and control groups as closely as possible. Essentially, the two groups must be as similar as possible. If they are not matched, then any differences we observe after the experiment has been completed could be due to differences that existed *before* the experiment began, and not to the experience of either participating or not participating in the program. For example, the experimental and control groups should contain the same numbers of females and males. Otherwise, any observed differences between the two groups might be due to sex differences. Similarly, the children should be matched in terms of age. This is especially true when dealing with deprived children, as it appears that these children suffer more and more from deprivation as they grow older (Hayes and Grethers, 1969).

Socioeconomic background should be matched, too. We can't put only high income children in our experimental group and only low income children in our control group because these factors will affect our results. Affluence as well as deprivation can confound our data. It has also been suggested that deprived children should be matched in terms of the *degree* of their deprivation. Matching for socioeconomic level is not always easy. Do we try to do it on the basis of parental income, geographical location, cultural heritage, or some combination of these elements?

Obviously, we have to tell the parents about the assignment of their children to one group or another. This can cause problems from an experimental point of view. For example, some parents will refuse, or demand that their child be assigned to a particular group. In either case, the balance of the experimental and control groups is threatened. Parents, knowing about the experiment, may become involved and change their behavior at home. This kind of behavior places the experiment in jeopardy, because we won't know whether the results we obtain are due to our program or to the artificial and perhaps temporary changes in parental behavior.

The children should be matched *before* the experiment on all the dimensions we feel might influence the results and on all the dimensions we intend to assess. As we have seen, good tests are difficult to find. Thus, even if we have a strong experimental design, we are still faced with a weakness in terms of assessment techniques. And even if we had good tests, we would have to make sure that the testers were competent and well trained. It is difficult to administer an intelligence test to a 3 year old. If the child is upset, or if there is a personality clash with that of the tester, the score will be affected heavily.

Statistics. Before the experiment is run, appropriate statistical tests should be planned. The particular tests that are used will depend upon the number of subjects involved, the numbers of groups employed, and the particular experimental configuration. Statistical analyses must be performed by qualified individuals and should be double-checked. The results should be interpreted in a cautious, conservative manner because, like anything else, experimental results can be read in different ways. Excessive usage of multiple, successive statistical tests should be avoided because, if we look long and hard enough, we can always find some significant difference—even in a pile of random numbers.

What to do? Given that rigorous experiments are difficult to conduct and perhaps beyond the interest and training of the average teacher, what should the individual teacher do with respect to program planning and evaluation? First, realize that new and more refined research methodology is being developed constantly. There is hope. The near future should witness an upsurge in carefully-gauged experimental efforts. Second, try to keep abreast of these research developments. Try to be aware of what elements have been shown to be effective program elements. Third, plan and conduct your program as best as you can, using what information is currently available. Remember that early childhood education is a service-oriented field and that we cannot all be, or even want to be, researchers. But the individual teacher should be aware of ongoing evaluative research even if she or he does not participate in it directly. Significant research findings should be incorporated into the growth process that is so essential to the future of early childhood education.

8

Issues in
Curriculum Development

We have adopted a developmental point of view in this text because we feel such an approach has value. According to this view, early childhood education, in all its complexity, is constantly growing and changing. By viewing all aspects of early childhood education in this manner, including its people, areas of concern, and programs, we do not miss the change and flexibility that is so characteristic of the field. This stage of education is not a complete and finalized entity. It is better understood as a dynamic, moving area of study that seeks to meet the evolving needs of a variety of people in a changing world.

It is from this point of view that we discuss the subject of curricula. Early childhood education curricula have not been finalized and perfected to the extent that everyone agrees on what they should and should not be. Curriculum can mean a different thing to different people. It may mean one thing for a particular group on a specific day . . . but then seem to imply something different on another occasion. Children, parents, teachers, administrators, and the community at large all influence what a given curriculum will and will not be at any specific time. Curricula, like the people that develop them, can and should change and grow; thus our emphasis upon "development" in the chapter title.

We will deal here with some general issues and concerns that relate to curriculum planning. Chapter 9 will deal with specific suggested areas of curriculum activity.

What Is a Curriculum?

Generally speaking, curriculum refers to a course of study, such as a sequence of courses taken in a university setting. It comes from the Latin word *currere,* meaning a course, a race. But in the early childhood situation, since there is normally no sequence of courses to be pursued, the term has taken on a slightly different and more diffuse meaning. It still refers to what is being taught to the children (or learned by them), but it lacks the connotation prevalent in other educational levels of a prescribed series of numbered courses. A curriculum of early childhood education is what people generally think of as the core of the educational program. As one teacher puts it, "The curriculum gets down to the real nitty gritty of teaching. It's what's happening in the classroom. It's what I teach."

In these two chapters we will discuss good curriculum planning and implementation. Like everything else in early childhood education, curriculum development is a complex area that must meet the varied and changing needs of many indivduals (Langenbach and Neskora, 1977).

Two Elements

A distinction between *content* and *process* is important in understanding the unique meaning of curriculum in connection with early childhood education. In general, content refers to what facts, concepts, and information a child learns, while process refers to how the child learns and what she or he can do with what is learned. Although some might argue that one of these two elements is more important than the other, many, and perhaps the majority (Biber et al., 1977; Weikart et al., 1971) would contend that both content and process are critical and that they are inseparable components of any curriculum. Essentially this means that *what* is learned by the children and *how* the child learns and uses information are equally important and intertwined. Even though, for convenience, we discuss the two separately, the reader should keep in mind that they are closely related.

Content

Content is the *what* of curriculum. Content is composed of facts, information, and concepts. You can get a feel for this by looking at your own curriculum as a student. What courses have you taken? Over the years you may well have studied mathematics, physical and social sciences, philosophy, education, English, foreign languages, history, government, music, art, theatre, dance, health, and physical education. This has been your course of study, the content of your education. Surprisingly (and fortunately) your course of study parallels quite closely the content of most early childhood education curricula. This may sound extraordinary to you, but it's true. There are elements of all these areas of learning in the everyday activites of the early childhood education program. Of course, the level of sophistication and the degree of rigor are very different.

Some samples may illustrate this fact. Suppose you and some of the children decided to cook scrambled eggs one day. If a recipe is involved, it may be read and explained before and during the activity.

This involves an exercise in basic language and mathematical concepts. The group must decide which bowl, pan, and cooking utensils to use. Here, at the very least, you are dealing with logic and the rudiments of science. Counting eggs and measuring ingredients involve further contact with basic content information. Colors, weights, smells, tastes, textures, and shapes will probably be discussed. The origin of eggs might be of interest. As the eggs cook, some children may want to know about heat and how it cooks the eggs. Once the eggs have cooked, of course, they must be served. This involves one plate and a spoon or fork for each child and the portioning of eggs. If you think about it for a moment, these activities involve elementary, but very definite contact with the basics of mathematics (one-to-one relationships, measuring, division, geometry) and science (biology, physics, chemistry). Furthermore, this activity provides a perfect opportunity for you to comment on the nutritive value of the food and on the digestive process, thereby bringing your pupils into contact with anatomy, biology, and the principals of health and nutrition.

What about building a snowman? Even though it seems a simple activity, it involves contact with many of your curriculum studies. Through discussion of the weather, snow, ice, size, volume, weight, shape, the construction of the snowman, and its decoration, you will be exposing the children to geography, climatology, physics, chemistry, mathematics, and art. Dramatic play and role playing with the snow figures might occur (drama, psychology, sociology). Some teachers and children might sing "Frosty the Snowman" and other winter songs, and a story might be read or told. Body movement and dance is everywhere. And, as in any human activity, there are social interactions to be worked out, rules made, and attitudes expressed. We have now included basics in music, drama, dance, physical education, psychology, sociology, language, literature, philosophy, and law.

You can probably see now how all those subjects you have plowed through can help form the content of your teaching curriculum. They can be useful after all. If you happen to be in school now, thinking about your eventual need for the information, it may help you in studying areas that seem unrelated to your major or that are "irrelevant." For instance, you may not care a great deal about evaporation and condensation; but when a 4 year old asks you later why plants dry out or how rain is made, you might feel differently.

The Content-Oriented Curriculum

Some schools emphasize content (*what*) over process (*how*). The content-oriented curriculum and some of its weaknesses are described by Karnes, Zerbach and Teska (1977) in this way:

> Content . . . is defined as facts, information, and concepts.
> *Concern here is for what a child learns rather than how he learns*
> *. . . In a content-oriented preschool program, the minimal content*
> *necessary for effective learning in later school has been identified*
> *and sequenced for presentation to the child. Such an approach*
> *establishes a finite body of material to be taught but may fail to*
> *provide the child with the opportunity to relate what he has*
> *learned to other tasks and areas. Further, since our society is*
> *changing at a rapid rate, considerable effort is required to ensure*
> *that the content is always relevant.* (p. 262)

Content Selection

Though one may not want to be overly content-oriented, no one would deny that content is an essential part of any curriculum. The next question, then, involves selection of content. How should it be determined?

Content selection depends on many factors: the type of program, the goals of the program, the location of the program, the clientele, and the teacher. For example, if you teach in a Montessori program, much of the content undoubtedly will center around the Montessori equipment and learning materials. Many seemingly trivial factors will influence content. For example, if your school is located in a desert or some other extreme climate, content will reflect it. If your children are of Native or Mexican-American heritage, you will want to include aspects of their backgrounds in the content. If your children are clearly lacking in any essential area, you will try to provide the appropriate experiences. If you have special skills or abilities, let the children enjoy and learn from the fruits of those talents. If the goals of your program include encouraging artistic creativity, then music, art, and dance will be part of the content of your curriculum. A particular theory of learning or child development adopted by yourself or the school may influence content selection. The owners of the school, the teachers, and the parents are all a part of the equation that determines content. In other words, the determinants of content are multiple.

Many content-oriented curricula emphasize content that will, presumably, prepare the child for success in the next school year or school experience. The attention is focused on the child's success *in the future* more than on the child's enjoyment of life today or on the child's development today. To some extent most programs have an eye on the future and on the child's place in it (e.g., most intervention programs are oriented toward helping the child learn how to succeed in public school later, and, finally, in adult life). In many content-oriented curricula the emphasis is upon acquiring, often through rote memory, the information and concepts needed to enable the child to function successfully as an adult in our complex, competitive society. For example, the children in a content-oriented school may "learn their numbers" from one to ten. They can count to ten, recognize the written numerals and possibly even write numerals one through ten. Essentially this information has been memorized. Sometimes it is acquired in formal drill situations. Unfortunately, following this sort of training, the children may not understand the logical implications of these numbers, nor be ready to apply the information to new situations in a flexible manner.

Herein lies the primary objection to the content-oriented school. Many argue that it does not provide the child with an *understanding* of, say, number concepts, and with the ability to use and relate numbers in everyday life. It is because of this sort of shortcoming that modern early childhood education programs emphasize process, and it is to this essential partner of content that we now turn. At the same time, *some* content would seem to be essential in any curriculum.

Process

What Is Process?

While content-oriented curricula focus on what facts and information are learned, process-oriented curricula are more concerned with how the child learns to learn, what learning skills are developed, and how these skills are applied to different situations.

Karnes and her associates refer to process as:

the ability to obtain, organize, manipulate, synthesize, integrate, and communicate information. *Programs that focus on process are concerned about the way in which children think, evaluate, and seek out new information. A preschool based on the* discovery *method is an example of a process-oriented school.*
(Karnes, Zehrbach and Teska, 1977, p. 261)

Clearly, a concern for process is a complex concern. This complexity is underscored by Berman who sees several skills and sub-processes in the overall process of learning. These include perceiving, organizing, creating, communicating, decision making, knowing, valuing, and loving (1968). Each of these sub-processes covers a lot of ground. Perception, for example, is the concern of an entire branch of psychology. Many universities have entire departments concerned with communication. And the questions of the natures of knowing and loving have puzzled scientists and non-scientists alike for centuries. In other words, we are just beginning to unravel the overall question of process.

Process-oriented curricula are concerned with helping children learn and with helping them enjoy learning *now*. The focus is on developing general learning skills rather than storing specific facts. Here, too, the hope is that a child who can succeed in the future will be produced. But a concern for process rather than content wants the child to be equipped with ways to learn and process information rather than with a *specific* body of facts that may or may not be relevant to the unforeseeable future.

Most preschool curricula are of necessity both content- and process-oriented. The two are woven together closely, although some curricula emphasize one over the other. Piagetian theory does not really distinguish between the two; they are inseparable. But as the child passes through later years of school, content will be stressed over process. One can only hope that the process skills learned in the preschool years may continue to help the children when they are required to deal with large bodies of information.

For example, if the process skills of perception, problem solving, and communication have been well developed in the early years, the child will be able to use these "old" skills in later school situations even though the new curricula may be content-oriented. Hopefully, the child will be able to perceive the problem clearly, to employ acquired problem solving skills in finding a solution, and to communicate the solution in an effective manner.

Unfortunately, many elementary school situations limit the amount of movement, manipulation, and spontaneous communication that still appears to be essential to children of the early elementary school age. But there have been and are some efforts to bridge the gap between preschool process-oriented curricula and content-oriented elementary curricula.

Teaching in a Process-Oriented Setting

When teaching in a process-oriented program, the teacher must consider the best means of attaining the goals of such a program. Generally, standing up in front of a large group and lecturing will not accomplish the aims of this sort of program. Although there are many different approaches, most would agree that the use of learning centers is one good example. Each center, containing equipment and materials suitable for a given activity area, is made available to the children. Then, singly or in small groups, the children explore and play in the center and teach themselves, or *learn by discovery*—with a little help from you, the teacher. They may be allowed complete free choice at times, or be structured in some activities to one degree or another. (One related issue which every teacher must face is the degree to which the learning process and content will be *teacher initiated* or *child initiated*. Who will choose what is done, where it is done, and how it is done? This issue is discussed further later in this chapter.)

"Moderation in all things" may be a good motto when deciding upon the stance you will assume as a teacher. Your curriculum will be both process- and content-oriented, but one can be emphasized over the other. You may also want to be concerned with the development of the whole child, promoting growth in all areas, physical, social, emotional, and cognitive.

Program Goals and Curriculum Development

Introduction

So far we have defined curriculum as what it is that is being learned, and have noted and discussed the distinctions between content and process. We have indicated how these two factors influence curriculum development, and have noted that they are interrelated. What else, in addition to a consideration of process and content, influences the nature of a given curriculum? Obviously, the many goals of the program will have a heavy impact upon the nature of curriculum. As indicated in chapter 7, a program is a general philosophy or orientation, accompanied by a set of goals, while curriculum is designed to implement those goals. In other words, the goals or strategy of a given program should dictate, in a direct manner, the tactics employed in the curriculum. Curriculum is what you do with the children to meet the general goals of the program.

Goals Influence Curricula

The direct influence of program goals on curricula can be illustrated by a few examples. For instance, Katz (1977) presents the following:

> A major goal of early childhood education is to help children make sense of their experiences and environments. In other words, we are responsible for helping young children to develop, refine, and improve, or deepen their understanding of the salient aspects of their day to day lives. (p. 64)

She then goes on to make some rather specific curriculum suggestions that might implement these particular goals:

> The intellectual vitality of our program can be strengthened when we encourage and help children to reconstruct these aspects.

*This can be achieved by actually building, making, and reproducing
some aspects; by dramatizing others; and by encouraging the
observing, recalling, recording, or discussing of their perceptions
and understandings of their experiences.* (pp. 64–65)

In other words, if an understanding of daily life is a program goal,
then that goal can be approached by developing a curriculum which
actually reproduces and reconstructs elements of the daily life within
the early childhood education setting where the teacher may aid in the
understanding of those elements.

Let's look at another example of the ways that program goals
can influence curriculum. The following rather extensive list of "goals
for all children" is suggested in one of Project Head Start's "Rainbow
Series" of pamphlets entitled *Daily Program I* (1973, p. 7).

To help children:
*learn to work and play independently, able to accept both help
and direction from adults;*

*develop their use of language-listening and speaking, and grasping
connections between spoken and written words;*

*exercise curiosity—asking questions, seeking answers, becoming
problem-solvers;*

*play with, and come to comprehend, mathematical concepts like
sequence, quantity, number, sorting;*

*widen their knowledge of the world—through science, books, field
trips, films;*

develop physical coordination and skill;

*grow in ability to express inner creative impulses—dancing, paint-
ing, speaking, singing, making things;*

*grow in ability to control inner destructive impulses—to talk
instead of hit, to understand the difference between feeling angry
and acting out anger, to feel sympathy for others in trouble;*

*learn how to get along comfortably with other children—each to
value his own rights and the rights of others;*

view themselves as competent and valued persons. (Stone and Janis,
1974, p. 7.)

In describing the general curriculum approach that might be suitable for the attainment of these goals at the 3 to 5 year level, the Head
Start pamphlet continues:

For preschoolers, the course is a general one; it covers wide knowledge about themselves and the environment. The study does not take place at desks, but rather in the context both of the children's self-initiated play and teacher-directed activity.

A child "studies" while exploring the room, getting help if he needs it, asking questions and putting the answers to use, hearing stories read aloud, discovering new words, engaging in conversation, conceiving new ideas, gathering new facts—all in a program tooled up with first rate materials and taught by responsive adults. This holds true for handicapped children, too, who may, however, need extra help (from grownups or older children) as they explore and learn. (pp. 14–15)

These examples of goal-based curricula emphasize several important points. First, they suggest that the child should initially learn about the world by learning about her immediate environment. One should help the child understand where she is living and her relationships to the people, things, places, and events found within her daily life space, whether it be a poverty, middle class, upper class, rural, or urban area. Help the child understand her immediate, personal environment.

Second, these curriculum suggestions emphasize the importance of avoiding rigid drilling while the children are seated quietly at desks. The children should be free to play and explore and to learn through self-initiated discovery, supplemented by teacher-directed activity. Third, the teacher should pay attention, and take seriously, even the most trivial questions and interests expressed by the child. The teacher must set up situations in which discovery is likely to occur.

By keeping these three curriculum elements in mind, many rewarding learning experiences can evolve. For example, suppose a teacher in a small coastal fishing community brings in some woodworking materials. This is a teacher-initiated event, based upon the knowledge that some children like to build and create things, and that they will learn by doing so. During the woodworking activities, one child decides to build a fishing boat. A friend decides to do the same. This is the child-initiated act, and it is directly related to everyday life in the community. A discussion of boats and fishing, centered around the woodworking, helps the children understand where they live and how adults earn a living in the community.

Taking the cue from the children, the teacher makes arrangements with someone from the local fishing community (possibly a parent) for a class field trip to the local wharf. Here the children can see the boats, ask questions, even climb aboard one or two of them. This experience is a blend of teacher- and child-initiated activity and exemplifies the way in which one learning activity can lead to another. The process can work in many ways. Suppose a group of children have been playing with blocks and have lined them up to form a train. Noting this activity, the teacher may introduce a new song about trains as they sit and play with their respective "cars."

In summary, general program goals determine specific curriculum activities. Because programs vary enormously, so, too, will curricula. Many modern curricula seem to include the notions that learning should not be accomplished through rigid drilling procedures, that play and spontaneous discovery are more important, that centers provide good learning environments, that a blend of teacher- and child-initiated activity is favorable, that the teacher should attend to the child's questions and interests carefully, and that the child's initial learning should occur in the context of everyday life.

Play

Play, Discovery, and Learning

Play assumes an enormously important role in an early educational setting (Bruner, Jolly and Sylva, 1976; Rubin, 1977). Even without the involvement of teachers and staff, children will engage in copious quantities of play. But because everyone within the field is aware of the importance of play, it takes on double significance. Even though play is not well understood, as we shall see in the next section, its importance is obvious. Specifically, most would agree that play can be the means by which the child discovers, learns, and creates. Through spontaneous as well as prompted play, the child wholeheartedly engages in a wide range of activities that foster learning and creativity. And we must not forget that play has value in and of itself; a playing child often (although not necessarily) tends to be a happy child, unworried and secure.

The marvelous quality of play is such that a child will learn things within its content that would not otherwise be learned so well. For example, a child may learn through play that it is easier to build small blocks on top of large blocks than the other way around. If you merely try to explain it, there may be no real understanding. The child's own manipulation and experimentation in play will lead to the kind of understanding that is real to her.

Through play, discoveries will be made that will have a lasting impression on the child. If the "discovery" is handed to the child without effort, its significance will be reduced. For example, a child's discovery that a bee is carrying "powdery stuff" on its legs as it moves from flower to flower, will have much more impact than a statement about pollen and pollination presented in dry, impersonal, biological terms by an adult. Many observers feel that the best and most effective learning occurs through individual discovery. Young children constantly discover so many new things, as so many of their daily experiences are new to them. And play is an important vehicle for this type of discovery.

In the next chapter we shall discuss specific content areas that are often considered to be important in an early educational setting (e.g., reading, math, science, etc.). It cannot be emphasized too heavily that much of the specific content learning occurs *within the context of play*. Children learn about number concepts during play. They discover biological, physical, and social principles during play. They exercise and improve their language skills as well as their physical skills during play. And they learn what they are curious about at their own level. They learn by doing. In other words, play rather than a rigid classroom situation can be taken as the principle forum in which preschool learning occurs. Thus, when we discuss specific content areas in the next chapter, we should keep in mind that a play context rather than formal instruction provides the best means of promoting learning and creativity.

Theories of Play

Although most would agree that play is important, we have not yet been able to develop a cohesive picture of its nature and function. Thus it behooves us to spend a little time thinking about various interpretations of play. Ellis (1973) has written extensively about the nature and function of play. Tables 8.1, 8.2, and 8.3 contain his interpretations of classical, recent, and modern theories of play, respectively. Although Ellis is keenly aware that our knowledge of play is, at present, very limited he feels the phenomenon is best understood through a combination of three of these theories: play as arousal-seeking, play as learning, and the developmentalist view of the child. The developmentalist point of view appears to be a tempered version of Piaget's position as found in *Play, Dreams, and Imitation in Childhood*.

Play Criteria

Although Ellis is skeptical about our ability to develop an adequate definition of play, he does, in agreement with Neumann (1971), feel that we can establish a set of criteria which will at least distinguish between play and non-play. In other words, we may not know exactly what play is, but we can identify it. The proposed criteria for play are as follows:

1. *Locus of control of the player.* Play occurs only if the child chooses what to do and how to do it. If someone else controls the behavior or

Table 8.1 *Classical theories of play*

Name	Play Is Caused:	This Explanation Assumes That:	It Can Be Criticized Because:
Surplus Energy (1)	By the existence of energy surplus to the needs of survival.	1. Energy is produced at a constant rate. 2. If stored, storage is limited. 3. Excess must be expended. 4. Its expenditure is made on overt behavior which is by definition play.	1. Children play when fatigued or to the point of fatigue, so a surplus is not necessary for play. 2. The process of evolution should have tailored the energy available to the energy required.
Surplus Energy (2)	By increased tendency to respond after a period of response deprivation.	1. All response systems of the body have a tendency to respond. 2. The response threshold is lowered by a period of disuse. 3. After periods of disuse, eventually all available responses should reach a low enough threshold to be discharged either by some stimulus events or spontaneously.	1. Some responses available to the persons are never used.
Instinct	By the inheritance of unlearned capacities to emit playful acts.	1. The determinants of our behavior are inherited in the same way that we inherit the genetic code which determines our structure. 2. Some of those determinants cause play.	1. It ignored the obvious capacity of the person to learn new responses that we classify as play. 2. The facile naming of an instinct for each class of observed behavior is to do no more than to say, "because there is play, there must be a cause which we will call an Instinct."

activity, then, according to this criterion, it is not play. (Obviously, our desire to give control to the child must be tempered by safety considerations, etc.)

2. *The motive behind the behavior.* If the child engages in a behavior purely for the enjoyment of the *process itself,* and not for a reinforcement from an outside source, then that behavior may be play if it meets the other criteria. There can be no anticipated "payoff" if it is to be called

Name	Play Is Caused:	This Explanation Assumes That:	It Can Be Criticized Because:
Preparation	By the efforts of the player to prepare for later life.	1. Play is emitted only by persons preparing for new ways of responding. 2. The player is instinctively prepared for responses that will be critical later. 3. The instincts governing this are inherited imperfectly and youth is the period during which these imperfectly inherited mechanisms are perfected.	1. Play occurs most frequently in animals that live in rapidly changing circumstances. 2. It requires that the player inherit the capacity to predict which responses will be critical later. This requires the inheritance of information about the future. 3. People do not stop playing as adults, when presumably they are acceptably prepared.
Recapitulation	By the player recapitulating the history of the development of the species during its development.	1. The critical behaviors occurring during the evolution of man are encoded for inheritance. 2. A person emits some approximation to all these behaviors during his development. 3. Since these behaviors are currently irrelevant they are play. 4. The stages in our evolution will be followed in the individual's development.	1. There is no linear progression in our play development that seems to mirror the development of a species. At one point, late boyhood and adolescence, there may be similarity between sports and games and the components of hunting, chasing, fighting, etc., but before and after there seems little relation. 2. It does not explain play activities dependent on our advanced technology.
Relaxation	By the need for an individual to emit responses other than those used in work to allow recuperation.	1. Players work. 2. Play involves the emission of responses different from those of work. 3. The emission of different responses eliminates the noxious by-products of work.	1. It does not explain the use of play activities also used in work. 2. It does not explain the play of children—unless they are clearly working some part of their day.

Adapted from Ellis, M. J. *Why People Play*, Englewood Cliffs, N.J., Prentice-Hall, 1973.

Table 8.2 *Recent theories of play*

Name	Play Is Caused:	This Explanation Assumes That:	It Can Be Criticized Because:
Generalization	By the players using in their play experiences that have been rewarding at work.	1. There are at least two separable categories of behavior. 2. The players transfer to play or leisure, behaviors that are rewarded in another setting. 3. To be useful we understand what rewards individuals at work.	1. It seems to exclude play of preschool children. 2. It assumes that at least some aspects of work are rewarding.
Compensation	By players using their play to satisfy psychic needs not satisfied in or generated by the working behaviors.	1. There are at least two separable categories of behavior. 2. The player avoids in play or leisure behaviors that are unsatisfying in the work setting experiences that meet his psychic needs. 3. To be useful we understand the mismatch of needs and satisfactions in the work setting (or vice versa).	1. It seems to exclude play of preschool children. 2. It assumes that work is damaging or does not satisfy some needs.
Catharsis	In part by the need to express disorganizing emotions in a harmless way by transferring them to socially sanctioned activity. This concept has been limited almost entirely to questions of aggression, and will be so here.	1. Frustration of an intention engenders hostility towards the frustrator. 2. This frustration or hostility can be redirected to another activity. 3. This hostility must be expressed to reduce psychic and physiological stress.	1. It is a partial explanation for only the compensatory behavior engendered by hostility. 2. The data show conclusively that sanctioning aggression increases it. 3. The planning of activities to provide outlets for aggression constitutes its sanctioning.
(1) Psychoanalytic	In part by the players repeating in a playful form strongly	1. Stimulating unpleasant experiences in another setting reduces the	

Name	Play Is Caused:	This Explanation Assumes That:	It Can Be Criticized Because:
	unpleasant experiences, thereby reducing their seriousness and allowing their assimilation.	unpleasantness of their residual effects.	
(2) Psychoanalytic	In part by the player during play reversing his role as the passive recipient of strong unpleasant experience, and actively mastering another recipient in a similar way, thus purging the unpleasant effects.	1. Achieving mastery, even in a simulated experience, allows the elimination of the products of unpleasant experience by passing similar experiences on to other beings or objects.	Both 1 and 2 ignore play that is not presumed to be motivated by the need to eliminate the products of strongly unpleasant experiences.
Developmental	By the way in which a child's mind develops. Thus play is caused by the growth of the child's intellect and is conditioned by it. Play occurs when the child can impose on reality his own conceptions and constraints.	1. Play involves the intellect. 2. As a result of play, the intellect increases in complexity. 3. This process in the human can be separated into stages. 4. Children pass through these stages in order.	1. It doesn't account for play *when* and *if* the intellect ceases to develop.
Learning	By the normal processes that produce learning.	1. The child acts to increase the probability of pleasant events. 2. The child acts to decrease the probability of unpleasant events. 3. The environment is a complex of pleasant effects. 4. The environment selects and energizes the play behaviors of its tenants.	1. It doesn't account for behavior in situations where there are no apparent consequences. (However this theory would maintain that there are no such settings.)

Adapted from Ellis, M. J. *Why People Play*, Englewood Cliffs, N.J.: Prentice-Hall, 1973.

Table 8.3 *Modern theories of play*

Name	Play Is Caused:	This Explanation Assumes That:	It Can Be Criticized Because:
Play as arousal-seeking	By the need to generate interactions with the environment or self that elevate arousal (level of interest or stimulation) towards the optimal for the individual.	1. There is a need for optimal arousal. 2. Change in arousal towards optimal is pleasant. 3. The organism learns the behaviors that result in that feeling and vice versa. 4. Stimuli vary in their capacity to arouse. 5. Stimuli that arouse are those involving novelty, complexity, and/or dissonance, i.e., information. 6. The organism will be forced to emit changing behavior and maintain engagement with arousing stimuli.	1. It is very general but it handles questions of work and play equally well. In fact it questions the validity of separating work from play.
Competence/effectance	By a need to reproduce effects in the environment. Such effects demonstrate competence and result in feelings of effectance.	1. Demonstration of competence leads to feelings of effectance. 2. Effectance is pleasant. 3. Effectance increases the probability of tests of competence.	1. For the organism to constantly test whether it can still completely produce an effect seems to require uncertainty as to the outcome. Uncertainty or information seem to be the very attributes of stimuli that are arousing. 2. It can be argued that competence/effectance behavior is a kind of arousal-seeking.

Adapted from Ellis, M. J. *Why People Play*, Englewood Cliffs, N.J.: Prentice-Hall, 1973.

play. The motivation must be intrinsic rather than extrinsic. It is often difficult to judge the nature of the motivation behind a given piece of behavior because extrinsic reinforcers can be very subtle. One obvious case is that where a child seems to be playing but is really aware of the adults watching her and is showing off in the hope of receiving social reinforcements. Parenthetically, it may be noted that behaviors acquired by the methods of behavior modification do not fall into the category of play.

3. *Constraints of reality.* The child's behavior need not reflect reality. Pretend play, fantasies, daydreams, and epistemic (knowledge-seeking) behaviors meet this criterion. The child's play *may* reflect reality, but it need not.

Although "pure" play, as prescribed by these criteria, is probably very rare, these guidelines can be useful in developing play-conducive curricula, environments, and methods. Basically the criteria suggest that we adults and teachers should provide a rich environment and maintain a low profile if we wish play to occur. The child should control the activity, should be allowed to slip in and out of his or her fantasy world.

Many people in early childhood education feel that play may be the single most appropriate activity for young children. Whether the play that actually occurs meets all these criteria may vary considerably from situation to situation. What is important is the fact that play in all its shades is critical for the development and well being of the child.

Play and Creativity

Play can lead to creativity. In fact, some have gone so far as to suggest that playfulness is creativity (Lieberman, 1965, 1966). In a more modern position Ellis (1973) comments:

> *the playful attitude, an indifference to extrinsic payoffs, allows a new response for the person or a new (for that person) transformation of information. Novel engagements with elements in the environment are self-reinforcing and sustain behavior leading to new knowledge. People do not need extrinsic rewards to engage with and learn about the environment.* (p. 121)

Ellis' position is consistent with Piaget's emphasis on the motivating quality of the moderately novel stimulus (see chapter 4).

Ellis also sees playfulness as an inherited trait which aids the individual and the species in adapting to the ever-changing world. One can be taught information and skills that will help one adapt today. But what about the *unknown* that lies in every child's future? It is more difficult to prepare the individual for situations not yet known. Ellis sees playfulness and the associated creativity as traits that will help one adapt to the unknown, and as traits that will allow the species to experiment and create effective ways of adapting to new situations as they arise.

Play, discovery, and creativity are closely related

Play and the Disadvantaged

The report of the 1970 White House Conference on Children pointed out that play may not be possible until basic, primary and acquired drives are met (see also Maslow, 1970). A child who is hungry, sick, cold, insecure, or otherwise uncomfortable will not be able to engage in play. This renders the child doubly disadvantaged—already deprived of basic need satisfaction, she will also be deprived of learning and growing through play.

Handicapped children can suffer in the same manner if suitable provisions for play are not provided. This is particularly true of children who are hospitalized or otherwise institutionalized. The handicapped need the stimulation, involvement, and learning experiences provided by play—preferably in the company of nonhandicapped children.

Special care must be taken in the cases of both handicapped and disadvantaged children to try to overcome these "two strikes" against them. If unable to grow through play and to deal more effectively with a disadvantaged situation or handicaps, the child is further hampered by her unfortunate circumstance, which in turn, precludes future play and growth.

Sociodramatic Play

As an example of the kind of play that can be extremely helpful to the child, we will discuss what Smilansky (1968) calls sociodramatic play. She feels this form of play has particular value in helping the child relate various experiences to one another, and in furthering their understanding of the environment. Sociodramatic play, according to Smilansky, can help the child discover ways to deal with the environment successfully. She observes that disadvantaged children seem to be lacking in this sort of role-play experience, while other children seem to pick it up at home.

There are several criteria which define sociodramatic play. At least two children must interact. Each takes on a make-believe role that imitates some person they have seen. Their actions and words take the place of the actual situations and objects. They must sustain verbal interaction related to the play situation, and must persist in the play episode for at least ten minutes.

For example, two or more children may engage in sociodramatic play centered around a fire station they have visited. The players pretend they are firefighters and have a make-believe truck, hoses, hats, and other equipment. For at least ten minutes they play their roles and create (or recreate) situations related to those seen or described during their trip. They may begin their pretend game by eating breakfast at the station. Then, upon hearing the alarm, they may don their equipment, climb on their truck, and race to the dramatic and successful completion of a firefighting and rescue mission, all within the space of twelve feet.

Smilansky feels children learn about the world through this form of role playing. It helps them think on a more abstract level and assists them in developing problem solving strategies. It also lets the child see things from another person's point of view. Teachers can benefit, too. They can observe the play and detect the children's attitudes toward people and situations in the environments. For example, children playing "school" may give a teacher a unique, if not completely flattering, glimpse into the child's interpretation of teachers, staff, and students. Parents receive the same opportunity when they see their children imitating them in games of "house."

Parenthetically, it should be noted that sociodramatic play is the last of several stages of play. In other words, play develops and evolves through several forms.

Conclusion

Play is an essential part of any effective preschool curriculum. It provides a context in which learning, discovery, and creativity may appear naturally and in a well-motivated manner, free from the debilitating constraints of imposed learning contexts. Play is where "it happens" and the effective curriculum will provide ample opportunity for this critical activity. The more formal subjects, such as science, art, music, mathematics, dance, language, and social studies can all be meshed into a good play context. The absorption of these may well be best when that assimilation occurs within a play, or play-related, situation. Social skills, and a positive self-image, may also be fostered within the realm of play. Clearly, physical development flourishes as well. The clever curriculum planner will use play as a basic learning crucible.

Centers

One of the issues which cannot be avoided in curriculum planning is the fact that what is done, and what is accomplished, in the early educational setting is heavily affected by the physical arrangements of furniture, space, and equipment. Thus curriculum planners must decide not only what they want to do but how to arrange the physical environment such that their curriculum aims will be best served. Even the best of intentions can be thwarted by poor or inappropriate physical arrangements. For example, we can't very well foster artistic activity if we have two easels and three brushes for thirty children located on a windy patio. And we may not have much luck encouraging an interest in biology if we bring in one toad in a small jar and hold it up in front of a room crowded with rows of 3 year olds.

One widely accepted solution to the problem of physical arrangements revolves around the concept of *centers*. In general, the center approach suggests that rooms and yards be divided into areas where particular activities can occur. Thus many schools have centers for books, housekeeping, blocks, music, science, art, and the like. Room dividers, shelves, and other devices can be used to section off the various areas.

Equipment and supplies for each activity can be stored within the appropriate center itself. Many supplies should be within easy reach of the child. If the material is neatly organized and easy to find, the children will adopt this organization; and cleanup will be greatly facilitated.

Centers may not always be rigidly designated; they may vary and change. For example, a particular space may serve several purposes at different times of the day. A "block area" may be a rather large area surrounded by shelves. At certain times block activities may occur here. But at other times, cleared of blocks and trucks, this same space may serve as a music center, a story center, or a nap center complete with cots. At the same time, children need the secure feeling that results from having some degree of certainty about where things will be and when they will be there. Too much change and turmoil can be disrupting (Featherstone, 1974).

Many different sorts of learning can occur in any given area. For eample, even though a book area might be primarily designed to encourage language development, other forms of information (e.g., mathematical, social) might also be acquired here. In other words, centers are flexible, not only in terms of what activity they contain, but in terms of the kinds of learning that occur within them as well.

It is important to think carefully about traffic patterns. Try to arrange major traffic routes such that they go around, rather than through, activity centers. It is terribly frustrating when a child builds a beautiful block structure only to have it tumbled down by a kick or push from a casual passer-by.

The size of an area will affect not only the kinds of activities possible but the numbers of children that can use the center at one time as well. For instance, housekeeping centers might be kept small so that only a few children can participate at once. But block centers might reasonably be larger.

Flexibility can be important when special or new activities are generated. When the size or shape of a center needs to be changed, then room dividers can be shifted to accommodate that need. Sometimes a child may wish to create a space of her own, and furniture that can be rearranged will facilitate the satisfaction of this need to be alone. Very often a blanket over two chairs or a table can be useful as a tent and a solitary place.

It is important to provide areas where "quiet times" can occur. A book area with some comfortable stuffed furniture is an asset—for both children and teachers. An adult-sized chair will be appreciated by the adults. Too often the poor teacher is forgotten, and required to crouch uncomfortably on tiny furniture. Pillows, stuffed animals, and blankets will increase the hominess of this cozy book area.

Safety is, of course, an important consideration in all yard and room arrangements. Teachers must be able to supervise all of the centers adequately. Room dividers should be low enough so the teachers can observe children in adjacent centers.

When planning a system of centers, adequate and appropriate water sources should be available for water-related play and for activities that require cleanup. Buckets of water can be used when water taps are inconvenient. Playing with water can lead to all sorts of cognitive and motor learning, as well as happiness and creativity. Electrical outlets for record players, hotplates, and the like should be located in appropriate areas. Windows and adequate lighting must also be considered. If your school is located near heavy traffic, quiet areas should be located as far away from the source of the noise as possible.

A bright, cheerful environment is more conducive to feelings of

Sometimes a child's need for solitude can be fulfilled . . .

contentment and happiness than is a dull and dreary one. This does not mean that your room needs to be gaudy and cluttered with decorations. However, nicely painted walls, cupboards, and shelves, along with attractive pictures, can help create a pleasant atmosphere. Some of your decorations can be composed of purchased materials. But, by all means, use the children's productions as well.

Structure

One of the issues facing any curriculum planning effort has to do with how structured (Prescott, 1978) the daily events will be. Depending upon their goals, some educators will want to move through a given set of activities, on a particular day, at a prescribed pace, no matter what happens. Others will prefer to be more flexible.

It is easy to sympathize with those who react strongly against a rigid, traditionally structured curriculum where the teacher has a daily plan that must be followed at all costs. However, a curriculum whose structure leads to confusion and even chaos may also be undesirable. A *middle ground* is probably the best solution. Here the teacher does plan the daily classroom and yard environments, does choose and prepare supplies and equipment carefully, and does have a daily schedule in mind. But, at the same time, she or he will try to be flexible in the execution

. . . in unexpected places

of these plans. Even though the teacher has very definite ideas about what types of activities would be best and tries to move toward them, there should be plenty of room for free choices by the children. By allowing the children to interact with the classroom materials, with one another, and with the teacher, the teacher will find that unscheduled but valuable activities will develop. If interesting activities do arise spontaneously, the teacher will adapt the schedule to include them rather than force the children to follow the predetermined schedule. Once these have been completed, the teacher can return to the pursuit of the preplanned schedule.

For example, a teacher may plan a nature walk with the intention of gathering colorful fall leaves. She knows that this activity will provide fresh air, exercise, raw materials for art work, and an opportunity to appreciate nature. However, on this particular day, the city's maintenance crew is repaving the road. They have their heavy equipment in operation —grading the road bed, laying the blacktop, and finishing the new surface. The sights, sounds, and smells capture the children's interest immediately. The teacher who insists on ignoring these fascinating events in pursuit of the planned nature walk is not only missing a *spontaneous* learning situation, but is inviting a minor rebellion. The children will be frustrated, as will the teacher; and movement away from the point of interest will be difficult.

In some cases no plan is made at all ahead of time. All activity is supposed to be of the spontaneous sort. Here dead spots can develop, events can get out of hand, and the teacher may find herself wishing for some plan to fall back on.

Interestingly, the highly structured approach has been emphasized in many traditional elementary, secondary, and college settings. In these schools teachers lecture at the head of the classroom. The learning process is passive rather than active. Everyone receives the same lesson, at the same time, in the same manner. Everyone is assigned the same work in the same text. Everyone is tested, in an identical manner, on the same material. Those who have retained the proper information, pass. Those who haven't, fail. Rote learning (and forgetting) is common. Little attention is given to the relevance of what is being learned, to its interest level, or to its suitability for the developmental stages of the learners.

For a few this unfortunate situation is changing, and the stimulus for this change seems to be coming, at least in part, from the field of early childhood education. Elementary and higher level teachers are beginning to realize that activity centers can facilitate learning. Open education is an alternative for some. Even some colleges and universities are experimenting with educational methods that are neither heavily structured nor overly content-oriented (Jones, 1978). In other words, the older, higher levels of education may learn something from the upstart early childhood education bunch.

General Guidelines

Introduction

Before moving to a consideration of specific areas of curriculum activity in the next chapter, we shall consider a number of general curriculum guidelines that may be helpful, in some situations, especially for the inexperienced teacher. Some of the seminal ideas behind these suggestions have already been discussed; some will be discussed in detail later. In either case, the guidelines are submitted in a spirit of suggestion; you, as a teacher, will undoubtedly apply your own knowledge and revise and supplement them in a creative manner. Obviously, these guidelines represent our own biases. Since programs do vary, these suggestions will not be appropriate in all settings.

Bring Their Life To The Classroom

We have already noted that many preschool educators feel that we should begin the learning process in the context of the child's environment and in the light of what the child already knows. To this end it is advisable

A cozy chair can be an asset . . .
even if it is occasionally used
as a launching pad for airplanes

to gather as much advance information as possible about each child before the semester begins. Through the school files and your initial contacts with parents and child, you can become aware of the home situation (e.g., ages, siblings, occupations, personalities). By familiarizing yourself with the children's neighborhoods, you can determine the general socio-economic range of the clientele and the overall characteristics of their community. Although you will want to expose the children to entirely new information eventually, it is desirable to begin with what they already are and what they already know.

Advance information can help you in various ways. For example, aspects of the community can be incorporated into the class materials and room decorations. If you work in a rural area, pictures of farms, barns, farm machinery, and animals can be placed around the room—even pictures of existing neighborhood buildings and scenes that the child will recognize. Block accessories and books involving familiar subjects and themes should be included. Sociodramatic play that incorporates farm activities and familiar rural roles can be encouraged. The cultivation of crops and the raising of animals will be familiar to the children and will provide a convenient learning context. No matter where you work, you can use the environment as a starting point for the preschool experience. Widespread development can be initiated within the context of these familiar areas of knowledge.

Walks and field trips within the community are valuable. In the process of seeing things they already know something about, they will ask questions, exchange facts, and begin to acquire new information.

Let the children see themselves, their families, and their school as integral parts of the community. Try to involve parents and other community members (young *and* old) in the school's activities. Provide male and female models for the children in a variety of community occupational roles.

Nutrition is important in beginning the preschool experience. If the children are victims of poverty and come to school hungry, you will want to serve breakfast, or at least a snack, as soon as possible. This is accomplished easily in Head Start, and other intervention programs, where substantial amounts are budgeted for nutrition, but may be more difficult in some private schools.

Consideration should be given to the cultural aspects of the food that is served. For example, Mexican-American children will feel most comfortable if menus include tortillas, beans, cheese, and other Mexican foods. Of course, new foods can be introduced gradually, but a representative sample of familiar food will be comforting (and will be eaten). Children can learn about and begin to accept different cultures through their experience with ethnic foods.

By emphasizing a familiar environment, children can be made to feel more comfortable in the strange, new school environment. The children can also gain a sense of self-esteem by realizing that the teacher not only knows about, but values, their personal origins.

As time passes, the children can be encouraged to bring items from home that might be of interest to the others. Sociodramatic play can be made more valuable if items with personal meaning are brought from home. Care must be taken, however, that "show and tell" times do not become "bring and brag" sessions.

Make It a Home Away From Home

For many children, especially those who attend full sessions five days a week, school will be a home away from home. Thus the school should contain the same essential love and security that makes a good home. You will become a kind of second mother or father as well as a teacher (the word "teacher" actually has very little meaning for the very young and inexperienced children). Considering the years of schooling that lie ahead of the children, it is important that their initial school experiences be as pleasant as possible. Try to create a warm, accepting, supportive atmosphere that says, "I love and appreciate you for what you are." Let them know people care about them at school, and will keep them safe. Let them know that you respect them and have confidence in them as learners. Be a good model for them, as you will have a strong influence.

Encourage them to explore and appreciate individual differences and similarities. Mainstream handicapped children into as many activities as possible. Try to help everyone understand that we *all* have strengths and weaknesses.

Recognize their individual efforts. Compliment them on the *ways* that they do things, not just their final products. Encourage them to try all activities, but don't be pushy. Provide many experiences where successes (however small) are guaranteed.

Give the children, and yourself, time to adjust to the new environment, and to each other. Don't expect too much at first. Concentrate on building trust and friendship in an easygoing, accepting manner. Hold the ones that need closeness and affection, but only when they are ready for it.

Use Centers

As we have already noted, many educators recommend that rooms and yards be arranged in centers. A few additional comments are in order. In these centers open ended, or raw, materials such as paint, sand, blocks, and water are often better than toys and games that can only be used in one way. When initiating the use of a center, begin with simple activities and then gradually add accessories to the raw materials. Include materials that are familiar to the children, and use activities and materials that the children suggest. Provide the best materials and equipment possible, but don't forget the *Beautiful Junk* (Warner and Quill, 1977) that is so useful and inexpensive. Broken toys need to be removed until repaired, unless they can be fixed on the spot.

Let Them Play

As we noted in the previous section, perhaps the most widely recommended learning context is that of play. If children are to play, we must: allow them freedom of choice and control; ensure that they are able to play for the sake of playing, and not for any extrinsic rewards; be sure they are able to break away from the constraints of reality if they wish (e.g., in pretend or fantasy play). Encourage creativity by allowing the children to play with, manipulate, and explore new materials. Let them experiment freely.

Use a Flexible Schedule

There are several additional hints that can be useful in connection with our discussion of flexible scheduling. For example, allow relatively large chunks of time for each activity. Sometimes it takes children quite a while to become involved in a task, and the frustration that results when an interesting effort is left unfinished is well documented. Provide a number of alternative activities so that those children with short attention spans, or "bad days" in progress, can move from choice to choice. Help the children extend their attention spans (Blank, 1973). Give them the opportunity to play alone and in groups. Provide quiet as well as active times. Encourage both large and small motor development. Be sure the children know well ahead of time that an activity change is approaching.

Some consistency in your scheduling is desirable. Consistency and predictability help the children feel secure; they need to know, more or less, what to expect. For example, you might want to keep the *sequence* of daily events constant while varying the amount of time given to each activity on any given day.

Let the children know well in advance when changes are coming. Provide plenty of time for transitions (e.g., cleanup, dressing, washing, toileting) so that these times do not cause anxiety or confusion. Don't rush them through meals and snacks. Keep the general atmosphere calm and relaxed. An easygoing pace helps everyone feel comfortable.

Eventually, you may want to discuss making schedules and rules with the children themselves. Rules are easier to accept and follow if one has contributed to their formulation.

Let Them Talk

We have a good deal to say about language skills in the next chapter. For now, it is enough to realize that verbal activity should be encouraged

A science center can be a fascinating place . . .

to learn about the world

whenever possible. Allow the children to express themselves freely as they work, play, and eat. Encourage them to talk to you, to the other children, and to themselves. Help them develop social skill through language (e.g., talking is better than fighting). Answer their questions as quickly as possible. Keep your answers both simple and honest. Provide verbal labels and simple definitions for things they don't know.

Help them verbalize instances of concepts such as color, shapes, sizes, texture, and numbers. Give them opportunities to sort and classify objects into different categories. Verbalize concepts of time, space, volume, and weight for them: "We sang songs *before* we ate." "Sharon is sitting *next to* Jason." "You have *more* milk left." "Sheila is *heavier* than Beth." Do your best to understand their ways of thinking—to evaluate their stages of cognitive development.

Their interest in language can be stimulated if you will read to them and tell stories. Let them "read" and tell stories to you. Label things within the classroom with printed signs. Write their names on their work. Familiarize them with letters, words, and simple sentences that have personal meaning for them (Kohl, 1973). Write down some of the things they say, then show them the writing and read it aloud.

As we turn to the next chapter, where we discuss specific content areas, keep in mind that these guidelines are appropriate in the case of each activity area.

9

Curriculum Development: Activity Areas

Most preschool educators agree there are several activities, or subject areas, that are desirable and appropriate for early childhood education curricula. Some of them correspond to the subjects found in higher levels of education, such as language skills, mathematics, and science. Others, such as water-related and block activities are essentially unique to the early childhood education setting, and form a context in which many forms of learning and discovery can occur. Although we shall discuss several of these activities individually, the reader should keep in mind that they often overlap and intermingle. For example, if the teacher is introducing the class to the rudiments of botany by growing and pollenating tomato plants on the windowsill, the rudiments of mathematics may also be introduced as the children count and compare the numbers of plants, blossoms, and fruits. Similarly, language skills will be exercised and strengthened in this same context. In other words, the potential for learning on many different levels is enormous in any activity that captures and holds the child's interest. Nevertheless, it is instructive to consider several activity areas separately.

Reading and Writing Readiness

Reading: When and How?

We live in an era in which there is great emphasis on success. Many see education as the key to that success. Children who are "high achievers" in school may well expect a greater degree of eventual success than children who are "low achievers." Basic reading and writing skills are usually considered to be essential for success in both school and later life. Hence, it is not surprising that reading and writing are stressed in the preschool experience (Clay, 1975; Wassermann, 1978). But even though the last decade has seen rapid growth in the emphasis upon cognitive development, there are those who still remind us that emotional, social, and physical growth are at least as important, and inextricably intertwined with, cognitive growth.

There is a controversy that surrounds the development of reading and writing skill which breaks down into two questions. First, should reading and writing be taught at a specified age level? The concern here is whether all children are prepared to learn these skills at the same age or whether they vary in terms of their readiness. The facts seem to point to variable readiness. Although children in this country do begin formal reading instruction in public school at the age of 6, Durkin (1970) sees this as a convention rather than a policy based on established facts about child development. Those in a position to observe young children can testify to the fact that some children can read as early as 3 years, with no formal school instruction, while others have trouble mastering basic reading and writing skills well into their teens. Some are clearly ready to begin reading and writing at 4, 5, or 6, while others have problems in the first-grade that seem to multiply as they grow older. And finally, Durkin points out that overall readiness to read revolves around an interaction between child and program.

The second issue within the overall controversy concerning the acquisition of reading and writing skills has to do with *how* we go about teaching them. Should we begin with the alphabet and phonetics? Should we teach one child at a time or in groups? Should the whole class be formally instructed at the same time?

What Does It Take?

Perhaps a reasonable way to begin our search for answers to the questions *when* and *how* reading and writing should be taught is to inquire about prerequisite capabilities and conditions. Clearly, extremely young children cannot be expected to read, no matter how brilliant they may be eventually. They just have not developed to the point that they can master the complex tasks involved. Similarly, there are essential emotional requirements for reading and writing. A terrified, hungry child will be unlikely to do well in any instructional setting.

Very fine visual and auditory discriminations are necessary for both reading and writing. And yet even newborns appear able to perceive many of the minute differences among written letters and words, and the tiny differences in phonetic sounds, that are necessary for reading. Thus, it seems that it is cognitive rather than purely perceptual development that must be awaited before the child is ready to read (Smith, 1977). For example, to read and write, the child must be able to understand symbols and their functions. *Written* letters, words, and numerals stand for, or are symbols for, *spoken* letters, words, and numbers. And both written and spoken language elements are symbols for objects, events, and concepts. Thus, it is not surprising that many first-graders have trouble mastering elementary reading skills. Most are still learning the meanings of spoken words, and building their basic spoken vocabularies.

Suddenly, they are asked to deal with a new symbolic system, that of written language, which they must relate to spoken language and to the referent world of objects and events.

Writing requires fairly sophisticated levels of eye/hand coordination. Drawing (writing) curved and straight lines in complex combinations is simply not possible at a very early age. The child must also learn that reading and writing proceed from left to right and from top to bottom.

The list of prerequisites goes on. For example, the child's memory capacity must be developed to the point where spoken and written symbols, as well as their referents, can be encoded, organized, stored, and retrieved effectively. A burden is placed on the child's attention span as well; this is sometimes short, even when applied to games, toys, and play. If a child is hungry, nervous, tired, unhappy or anxious, learning anything is difficult. The performance of children who lack confidence in themselves as learners may suffer from fear of failure, particularly in this area where they have been told learning is so important.

Obviously physical handicaps (visual and auditory problems in particular) will add to their difficulties, and their perception of themselves as learners. A lack of motivation can also hamper efforts to learn to read and write.

In other words, children need to develop physically, and need to gain considerable experience, before they will be "ready" to learn to read and write. They need a foundation of prereading and prewriting skills upon which to build actual reading and writing capabilities.

Readiness Activities

One solution to the problem of the need for prereading and prewriting skills has been the development of readiness activities. These have been taken by many to be the most important contribution that the preschool experience can make to the overall learning process. They concentrate on the development and exercise of the skills and capabilities that must be present *before* the acquisition of full-blown reading and writing activities can occur.

Many preschool educators feel that, if a youngster can be given a readiness to read and write by the time he or she is through with the preschool years, then that is sufficient progress. Of course, there are exceptions; some children are ready before or after others. But, in general, a readiness to read is seen as a reasonable goal in the preschool years, with actual reading and writing instruction being delayed until first grade.

Readiness activities are quite varied. Obviously *talking* is an activity that is critical to the eventual acquisition of reading skills. Since we have discussed language development in detail in chapter 3, and have outlined some activities that foster speech (Engel, 1968; Tough, 1974), we will concentrate here on activities more directly related to reading and writing activities. But remember that speech precedes reading and writing, and anything that fosters speech will eventually assist in the acquisition of reading and writing skills.

We have pointed out that fine visual and auditory discriminations, as well as good eye/hand coordination, are essential for reading and writing. Any number of activities within your classroom will foster these important areas of development. Painting, working with clay, cooking, woodworking, puzzle assembly, and the use of any small manipulative materials will provide practice in making fine visual and spatial discriminations, as well as an opportunity for verbal activity. Certain types of matching and classification games will help develop visual discrimination ability, as well as concepts such as shape, color, and size. For instance, the teacher can remark, "Susan has on a red skirt. Who else is wearing something red?" Or, on a more complex level, the teacher can say, "I have a small green ball of clay. Who can make a large green ball of clay?" Number games are helpful, too. "How many children are in the block area?" "How many buttons are on Jim's shirt?"

Without doubt, reading to children helps them become more ready to read themselves. They see the obvious value of being able to read. They develop the abilities to sit, to listen, and to follow a story line. They are exposed to new words and ideas. They can be shown that one reads from left to right and from top to bottom by pointing to the words that are being read from time to time. The teacher can give them "left to right practice" by discussing features of pictures from left to right.

Poetry and songs give children experiences with sounds and tones. Rhyme games help develop auditory discrimination abilities. For example, you may say, "Book rhymes with cook. What other word rhymes with cook?" Taping children's voices and playing them back helps them hear sounds and tones. Writing down their words and stories (pointing out that you are writing from left to right) helps them see that printed words have meaning for them, and not just for adults.

Children often learn their own name as their first written word. This is especially true if teachers and parents label their art work, their clothing, their lunch boxes, their cubbies, and their chairs.

It is also a good idea to inform the parents of the type of printing you are using. Ask them to use the same style so the child will not be confused by seeing their names written in too many different forms. Give the parents a copy of the standard printed alphabet so they can brush up on their printing skills once again. As adults we all develop our own writing styles over the years. To a child, these idiosyncratic chicken scratches can be terribly confusing. It is best to relearn standard printing skills when working with young children.

Other reading readiness activities include following directions, putting pictures in cartoon sequence, finishing a sentence or story, retelling a story, dramatizing a story, and imitating sounds.

Eventually, through varied exposure to language, children will write letters. In a most natural manner they will begin to recognize letters and words that have become familiar to them. This type of progress is a sure sign that they are becoming ready to read and write. In fact, they have already begun.

Kohl, in his book *Reading, How To*, (1973), makes a number of points that are germane to the issue of reading readiness. First, learning about reading and writing should take place in a noncompetitive atmosphere. Reading may be thought of as something that everyone can and will learn—just as almost everyone learns to walk, talk, and ride a bike. Second, the *value* of reading and writing needs to be emphasized. After all, once a young child can read, a whole new world opens up. She can read books, nursery rhymes, signs, labels, letters, notes, record covers, posters, bumper stickers, invitations, and T.V. schedules. As she progresses she will be able to absorb game rules and hobby project instructions. The equally obvious advantages of writing should also be made clear to the child. Once the child understands that being able to write will allow her to send notes and messages to friends, to write her name on her possessions, and to create stories, rhymes and jokes, her motivation to learn will be enhanced.

Third, Kohl points out that children can help one another learn to read and write, even though they themselves may not yet be completely skilled. For example, a 4 year old may not know how to read, but she may be able to show her younger friend or sibling how to hold a book right side up, and how to turn the pages in the correct order. A child who recognizes her own name may show it to another child and say the letters aloud while pointing to them. Naturally, the more the child knows, the more he or she will be able to pass along.

Fourth, Kohl recommends that reading begin with subjects that are familiar to, of interest to, and valued by the child. Don't begin with African prehistory. Names, street signs, familiar labels, and favorite books can all be sources for learning letters and words. Ask the children what words they would like to learn. Play word games with them, such as rhyming exercises, and labeling games. Write down and show them their own words—what they have just said as well as what others have said. As the children grow, jokes will become favorites and can be written down for them. The words to their favorite songs can be written and given to them. Either serious or amusing printed labels can be made up for objects in the room and yard.

Fifth, Kohl points out that printing sets, stencils, label makers, typewriters, and tape recorders are all valuable adjuncts to the process of learning to read and write. Magazines and newspapers can be cut up and used to create phrases, stories, or poems.

In other words, even though Kohl's book is directed primarily toward older pupils, he has some valuable suggestions for the preschool teacher. Keep it light and noncompetitive, emphasize the value of reading, let them know that there is plenty of time to learn, and that, just as they gradually learned to walk and talk, they will gradually learn to read and write. Take your time and let them take theirs. As we will see, there are many opportunities to encourage reading readiness embedded in almost all other early educational activities.

How to Read a Story

Schickedanz (1978) underscores the importance of reading stories to children. She adopts, in contrast to a strict reinforcement interpretation of learning, a cognitive view of the learning process. Specifically, she feels that the child is an active processor of information. The child is assumed to build, construct and organize information about reading in an active, highly self-motivated manner. To obtain information about reading the child must have close contact with actual reading experiences, and not just with tangentially related readiness activities, or with drill. Having a story read, according to Schickedanz, provides the necessary contact with actual reading events.

Schickendanz points out that, if we are to maximize the child's useful contact with reading, we must do several things when reading:

1. *To be most effective, story reading should allow the child to see the print. Reading to a group deprives the child of this essential experience with the relationships between written and spoken language.*
2. *Allowing the child to turn the pages may help the child sequence the information and match a rote memory of the story with the printed words in the book.*
3. *The same story should be read many times; it is only through repeated presentations that the child can begin to match a verbal memory of the story with the printed story.*
4. *At least occasionally, the reader should point out printed words that are being spoken.*
5. *Children need free access to the stories when they are not being read. This allows them to practice matching their "by heart" memory of the story with the printed material.*
6. *The teacher should encourage the children to compose stories*

and should write down and read these stories. These provide helpful exercises in matching printed and spoken words.

In general, Schickedanz is suggesting that, instead of teaching reading, we should provide experiences that allow the child to discover, construct, and order the essential elements of reading.

Books

Clearly, if one is to stimulate reading and writing readiness, one must have books readily available. We have already emphasized the importance of a comfortable and attractive book center that invites children to spend time there. But what can be said about the actual books contained in this center? Books need to be arranged attractively on shelves, and should be within easy sight and reach of the children. Avoid stacking books on a table, placing them in a corner, or keeping them out of view. Think of them as flowers and the children as bees. Also, children will have more regard for books, and take good care of them, if the teacher does too.

The books themselves are best if they are sturdy and attractive, inside and out. Colored pictures that follow and illustrate the story clearly are best. The younger the children, the better it is to have many pictures. Books with thick pages are desirable for the very young. Pages that tear easily can be very discouraging, even frightening to some children.

We have already discussed the fact that the books should be nonsexist and multiracial in chapter 3. It is also generally accepted that most of the books should be concerned with objects and events that are real, and are familiar to, the children. At this point books are best when they help children understand things they have already experienced or been exposed to. Books that introduce completely new and unfamiliar subjects might best be kept at a minimum. If a child can relate to the contents of a book, then he will be more interested in, and pleased by, that book. For example, very young children love books about babies, children, mothers, fathers, and familiar animals. Book covers displaying cars, boats, aircraft, mailpersons, doctors, grocery stores, and toys also seem to attract children.

Although some fairy tales and fantasy stories can be included, particularly as the children mature, others might be excluded. *Snow White and the Seven Dwarfs, Little Red Riding Hood, Jack and the Beanstalk,* and *The Three Little Pigs* have been traditional favorites for children over the years. But now many preschool educators feel that stories containing witches, giants, wolves and other frightening creatures and events are inappropriate for very young children. Evil characters and situations of this sort can frighten young children quite badly as they are not yet fully capable of distinguishing between reality and fantasy. Even though you tell them monsters and the like don't exist, they are not quite sure they are safe from such apparitions. The *Pied Piper*, by taking all the children away from their parents, can become a frightening symbol to the young child. As the children mature, and become more able to distinguish reality from make believe, you can use your judgment as to which of these "oldies but baddies" you want to include. There is enormous value in imagination, so some fantasy has a place in the early education library.

Books of poems, rhymes, riddles, and jokes should be included in your book center. And the inventive teacher will supplement the book collection with original stories told to eager listeners—keeping them appropriate to the ages and experience of the children.

It is difficult to read or tell stories to large groups of children. Interest wanders. Groups of from two to five are best. By limiting the size of the group, each child can see, hear, and not be distracted by restless, disinterested children who are forced to sit through the story. Be sure to speak clearly and slowly, keeping in mind that the listeners are still learning the language as well as the story. Use emphasis and tone to make the meaning of the story clear and interesting; avoid a boring monotone. Be sure your books contain language that is not over their heads.

Your collection of books must not be stagnant; it needs to be supplemented and varied as much as possible. Although there will be favorites that remain, new books can be obtained in a number of ways. Your school may have a library budget. Public libraries, and librarians, are helpful in maintaining a good collection of books. Encourage the children to bring books from home from time to time. If possible the children should be allowed to check out books on an overnight basis. Ask the children what sorts of books they would like included in your library.

Mathematical Readiness

Introduction

The concept of readiness seems to guide preschool curricula with respect to mathematics just as it does within the realms of reading and writing. Here again the emphasis is not so much upon teaching ordinary mathematical skills but rather upon *preparing* the child for what she or he will encounter upon entering elementary school.

When one hears the words arithmetic, mathematics, or math, one is inclined to think of children learning to read and write numerals and solving increasingly difficult problems. We think of addition, subtraction, multiplication, and division. But before a child can engage in these rather advanced mathematical activities, she or he must have acquired a great deal of background that is not obvious. Just as there are many areas of readiness that have to be developed before a child can read, so, too, the child must be ready for mathematical training. It is the development of this readiness that is emphasized in the preschool experience, rather than the acquisition of what we normally think of as mathematical skills.

Understanding Relationships

No one truly understands how thinking in mathematical terms comes about: the process is just too complex. But there are certain things that the teacher can watch for, and encourage, that seem to aid the overall process of development. Specifically, the teacher can help the child understand a wide range of relationships that are essential for later mathematical thinking. If the child understands these relationships then she or he will be ready to handle more formal modes of quantification and measurement.

For example, *distance* relationships must be understood before a child can be expected to use exacting methods of measurement. Rudimentary concepts such as *closer, farther, near, long,* and *short* must be understood before inches, kilometers, and light years will make any sense at all. The children will discover some distance relationships in the course of their play, but the teacher can refine their understanding by discussing and introducing instances of these concepts into the classroom setting.

Weight relationships are essential for a state of mathematical readiness. "Is this ball of clay *heavier* or *lighter* than this one?" Once the general concept of weight and weight differences is established, then quantification of these differences can begin to be understood (e.g., pound, gram).

Fractional relationships are also essential for a later understanding of more complex mathematical manipulations. "Do you want a *whole* glass of milk or a *half* a glass of milk?" "We shall each have a *piece* of cake."

An understanding of rudimentary *size* relationships can be encouraged by pointing out size differences and using appropriate vocabulary. "Elephants are big and rabbits are small." "We need a *larger* person to be able to lift this table."

We don't expect preschool children to be able to quantify *volume* in an exact manner—such as measuring out a quarter of a cup of milk exactly. But they can be introduced to general volume concepts by using vocabulary that includes words like *more, less, quart, cup,* and *teaspoon.*

Neither do we expect preschool children to be able to tell *time* with any accuracy. But a readiness for this essential activity can be encouraged by using vocabulary that expresses temporal relationships. "Did Billy come in *before* or *after* you today?" "That was a long time, wasn't it?" "We will be taking naps very *soon* now." By using the words *second, minute, hour, day, week, month* and *year*, without requiring or expecting a true understanding of these complex temporal units, we will at least be providing essential vocabulary. If the child grasps that days are longer than hours, and hours are longer than minutes, he will be on his way toward a full understanding of time.

The rudiments of *temperature* measurement can also be instilled at an early age by demonstrating and labeling *hotter, colder, warmer,* and *cooler,* as well as talking about the four seasons. Before degrees of temperature can be comprehended in later educational levels, these simple basic temperature relationships must be understood.

Monetary values and the uses of money can be introduced, although it takes a long time for all those dimes, nickels and pennies to be sorted out. Introduce concepts like *buy, sell, trade, pay,* and *rent.* Talk about the monetary denominations, naming them and labeling their values, but don't expect them to be understood clearly at an early age.

An understanding of *shape,* and a readiness to understand later specific forms of geometry such as equilateral triangles and the like, can be developed by using and talking about *circles, squares, triangles, thin, fat, tall, short* and *round.*

Once the child understands these general dimensions (distance, weight, fraction, size, volume, time, temperature, money), exacting measurement of these dimensions can be more easily understood at a later time. Inches, pounds, sevenths, liters, milliseconds, eons, degrees, and mils will all come later. What we want to do is prepare the child for an understanding of these systems of unit measurement by ensuring that he comprehends the underlying dimension to which units are applied.

Numbers and Counting

Finally, and perhaps most importantly, any program of mathematical readiness will want to deal with *numbers* and *counting.* The ultimate goal is the ability to think in terms of, and manipulate, numbers without reference to objects or things—to think abstractly in terms of, and about, numbers. But that skill is a long time in coming. And it does not develop in an abstract context. It occurs in a *concrete* context where the child learns the concept of *oneness, twoness, threeness,* and so on, by dealing with groups of one, two, and three known objects in the immediate environment. "How many eyes do you have?" "How many mommies do you have?" Have the child touch each object with her finger when she first begins to count. Identify things in terms of number: "Now, we have two tricycles here." "Please bring me those two boxes over there on the table." Play games that require the use of numbers. "Who knows how many blocks I have here?" But don't be surprised if the acquisition of single number concepts takes a long time. Don't make the acquisition of number concepts a competitive one. Allow the children to move at their own rate.

The ability to count by rote does not imply an understanding of number concepts. A child may be able to count to ten, but may not truly understand what a group of three is. It is not bad to have children learn to count by rote. It is just not enough.

As Piaget has pointed out, a child may well think that six pieces of candy spread out on a table are more than six pieces closely spaced on the same table. There seems to be some kind of confusion between number and space here. But through play and interaction with concrete objects, the child will eventually grasp the essentials of numbering.

By the time children enter elementary school, they may have a fairly good grasp of oneness, twoness, and so on. But most children will still be tied to concrete manipulations of objects, and will not be ready to deal with number concepts on an abstract level. As Piaget points out, many children entering elementary school are simply not ready to deal with abstract concepts. This suggests that at least some children should be allowed to continue their play and discovery activities, and their inter- actions with objects and situations beyond the preschool years.

Helpful Vocabulary

When one thinks about it for a moment, the vocabulary that is essential to a state of mathematical readiness is extensive. The words in table 9.1 represent just some of the concepts, objects, and relationships that can facilitate the later learning of formal mathematical manipulations.

Discovery and Time

Many of the child's own actions and discoveries provide training in mathe- matical readiness. Whoever decides how many chairs are needed to build a fort is learning to count, as well as estimate size and shape. A child dividing clay into equal pieces for herself and a companion is experiencing sameness, division, and number. Following a recipe is an excellent exer- cise, with the teacher leading the way. Setting the table for snacks pro- vides experience in counting and in understanding one-to-one relationships (one utensil of each kind for each place setting). Serving and dishing out food can be valuable.

Piaget has emphasized the fact that it takes children a long time

Table 9.1   *Useful words*

count	before	take	front	warm	nickel
measure	after	divide	top	day	dime
small	front	piece	seasons	week	buy
big	next	whole	temperatures	month	sell
many	behind	double	times	year	pay
some	middle	half	soon	teaspoon	charge
much	together	alike	later	pounds	multiply
all	how many	circle	some	ounces	subtract
group	pairs	square	sometime	weigh	change
bunch	partners	triangle	some day	weight	cost
light	add	full	cups	scales	trade
tall	thin	empty	pints	balance	cool
short	fat	into	quarts	even	dollar
heavy	wide	out of	hot	uneven	angle
first	narrow	inside	cold	penny	into

to be able to classify objects according to shape, size, or color. The ability to *reverse* mental procedures, so essential in mathematical thinking, is also slow in coming. The same is true with most mathematical readiness requirements. The children need time to manipulate and experiment with many relationships in a familiar environment, in their own way, and at their own speed.

Piaget also points out that a child's definition of words begins in a very personalized way and that it takes time for the young child to arrive at a personal definition that concurs with the standard definition. In chapter 3, we saw that modern linguistic theory holds that the child makes hypotheses about linguistic reality, and then proceeds to test those hypotheses. All of this takes time and requires conversation with adults. This time-consuming process must also occur in connection with mathematical vocabulary and concepts. False starts and trial-and-error efforts are to be expected.

Preschool programs vary enormously in terms of the amount of emphasis they place on mathematics and/or mathematical readiness. Some programs reflect the opinion that readiness should be achieved through play, interaction with children and teachers, and discovery. These programs do not emphasize written numbers. Other programs introduce and encourage written numbers in a variety of ways—in puzzles, games, books, and so on. Recognition of written numbers is a goal for some programs, while others stress writing of numbers as well.

One bit of advice would be to adopt an approach that considers the individual child. If the child wants to learn to write numbers then perhaps the writing of numbers would be a good idea. But don't expect too much in any case. If the child seems to have difficulty then you may be ahead of his level of readiness. Take it "slow and easy," for if he believes that learning mathematical material occurs slowly, and is taken in relatively simple steps, then that attitude will transfer to future learning situations.

Science: Physical and Social

Positive Attitudes

Because of their enormous curiosity about the world around them, pre-school children can easily be caught up in an appreciation of both physical and social sciences (Roche, 1977). You will find that your high school and college courses in subjects like biology, anatomy, chemistry, physics, geography, ecology, nutrition, and sociology will help you a great deal in fostering a positive, constructive attitude toward scientific inquiry. Paren-thetically, each time you take an additional science course, try casting the incoming information in terms that a preschooler might understand, because you will have to translate adult scientific language for them. Your attitude toward science will color and shape their attitudes. Your general approach to problem solving, to experimentation, and to information-seeking will influence them. You need to be not only enthusiastic, but as rigorous as you can be in dealing with scientific matters.

Sometimes teachers find it necessary to temper or control their feelings in certain areas, because the children will take on negative atti-tudes if they observe them in their teachers. For example, a certain pre-school teacher may not find any redeeming qualities within the world of insects. His reaction to this segment of the animal kingdom is to kill, maim, and/or escape. Caterpillars, spiders, flies, beetles, and the like, may be repugnant to him, and yet he knows his attitude is emotional and far from the sort of interested, rational approach demanded by scientific logic. He knows there is much to learn about, and from, these creatures. So he must watch himself, and be careful not to pass on his overly emo-tional reactions to the children. Of course, harmful insects can be iden-tified as such, but there are many harmless insects that can be the object of careful, first-hand scientific scrutiny.

The weather provides another area where negative attitudes can be passed along if the teacher is not careful. Many people, including tele-vision and radio weather forecasters, seem to feel that any weather that is not hot and sunny is bad. And how sad this is, because weather changes can be among the most exciting events in our day-to-day lives. One teacher was heard to say, "Oh dear, it's windy today. That means we'll all be crazy." It is interesting to speculate about what a 4 year old would make of that statement. Many people hate cloudy days and almost automatically go into a depression over the prospect of a "gloomy," rainy day. These negative attitudes and reactions can be transmitted to, and adopted by, the children. So be careful if you have strong weather preferences. Try to pass along the interesting, exciting aspects of all weather situations. Explain, as best you can, the reasons behind all weather conditions. It is far better for children to hear about the causes of rain, snow, hail, clouds, and wind, about adjustments that animals make to weather, and about how plants are affected by weather than it is for them to hear a careless comment about how hateful the rain is.

Physical Experiments

Providing children with scientific information by *telling* them is not enough. If they are to understand the concepts involved, the children must be given the opportunity to engage in rudimentary experimentation, and should be allowed to deal with scientific concerns on a concrete level.

There are many areas where good solid, if introductory, experimentation may begin. For example, rather than telling children that some large things weigh less than certain small objects, a teacher can say, "Let's find out which things weigh the most." She can let the children scurry about the school finding objects to weigh and compare. The teacher can help them by keeping a record, or making a chart, of the noted weights. Similar *actions* on the part of the children can help the children discover what kinds of things magnets will attract, and which objects will float. The informed teacher can help them speculate about causes. Melting ice or snow, and then boiling off the water, will demonstrate how water can assume solid, liquid, and gaseous forms. *Seeing* and *doing* these sorts of things appear to be much more meaningful than merely hearing about them.

Children love to watch things grow—plants as well as animals. A garden, or some potted plants in a window, provide a great deal of information about growth. Pets such as rabbits, guinea pigs, mice, frogs, goats and the like can be included whenever possible. Of course, pets, like plants, put an extra burden on the teacher, but they are well worth it. Trips to farms and zoos are engaging and informative, particularly for your children who are fascinated by babies, growth, and their own place in the world. Maintenance of an ecological balance and the dangers of pollution are good topics for study also.

Good equipment can greatly facilitate physical experimentation. Certain pieces of equipment are particularly valuable, including thermometers, windmills, kites, scales, pulleys, microscopes, telescopes, sundials, measuring cups, rulers, compasses, yardsticks, magnets, siphons, straws, and, of course, a full array of kitchen implements. But even more important than the best equipment is the teacher who has the knack of involving children in action and experimentation of their own.

Of course, the teacher will have to consider how much guidance to provide in each situation. Some "experiments" can be dangerous if totally unsupervised. The obvious areas of concern are those that involve the use of stoves, hot plates, and breakable glass.

The teacher can help the children verbalize what they are doing, and assist them in perceiving effects—but only when verbalization from the children is lacking. In general, the teacher can let the children experiment and think about causes and effects on their own. Verbal explanations will not necessarily be of much help. The child's own actions and manipulations are the important factors here. The teacher's role might best be limited to making a few suggestions, to asking a few questions, and to ensuring the safety of the children.

Social Information

In learning about the world, children begin to question the meaning and nature of social relationships. For example, they will want to know about families, marriages, friendships, and animal relationships as well. Although experiments are difficult to conduct in this area, the teacher can provide straightforward, honest answers to their questions.

As the children you teach may come from a variety of family backgrounds, it is important to avoid implying, even inadvertently, that the two-parent family is the best or "most normal" one. Many children live with single parents, in extended families, or with adoptive parents. Each family style should be studied and accepted. Let the children know that all family situations have their advantages. Don't denigrate any lifestyle.

The subjects of birth, death, and the general life cycle will come up. Questions need to be answered immediately and honestly. Avoiding these subjects will only make them more mysterious, frightening, and allow them to take on an unfortunate taboo-like quality. Ask the children how they feel, and what they know, about these subjects. By estimating what they do know, the task of correcting misconceptions and supplying new information will be simplified.

Art

The Art Center

The art center is the scene of great fun, creative expression, and learning. It is also an area where self-confidence and self-esteem can grow. But organization and careful planning are essential for a successful art center.

The center must allow freedom of choice. It should contain child-sized tables, chairs, and easels. There should be room to work on the floor. Newspapers or plastic can be used to keep at least some of the paint and glue off the floor. A constantly replenished stack of newspapers can be handy for both teacher and child. The art center is best placed near windows for natural lighting. Materials need to be neatly organized and readily available to the children.

Older children may be able to take care of their own needs quite readily. They can help you mix paint, make playdough, and can put on their own protective clothing. They can sometimes help with the younger children. But with the younger ones, you will want to set up their materials and help them don their smocks and aprons.

Of course, the more materials the better. It can be quite frustrating for the young child, encountering art activity for the first time, to have to wait for an easel, a spot at the table, or certain materials.

As the children gain experience, they will discover new ways of combining old materials, and creating new effects with familiar substances. As they expand their modes of expression, they will experience a growing sense of competence. For example, they will enjoy inventing new colors by mixing old ones, by adding food coloring, and by thickening or thinning existing colors.

Large Is Good

Because of their initial lack of fine motor development, preschool children often use large muscles to do what smaller muscles will do later. Large sweeping strokes with paint brushes will be common. Because of this, they need *large* working spaces, and large pieces of paper. Remember this rule of thumb: the smaller the child, the larger the piece of paper. Sometimes we see small children struggling with small pieces of paper. This situation often comes about because the school has collected scrap papers of various sizes, colors, and shapes; and the teachers give them to the children with the intention of providing variety. But these small pieces are more appropriate for older children, or for the creation of collages.

Freedom and Progress

Another point that can't be stressed too heavily is that the children must be allowed to use the materials in *their* own way, and at their own speed. Let the children create what they want to create; don't try to mold their art to any preconceived ideas of what it should be. Their art need not be required to conform to any standards—whether it's painting, clay molding, pasting, chalk drawing, or pen drawing. Let them do what they want to do. This includes allowing them to sit, stand, walk, lie down, and talk as they work.

Helen Buckley's poem makes the point:

THE LITTLE BOY

Once a little boy went to school.
He was quite a little boy,
And it was quite a big school.
But when the little boy
Found that he could go to his room
By walking right in from the door outside,
He was happy,
And the school did not seem quite so big any more.

One morning,
When the little boy had been in school awhile,
The teacher said,
"Today we are going to make a picture."
"Good!" thought the little boy.
He liked to make pictures.
He could make all kinds:
Lions and tigers,
Chickens and cows,
Trains and boats—
And he took out his box of crayons
And began to draw.

But the teacher said: "Wait!
It is not time to begin!"
And she waited until everyone looked ready.

"Now," said the teacher,
"We are going to make flowers."
"Good!" thought the little boy,
He liked to make flowers
And he began to make beautiful ones
With his pink and orange and blue crayons.

But the teacher said, "Wait!
And I will show you how."
And she drew a flower on the blackboard.
It was red, with a green stem.
"There," said the teacher,
"Now you may begin."

The little boy looked at the teacher's flower.
Then he looked at his own flower.
He liked his flower better than the teacher's.
But he did not say this,
He just turned his paper over
And made a flower like the teacher's.
It was red, with a green stem.

On another day,
When the little boy had opened
The door from the outside all by himself,
The teacher said:
"Today we are going to make something with clay."
"Good!" thought the little boy,
He liked clay.
He could make all kinds of things with clay:
Snakes and snowmen,
Elephants and mice,
Cars and trucks—
And he began to pull and pinch
His ball of clay.
But the teacher said:
"Wait! It is not time to begin!"
And she waited until everyone looked ready.

"Now," said the teacher.
"We are going to make a dish."
"Good!" thought the little boy,
He liked to make dishes,
And he began to make some
That were all shapes and sizes.

But the teacher said, "Wait!"
And I will show you how."
And she showed everyone how to make
One deep dish.
"There," said the teacher,
"Now you may begin."

The little boy looked at the teacher's dish.
Then he looked at his own.
He liked his dishes better than the teacher's
But he did not say this.
He just rolled his clay into a big ball again.
It was a deep dish.

And pretty soon
The little boy learned to wait,
And to watch,
And to make things just like the teacher.
And pretty soon
He didn't make things of his own anymore.

Then it happened
That the little boy and his family
Moved to another house,
In another city,
And the little boy
Had to go to another school.
This school was even bigger
Than his other one,
And there was no door from the outside
Into his room.
He had to go up some big steps,
And walk down a long hall
To get to his room.

And the very first day
He was there,
The teacher said,
"Today, we are going to make a picture
"Good!" thought the little boy.
And waited for the teacher
To tell him what to do.
But the teacher didn't say anything.
She just walked around the room.

When she came to the little boy
She said, "Don't you want to make a picture?"
"Yes," said the little boy,
"What are we going to make?"
"I don't know until you make it," said the teacher.
"How shall I make it?" asked the little boy.
"Why, any way you like," said the teacher.
"And any color?" asked the little boy.
"Any color," said the teacher.
"If everyone made the same picture,
And used the same colors,
How would I know who made what,
And which was which?"

"I don't know," said the little boy.
And he began to make pink and orange and blue flowers.

He liked the new school
Even if it didn't have a door
Right in from the outside.

Reprinted from *School Arts* vol. 61 no. 2, October 1961, with permission of the author.

Young children do not begin their long series of creations with representational art. The first recognizable horse, person, or tree will be a long time in coming. In fact, at the very beginning children don't seem particularly concerned with the outcome of their efforts at all. They lock in on, and love, the *process* of testing and manipulating the medium, whatever it is. For example, they will have a fine old time just applying paint to a large sheet of clean white paper. They will scribble in their initial, fascinated moments with a new set of crayons. They will try out the medium, and see what it can do for them.

The next step seems to be one where they begin to recognize objects in what they have created *after* they have created it. They don't plan ahead at this stage. And as they continue, say, painting, they will see different things in the same painting—first an elephant, then a building, and so on. Of course, they eventually begin to decide, in advance, what they will create; but this stage can require considerable growth and experience. And it takes even longer before the representational qualities of their works become distinct. Of course, some work remains abstract, as it should, at any age.

According to interpretations of Piaget's research by Kellogg (1969) and Lansing (1966), children pass through several stages in their artistic endeavors. In general, children scribble first (from 2 to 3 years), then begin to draw some outline shapes (3 to 4), and finally advance to some representational art between 4 and 7. The child must develop concepts of size, shape, time, and space, as well as an understanding of color and an advanced level of physical skill in handling a given medium, before much representational art is possible. Of course, this is not to say that representational art is a necessary goal; art is self-expression and has value in any form and at any stage.

Reinforcers?

Although we don't want children to engage in artistic activities for nothing more than social reinforcers, it is usually difficult to pass up the chance to do a little ego building by praising their work. This is particularly true with children who seem to lack confidence.

Paint smocks can be made from adults' old shirts. Cut off long sleeves, put them on backwards, and button the second button from the top. Most children love them

Because we want to help the children feel good about themselves and their achievements, a moderate level of social reinforcement would seem to be acceptable. Your comments about their artistic creations should show that you are interested in, and recognize, what they have done. "I like the way you pasted that piece of yarn on your picture, Sheila." "What a nice red painting, Adam!" "I think you really liked the clay today, Wendy." "Look at all the colors you used in your painting, Gregg. What a colorful picture."

We can also ask questions. "I like your picture. Would you like to tell me about the colors you used?" But we should avoid asking things like, "What is it, Lisa?" and, "What did you make, Richie?" If we do ask questions such as these, we run the risk that the child may not know what she made, or that she will feel a sense of failure because her clearly recognizable cow drew a total blank from the teacher. She may think her work is not good if you can't recognize what it is.

Some Artistic Activities

Even though children should explore on their own, there are certain things you can do to increase the chances of certain discoveries being made. For example, if we put out only yellow and blue paint on a particular day, and then withdraw into the background, we may very well hear a cry of, "It's green!" I painted blue in my yellow and now it's green!" On the other hand, don't be surprised if the discovery is not made either. You may want to call this color mix to their attention if it occurs in their work, but it means more when a child discovers it.

Certain accessories and mediums can be introduced as you attempt to diversify artistic activity. For example, fingerpainting is always a great favorite. Cookie cutters, sponges, rollers, and potato slices can be dipped into paint and pressed on paper, yielding many wonderful print effects. Dramatic effects can also be obtained by dropping paint-soaked pieces of string onto paper. Halloween, Thanksgiving, Christmas, Easter, Valentine's Day, and Cinco de Mayo, can be marked by providing appropriate colors and materials. Large precut pumpkins, turkeys, Santas, bunnies, and hearts can serve as surfaces for painting, pasting, and making collages. Older children can cut their own shapes. Many educators feel that predrawn pictures, such as those found in coloring books, are not nearly as appropriate as shapes and figures created by the children themselves.

It goes almost without saying that a great deal of learning can go on within the context of artistic activity. Colors, shapes, sizes, numbers, and spatial and temporal relationships, are all integral parts of the artistic experience. "*Green* is on the *top*." "*First*, I used *blue*." "I made *two big* lines and *one small* one."

Collages provide a great deal of instructive fun. Again, experiences with colors, shapes, positions, numbers, and sizes are common. Classification and sorting go on in the construction of a collage. Deciding which pieces go where, and when, can be a stimulating challenge. Which things go together? What is on top? What is next to the little blue piece? How many green ones are there? Collages can involve almost anything—paper, toothpicks, wood scraps, buttons, pictures from magazines, cloth, plastic, leather, cellophane, and tissue. The potential for satisfying creation is almost limitless. For the toddler, one piece of paper pasted to another is a terrific result. For the kindergarten child the creation will be more complex, involving, perhaps, wood scraps nailed into the shape of a wonderful castle, or genuine monster, and painted in vivid colors. Anything goes.

Playdough is a favorite, and children can help make it. The recipe for playdough is: 4 cups flour, 2 cups salt, 4 tablespoons vegetable oil, 5 drops vegetable coloring. Mix with enough water to produce desired consistency. It can be prepared in any color, and its texture can be varied too. Completed objects can be dried and taken home. Playdough can be stored in a plastic bag in the refrigerator and used on successive days. Playing with playdough sometimes appears to soothe young children. It can be a major prop in dramatic play. Cooking a playdough dinner is a great challenge. Spaghetti and meatballs, hamburgers, hot dogs, pizza, tortillas, bagels, and egg foo yong are easily made from playdough. Rolling pins, cookie cutters, pie pans, and silverware add to the dinner possibilities.

Tie and dye, mobiles, plaster of Paris, pottery, costumes, and and endless number of activities, can be added at the art center. The children can be allowed to paint with their feet. Shaving cream can be used for finger painting. Paper bag puppets can be made and used. Macaroni can be strung on string and/or glued to paper.

In a publication entitled *Responding to Individual Needs in Head Start* (1974), the federal government points out that the following kinds of "beautiful junk" can be very useful in supplementing your classroom supplies. Parents can be asked to contribute what they have. (Caution should be exercised in using certain of these materials, such as sequins, with very small children.)

beads	food coloring	cans	sand
sequins	aluminum foil	nails	rope
shells	cardboard	wood scraps	frames
crayons	magazines	bottle tops	old clocks
wheels	newspaper	plastic bottles	old jewelry
keys	margarine	sponges	seeds
plastic spoons	containers	hair rollers	burlap
sandpaper	empty boxes	baby-food jars	shoe laces
paste	paper towels	cotton	balls
crates	old ribbons	drinking straws	string
carpet scraps	cookie-box trays	popsicle sticks	toothpicks
funnels	egg boxes	wallpaper	corks
cups	plastic film	buttons	clothes hangers
squirt bottles	spools	floor tiles	pine cones
pill containers	containers that	screening	artificial
thread spools	slide open	tongue	flowers
old socks	wrapping paper	depressors	birch bark
paper bags	cereal boxes	yarn	clothespins
dried beans	milk or juice	candles	old telephones
cloth	containers	zippers	eggbeaters

Cooking

Cooking is one of those activities that, while being fun in and of itself, helps the children in a number of areas of development. For example, while chattering happily in the cooking area, the children are honing any number of language skills. In addition, they are improving their grasp of number skills through such activities as counting and measuring.

Their fine motor coordination is helped by cooking activities. Their understanding of some of the more basic physical principles can be enhanced as well. For example, they can observe, first hand, the processes of boiling, evaporation, condensation, expansion and contraction, and so on.

The Head Start booklet mentioned in the previous section lists the following simple, entertaining, and useful cooking activities appropriate for many handicapped as well as nonhandicapped children.

1. *Sandwiches* Spreading and cutting are good developmental skills. Children love making sandwiches.
2. *Chocolate milk* Pouring, measuring and stirring are all skills that can be developed through making this.
3. *Jello* Helps understanding of transformation. Changes from warm liquid to solid right before your eyes. Making it involves careful pouring which helps coordination.
4. *Pudding* Quick and easy. Stirring the pudding over a low flame brings about a gradual change in its consistency.
5. *Frozen juices* Need to be shaken and children like doing it.
6. *Popcorn* Easy to make and children like the popping noise of the kernels. The kernels are changed from small, yellow dried seeds to large, white popped corn.
7. *Lemonade* Squeezing lemons to make lemon juice helps to develop manual strength and coordination.
8. *Fruit salad* Children enjoy cutting up all kinds of fruit and mixing them together. This activity helps your class learn the names of different goods as well as how to cut various fruits.
9. *Butter* Heavy cream in a jar with lid and shake.
10. *Whipped cream* Just shake heavy cream in a jar or use an egg beater with some heavy cream and add a little sugar, maybe some vanilla and you have a great topping for cakes, jello, practically anything. Shaking involves grasping, wrist and/or arm movements. Egg beaters also require wrist movements and grasping.
11. *Applesauce* Peel and core apples, cut them up and cover them with water. Your class will enjoy cutting the apples, stirring the sauce and eating the end result of their work. Through this activity they will also improve their manual skills.
12. *Tuna fish salad* An easy, fast cold dish. It involves cutting up vegetables (i.e., celery), measuring and mixing.
13. *Hard-boiled eggs* Easy to make. Children enjoy learning the difference between liquid and solid eggs. Peeling these eggs also helps enhance manual coordination.
14. *Vegetable soup* Beef or chicken broth with cut-vegetables; children learn the names of vegetables that they eat. It's fun to introduce new foods through class cooking projects.

15. *Scrambled eggs* Children like cracking the eggs, pouring, stirring and eating them.
16. *Complex cooking activities* The following are a little more complex than the others. Because of this, these activities require the teacher to take a more active role and provide more equipment. These recipes involve measuring, pouring, mixing, kneading (bread), cookie cutters (Christmas cookies), and decorating.
    Birthday cakes
    Jimmies (sprinkles, shots)—for decorating cakes and cookies
    Cookie dough
    Bread dough
    Christmas cookies
    French toast
    Pancakes

Music and Dance

Musical Abilities Develop

Music and dance are forms of self-expression, avenues for creativity, sources of great fun, and contexts in which learning can occur. Cognitive, physical, social, and emotional development may be enhanced through these activities. Many educators feel that music and dance should be included in the daily preschool schedule.

It seems clear that the development of musical abilities depends upon a combination of maturation and experience. While studies have shown that infants will listen to music, and sometimes attempt to vocalize musical intervals within the first year, it is not until several additional years have passed that the child can carry a tune, or move to the rhythm of music (Ostwald, 1973; Michel, 1973; Shuter, 1968).

McDonald and Ramsey (1978) summarize the sequential stages of tuneful singing in the following manner:

> *First young children attempt to use the range of their speaking voices to reproduce songs. Next, they might exhibit inconsistent melodic direction. Gradually gaining vocal control, they may become accurate directionally, but inaccurate in interval reproduction. The hoped-for final stage is the accurate reproduction of a melody within a given tonality.* (p. 28)

It has also been found that young children have less trouble copying *pitch* if a voice rather than a piano is the model (Hermanson, 1972). Many of the songs taught to young children should be limited in *range* from approximately B_3 to A_4. Surprisingly, your children have less trouble reproducing low notes than high ones (Boardman, 1967; Smith, 1970).

Musical Activities

Because musical ability develops, and does not spring forth fully formed, the child must be given the chance to explore, experiment, and discover on his own. Singing and dancing are not simple activities. They require the ability to discriminate differences in tone, volume, and rhythm. Lyrics must be mastered as well. And bodily movements, which we shall consider in detail in the next section, must be under control and finely tuned.

A special music and dance center within the school is a good idea. Instruments, records, songbooks, and dance accessories such as costumes and scarves should be permanently accessible to the children. A full-length mirror is also helpful.

Special song and dance times can be established. But spontaneous activities of this sort should be allowed, and encouraged. Children need to be able to choose as to whether or not they wish to participate. Most children enjoy music and, even if they do not wish to participate, they will often enjoy watching and listening.

During a musical session the teacher might play a piano or a guitar while the children join in with bells, cymbals, drums, xylophones, recorders, and small guitars or ukeleles. Various homemade instruments can supplement the collection of instruments. For example, oatmeal boxes can be used as drums, and rubber bands around an uncovered shoe box will serve as a guitar.

Many children enjoy body movements that imitate animals, other people, or machinery such as planes, cars, and steam shovels. It is important to encourage this form of expression, with or without musical accompaniment.

Of course, learning and singing songs remains one of the favorites of both children and teachers, but the resourceful teacher will gather together a list of alternative musical activities. It is recommended that these activities allow the children to experiment with singing, with instruments, and with dance. Let them explore at their own rate, and in their own way. Don't push, but be supportive and encouraging. Let them ease into music and dance if they are hesitant.

Music and Emotion

The teacher can use music to explore feelings and moods. For example, she can play a particular piece of music and say, "This kind of music sounds very cheerful, and makes one feel happy and bouncy. Now I

Music sets the mood

will play another record and you can tell me, or show me, how it sounds to you."

Because music can affect mood, it can be employed in a variety of useful ways. For instance, after a period of active, exhausting outdoor play, children often enjoy listening to quiet music in comfortable surroundings. Slow, settled dancing can sometimes help wind them down and relax them. Soft music and lullabies at naptime will often soothe restless children. On the other hand, a march, or some rock music, can perk up an otherwise listless, bored group and inspire them to active, expressive movements and dance.

McDonald (1970) suggests that music may hold an important position in the emotional well-being of some children. Certain songs, or types of songs, can become associated with the child's home life. They may be classically conditioned stimuli for any number of emotional reactions. When these songs are heard at school, they may elicit many of the feelings experienced at home. A child's favorite song may help bridge the gap between home and school, and may help the child feel relaxed in the new school environment. Teachers might do well to ask children and parents about "family favorites," and incorporate them into the school routine.

Motor Development

Large Muscles

Children need to exercise their bodies, and to improve their coordination. Both indoor and outdoor activities can promote physical development. But in either case, the children need *time, space,* and *freedom* to become active, exuberant, boisterous, funny, interested, and stimulated. In other words, they need room to *play physically*.

Running, jumping, hopping, skipping, balancing, and climbing comprise a major portion of children's activity. Any equipment, or form of encouragement, that will facilitate these activities should be considered Bouncing balls, riding bikes, moving carts and wagons about, digging, and sweeping are also appropriate activities. As the children play they will be acquiring a vocabulary appropriate to their actions: up, down,

Jumping is a pleasurable way to aid large muscle development

over, under, around, through, first, last, high, low, fast, slow, short, long, and so on.

Obviously, swings, slides, jungle jims, teeter-totters, tricycles, and wagons are enjoyed by children. But certain materials, not designed as toys, can also be enjoyed. For example, old tires are fun and can be used for rolling, for sandboxes, and as swings. Empty appliance cartons serve very nicely as houses, tents, caves, hideouts, and puppet stages. A simple piece of rope can be good for a lot of laughs when captured by a child's imagination; ropes can be jumped, swung on, and used as pulleys —not to mention the fact that they are useful in binding Martians and other assorted bad guys.

Humankind's fascination with the rubber ball extends into the preschool setting. Pleasure, exercise, and learning all accrue as balls are bounced, thrown, hit, kicked, batted, caught, chased, carried, held, released, and lost. Empty milk cartons can serve as bowling pins in an improvised bowling alley. Tagball and dodgeball are fun. Tossing balls (and bean bags) into baskets can be entertaining.

Trees can be an asset. A facsimile of a car, boat, or aircraft big enough to enter and "operate" is always popular. Balancing beams angled upward from the ground can increase skill and self-confidence.

And the old, standard games still hold their edge. Ring-around-the-rosie, follow the leader, tag, hide and seek, London bridges, and Simon says are all fascinating. Don't forget hula hoops. In other words, anything that will encourage normal, active physical play is worthwhile.

Small Muscles

Just as the large muscles need exercise, so do the small. Eye/hand coordination will improve as the child engages in fine motor activities. Again, vocabulary, concepts, and self-confidence will grow with each accomplishment.

Legos, tinkertoys, Lincoln logs, and erector sets provide the children with the opportunity to build structures, and to engage in dramatic play inspired by the finished products. Puzzles and pegboards are good, as is much of the Montessori equipment.

Fine motor development leads to the acquisition of certain skills that are not only useful to the child but a source of pride as well. For example, being able to lace and and tie one's shoes, button and unbutton clothing, open and close zippers, and work snaps can be an enormous source of self-confidence.

Additional equipment suitable for fine motor development includes dominoes, telephones, jack-in-the-boxes, nuts and bolts, and screwdrivers. Stringing large beads can be a challenge. Rubber bands or string can be strung in designs between nails fixed to a board.

Simply holding *scissors can be difficult when you are 2*

Of course, fine motor development is encouraged by many of the preschool activities not specifically designed for that purpose. Still, special attention should be given to this essential developmental ingredient.

Mud, Sand, Water, and Snow

We turn now to some activity areas that do *not* parallel the subjects normally taught at higher educational levels. These areas of activity are unique to the preschool level. Activities involving mud, sand, water and snow are not usually found beyond the preschool level, but in the early education setting these resources can be invaluable. When children interact with these materials they are amused, and they learn. In a sense, these materials provide an entertaining context in which all the traditional curriculum subjects—reading, mathematics, science, art, social behavior, physical development—can be explored and exercised.

In a book that suggested the title of this section, Dorothy Hill has outlined many of the valuable qualities of these elements, and has provided helpful suggestions concerning their use. If the weather is hot, then sand, mud, and water play can proceed freely outdoors. Children can strip down to their underwear, use a bathing suit, or wear their extra set of clothes kept by the school. Boots or baggies over shoes will help if, for some reason, they can't go barefooted—which is the preferred mode. Snow activities require, of course, warm clothing and an awareness by the teacher of when the children are becoming too cold and wet to continue safely and happily.

Sand, mud, and water play in the yard do not require extensive equipment. A sandbox, a large tire filled with sand, or a muddy area, and some water provide all that is needed. If water faucets and hoses are not close by, then water can be brought to the area in buckets and plastic containers.

As we have noted before, it is best to begin with simple activities, and build complexity as the children gain experience in manipulating the raw materials. Don't overwhelm them with accessories, or games, or suggestions at first. Just let them get in there and find out what mud, sand, and water will do. A variety of containers, and other utensils can be introduced gradually. For water play, plastic squeeze bottles, basters, tubes, straws, funnels, and large paint brushes all add to the fun and excitement. Measuring cups, scales, and magnets can be used, too. All supplies should be stored nearby and within easy reach of the children—except for materials that are to be introduced at a later time. These should be kept out of sight until the appropriate moment of introduction.

Snow conveniently covers the entire yard. Hence snow activities are not restricted to one spot, and can occur over the entire area. Observations about the way snow changes the appearance of the environment will be made. Questions about what snow is, and how it is formed, will need to be answered. Like sand and mud, snow can be dug, contained, formed, shaped, and measured. In addition, it can be melted! Basic scientific facts, as well as language skills and social interaction will all be involved in these elemental forms of play.

Time and space are needed for these activities. Leave plenty of time for mud, sand, water and snow play. It often takes children quite a while to become enmeshed in these forms of educational play. Some children dive right in (actually, as well as figuratively). But others ease themselves in more cautiously.

If given enough time, children's thinking can develop in many ways while they play with these materials. They experience the processes of testing hypotheses and solving problems as they experiment with these materials. They explore concepts of weight, volume, size, shape, time, force, gravity, equality, evaporation, melting, and number. Social and emotional development takes place in this play context. Large and small muscles are exercised. Coordination is improved. Although the children should be left pretty much to their own devices, the teacher can help by occasionally asking questions or making observations that might lead to further discovery and useful vocabulary.

Cleanup should be a normal part of the activity. Tell the children, well in advance, when playtime is almost over. Children and accessories should be cleaned. Hoses can be helpful in this cleanup process with mud and sand. Well organized and labeled storage areas facilitate the straightening process. If the teacher is cheerful and helpful during the cleanup period, the children will be, too. Leave plenty of time for cleanup.

Dressing and undressing takes more time than one would imagine, too. Although many children will eventually learn to dress themselves, there are always buttons, snaps, zippers, and the like, that need the teacher's attention.

Sand, mud, snow, and water activities can occur inside, too. It's a little more difficult, but it can be done. Papers or plastic sheets on the floor make the eventual cleanup process a little easier. Plastic tubs or buckets can be used to bring the material inside. Special trough-like tables can be constructed to hold sand, water, snow, flour, rice, beans or any other material that is suitable for manipulation, if it can be contained. Small plastic portable swimming pools are also suitable as indoor containers.

Water play can be enhanced by the addition of bubble solutions and accessories. Hill recommends the following recipe: ¾ cup liquid soap, ¼ cup glycerine or sugar, 2 quarts of water. Young children need to be reminded to blow out instead of sucking in. Bubbles can be made to float on water or to sit in styrofoam cups. Bubbles can be blown through pipes, straws, and bent wires dipped in the solution.

Soap films of various shapes can be made by inserting a pipe cleaner all the way inside a plastic straw, and by bending the straw. The pipe cleaner inside will hold the straw in any shape, such as a triangle or square. When dipped in the solution the resulting, colorful film will amuse the children.

Even rainy days can be a source of water play if the children are appropriately dressed. Dripping eaves, rushing surface water, drops on roofs, and occasional rainbows, introduce the children to new wonders. The processes of erosion can be introduced within this context. Remember, time, materials, accessories, and the freedom to use them are essential.

Block Activities

Although the activity might seem to be a simple one and may not correspond to more traditional conceptions of curriculum activity, block building is a complex, useful activity. By playing with blocks the child can benefit physically, emotionally, socially, and cognitively.

When playing amid a scattering of blocks, the child comes into contact with any number of mathematical, scientific, verbal, social, and physical elements. Blocks also provide children with the opportunity to recreate, and dramatize important aspects of their lives. Social relationships often form and evolve while children are playing with blocks. Successful block play can lead to an increase in self-esteem, too.

There are several useful hints concerning block play:

1. Be sure the children have plenty of *time* and *space* for their block activities. Hirsch (1974) actually recommends that a full one-third of the classroom area be given over to block building. Of course, the same area can be used for other activities at alternate times. Hirsch also feels that the chances for interrelated dramatic play will be increased if the block area is located near the science and/or housekeeping areas.
2. Traffic patterns should go around and not through the block area.
3. Simple rules should be developed with the children. "Blocks may not be thrown. It's too dangerous." Respect for one another's creations should be fostered, too.
4. Encourage the children to build away from one another, and away from the block shelf. In this manner their constructions will be less likely to be knocked over.
5. Blocks should be stored in such a way that they are easy to see and easy to reach. Keep shelves low and arrange the blocks so that they are neither too sloppy nor too neat.
6. Let the children use the blocks in their own way. Give them freedom and encourage them to experiment and create.

Teaching children to carry blocks away from the block shelf can reduce the chances of confusion and possible conflict in the block area itself

7. Add accessories slowly as the children seem ready for them. Save special or more complex accessories for later in the year, or for older children. Accessories may be purchased, made, or donated. Useful accessories include people and animal figures, cars and trucks, miniature furniture, trains, larger blocks, pieces of wood, boats, and planes. A growing variety of blocks is always good. Wood and plastic are among the safest and most durable materials for block accessories. Of course, children can be encouraged to pretend, or use symbolic accessories, too. They can pretend that a rectangular block is a car, or that a cylinder is a human.

8. After being alerted in advance that cleanup time is approaching, the children should put the blocks away. Even children that haven't been playing with the blocks can be encouraged (not forced) to help. In this way, some children that have not felt comfortable in the block

area can be introduced to it—and it avoids penalizing those children who make large, complex structures. Teachers should help, too. They can hand things to the children, or suggest how many should be carried at once (number concept).

The process of sorting the blocks onto the shelves involves classification, seriation of size, shape, number, and spatial relationships. Some children will enjoy loading blocks into wagons, or onto chairs, and then pulling or pushing them to the shelves.

9. The children will probably begin playing with blocks in a parallel fashion, but they will eventually begin to work and play together. They will copy one another, and learn from each other. The teacher can be helpful in encouraging their work, and in stimulating social interaction. "Your building is very strong, Mike." "You and Janet made a nice home, Billy."

10. As the children build more complex and representational structures, dramatic play will become an important block area activity. The teacher should support this activity, and reward it warmly.

11. Language skills should be encouraged in the block area. For example, reusable labels can be made to attach to structures when requested. Older children will, in the process of becoming ready to read, learn to recognize the words on these labels, and may actually make some of their own. And finally, the children should be encouraged to talk while they play with blocks. It should be a noisy, happy, chattering area.

10

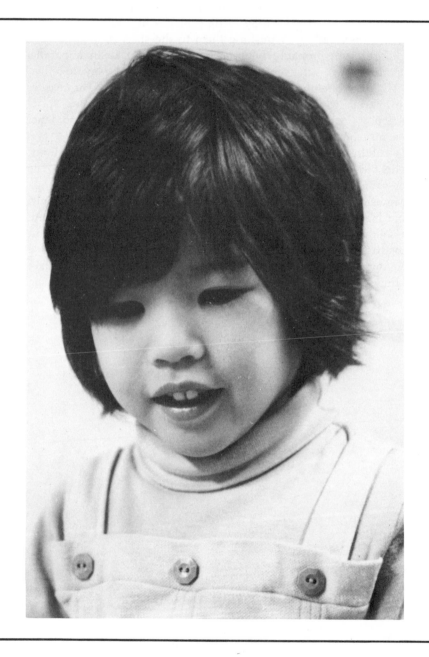

Working with Parents
and Other Caretakers

People entering the field of early childhood education often say they are doing so because they "like working with kids." This is, of course, a very sound reason. But the tendency to focus upon the children underlines the fact that many of us are unaware of, and unprepared for, one of the most important aspects of our chosen career . . . working with *adults*. The last two decades have produced a growing feeling that working with parents and other caretakers close to the children is one of the most important functions of the early childhood educator (Bronfenbrenner, 1970 and 1974; Karnes and Zehrbach, 1977; Lazar et al., 1977; and Levenstein, 1977.) We can't just ignore those large people who so often bring the children in each morning.

For many teachers, working with the parents may turn out to be their most challenging function. For others it can be the most unexpected and, sometimes, the most frightening and difficult. But with a positive attitude, and good preparation, it can be done. Just as working effectively with children is learned, so is dealing with parents. This too takes time, study, thought, preparation, and experience. But it's not a *totally* different ballgame. After all, children and adults are all humans, and they can be thought of as individuals at different stages in the same process of development. Both are subject to many of the same principles. For example, children and adults both respond to rewards, even though they might be different rewards. Some rewards appear to work with both adults and children. While a paycheck may mean nothing to a child and a chance to play in the sandbox may mean little to an adult, praise and affection can be effective rewards with both grown-ups and youngsters.

Thus there are certain principles which apply to both children and adults. On the other hand, there are some additional elements which must be mastered if the instructor is to deal effectively with parents. It is these ways of dealing with parents and other caretakers that are the focus of this chapter.

Who Are All These Adults?

In the past, a teacher could usually assume that children, unless in rather rare circumstances, were raised by their mother and father. Generally, the father played the usual role of financial provider, while the mother took care of the home and children. These assumptions can no longer be made. Today, families assume many forms. Now childcare is often provided by a variety of people in both traditional and non-traditional roles.

Two-Parent Families

Many children are still being raised in families where both parents are present, and, in some of these, the parents still assume the traditional roles described above. However, even though there are still two adults in these families, the male and female roles are changing. Increasing numbers of mothers are preparing for, or are involved in, careers of their own. Many fathers are choosing to assume a larger part of the childcare role. Some are even exchanging roles with the mother entirely.

Increasing numbers of children have parents who both work either part- or full-time. This means that for a significant portion of the day the child is being cared for by someone other than the parents, such as relatives, housekeepers, or sitters. Many are attending some sort of early education facility. Others are being cared for in home-based intervention programs by teachers, tutors, and researchers in connection with the parents and families (Levenstein, 1977; Schaefer and Aaronson, 1977; Nimnicht, Arango, and Adcock, 1977). In other words, children are being cared for in an increasingly varied number of circumstances even when living with both parents.

In order to understand a child, the teacher needs to be aware of the kinds of roles the parents have assumed. It is only with this understanding that the teacher can provide support for, and work toward common goals with, the parents.

New Roles for Parents and Other Caretakers

But there have also been changes in childcare that are more dramatic than those within the two parent setting (Hamilton, 1977; Levine, 1976). Our society has seen many changes in the past decade or two that have led to some new and unexpected roles for many. Children today often grow up under circumstances that simply did not exist when many of their teachers were children.

For example, although divorce is not new, more and more children now have parents who are divorced. In divorce cases mothers have traditionally been given custody of the children. Fathers have visitation rights, provide child support, and sometimes pay alimony. So the children live with their mothers, but visit or are visited by their fathers. For those children at the positive end of the continuum, these visits are on a regular basis, are pleasant and rewarding, and everyone gains from them. The children and their fathers see and enjoy each other. The mother is refreshed with some time off from her childcare role. But for other families, divorce might be highly traumatic. The parents may continue to fight. The children are caught in the middle and manipulated by the parents. Still other children are separated by time and distance from one parent, whom they rarely see. Few divorces are totally bad or all good. Like everything else in life, they have mixed consequences. By understanding the particular nature of a given divorce, the sensitive teacher can go a long way toward easing the youngster's adjustment to that divorce. And by helping the child, the teacher can aid the parent as well.

There have been a few recent cases in which full or joint custody of the children has been given to the father. Sometimes this is because the father is more able to support the family financially; the mother may never have had a job and may need and want to go back to school or begin training for a new job or career. Sometimes the father is judged to be more suited to children than the mother. For whatever the reason, more children are now living with divorced fathers than ever before.

As our divorce rate rises, there is a corresponding increase in the number of new relationships that the divorced parents, and consequently the children, become involved in. The phrases, "My Dad's girlfriend . . ." or "My Mom's boyfriend . . ." are becoming more and more common in the vocabulary of young children. The options open to the divorced parent are many. They may date a variety of new people, become involved seriously with one individual but live apart, live with someone, remarry, or experiment with any number of new living arrangements. And as the divorced parent goes, so goes the child of that parent. It is sometimes very helpful to know about the living arrangements of the divorced parents of your students.

More and more children are becoming involved with new people who are themselves playing new and unfamiliar roles. Think about all those who, without children of their own, become involved with divorcees, and hence with their children. These new friends and lovers of divorced people suddenly find themselves in positions that are, as yet, poorly defined and poorly understood. They are placed in direct and immediate contact with children who are not their own. And yet these children will directly influence them, and, in turn, be influenced by them. In some cases, two divorced people, each with children from a previous marriage, get together in relationships that involve themselves and all the children. "My boyfriend's kids" or "my girlfriend's kids" are also becoming more commonly used phrases. Obviously, an endless variety of positive and negative situations can evolve in these circumstances. The teacher must be sensitive to these complexities in an effort to understand and support both child and parent.

Very young children have enough trouble keeping traditional relationships straight, such as aunts, uncles, cousins, and grandparents. Many of these newer relationships don't even have names. (Does a 34 year old woman call the 40 year old man she has been living with for years her "boyfriend"?) They don't fit into familiar categories. As far as the adults are concerned, this uniqueness may be advantageous and appealing. But the young child may need help in understanding and living comfortably with these new arrangements.

The parent who does not have custody of a child may enjoy an invitation to visit the school from time to time. He or she may want to confer with the teacher, or to attend parent groups or meetings. The teacher must be sensitive to whether or not such an invitation will create conflict with the parent who has custody.

Some of the people with whom divorced parents are involved might also enjoy accompanying the parents to various school activities. By doing so, they may gain valuable insight and feel supported. Equally important, the teacher will have the opportunity to meet and become at least superficially acquainted with people who may be deeply involved with the students. However, when the divorced parents are at odds, the teacher must consider the pros and cons of these visits carefully. The idea may have to be abandoned, at least temporarily.

There are additional people who may form important caretaker relationships with the children of married, divorced, widowed, or single parents. They include babysitters, housekeepers, servants, older siblings, and other relatives. From time to time, the teacher may wish to extend an invitation to these individuals to visit the school. Again, the parents should first be consulted.

Another childcare role that has become more common in recent years is that of the single, never-married parent. These individuals are usually female; but, more recently, some males have taken on this role. Rather than enter into an unwanted marriage or give up a child born out of wedlock, an increasing number of single parents are opting to keep the child and raise it alone. Similarly, single individuals occasionally adopt a child. Besides the normal problems that parents face, these parents are often confronted with disapproval from their family and friends. Such social pressures can be a strong, negative force in their lives.

Other parental situations that need to be considered and understood by the teacher are those of step-parents, foster parents, and adoptive parents. Some of these, too, will be married, while others will be single. And all will require understanding and support from the teacher.

Of course, there are many other factors such as socioeconomic status, bilingualism, cultural differences, and job transfers that must be taken into consideration when dealing with parents. But the various roles just outlined form one of the important, and sometimes most perplexing, sets of elements in the instructors' efforts to aid both child and parent. It behooves the teacher to try to find out what kind of home situation each child faces so his or her action and thought may be understood in that context. Of course, this is not always an easy task, sometimes not even possible. Without an extensive building of trust this sort of information may be difficult to obtain.

The Stresses and Strains of Parenthood

What is involved in parenthood? Fulfillment? Responsibility? Hard work? Fun? Surprise? Anxiety? Excitement? Growth? Stress? Guilt? Satisfaction? Pride? Probably these and more. If you are a parent, you have a headstart in being able to identify with the parents of the children you teach. You have already experienced some of the joys and sorrows of parenthood. We need not explain.

However, we assume that many of you have not had children of your own. Hence a few comments concerning the mental and physical states of parenthood seem in order. If you have some idea of what the parent is experiencing, it will be easier for you to identify, to communicate, and to empathize with her or him.

Let's try to get some idea of what has led up to the day the mother or father leads, say, the little 3 year old into school for the first time. For the past several years, this parent has been through some intense and novel experiences centered around that youngster. The emotional involvement has been heavy. What have they been through together, and what are they experiencing as they stand on the threshold of your classroom?

In this section we focus upon some of the pressures, fears, problems, and anxieties that are common during early parenthood. Two points must be made very clear. First, by emphasizing some of the negative aspects of early parenthood, we do not mean to imply that parenthood is an essentially unpleasant experience. On the contrary, it goes without saying that parenthood can be one of the most rewarding and satisfying of all human experiences. We underline some negative aspects of parenthood because of our purpose . . . to prepare the early childhood educator for problem cases and to sensitize the teacher to the number and type of difficulties that the parents may be experiencing. Second, we cannot provide a full psychological profile of all the difficulties that can and have occurred during early parenthood. We have selected a few of what appear to us to be some of the more common problems that arise.

The very first thing to realize is that the parent or parents standing before the teacher with this small child in tow probably went into parenthood knowing next to nothing about what it would involve. Essentially, they have had to go it alone in their struggle toward this day. In spite of their cheery faces, the teacher must realize that behind them lies a long period of experimentation, discovery, frustration, and growth.

In our society, people are not well-prepared ahead of time for the reality of parenthood. The responsibility of raising and educating their children is not explained before it is upon them. Although many people in our society grow up expecting and wanting to have children "someday," little is done in terms of readying them and their partners for what parenthood entails. Just as no-one ever seems to tell young people what marriage is truly like (an admittedly difficult task), no-one seems to give young people a realistic view of parenthood, or any training for it. This is the subject of a great deal of recent thought and research (Lally and Honig, 1977; Lane, 1975.)

Because no-one has made them aware of the need, few young people take classes in childcare, parenting skills, or the like. In fact, few classes such as these are offered in high schools or junior high schools. And unless one is majoring in a related field, few college students want to waste the units taking child development courses.

Until very recently boys and men in our culture have not been encouraged to take an interest in childcare. In fact, as we have seen in chapter 5, boys don't play with dolls, and have been systematically barred from most activities that might prepare them for their roles as future fathers. Hence, as new fathers, they are often nonplussed or aloof with respect to this very live newcomer.

Females, on the other hand, have been educated to want marriage and children. But even they have not been realistically prepared for motherhood. They have been encouraged to want children but not educated in how to care for them. They have to discover as best they can how to handle the new child and promote good development. The burden on young women today is twofold. They are not only expected to be good mothers without having been given very much guidance, but they are finally being given a chance to develop a career as well. Role training for a career is also minimal. Many are trying to handle two complex, unfamiliar roles without adequate preparation for either.

A second element that the teacher should be aware of is the child that is the result of an unwanted pregnancy. Although greater numbers of people are now in a position to plan their parenthood and many people have children when they want them, a significant portion are faced with surprise pregnancies that can have important implications for the future well-being of the child.

Clearly, if a child is the result of an unwanted pregnancy, there exists the danger the parents will harbor negative feelings and resentment. Admittedly it is a danger that does not always occur, but it is there and it can affect the adjustment of the child. These parents need understanding and help in adjusting to this problem.

Another type of stress that acutely affects new parents is the loss of freedom and choice that is imposed upon them by the birth of a child. By the time the parents bring the child to you at school, they have been living through a number of very restricted years. Their options have been severely limited by the necessities of childcare. Social lives, vacations, career plans, and their time alone together have all been heavily affected by that adorable little creature. The child forces them into a narrow band of life experiences. Some parents don't mind, in fact even revel in the wonder and pleasure of childrearing. Others bridle under the repressive demands of the parent role.

The child can sometimes be a wedge between partners, turning them away from each other. Children can and do, unintentionally of course, represent a factor in the breakdown of many relationships. The couple who has been free to travel, to go out at night, and to plan and indulge in wonderful and rewarding experiences now has neither the time nor the money (nor even the energy) for any of them. By the time they arrive at your doorstep they may be angry, frustrated, disappointed, worn out, and near the breaking point. They may be pretty unhappy about that young child clinging to their hand.

Of course, we don't mean to imply that all parents have negative feelings about their child, their partner, and themselves. Excitement, intrigue, and wonder may fill their heads and hearts. But the teacher should be aware that these problems can exist.

The baby has been their responsibility every minute of every day for several years—and this may not be their only young child. Nursing, feeding, sleeping, and play schedules have been endlessly worked and re-worked. Diapers, bathing, formulas are every day, hour-by-hour events. Appointments with the pediatrician and dentist for checkups and shots have had to be arranged. The parents find they must constantly center their activities around the baby's needs. If there is any time left, and if the parents aren't too tired or keyed up, they can play together.

Freedom from childcare has occurred from time to time, *if* the parents have been able to find a babysitter whom they both trust and whom they are able to afford, and *if* the timing has been worked out.

Then, of course, there has been the worry about how to interact with and raise the new child. Parents anxiously read books by pediatricians, psychologists, and educators. They discuss ideas with their partners, their friends, and their relatives, all or none of whom may agree with them. They work and play with the child. They receive all sorts of conflicting advice. No-one has the final answer to how children should be raised. The uncertainty of it all makes the parents worry about how well they are doing. They watch their child's progress and development, and hope to God it's normal. They fear that something may go wrong or that they are to blame when things do go wrong. They worry about every little developmental change they see. Is it on time? Is it normal? Is is good enough? Why isn't Jimmy talking yet when so many other children are? Does Jimmy walk a little off-balance? They search for confirmation of their hope that things are not only normal but perhaps better than average. They read Dr. Spock with a sigh of relief. They compare their child to other children, secretly hoping the comparison will be in their favor. The pressure is considerable, and it should not be difficult for the teacher to sympathize with them. After all, things do go wrong; life does have its troubles; and the new parent will, essentially, be responsible for this new human for the better part of two decades. It's not an easy task.

If the child is not "normal" in any way, the parents may feel guilty, depressed, and angry. "Why me?" might be their reaction. Special medical treatment may be necessary, entailing more expense, more scheduling, more worry and less time for their own needs. And more stress in the adult relationship.

Sometimes parents feel exhausted, and at a loss to cope. Their patience with the child, the partner, and themselves runs very thin. At times they fear that if the child doesn't stop crying, demanding, and spilling things, they may lose control and do something rash. It's times like these that can lead to child abuse or the abuse of one's partner. Even when the parents restrain themselves, they may feel guilty about having thought about hurting the child or partner.

By the time the child is old enough for a preschool program, many parents desperately need some time off. They many want to go back to school, find a job, or just spend time on their own. They love the child but need to interact with adults. Many a mother complains about not having spoken to anyone over the age of 4 for what seems like endless periods of time.

But the age when the child can attend an early childhood education program brings new worries and anxieties, as well as the potential for relief. The parents must now face the difficult task of finding a suitable school with an appropriate program and good teachers. Not an easy assignment. How can one ever be sure they are making the right choice? Many parents read up on the subject and ask around. School reputations are often passed around and maintained by word of mouth on a kind of "young mother grapevine." But there is always the possibility that the information in the grapevine is inaccurate, outdated. When they leave their child with you, they are taking a big step. How will they ever know what you do to their child? The child is too young to report accurately. For all the parent knows, the child may sit in a corner all day.

It is at this point that the skillful teacher can be of immense help. The teacher must assess the new parents' suspicions and level of anxiety, and attempt to alleviate their fears. Being totally positive and effusive won't do it . . . parents may wonder about phoney enthusiasm. On the other hand, the parent does want a display of interest. There is a thin line here between genuine, warm, professional concern for the new little student, and over-enthusiastic behavior that will put off the parent. Perhaps confidence on your part is what most parents seek. They are uncertain and worried about what they are doing to their child. If you can assure them that it is in the best interest of the child, and that you know your job, you will be on the way towards a successful arrangement.

Parents worry about a number of other things at this point. They wonder how their child will compare with other children of the same age. They may feel they have done a pretty good job of raising their child, but they can't quite help feeling that perhaps they haven't done enough. They feel guilty about putting the child in school at such a young age. Your task, as a teacher, is to assure the parent that the child will benefit from the school experience and from having a happier, more fulfilled parent.

Parents are also concerned about whether their philosophy of child-rearing will match up with the teacher's. How will the teacher like their child? How should they act when they visit the school? Can they trust the school and teacher enough to leave their child there? What are the other children and parents like? Could any of the other parents have the same problems and feelings?

And parents worry about worrying. Are they being over-protective, or too rejecting? Their basic need is for certainty. They want to know, good or bad, what is going on. As they face you for the first time, be aware of these sorts of concerns. Of course, some parents worry very little, but many worry a lot. By knowing what they are concerned about, you can project an aura of confidence; and you can assure them that everything is not only all right but downright fine.

Some people forget that all humans go through childhood and that most of us make it through somehow. They do not have the perspective you will have, having steered any number of children along the way. To the parents, their single offspring is the most important thing in the world, and their worry is natural. You must convince them that danger does not lurk behind every door, that their child is entering into a new, exciting, and essential phase of development, and that you can, and want to, handle the job. And they are invited to be a part of it all, if they wish to be.

Your First Day

Though you are confident of your abilities, you are nervous as the first day begins. Children and parents begin to arrive. Your room is prepared and there are many activities from which the children may choose. There is an air of excitement as the new school year opens. It doesn't take long before you realize you are not alone in your nervousness. Though some of the children, parents, and other teachers have been through this before and are calm and happy, others greet you with anxiety. Some talk nervously. And some are frozen into silence. Some of the children easily move about the room and become involved in the activity areas you have set up for them. But not all of them. Others are held back by uncertain parents or by their own inhibitions. One or two children arrive crying; others start to cry after arriving. Some parents move around the room with their children and some of the other parents. Other parents appear stiff, uncomfortable, and awkward.

As you greet each new arrival, there are questions from both children and adults. Things are happening quickly. Your attention is needed in several areas. Perhaps you have an experienced teacher with you who begins dealing with anxious parents and children, talks calmly and confidently as she moves from one need to another, and promotes a trend toward friendliness, relaxation, and fun. But perhaps you are the one who must do this, alone. There is a definite need for leadership here—and fast.

What attitude will you have toward the parents? Will you invite them to stay, or work toward their leaving? Do you feel you are the expert here and that this is your domain? Or do you recognize their importance, their own expertise, and their needs? You may have many ideas about how to deal with their children, but how will you work with parents? What sort of relationship do you wish to establish with them? Again, forethought and preparation are needed; and it is to this preparation that we now turn.

The Parent/Teacher Relationship

Before you begin that first day, you really need to think about the relationship you wish to establish, beginning immediately, with the parents of the children you will be teaching. Most of the literature in this area suggests that the most desirable and beneficial teacher-parent relationship is that of a *partnership* with the teacher taking an initial leadership role in establishing feelings of acceptance, friendliness, support, and confidence (Almy, 1975; Biber, 1969 and 1977; Nimnicht, Arango, and Cheever, 1977; Weikart, 1967; White and Watts, 1973).

Recent thinking and research points out that the teacher cannot take on the role of an authority and merely dispense wisdom to the parent and child. The teacher does not and cannot know all the answers. The teacher must listen to, and respond to, the parents' ideas and initiatives. The parent should be encouraged to become caught up in the educational process. Working together, as equals, seems to be better than the situation in which the teacher takes an undisputed authority role. In many ways, because the child really only spends a relatively small portion of her time in the early childhood education setting, the teacher can only be an aid to, and secondary to the parent. This is especially important in intervention programs that take place at least in part in the home setting (Karnes, 1969; Karnes and Zehrbach, 1977; Nimnicht, Arango, and Adcock, 1977). One must be very sensitive to the parents' true role and not make them feel in any way inferior.

It seems clear now that the parent must become involved in the educational process. Recent research in intervention has raised our awareness that, if education is to "stick," the parents should be involved in both the planning and the execution of the child's education (Bronfenbrenner, 1974; Lazar et al., 1977). In this sense, it is the teacher's job to involve the parent and to break down the passive role of the parent in which the parent simply gives the child to the teacher to be educated.

There are many reasons for trying to develop a partnership. To help the child grow, both parents and teacher need to understand the child as well as possible. They both benefit from understanding the child's home and school environment. Whereas the teacher knows best what goes on at school, the parent is the undisputed expert on the child's home life. As part of their partnership, parents and teachers should exchange this information and try to interpret together what it all means to the child. The teacher should initiate these information exchanges and show an interest in what the parent has to say.

If they have a strong partnership, parents and teachers can discuss problems that arise at home and in school. They can work together toward solutions that draw upon the expertise of both. It is important for the teacher to express confidence that solutions will be found, however slow and painstaking the process may seem. The parents and teachers can discuss the goals they have in mind with respect to the child's education. The teacher must listen to the parents (Greenberg, 1969). The partnership will be strengthened by the fact that, in spite of some differences, they will probably discover that they share many of the same goals (Knitzer, 1972). Together they can work toward attitudes, methods, and curriculum that will foster them. The teacher should encourage parents to consider carefully, and to articulate, what they want for their children. How much and what kind of emphasis do they wish to place on academic achievement, social development, physical skills, and so on? The teacher can help the parents express themselves and can encourage them to believe in their ability to attain these goals.

The parents' feelings, moods, and attitudes clearly affect the child's sense of well-being. A happy, confident, growing parent will be a good model for the child, as well as a source of security. If the teacher can help the parents find solutions to their problems and can support them on their road to self-fulfillment, the child will also benefit. Parents need to hear that promoting their *own* happiness, as well as the child's, is good for the whole family. For example, in families where both parents work or are going to school, the parents may feel that they are not spending as much time with their children as they should. A teacher can point out that the *quality* of the time spent with children may be much more important than the *quantity*. This idea was expressed decades ago by Dr. Montessori, and it is currently gaining support from the Women's Movement (Friedan, 1974). It seems far more beneficial to have happy, interested parents with their children part of the time, than bored, angry, resentful, self-involved parents around all of the time.

If you work in an area where poverty and deprivation are common, your interactions with parents are even more important. Recent research indicates that in intervention programs designed to assist the underprivileged, the development of an effective and lasting parent/child relationship may be crucial in maintaining any gains made by the educational program (Bronfenbrenner, 1974; Lazar et al., 1977). You may be just the person to provide the parent with the confidence and the information needed to develop an effective parent/child relationship. Without this relationship Bonfenbrenner argues that any gains made in the intervention program may be lost. Again, care must be taken not to make parents feel that their methods have been inferior or damaging to the child. Rather, one must help each parent build an ongoing relationship.

Forming and Maintaining the Parent/Teacher Partnership

How does one form and maintain effective parent/teacher relationships?. Very few important relationships are born instantly, and full-blown. Patience, time, effort, planning, and commitment are generally needed. The teacher can take on a leadership role in the initial stages to get things moving.

There are many ways of beginning and maintaining partnerships. Your choice of techniques will depend, to a certain extent, upon the facilities, the program, and the procedural policies of your school. To provide a broad background, we shall discuss techniques that are currently being used in many kinds of schools. Some of these methods will work with some groups or individuals and not with others. No-one needs to use all of them, and some may appeal to you more than others. And, of course, there is always room for creativity and ingenuity on your part.

The important thing to remember is that a partnership, in which you learn as much from the parents as they learn from you, is probably the best way to approach this situation. The teacher cannot be the source of all truth and authority. Educators do not have all the answers concerning childrearing. Far from it. And, after all, the child will be living with the parent and not you; so the thoughts, values, and goals of the parents must be taken very seriously.

Working together as partners, parents and teachers can be most effective in meeting the needs of the child

The Initial Encounter

Forming an effective parent/teacher relationship can begin the very first moment you set eyes on each other. The circumstances under which you first meet parents will vary. Sometimes you will meet in an orientation session at the school. At other times you will meet in the school's office, in an interview, in your classroom or out in the yard. At still other times you may meet as the parents visit the school for the first time, in a pre-arranged home visit, or at the classroom door on the first day of school.

Wherever you do first meet, remember that there is some truth in the old saying that first impressions (yours and theirs) are important. At the same time, realize that first impressions do not always provide the most accurate picture of what a person is like. Try to be friendly and confident. Make the parent and child feel welcome. Don't prejudge them. Remember that parents, whatever their outward appearance, are most likely a bundle of hopes and fears at this important time in their lives.

Parents, like everyone else, are complex people who can become anxious and appear unfriendly or negative in an unfamiliar and potentially threatening situation. You need to take your own fears in hand and assume a friendly leadership role in your first encounters. Let them know that they are as important to you as their children are. Tell them you are happy to see them and hope to see a lot more of them in the future. Let them know you want to hear their views and work with them for the good of both their children and themselves. Don't be gushy.

Take the initial encounter in your stride. Do the best you can to project an image of confidence and interest. Don't worry if your ideal first encounter is not achieved. Remember, Cleveland was not built in a day.

Parent Orientations

If a new semester is about to begin, your school or center may arrange an orientation session for the parents. These sessions often afford you the opportunity to become further acquainted with the parents (if you have already met) and to begin to build your partnership with them. Here the parents (with or without their children, depending on the school policy) are shown the facility, the general program is outlined for them, and they have a chance to meet the teachers briefly. Sometimes the teachers are asked to introduce themselves to the group as a whole. Sometimes they meet the parents individually in their classrooms during the course of the tour.

In this situation you want to convey a feeling of friendliness and goodwill. Express your appreciation for their coming. Make them feel welcome, encourage them to look about the classroom, and suggest that they ask questions. This is a good opportunity to let them know that you welcome group and individual parent participation. Sow the seeds of the partnership at this point. Try to speak briefly to each parent. Avoid spending all of your time with the interesting, talkative, and comfortable ones.

Parent Application and Interview

Some schools may require that the teacher be present when the parents are deciding whether or not to apply to the school. You or the director may briefly explain the program and answer questions. The school rules and regulations concerning fees, school routine, safety, and health requirements will be explained. The teacher may go over the application with the parents as they fill it out.

This session can be useful beyond the conveyance of this sort of administrative detail. It offers a golden opportunity for you to instil the idea of a cooperative partnership. Take this opportunity to tell the parents that you welcome, and need, their participation in the school. It may seem to you that this is unnecessary. But it is essential that you be explicit, as the parents really have no way of knowing what to expect unless you tell them. Inform them you want to be a partner rather than a boss or an authority figure and that they can consider this initial exchange of school and home information as their first working session together.

Do not overreact to any information they may give you at this point. Be nonjudgmental and supportive. Do not go into details of your own personal life. Remember, this is a friendly, but professional relationship.

Home Visits

Your school may encourage or require that teachers visit the homes of new students. This can be a very useful tool in bridging the gap between home and school, especially for the very young child, for the child who has never gone to school before, or for the child who has had a bad experience with a previous school. It can be equally beneficial to the young, inexperienced, and/or anxious parent. And it allows the teacher to move closer to the parent in a one-on-one situation on the parent's home ground.

Once the parent has enrolled the child in school, but before the child begins attending, you can call to arrange a convenient time for the visit. Explain that this is a chance for the child to meet you on her home ground instead of in the unfamiliar and perhaps disquieting atmosphere of the school. (The child may have met you briefly in a school visit, but most likely did not have a chance to really focus in on you as someone special.) Explain that by becoming acquainted with you in their familiar home surroundings, you will all be more relaxed when you all meet again at school.

The home visit then provides a good opening topic of conversation when they finally arrive at school for the first day. "Remember when I visited your home, Joey? You showed me how you can ride your rocking horse?" Typically, the child feels comfortable remembering that you have a past together.

The home visit should be kept on a rather light level. Avoid heavy, serious, and ponderous discussions. Think of it as a chance to work toward the trust and understanding that will form the basis of your relationship with the child and the eventual parent/teacher relationship. The child should be encouraged to participate, or to play nearby where she or he can watch the friendly interactions between teacher and parent. Problems should not be discussed unless the child is out of hearing range.

This is also a good opportunity for the teacher to gain insight into the child's home and family life. You will see firsthand whether the child lives in a slum tenement, in an average suburban home, on a farm, or in a spacious, luxury home. Other members of the family, and perhaps servants, may also be present. The teacher can see firsthand how they relate (or don't relate) to one another. A home visit can be an invaluable experience for everyone involved because so much information is exchanged above and beyond what is actually said.

However, if the parent prefers not to have you visit, don't push it. Some may consider this an unnecessary invasion of their privacy. Others may not want you to see the poverty conditions in which they live. Still others may just prefer to get to know you better before they invite you into their home. Be sensitive to their feelings in this matter. Be patient, understanding, and supportive.

Casual Encounters at School

Many of your encounters with parents will be informal, brief meetings, when the child is being brought to or picked up from school. This may actually be the *only* time you will see some of the parents (especially fathers on their way to work), so you may want to make the most of these encounters whenever you can. But your main concern at these times will be the children. Therefore, many of these contacts with parents must be brief. Even so, a friendly greeting, and a, "How are you today, Ron?" or, "How's everything, Ron?" will show your concern for him as an individual and not just as "Jody's father." By greeting the parent in this manner you are, in effect, inviting him to tell you anything he feels you should know. For instance he might say, "Well, actually, I'm beat. The new baby cried so much last night, none of us got much sleep. So if Jody isn't quite herself today, you'll know why."

A simple statement like this can key-off a variety of thoughts in the alert teacher. For example, you will want to make sure Jody has ample quiet time and a nap during the day to make up for her loss of sleep. You will also want to help her through any grouchy times she may experience. You will understand that, if she fights during the day, it may be due to her lack of sleep. You can explain to her and to others that she might be feeling a bit cranky because she didn't get enough sleep.

Then, too, the father's brief statement will remind you that there is a new baby in Jody's household. This may inspire you to read a book about babies to your group and to talk about babies with them. This topic seems to be a favorite. Children usually love babies and are very curious about them. Discussions about babies let the children know the tremendous progress they have made since they were babies, and shows them that they are "growing big."

In your conversation with the children you can point out how much care and patience babies need. You can tell the children that all new babies, sooner or later, cry at night and keep everyone awake, even though they don't mean to. Through these discussions and stories, you can get a feeling for how Jody and the other children with baby brothers and sisters are adjusting to the new family members. If someone seems to be having problems, you might want to discuss the subject with the appropriate parents.

So you can see that a brief exchange in the morning can have some important implications for the rest of the day. Similar exchanges at the close of the day can also be brief but valuable. In the afternoon it may be you who has a message to send home. "Mitch painted a great picture with three different colors. It's in the room on the bulletin board. He may take it home if he wants to or leave it for us to look at again tomorrow." "Lisa learned how to ride a tricycle today. Isn't she terrific!" "Jessica just couldn't get to sleep at nap time. She was so excited about her birthday party at school today. Don't be surprised if she gets tired early tonight." And so on.

As you and the parents become more familiar with each other and as your partnership grows, you can each learn to utilize the brief encounters to both give and receive clues about the home and school conditions the child is coming from and hints as to possible effective ways of reacting to the child at that time. You can help one another understand the child.

Parents can use support and reward, too. "The kids sure enjoyed your visit last week when you played your guitar and sang with us. They still haven't stopped talking about it. Do you think you might do it again sometime soon?" "Our trip to your grocery store last week was a hit with the kids, Marion. They've been playing 'store games' all week, taking turns stocking our shelves and checking each other out at our toy cash register. It was a wonderful experience for them."

These moments can also be used to remind parents of coming events. "Don't forget the parent meeting tonight. I hope you'll be able to make it." "I'm looking forward to our conference this afternoon." Printed announcements of future events can also be distributed during these times.

S.O.S. Calls

A parent may arrive with distress written all over her or his face. Once the child is out of hearing range, he may say, "My wife was in a terrible accident last night. The doctor thinks she will be all right. Jenny doesn't know yet. I didn't know whether to bring her to school or not, but I'm so worried I didn't think I could cope with her at home."

Another distressed parent might say, "My husband left me last night. We had a terrible fight, and he just walked out. With three kids and no job, what am I going to do?"

Or a panic-stricken parent might say, "I think I'm losing it. I can't cope. The kids are driving me crazy. I . . . I almost hit the baby this morning. I just wanted her to stop crying. I'm afraid I'm going to do something terrible. I can't cope."

It's good to think about what to do in these kinds of situations ahead of times, as they will occur. This is a good topic of discussion in your staff meetings. What are your options? What services are available? You may want to ask your director or anyone else on the staff who is available, to fill in for you while you talk privately with the parent to give emergency support. If feasible, arrange for the parent to meet you for a coffee break or lunch break if no substitute is available for your class. If there is a teacher's room, lounge, or office, the parent might wish to wait till you are free to talk. Perhaps you can refer the parent to a social worker, psychologist, or other human resource person affiliated with your school, community, or college campus. Your director may prefer to talk with and help the parent. Possibly another family member or friend could be called for assistance. Recognize the parent's dilemma and do whatever you can, as soon as you can. Don't let the parent leave without some help.

There are also times when parents may see that you are not your usual organized and cheerful self. In other words, *you* may be sending out S.O.S. signals without knowing it. If your partnership is progressing, it will be further cemented if the parent instinctively gives you a little support. For example, the day may come when you oversleep and arrive late after a night of problems of your own. On the way to work you hope that your co-teacher or assistant has already mixed the paints and set up the room or yard for you. Instead, you find that she or he has a flat tire and won't be in for another hour. The kids begin arriving, and you're totally disorganized. In those situations there often seems to be at least one parent who sizes up the situation, lets you know you have a friend, and volunteers to stick around for an hour or so to help you turn a near-disaster into a very pleasant day.

As you can see, these casual and S.O.S. encounters can be extremely valuable for you, the parent, and the children. In a sense, they can form the backbone of the parent/teacher relationship.

Parents at School: Observation and Participation

One important way to involve parents in the concept of a working partnership is to encourage them to come to the educational facility during school hours to partake of the ongoing educational process. Whether these visits are strictly observational, primarily of a participating nature, or both, the parent is sure to feel a part of it all.

It is a good idea to invite the parent to observe the school at an early date. Directors and teachers should give the parents a rough idea of the program for the day, should encourage them to move about freely, and should suggest that they join in if the spirit moves them. Some will prefer to remain in an observational role. But even this limited role can be very valuable. The parents will see their child in a new light. Perhaps for the first time they will see their child as one of a group of children. They will be able to get some idea of where their child's development stands relative to the other children. If problems arise, the parent and the teacher can work together toward solutions. And, more than likely, the parent will meet some of the other parents. They will all quickly realize that they are not alone in their hopes, fears, anxieties, and pleasures in the parent role.

Observational visits provide an opportune time in which to bridge the gap between parent and school. Directors and staff alike should indicate to the parent that they feel the school is a good one, with a good program, but that everyone involved realizes perfection has not been obtained. In dealing with the many complexities involved, every school has some problems, and makes some mistakes. The parents should be informed that the school sees itself as a developing, growing, and changing facility. The parents should understand that you do not have all the answers, or even all the questions. Encourage the parents to look for strong and weak points in your program, and suggest that, by doing so, they can help improve the school. Welcome their questions and suggestions. They can contribute to the ongoing process of updating, revising, and further developing the program. Convince the parent that you have nothing to hide and that, in fact, you welcome their constructive criticism.

While many visiting parents prefer the observational role, and it is a useful one, others either choose or fall into a role that involves more direct contact and participation. It is probably safe to say that anyone entering the preschool classroom or yard becomes a participant in at least some small way. Many preschool children characteristically interact with whoever happens to be there . . . kids, teachers, aides, custodians, plumbers, directors, inspectors, and, last but not least, visiting parents. Of course, many children are too shy or too absorbed in other things to notice the visitors. But there are always a few who simply assume that whoever is there is part of the school. They have a charming way of drawing everyone into their world.

Parents who had planned to observe or to help their own child adjust to the new situation, often find themselves approached, and captivated, by other children. Some children will be aware that the parent is a stranger and ask, "Whose mom are you?" Others may need help with something, and appeal to the nearest adult. If a button needs buttoning or paint shirts need to come off, there is nothing like the nearest, convenient adult to get the job done. Some children will unabashedly climb into an adult's lap with a book and say, "Read me a story." For the parent who had intended to observe and remain aloof, this may be a bit flustering; but more often than not it helps cement the attitude that the parent is a partner in the educational venture. Some parents join in freely. Others first glance at the teacher uncertainly, and wait for approval. But few can resist, and many love it. Sometimes parents become acquainted with certain children before their own child does.

Again, the teacher needs to let the parents know that parent participation is not only welcomed, but encouraged, and that they are free to relax and interact in their own normal manner with any or all of the children. This form of participation can provide considerable insight into the children's behavior and the program. And both the children and the teachers gain from the smallest parent contribution.

Eventually, a parent may want to take a further step in participation. For example, she or he may know how to play an instrument and volunteer to bring it in, and then tell the children about it, let them touch it, and play a song or two. Everyone may sing one of the group's songs accompanied by the new instrument. In some cases, the children may have a chance to play the instrument themselves. Other parent skills can be shared with the children, including cooking, crafts, working with tools, dancing, and many more.

Of course, activities of this sort need careful planning and preparation. The teacher and parent must, as partners, be sure that the children's attention span is not exceeded. There is nothing more frustrating than a group of children whose information-processing capacity has been overloaded. In addition, parent and teacher must be sure that adequate and safe equipment is available. The parent may be well-advised to start with something simple.

Parents who belong to a particular ethnic group may want to share some of their cultural heritage and customs with the children. In one school, a mother of Mexican descent planned several days of activities centered around the festive Mexican holiday, Cinco de Mayo. One day she prepared tacos and other foods with the children. Another day she brought in records and taught them the Mexican hat dance. Still another day she talked about the Mexican countryside, Mexican customs, and Mexican children.

Another parent with a Native American background enjoyed telling and showing the children about the ancient Indian way of life. Arrowheads and other artifacts were shown. She demonstrated the grinding of corn and nuts with stone tools, and let the children try it themselves. She brought in some woven rugs and beadwork and explained in a very simplified manner how these items were made.

Of course, these are rather elaborate examples of parent participation, and a great deal of thought and preparation was necessary for them. But when they are well done, the children love them and remember these sorts of activities. And, of course, the parent's experience is one of accomplishment, pride, and participation. The contribution has been valuable, and the sense of partnership grows. This is true not just for the elaborate forms of participation, but for the simple ones as well.

When a parent has a project in mind, the teacher should set up an appointment to discuss it. By working together, they can increase the chances of the project being a success. During the actual presentation, the teacher should be supportive and helpful. Let the parent be the leader of the project unless she or he prefers you to assume that role. Build their confidence: express appreciation for their efforts in the presence of the children (who will, no doubt, join in with their own applause). You may want to discuss the experience with the parent after it is over.

In summary, the partnership between the parent and teacher can be strengthened immeasurably through parent participation in the school process. In effect, they become teachers, your equal and your peer, when they engage in these forms of participation. You, the children, the parents, and the school can only benefit from this type of contribution.

Parent Conferences

Most schools want their teachers to confer with the parents on an individual basis at least once or twice a year. These conferences can be anxiety-producing for both teacher and parent, especially for the inexperienced teacher. At the same time, they represent one of the most effective means available for bringing the teacher and parent closer together, for building the desired partnership. The first thing the new teacher must realize is that no one has all the answers to all the questions we have about how a conference should be conducted. There are no set formulas that meet with everyone's approval. With thought, preparation, and experience, your skills in this area will grow. You will develop techniques that work for you and the particular people with whom you are working.

Schedule each meeting at a time that is most convenient for the parents. Encourage both parents to attend. Reassure them that the conference is no cause for alarm and that conferences are routine for you and not stimulated by difficulties that the child is having. It helps to tell parents about these conferences when the child enrolls. Some parents may immediately associate conferences with problems. Reassure them that these are periodically scheduled meetings for the purpose of discussing, as partners, their child's progress in school and at home. They are supposed to be positive, helpful experiences. Inform them that the meetings will help you understand each other better in terms of your ways of working with their child. The conference is an opportunity for the parents to ask questions and discuss any problems they may be having.

Preparation is absolutely essential for an effective conference. To go into one cold is to court disaster. There are some hints we can provide concerning effective preparation.

Go through the child's school file. Refamiliarize yourself with pertinent background information such as the parents' application, the child's health and attendance record, the parents' occupations and interests, how many siblings there are, and so on. If you are familiar with this sort of information, your conference will progress more smoothly and be of more help to you and the parents.

In addition to the school file, many teachers keep their own file on each child. This file may contain notes on significant events in the child's school career, samples of the child's work, and a running evaluation of the child's development. If you have not kept such a file, the period of a few days or a week between the day you made the appointment and the day of the conference itself may be a good time to start one. Focus on that child in particular at different times of the day and in a variety of situations. Jot down and date comments to yourself regarding the kinds of activities the child enjoys or avoids and how he interacts with the other children. Does he approach new activities easily, or avoid them or seek help? Is he outgoing or shy? In general, is this a happy child? Does he talk to you, to the other children? Does he verbalize needs, questions, ideas, and problems? Are there certain areas in which he excels? Are there areas that give particular difficulty? If so, what are some of the ways you and the parents may want to work together to help the child? During the conference, you can refer to these notes.

It is a good idea to keep an occasional (dated) sample of the child's work in the file. Progress is easily seen from this sort of record. Jot down occurrences which you think the parents may enjoy hearing about at the conference, or that may give the parents particular insights into the child's life at school. For example, you might note that, "Jeffrey discovered the wonder of playdough today. He could barely break himself away from it, even for a snack. Perhaps his parents would like the recipe so that they can make it at home." Or, "Today, I found Michelle in the housekeeping corner showing two of her friends how to take all the handles off the pots and pans. On seeing me, she announced proudly, 'My daddy showed me how to use a screwdriver yesterday,' to which I said, 'Well that's great. Now maybe you can show Beverly and Michael how to put the handles back on.' She said, 'Okay,' and she did." A story like that will go a long way in reassuring a set of parents.

Some beginning teachers observe a few conferences held by experienced teachers or the director of their school before they try one on their own. Assistant teachers can help in the planning of, and participate in, conferences led by head teachers. You may want to discuss conferencing with your director or at a staff meeting. Remember, good preparation is your best insurance.

As the conference begins, thank the parents for coming, and compliment them for taking an interest in their child's progress at school. Reaffirm your desire to work with them as partners in attaining mutual goals for their children. Sometimes you can begin the discussion by asking the parents, parent, or other caretaker how they themselves are doing. How are things going at home, at work, etc.? If something is important to the parent, it naturally has an effect on the child, so you will want to know how they are feeling. Some will simply say fine, and move on to a consideration of the child. But others will be more than ready to tell you about significant developments in their lives that will affect the child's well-being. You may hear about job promotions, house guests, deaths, marital problems, problems with any of their children, job losses, transfers, health problems, pregnancies, and any number of other events . . . some good and some bad.

If everything seems good, you can remark that you are happy to hear that things are going so well for them. On the other hand, if they are having difficulties, you will want to be sympathetic and supportive. Don't begin by throwing out advice. Encourage them to explain their efforts for dealing with their problems. Discuss any alternatives *they* may be considering. Remember, you are a partner and not a know-it-all. Consider whether or not they would be willing to accept suggestions from you. Many people will be irritated and miffed if you begin offering advice of any sort. If you think they would accept suggestions from you, present your ideas as additional alternatives that they may want to consider and not as "the answer." Express confidence that a solution will be found even though it will take some time. Offer to try to help. Don't be pushy.

If your school provides services that might be of assistance in their situation, you may suggest them as alternatives. Community or governmental agencies may be of some help. For example, if a parent has lost a job and is in need of assistance, you can suggest that they apply for unemployment and food stamps. Show them the way to work through the bureaucratic maze.

Much of your conferencing time will sometimes be taken up with the parents' problems without ever getting around to the child. If this is necessary, do it because the parents' problems affect the child. However, in most cases the discussion will eventually center on the child. In fact, sometimes you will decide to discuss the child first, before you consider the parents' situation. As you become more familiar with each family, you will have a better idea of what you want to do first.

Begin discussing the child on a positive note. Since many parents are quite anxious, you can help them relax by demonstrating their child's areas of competence and your awareness of those areas. Show them that you like their child and that you are happy to have her in your group. Tell them about some of the activities the child likes and how she handles herself in those activities. Some teachers bring in samples of things the child has made or helped to make in the group. Encourage discussion of the child at home. Does she enjoy the same things there? Is her behavior similar at home and school? Often a child who is quiet at home will be outgoing or aggressive at school, and vice-versa.

If the child is having difficulties in some areas, refer to these as areas of development that should be focused upon. Ask the parents' advice about how to handle a particular situation. For example, "Jason seems to have a hard time sleeping at nap time. How do you get him to sleep at home? Does he have a favorite blanket or toy that he sleeps with at home? Do you think he should bring it with him to school?" You may learn that Jason doesn't sleep at home either and that a rest without actual sleep is adequate and normal for him.

Discipline is an issue you will have to discuss occasionally. Ask the parents how they feel consistency can be maintained in this between home and school. They may well have better ideas than you do. Discuss the school's policy regarding discipline, also. Some states have regulations regarding discipline that must also be followed. For example, many disallow corporal punishment and punishment that involves withholding of food.

The notes and anecdotes you have in your file can be used to keep the conversation from bogging down, or from sounding too negative. It is helpful to have a good anecdote for the end of the conference. When the conference is over, thank the parents again, and try to see that they leave with a positive feeling. Tell them you are happy to have had such a good work session with them. Express confidence that you are all beginning to work well together in the promotion of the child's development. Invite them to browse around the school before they leave.

Parent Meetings

Parent meetings, or meetings between staff and groups of parents, can vary considerably in their goals, activities, location, and number of participants. But, in all forms, they can be very helpful. They all promote a sense of partnership. Again, planning is important. In fact, parent participation in the planning stage is often a key to the success of any given meeting. Inquire as to the parents' interests and needs. Let them know you welcome their suggestions as well as their participation in the organizing of parent meetings.

Some meetings, such as orientation meetings, may involve all the teachers and as many of the parents as possible. Other large group meetings may be for the purpose of hearing a speaker or seeing a film.

A large meeting may be called to invite parents to hear a progress report on the school itself, or to obtain parent input on a policy-making decision.

In some cases a once-a-year workshop is planned. In these situations the school's classes and yard are arranged in the normal, every-day manner. The only difference is that on this day the *parents* take on the role of the students. They paint, build with blocks, rediscover the fun of clay, read children's books, sing songs, play with puppets, and have a snack. Adult enthusiasm is often suprisingly high. Although it represents no more than an hour or two of the child's day at school, this experience can give the parents a feel for their child's school world. It also provides an opportunity for the parents and teachers to become acquainted in a relaxed and often hysterically funny atmosphere. To say nothing of that great snack.

Other kinds of workshops can be planned for the purpose of mending toys and books, building shelves, and improving equipment and supplies. Most schools are on very tight budgets, and need to repair rather than replace whatever they can. Parents who are carpenters, bricklayers, seamstresses, painters, carpet or tile layers, or in other such crafts are often willing to volunteer their time and efforts. Sometimes they can bring in surplus supplies either free or at reduced rates. A new coat of paint for walls, cabinets, or toys can do wonders. It makes the school look nicer, and those in it feel better.

This is also an ideal opportunity for parents and teachers to all get to know each other better. And it's a chance for parent leaders to appear. In addition, parents who do not feel comfortable in other forms of parent participation may find this an excellent way in which to make their own kind of contribution to their child's school. Many parents enjoy an active meeting far more than those in which they are the audience.

It is difficult to get parents to attend meetings. Work schedules often make attendance impossible. Arranging baby sitting can be difficult and expensive. Some parents would like to come but are too shy and intimidated by large groups. Others are simply not interested.

To counteract some of these deterrents, several steps can be taken. First, the meeting can be advertised (on bulletin boards, handout sheets, etc.) in a way that makes them sound informal and easygoing. The social aspects of the affair should be emphasized. Dress can be casual and refreshments—even if it's just coffee and cookies—should be served. In areas where poverty is prevalent, the announcement that a meal will be served may induce many to come, especially if provisions for children can also be provided. A pot-luck dinner, with the school providing several dishes, is a possibility. Games or dancing at the end of the meeting may appeal to many. They make the meeting sound less serious and more fun, especially for parents who have little social life.

Parent Groups

As parents become acquainted with one another through various school activities, they may begin to see that they have a number of things in common, and that they might enjoy and profit from the chance to get together. And, as they get to know each other, they may see that they share some very serious concerns. What may start out as a few parents going to lunch together or meeting at someone's house for coffee, may turn into a discussion and support group that meets on a regular basis. These groups should be encouraged by the school as they represent an important form of parent participation. Within a very short time, these groups will have discussed a wide range of topics, including praise and criticism of the school, parental hopes and frustrations, marital problems and solutions, divorce, sexism, careers, babysitters, servants, financial problems, alcoholism, theories of child development and education, birth control, and child abuse, to name but a few.

For parents who have been spending a major portion of their time in the company of preschool children and have been somewhat isolated from adult consideration of these topics, the parent discussion group can be a heady experience. The meetings can be exhilarating and will leave many parents stimulated and ready for more of the same. Sometimes these groups continue to discuss things in a rather spontaneous way. At other times they may decide to pick a new topic each week (e.g., fire prevention in the home, neighborhood trips). The group may become too large and eventually divide up each week according to subjects of common interests.

They may invite staff members of the school, or not. They may or may not ask to meet at the school. It is important that they be able to meet without interruption by their children or other family members. They need a place where they can speak in an uninhibited way. If the school cannot provide appropriate space at a convenient time, perhaps you can suggest an available facility within the community, such as a community center, a YMCA, or a room in City Hall. President Carter launched a program to encourage communities to make public buildings, such as public schools, available for use by community members "after hours." After all, tax dollars pay for these facilities. It may be appropriate for the parents to make such a request in their community. Whenever possible, the school and staff should cooperate with and support these groups (Honig, 1975; Lally and Honig, 1977). If the group is open to other parents, teachers should help spread the word.

Many of the parent groups decide to work together for the benefit of the school. They start fund raising projects. They collect and make things for the school. Certainly, these are terrific ways to help stretch the school's budget. Staff support and input can help the parents determine what the school needs most.

These groups can have problems in terms of competition among members for leadership roles. The teacher may be able to suggest voting for leaders or rotating leadership roles. Where no leaders appear, teachers can suggest they list all the jobs needed to be done for completion of a project and draw straws to see who does what. Sometimes there is a great deal of disagreement as to what should be done for the school and how to do it. Sometimes parents get carried away and become involved in projects that are just too complicated. With experience, the teacher may be able to break down unrealistic or highly complex goals into smaller, more manageable units that will be equally beneficial to the school.

Sometimes, smaller is better. For example, after several unsuccessful attempts by a large, well-meaning, but highly competitive and disorganized group of parents to raise money to buy a piano for a particular school, two women decided to try something on their own. They arranged to photograph all of the classes with their teachers. By photographing each class every day for a week, they ensured that all the children would eventually be photographed regardless of the days they attended school. They picked a good spot—a hill on the playground—and took pictures all that week. What a team they were . . . one amusing the children and teachers with her playful antics while the other snapped the pictures. Within another week they had the pictures developed and had given samples and order blanks to all the teachers. The teachers displayed the sample pictures, took orders, and collected the nominal fee. Most parents were not only willing to cooperate in the fund-raising effort, but more than willing to buy the excellent pictures as well. Many ordered several copies. Within another week the two mothers had located, purchased, and delivered a good, second-hand piano with a five-year guarantee.

Understandably they were very pleased with themselves. They had given themselves a sense of accomplishment, the school a piano, and the parents some fine school photographs. Everyone agreed it was a most impressive feat. Clearly, there is much to be gained by encouraging and occasionally guiding parent groups of all types.

Parent Education

We have already noted that our culture does not provide much in the way of adequate preparation for parenthood at the time when it would be most valuable . . . *before* one becomes a parent. And education after the child's birth is also lacking. Parents could profit from the information contained in the fields of education and psychology, but many of them simply cannot afford the time and expense necessary for a formal education. Many are not motivated to pursue such study on their own. For others, language or health problems may interfere with their efforts to learn about parenthood.

Today early childhood educational facilities are beginning to recognize that parents need additional educational opportunities in the areas of parenthood, childcare, child development, and prenatal care for present or future pregnancies. In fact, some require that parents attend classes and that they work for a number of hours in the facility each week. Some programs provide training in the home. Others provide study and discussion groups led by teachers, directors, or administrators. Some provide guest lecturers.

At the very least, a facility provides a library for teachers and parents. It may be no more than a bookshelf in a corner containing appropriate resource materials and reference lists. It may be as much as a full room containing up-to-date resource material and a quiet place to read. Sometimes a school can provide a small budget for the purchase of new or used books and materials. Sometimes parents can donate or lend their resources to the school. Teachers might be willing to lend textbooks and materials from college courses they have taken. Fund-raising projects may provide library materials.

Regardless of how a facility promotes education, care must be taken to ensure that parents do not feel that they are inferior or in any way the recipients of charity. You want to convince the parent that they are doing a good job with their children, and that they are also invited to share in the continuing process of self-education that absorbs the staff and other parents. Let them know that the school always tries to keep up with new developments and that parents and teachers are invited to do the same, for the good of the children and themselves. Again, this is an area where your creativity and innovations can help enrich the program for everyone.

Conclusion

Without doubt, the days of the isolated, authoritarian, early childhood teacher are gone. No longer can the instructor deal with the children in a vacuum. The parents or caretakers of the child must be involved in the overall educational process. What happens in the school should not be isolated from what happens in the home. The teacher should strive to form a working relationship with the parents so that the expertise of both can be brought to bear on the educational process.

At the same time not all of us can work as effectively with *both* children and parents as we would like. Furthermore, we sometimes find certain parent problems that we are simply not equipped to handle (e.g., alcoholism, violence). In these cases the teacher needs to know about community resources that can provide appropriate professional help. Perhaps the best bit of advice is to try a *variety* of parental involvement techniques that will, in all probability, work with some of the parents, some of the time.

11

Teachers
and Their Concerns

In a sense, this entire book has been about teachers and their concerns (see also Kohl, 1976). But there remain a few additional topics that are of particular interest to both the new and the experienced teacher. This chapter looks at several issues which most teachers must address sooner or later. Some of these are theoretical, but most are practical. Some are straightforward, while others represent real problems that require difficult decisions. Basically, in this chapter we attempt to discuss substantial issues that will confront the teacher outside the college classroom, and under actual working conditions. In other words, this chapter attempts to bridge the gap between textbook learning and the reality of a career in early childhood education.

Reality: The Classroom

It is all well and good to write about issues and problems within the area of early childhood education. But nothing can quite prepare the novice for the joy, confusion, frustration, change, complexity, and satisfaction that characterize the actual classroom experience. In general, events move so rapidly within the classroom that it is often difficult to remember what kinds of advice one has previously acquired or how to apply that advice in an effective manner. We are suggesting that it is reasonable to feel uncertain and confused when you first face a class of a dozen or even two dozen active, complex youngsters, and you should expect a period of adjustment before things will be going smoothly. In this section we will attempt to provide a feeling for, or the flavor of, a typical classroom experience. In the next section we will describe some of the stages the new teacher may expect to pass through as she or he adjusts to the position of preschool teacher.

Imagine that two teachers, Karen and Charlie, are working with a class of fifteen 3 and 4 year olds. The classroom is arranged in centers, one each for art (paint, playdough, collage material), housekeeping, books, a sand table, manipulative toys (puzzles, Leggos, Lincoln logs, etc.), and blocks. Charlie stations himself in the art center where he can easily see most of the rest of the room. Karen stations herself in the block area where she can also see the other areas. As we join them, most of the children have been greeted and had their health checked. Parents have left, and the children are beginning to get involved in various activities. Charlie is immediately asked for help in putting on paint smocks, even though he is already in the middle of making playdough with several children. Like all early educators, Charlie must be able to do several things at the same time. And he must always keep track peripherally of the children in the surrounding areas. Although easels were set up ahead of time and some paints premixed, Jessica needs blue-green. So Charlie guides her paint mixing. As art projects are finished (and they are usually finished quickly), he writes names on them. He helps younger children hang pictures up to dry. Simultaneously, the playdough is being measured, poured, mixed, felt, squeezed, and appreciated on a tactile level. A lot of discussion leads up to the choice of a color for the playdough.

As Charlie is so occupied, Karen is supervising the beginning of block-building projects. She suggests that the children consider spreading out so they will all have plenty of room. Some children are getting out carts so they can load them with blocks and build some distance from the block shelves. Lisa, one of the smaller children, climbs into Jeffrey's cart and wants a ride. Jeffrey protests, but to no avail. He resorts to pushing and shoving her out of his cart. As Karen helps them verbalize their needs and discuss possible solutions, another child arrives, crying. Seeing that the crying child is Roger, who loves playdough more than anything, and that Karen is occupied, Charlie greets him and informs him that today's playdough is *orange*! He invites Roger to fill a vacant place right next to him at the table. Roger's mood takes a noticeable turn for the better. Karen signals her appreciation to Charlie.

While all this is going on, Sarah has the cozy book area, with its big, comfortable chair, all to herself. She has several books on her lap and is paging through one of her favorites with the concentration of a golfer about to attempt the winning putt. Jason, Kimberly, and Arnold are playing restaurant in the housekeeping area. Arnold, the waiter, is taking down their orders on his imaginary, or real, pad of paper. Jessica is making a puzzle.

Suddenly a loud crash is heard from the block area. Wails of frustration and anger fill the room. Linda, for lack of any other involvement, has taken to destroying block constructions. She has knocked down Karla's and is heading for another. Karla is chasing her, swinging a block in her hand. Karen alertly and quickly stops them both, just in time. She encourages another discussion of feelings, including Linda and her victim's. Then Karen suggests to Linda that the restaurant is in need of a cook and walks over to the housekeeping area with her to ease her into the game there. Karla goes back to assess the damage, and begin rebuilding.

Simultaneously, Jessica spills paint and the two children at the sand table begin a new game—throwing sand straight up in the air and watching how nicely it covers everything around them (including themselves). Charlie and Karen are off to the rescue again, each handling one crisis. Now Jessica, who has been making great gains in her toilet training efforts, suddenly realizes she has to go to the bathroom. But she can't get her belt unbuckled. Fortunately, Karen enlists help from Jessica's friend, Sarah, who gets Jessica to her destination just in the nick of time. Both girls giggle at the close call.

Time is flying and soon it will be time for cleanup, some songs, and a snack before they go outside. A "first call" warning is given to all the children. Charlie leaves for a quick break, and returns with the snack tray. Another warning is given and some cleanup is begun, with teachers helping. Karen gets out her guitar and begins to sing with the children who are ready. Charlie helps with the rest of the cleanup, giving block builders a little more time to enjoy what they've made. He and the builders put signs on structures to be saved. Most of the children are singing now. Eventually Charlie joins them as Karen takes a helper or two to set up snacks.

The remainder of the day is filled with similar activities, incidents, and emergencies, both large and small. There are pants to be changed, juice spills to be cleaned up, scratches and scrapes to be washed and bandaged, children to be held and cuddled, new activities to be introduced, parents' and other visitors' questions to be answered, observations and messages to be jotted down, crying children to be soothed, arguments to be worked out, and last but not least, a curriculum to be pursued.

The point is that events occur rapidly. Teachers must be alert and react quickly to all the necessities that so quickly arise. There is often little time to stop and think. One must move, *now*. One must be able to keep track of and do many different things at the same time.

Because so much of the teacher's time is spent meeting immediate and undeniable needs, it is a good idea to have the room set up so that most of the children can function independently and can learn in their own way with only occasional help from the teacher. Besides meeting the developmental needs of children, centers also meet some of the practical needs of teachers. Let's face it, fifteen children can keep two teachers hopping even if they each only need occasional help.

On top of all this ongoing maintenance work, Karen has ideas about what she would like to be doing with the children. She wants to work in, and introduce, new materials and activities. She wants to become involved with certain children who are having particular problems. She wants to participate with the children, make observations, give individual recognition, and hold and talk to the children in a relaxed and easy manner.

Of course, the days will vary. Sometimes things go very smoothly and teachers have time for more than what seem like simple maintenance tasks, which they quickly learn to make the most of with the children. But even then, the teacher is very busy responding and making quick decisions.

Meanwhile the children go about the business of learning through play and discovery. As far as they are concerned, the most hectic day can be an interesting, calm, average day. The teacher may be tied up in knots by the end of the day, but the children are already looking forward to tomorrow.

Even though all of this sounds hectic and confusing, the experienced teacher has learned to handle most of it calmly and effectively, and is able to promote an atmosphere of explanation, discovery, and industry. Just how a teacher reaches this state of serene effectiveness is the subject of the next section.

The Teacher's Developmental Stages

One does not become a relaxed, effective preschool teacher overnight. Experience and practice are necessary. The most important thing to remember is that periods of discouragement must be expected on the long road to teaching maturity. Don't expect too much too soon. Just rest assured that the job becomes easier and more rewarding as time goes on.

Just as the child develops so, too, does the teacher. Katz (1977) sees teachers as moving through four developmental stages on their way to maturity. She describes the feelings and events associated with each stage, and cites specific training needs appropriate to each stage. Figure 11.1 contains the training needs associated with each stage, while the following sections discuss the four levels of teacher development.

Stage 1: Survival

Every new teacher begins her or his career by being brought face to face with the reality of dealing with small children all day long. It is not an easy experience. It takes energy, patience, the strength of ten, a sense of humor, and as much confidence as possible. Even though time often seems to fly by, there is absolutely no doubt in your mind at the end of the day that it has been a long and hard session. Every aching bone and muscle in your body will tell you that. Your poor sore feet have a tale to tell as well.

The initial experience can lead to worry and self-doubt. How did I do? How will I ever do it again tomorrow? Is this really only Monday? Have I really gone to college all these years just to qualify for a day of torture? How will I ever survive this job—never mind enjoying it

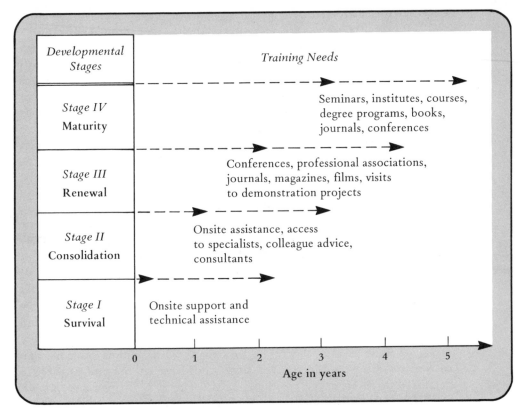

Figure 11.1 Stages of development and training needs of preschool teachers (Adapted from L. G. Katz Talks with Teachers, *Washington, D.C.: NAEYC, 1977)*

and getting a feeling of satisfaction from it? I made so many mistakes, the director must have added me to her idiot list. Will my replacement be here tomorrow?

But not to worry. All of these feelings are to be expected. Even though it is a demanding job filled with responsibility, you will survive and come to enjoy it. It takes a bit of time, a lot of thought and planning, and practice. But doesn't everything? You'll learn by doing, a difficult but effective means of acquiring skills. Don't be afraid to ask more experienced teachers about every facet of the experience. Seek as much feedback, and as many suggestions, as possible. Go to staff meetings. Watch and listen. You will survive. Get a lot of sleep (as if you could do anything else at night the first few weeks), and eat well. Keep your sense of humor. You can do it.

Stage 2: Consolidation

Although teachers vary greatly in how quickly they advance through these stages, Katz feels that most teachers make it through the survival stage by the end of the first year. At this point teachers see the gains they have made and can consolidate what they have learned so far. During the second stage teachers make use of techniques and skills acquired during the survival stage. They begin to be able to focus on the kinds of things they want to learn and want to do, rather than upon mere survival.

By this time teachers usually have a pretty clear grasp of the ways that most normal children behave, and they can identify children whose behavior deviates from the norm. Although they may have been too busy during the survival stage to help those children, they can now begin to move toward a resolution of some of these special needs. They can now focus upon particular children and upon certain kinds of problems. For example, a teacher might decide to explore ways of helping a particularly aggressive child develop nonaggressive modes of problem-solving. Or a teacher may decide to concentrate on developing effective ways of using puppets in the elicitation and expression of emotions and feelings. This is a time when teachers turn the corner from merely coping to finding ways of working effectively with children, parents, and co-workers. In a sense it's the time when the teacher moves from a defensive to an offensive position. It is a period of tremendous growth and a time when plans and interests develop rapidly.

Stage 3: Renewal

According to Katz, by the time the teacher has been in the job for two, three, or four years, she or he may feel the need to add new things to the repertoire of activities, skills, and techniques. This may be a time to catch up on the related reading that there was never enough time to do as a new teacher. One may want to familiarize oneself with new research being done in the field.

Although the children may be thoroughly happy with the activities a teacher uses each year, the teacher may be bored by the repetitive quality of it all. She or he needs to be stimulated again. If one can find ways to rearm oneself, and to perk flagging interests, the children will benefit as well. A bored teacher can be boring.

Stage 4: Maturity

Eventually, a teacher reaches a stage of maturity, where one comes to terms with oneself as a teacher. After the stage of survival, that of rapid growth, and the third stage of revitalization, the teacher may now find herself or himself becoming more concerned with abstract, philosophical questions and issues. The history of early childhood education and epistemological questions may be of great interest. The teacher may adopt a reflective, thoughtful attitude that goes far beyond the concerns of everyday classroom events. Questions such as, "What is the purpose of education?" and, "What place does education have in differing societies?" may now be asked.

As figure 11.1 indicates, the training needs for each of these stages are very different. The teacher should be aware of these training needs and should not ignore them. They are important to the development of the teacher. Like the child's developmental needs, those of the teacher must be taken seriously, and must be provided for at the proper time.

Reality: Working Conditions and Loyalties

Just as sometimes there is a gap between what one reads about the classroom experience and what one actually faces on the first day of a new job, so, too, there can be a gap between what one reads about the duties and roles of the preschool administration and what one encounters in the "real world." In other words, new teachers would be well advised to anticipate and expect occasional problems in their work situations and in their relations with the school administration. We do not intend to portray the average preschool administration in a negative light; to the contrary, most teacher-administration relationships are rewarding and mutually satisfying. But there is no doubt that problems can arise, and the teacher who has some idea of what kinds of difficulty there are may be better able to head them off, or at least be more able to handle them effectively, if they do develop. So, in this section we outline some of the more common kinds of problems that new and old teachers occasionally face. You may never have to deal with these sorts of situations; but, then again, they might be present during your first work experience.

Ideal Working Conditions

Just as you may never find the perfect love, the perfect house, the perfect pet, the perfect car, or the perfect spaghetti sauce, you may never find the perfect teaching position. Look for the best that's available and then adjust to the realities of that situation. As you begin to work, you will probably discover quite rapidly that while ideal ways of doing things are discussed in many textbooks, "real life" teaching positions often deviate from that ideal. Some examples might help illustrate this point. Let's look at one *ideal* teaching situation.

Your new employment agreement specifies that you will be paid for a period of time during which you set up your room and materials *before* the children arrive. You will also be paid for the time required to clean up your room, to plan and evaluate, and to attend staff or parent

A teacher's concerns . . .

. . . are many . . .

meetings *after* the children have left. Your school is well-equipped and you can obtain adequate supplies easily. Your group has a well-equipped room which does not have to be shared at any time with any other group. You can use the yard for any kind of activity at any time. The children arrive at and leave school at the designated times. The staff, administration, and parents all get along well. Training opportunities are plentiful. Morale is good. You work with a co-teacher who is cooperative, creative, has a positive attitude, and shares your point of view. You have a competent aide or student teacher who is intelligent and helpful. The three of you easily work out a schedule of activities, breaks, and lunches that best meet the needs of the children and adults. All of the children take a nap or rest quietly on cots. Parent and child interest and cooperation are high.

Actual Working Conditions

This rosy picture is seldom realized in real life. For instance, you may end up with little or no paid time for setting up, cleaning up, planning, evaluation, or attending meetings. You have a choice—either set up after the children have arrived or come in early and stay late on your own time. You may have a room that must be shared with another group. You get it part of the day; the other group has it the remainder of the

. . . and varied

time. Normal scheduling—not to mention "rainy day" scheduling—can be a real challenge. You will most likely share the yard with other groups, also, or be designated a specific time when your group can use it alone. The room and yard are inadequately equipped, and less than bountiful supplies will be ordered by the director.

Most of the staff members cooperate, but competitiveness, jealousies, differences in opinions can arise here and there. Your co-teacher may not always share your point of view, and may have a style that conflicts with yours. Sometimes the two of you will be compatible, but not always. You may not have a trained aide at all. Volunteers or participating parents may be some help, but they may also need help themselves. Rest periods for the teachers may not be clearly organized and you may have to take five minutes when there's a "break in the action." Even though a cook may prepare lunch, you may have to ready snacks yourself, and while watching fifteen children. Sometimes this is a good learning experience. Sometimes it's a great inconvenience.

Most of the children arrive within half an hour of the designated time (before or after), but some will arrive much earlier or later. And there always seem to be children who are picked up late at the end of the day. These very early or very late children must either be cared for by you or you must arrange for them to be taken to the extended day-care group. Most of the children nap. However, some never sleep and need quiet activities. Parents and children vary enormously in interest and cooperation. Scheduling to meet everyone's needs is a major problem.

In other words, the new teacher who is expecting to teach in a perfect situation may be in for a shock. The one who expects the unexpected, and is ready to be alert and flexible, is the one who will flourish.

Conflicting Loyalties

Teachers sometimes find themselves in a position where they are torn between conflicting loyalties. As one becomes an experienced teacher in a particular school, many loyalties develop—to the school, to the parents, to the children, to other staff members, and to oneself. But what does one do when these loyalties come into conflict?

For example, imagine that, to save money, a new administrator drastically cuts the budget for supplies and begins to add more children to each group without a corresponding increase in teachers. Parents have been promised the lower ratios, and they are not told of the changes. Because they are in and out of the school quickly and have trust in the school, they do not notice these changes at first.

The teachers begin to have conflicting feelings. They want to support their school and help solve the budget problems, but they feel adequate supplies and low ratios are essential. They suggest to the administrator that other methods may be preferable. They feel parents should be informed of, and involved in, the difficulties and their resolutions. But the administrator disagrees and becomes quite intimidating. He informs the teachers that he expects their complete loyalty. They are told that to alarm parents is unprofessional and that "this school wants only professionals on its staff." Teachers become confused and morale begins to deteriorate.

Of course, this is an extreme example, but it illustrates the sort of things that can happen. What would you do in a situation such as this? When? And how? Remember there are certain hard realities involved. Specifically, the administrator, in his need to economize, is not above deluding the parents. Unfortunately, he does not view the parents as partners or as sources of cooperation and help. Rather, he fears their power to take their children out of his school if they see problems arising. The teachers understand that their jobs may be jeopardized if they openly oppose the administrator. Furthermore, they are being asked to do several things that go against their beliefs about what constitutes a good program. The quality of the program is beginning to deteriorate and yet the teachers are being told to act as if nothing is changing. They are being asked to betray the trust of the parents and children. What would you do? What is the professional thing to do?

There is no simple answer in a case like this. Each individual must decide personally what to do. Some may be willing to lose their jobs if that is what it takes to bring these sorts of difficulties out into the open, but this is a tremendous sacrifice to ask of someone whose livelihood depends upon a preschool position. At the very least, talk and communication are essential in this sort of problem. Secrecy can lead to nothing more than deeper problems. Without open, free communication and a willingness to admit problems, there is little hope for rapid improvement.

Seeking Employment

Volunteer and Substitute Work

Most of the readers of this book will to some degree be considering a career in early childhood teaching or research. Many will complete a four-year college program. Others will gain state or local certification by taking twelve to fifteen units of prescribed early education courses. Some readers, already working, will continue to take additional courses for both self-satisfaction and career advancement. In other words, many of you are already on your way toward a successful career. Still, it is helpful to outline some of the steps that can be taken on the path toward meaningful employment.

There are many ways to gain experience and to learn about employment opportunities. Talk to your instructors about local, state, and federal programs. If you find a program that interests you, find out what it would take, in terms of requirements, for you to become a member. Find out what your chances would be of being taken on if you did meet the requirements. In general, be certain that the kind of training and education you are planning will qualify you for the kind of position you want. Find out ahead of time; there is nothing more disheartening than to discover you need one more course, or set of courses, to qualify for a given position.

In many programs you must start at the bottom and work your way up. In these cases, you may want to begin working on a part-time basis, or as a volunteer, while you are still in school. Volunteering or being placed on a substitute list are excellent ways to get to know a school, and for the school to get to know you. By volunteering, you can gain a realistic impression of the program before you agree to take a position. You will meet staff, children, and parents. You will see the program in action. You will be able to tell if this is or is not what you want.

It is also good that the staff, parents, and children can see you in action as a volunteer or substitute. By serving in these capacities, you are no longer just another name on an application blank. You are someone that they know personally. They can observe your particular working style. You will be seen as a person with talent and potential. You are not an unknown. They will come to know that you can be depended upon and that you will be there when they need you.

Of course, you don't want to volunteer indefinitely. Let your potential employers know that you are willing to volunteer on a temporary basis so you can both get an idea of what the other is like. While doing volunteer work, the trick is to make yourself invaluable to the school. Do your very best. Show that you are reliable and that you can work well in their program. Let them know what your educational and professional goals are. Keep them informed of your progress, and obtain as much feedback from them as possible. Let them know you are willing to learn from them and that you are flexible enough to fit in where you are needed. Be sure they understand that you are serious about your work and your goals.

If your volunteer work is good, your chances for future employment will be increased immensely. It's not an easy job to hire teachers or researchers without first observing them under working conditions. Trying to hire the best people for the right job is a tremendous responsibility. Employers can't really learn very much from an application form. They can't be sure that a particular applicant will be liked or disliked by the children, the parents, or the rest of the staff. They don't know if you will be reliable, responsible, warm, friendly, creative—or the opposite. But if you volunteer, you are showing real interest and determination.

If you can be flexible enough to be a substitute, your talents will be well-appreciated. Many schools have great difficulty in maintaining a reliable substitute list. And in a profession where everyone—children, staff, and parents—tend to share colds and flus and whatever else happens to be contagious that week, a good sub is an invaluable person. By substituting in a variety of classes, you will gain insight and experience in working with various age groups and with various teachers. Many times staff members who like working with you as a substitute will recommend you to the director and the other teachers. If you have done well, teachers will ask for you when openings occur. Since directors and administrators know it is important for their teachers to like one another, this can be helpful.

In other words, volunteering and substituting are two good ways to get your foot in the door. They are legitimate, important mechanisms whereby both the employee and potential employer can evaluate one another before a firm commitment is made by either party.

The CDA Program

Let's say you have worked in early childhood education for a while and have done well. You know you are a good teacher, and you enjoy the work. However, you have no degree, no certificate, and will not be able to go on in your formal education—at least not for quite a while. But you would like to have some professional standing, something that vouches for your ability and experience. What you need is something that will convince potential employers that you are a qualified teacher even though you do not hold a degree.

Many people find themselves in this position. Requirements for working in preschools have been variable over the years. As a result, many excellent teachers, with years of experience, have no concrete credentials. People who have worked their way up in Head Start and similar programs find themselves in this position. They have proven their ability but have no way of documenting that ability in a concrete manner.

However, the situation is changing. Recently, a federal program has been developed whereby persons can obtain training and professional status based upon their ability to work with young children rather than upon formal academic training. The Child Development Associate (CDA) program was developed in the early 1970s and is now regulated by the Child Development Associate Consortium. Under this program, early childhood education workers are awarded a credential when they meet the requirements of the consortium. The credential designates the recipient as a Child Development Associate. Recognition of this credential has been increasing steadily since the first one was awarded in 1975. The credential recognizes, and gives professional standing to, those who have not had the opportunity to complete formal academic training in the field but have demonstrated their ability to work *effectively* with young children. At the present time the credential can only be earned by people working in centers with 3 to 5 year olds. But, in the near future, the credential program may well be extended into different learning situations and age groups.

In order to receive the credential, each candidate is assessed by a Local Assessment Team (LAT). The LAT is composed of the candidate, a trainer (often the director of the center where the candidate works), a parent-community representative, and a consortium representative. The trainer and the parent-community representative are chosen by the candidate. Their specific functions include observing the candidate as she or he works with children and parents and collecting information pertinent to the candidate's work experience. They also participate in a final, decisive LAT meeting. The candidate's duties include applying to the CDA program, preparing a portfolio that demonstrates competence in childcare, contacting and coordinating the actions of the chosen team members, and arranging for the final LAT meeting. The consortium representative's responsibilities include participating in the final LAT meeting, verifying that all procedures have been followed properly, and collecting and mailing all LAT materials to the consortium. The LAT recommends that, "the candidate is competent and should be awarded the CDA credential or the candidate needs more training and is not recommended for the CDA credential at this time." (Child Development Associate Consortium, 1976, p. 9).

The LAT must provide feedback to the candidate in the form of a profile. This profile includes a summary of the candidate's strengths and weaknesses. It contains specific suggestions concerning ways in which the candidate might improve, even if the credential is awarded.

Figure 11.2 shows the CDA Consortium Competency Structure. This figure provides some idea of what it is that the LAT will be looking for in the CDA candidate.

The following is a list of requirements that must be met before one can become a candidate:

1. Be at least 16 years old.
2. Know of a center where he or she can be observed working with children.
3. Have at least eight consecutive months of full-time experience or sixteen consecutive months of part-time (less than three days a week) experience working with three to five year old children in a group setting with their parents.

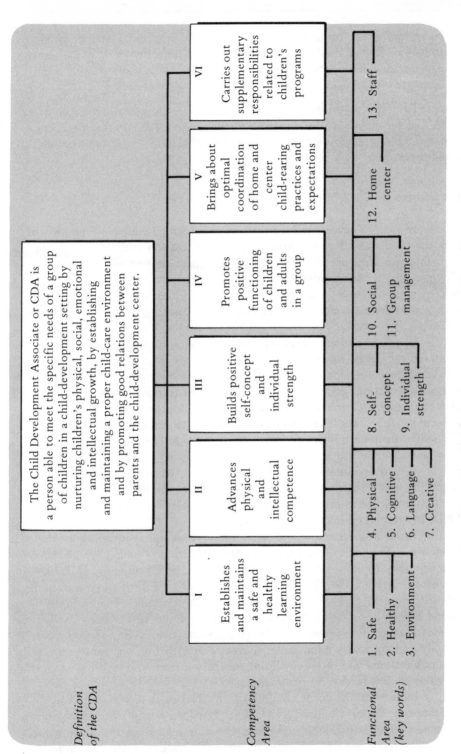

Figure 11.2 The Child Development Associate Consortium competency structure (Adapted from The Child Development Associate credential and the credential award system, Washington, D.C.: CDA Consortium, 1976)

Definition of the CDA

The Child Development Associate or CDA is a person able to meet the specific needs of a group of children in a child-development setting by nurturing children's physical, social, emotional and intellectual growth, by establishing and maintaining a proper child-care environment and by promoting good relations between parents and the child-development center.

Competency Area

I   Establishes and maintains a safe and healthy learning environment

II Advances physical and intellectual competence

III Builds positive self-concept and individual strength

IV Promotes positive functioning of children and adults in a group

V   Brings about optimal coordination of home and center child-rearing practices and expectations

VI Carries out supplementary responsibilities related to children's programs

Functional Area (key words)

1. Safe
2. Healthy
3. Environment

4. Physical
5. Cognitive
6. Language
7. Creative

8. Self-concept
9. Individual strength

10. Social
11. Group management

12. Home center

13. Staff

333

4. Have had either some formal training (in a university, college, junior college or high school) or some informal training (in workshops, seminars or in-service programs) in early childhood education/child development. (CDA Consortium, 1976, p. 1)

For further information about the CDA program write to: The CDA Consortium, 7315 Wisconsin Avenue, Suite 601E, Washington, D.C. 20014. This is a growing program whose credential is becoming recognized throughout the country.

Job Sources

There are many sources of information about employment. First of all, pick the brains of all your instructors for information and referrals. Second, find out if your school or university (past or present) has an employment center for students and alumni. They will help you start an employment file, give you helpful hints about filling out applications and going on interviews, and will send you to any openings for which you are qualified.

Check your local want ads and subscribe to newspapers in other geographical areas of interest. Local women's groups, parent groups, the Chamber of Commerce and other community groups may know of openings in various schools and centers. Parent co-ops can also be located and contacted. Check the Yellow Pages for locations and descriptions of local schools. Visit local preschools and get to know the administrators and staff. Contact the United Way for referrals to family service agencies. Any contact may prove to be valuable.

If you are interested in research, check with your student counselor, the early childhood education department in your college or university, and write to other colleges and universities regarding master's and Ph.D. programs, grants, and scholarships.

Write to local, state, and federal governmental agencies about their programs. The U.S. Government Printing Office is a source of information on many topics. Write to: Superintendent of Documents, U.S. Government Printing Office, Washington, D.C. 20402. Tell them your area of interest and ask for a catalogue of available publications. For example, "I would like to know of any publications available on Head Start." Many publications are free, most are relatively inexpensive. They respond very quickly and are a very good initial source of information on many subjects. The publications you receive will undoubtedly inform you of other sources to write to for further information.

Inquire at the local chapter of the National Association for the Education of Young Children (NAEYC). They may be able to refer you to other sources of valuable information. Become a member and go to meetings. The more people you know in the field, the better your chances are of hearing about upcoming or present job openings. If you don't know how to contact the NAEYC chapter for your area, write or call the head office: National Association for the Education of Young Children (NAEYC), 1834 Connecticut Avenue, N.W., Washington, D.C. 20009.

As you can see, there are many ways to obtain the information you need. It may seem difficult to get started, but once you do, it begins to snowball; and, suddenly, you have all sorts of information flowing in. Just start—*now*. The sooner you start, the faster you will build up contacts and sources.

Intervention Teaching

Because intervention programs are so influential today, and because they represent a unique challenge to the teacher, we shall spend a little time discussing the teacher's position within them. Teaching in an intervention program makes special demands upon the teacher. Not every teacher could, or would want to, work in this demanding situation, for it takes a special kind of commitment, understanding, and even courage. Working in an intervention program usually means working in a poverty area with people who live under a great deal of stress. Let us look first at the intervention setting, next at the people, and finally at the teacher's role (Comer and Poussaint, 1975).

The Poverty Setting

Intervention programs are, very often, located in urban areas. Physically, the neighborhoods may be dirty, run-down, smoggy, noisy, and congested. Homes and tenement buildings are often overcrowded, long in need of repair, and infested with vermin. Poor lighting, ventilation, and plumbing are common. Tended, suburban-type yards and parks are uncommon: children play where they can, on sidewalks, in streets, and in alleys. In short, these areas are not pleasing to the eye. Unless one has lived or worked in such areas, they can be shocking and frightening. The fact that these areas often have high crime rates can unsettle the new teacher. Whites visiting black or Mexican areas often feel that they "stand out," and sense that they are potential targets. In other words, the new intervention teacher must anticipate a certain degree of uneasiness.

People

Honig (1975) has described some of the problems teachers face in dealing with the parents of intervention program children. First, these parents are often suspicious of, or intimidated by, any institution or power structure. In their minds teachers and schools are things to be suspected. The motives and methods of teachers and schools are often regarded with deep distrust. Second, these low income parents often have so many other problems that they have little time or energy to think about, or take part in, their children's education. They may miss appointments or fail to bring their children to school on time. They may have trouble believing in the value of the program, and in themselves as valuable participants. They often lack confidence in themselves, their children, and the teachers. Third, overcrowding at home may add to the difficulties and frustrations. Because of a lack of money, health and emotional problems are often neglected. The children will reflect these conditions in their thought and action.

Honig points out that patience is essential because people can change only gradually. But they *do* change. The gradual change that can occur in parental attitudes is illustrated by the following quotes from parents participating in a number of Parent and Child Centers (PCC) around the country.

PCC made me a mother—before that I just gave birth—I used to run around with men a lot and felt the kids just bogged me down —but now I really enjoy them.

Made me feel a lot more comfortable about being a mother—I used to whip the children—but I don't do that any more.

With the children I used to lose my patience. They taught me how a child of certain ages should act so I gradually became a better mother. I was able to control my temper and respond in a better attitude. I didn't know how to handle their fighting and screaming. Then I saw how the PCC teachers operated and I learned.

I've learned that kids are individuals—before I just raised them— clothed and fed them. Now I'm aware of even little differences and praise them and give them credit for what they can do at their own speed. I feel therefore I'm a better parent and an important person. Before I felt that anyone could do this job.

I used to whip first and ask questions later.

I love the children a lot more. There are things that you don't appreciate until you learn about them. You appreciate them for what they are, little individuals. You can't love a child enough. Before I didn't really like children.

I feel more adequate as a person, my life has meaning to it. My relationship to my husband has improved because I have been able to stand up to him in showing him how important a woman's role is.

I'm the best example. Three years ago I didn't talk to anybody. Now I'm on the school board, and the welfare board, and now I speak to anybody.

(Honig, 1975, pp. 60–61)

Intervention Teachers

It is no simple matter to be an effective intervention teacher. Qualities that are essential in any educational setting are doubly important here. Patience, understanding, courage, persistence, and commitment are vital for work with low income families. As we have seen, if parents are not committed to the program, it probably won't succeed. Hence it is absolutely essential that the intervention teacher make a significant positive impression upon the low income parent. Anyone interested in intervention teaching can gain insight into what is and what is not a good intervention teacher by reading the following statements made by low income parents about intervention teachers (Honig, pp. 53–54):

I feel I'm equal to her. She never puts me down. And you know that she has the same problems—just normal everyday people who don't try to run your life. She knows that everyone is different.

She has always been friendly and helpful in anyway she could. Always there to contact for any problem.

She's very understanding. She's gone through a lot with me. I don't answer the door or phone. It takes a person with a lot of nerve to try to see me. If she weren't so patient and understanding my child wouldn't be in the center. I don't think most people would put up with someone like me. I know I wouldn't.

She's patient. I'm awfully moody at times.

She's never down or mean though she has problems, too.

She's given help on personal problems and taken us to her home. She's helped me out of certain personal jams.

She's frank with you. She tells you what she thinks about things. You can believe her. She doesn't twist things.

She's not afraid to come into my house and eat my cooking.

She worked her schedule around mine.

The way she puts things gives me choices; though she tells me when she's upset by something I've done.

She's always there to contact for every problem.

She likes her job more than just for the money.

She's one of the best friends I've got.

As you can see, it seems essential to the success of intervention teaching for the teacher to convince the parents that she or he is honest, committed, trustworthy, and an equal.

Intervention teachers must also be able to cope with the fact that, no matter how hard they try, they will not be able to effect a great deal of immediate change. They must be willing to keep on striving for improvements, no matter how small or infrequent. Poverty and its associated problems are complex. Although we wish it were the whole answer, intervention can only be a part of the final solution.

Finally, a good intervention teacher must be nonjudgemental. Many new teachers are surprised to discover that they are not quite as fair or as neutral as they had thought. They discover that they must acquire, and tune finely, this quality, as they deal with low-income individuals.

Working with the Financially Advantaged

Just as there are unique problems associated with working among low income clientele so too are there some unique problems that can arise in dealing with the other end of the socioeconomic spectrum—the high income clientele.

Groucho Marx has been credited with saying, "I've been rich and I've been poor, and rich is better." Probably most of us believe that, but most of us will never have the opportunity to find out for sure. Feelings of envy and/or resentment towards those who are well off do exist and can become a problem for teachers working with children from high income families. If one is teaching in a school whose clientele falls into the upper income bracket, then one may well have to come to grips with negative feelings.

We may say that we want all children to have the best life can offer. We want children to have books, toys, and nice homes. We want them to have wonderful experiences traveling, and to learn about the world. We want them to have positive attitudes about themselves and life in general. We want children to be able to express their needs and their feelings. We want children to look toward the future with hope and confidence.

But, somehow, many of us have trouble dealing with children who *do* have all these advantages. When children arrive at school in Mercedes and Rolls Royces (some of them complete with chauffeur), talk about maids and gardeners, and occasionally speak to teachers as though they were servants, some teachers have a little trouble in being nonjudgemental. "Spoiled brat" is a phrase that is sometimes whispered during school hours and shouted in frustration after the children have left. Some teachers find it difficult to cope with wealth, and the complacency that appears to accompany it, when they know that there are so many people who have nothing at all. Adjusting to wealthy clientele can be as difficult as adjusting to low income clientele.

But it can be done. The trick is to realize that high income people have their troubles, too. As the old cliché points out, money doesn't necessarily bring happiness. The problems of some high income individuals may seem more comfortable than those faced by the low income person, but they are real and serious problems nonetheless. For example, some (not all) high income people are trapped in highly competitive worlds where achievement is expected and failure leads to misery. These people sometimes live under great pressure. They must constantly try to do better, to succeed, to win, to accomplish, and to acquire. More, more, more. Sometimes they are so busy trying to maintain their status that they really have little time to relax and enjoy it. Husbands often spend long hours working, isolated from their homes and families. It is the famous high blood pressure, early heart attack rat-race.

Wives are often busy with their own pressured careers, or are trapped in large homes where they try to fill their hours supervising servants, planning social events, and generally trying to project and protect an image of style and wealth. They may be fairly involved with their children, but many have live-in maids or governesses. These women, in spite of all the expensive trappings, can feel they are living empty, fruitless lives.

The children, of course, can pick up the stress placed upon success and winning at a very early age. By the time they reach preschool age, they may already be suffering from the pressure, and inevitable sense of failure that accompany a competitive orientation.

Of course, this has been a stereotyped description of the high income family situation. Many people can, and do, cope with money and success, and have very happy, well-adjusted children. Still, everyone, including the wealthy, must deal with the complexity of interpersonal relationships and life's uncertainties. And all children need help in understanding and learning about their own world—whatever it may be. The teacher of the advantaged must be understanding, patient, and as nonjudgemental as possible. Whatever the situation, rich or poor, the teacher will have to deal with needy people.

There is an old joke about the man who complains that his brother thinks he is a chicken. When the doctor asks, "Why don't you get rid of him?" the man replies, "We can't. We need the eggs." We all need the eggs in life and love. The preschool clientele, no matter what the financial situation, is no exception.

The Fun of Teaching

Teaching is serious business. We think we've made that point quite clearly. It's a great responsibility that cannot be taken lightly. But teaching is pleasurable, too, and we'd like to close this book with a few examples that show just how rewarding, and how much fun, teaching can be.

It's wonderful when:

An "I can't" child finally says, "I can."

A child who felt rejected by you when he was promoted out of your class finally says, "I'm ready to be your friend again."

A 4 year old tells you that your buckteeth can be fixed if you have bracelets put on them.

You come to school feeling low, and one very perceptive 2 year old hugs you and asks you if you're okay.

The kids come in and discover the brown finger paint is chocolate pudding.

A child makes it to the potty in time, for the first time—and feels proud.

The children arrive first thing in the morning and run to give you a hug and excitedly tell you their news.

Everyone gets ready to go home—and no one has lost a sweater.

Everyone agrees the playdough should be purple.

A child sticks up for himself for the first time. You hear the words you taught him shouted: "Don't hit me! I don't like that!"

You planned a parent meeting and nearly half the parents came.

You took fifteen children and five parents to the zoo and came back with fifteen children and five parents.

Your director says, "You're doing a great job"—and you agree.

A child shares something with a friend for the first time.

A child has gone on vacation to a national park and brings you a stick as a souvenir.

It's Monday and you've had a great day.

You've had a bad day—but it's Friday.

It's the last day of the school year and you're sorry to have your group for the last time—and so are they.

You didn't think you'd like the 2 year old group, but now you find them irresistible.

The children are chopping down an imaginary tree and one shouts, "Kimber!"

An injured, crying child needs only your hugs to make her feel better. Plus a Band-Aid.

You're 30 years old and a child asks if you have any grandchildren.

When you overheard one little girl bragging to another, "Ha Ha. I have more fingers than you do!"

A childs asks you, "Where did I come from?" After a brief discussion about babies, she says, "Joey came from Cincinnati. Where did I come from?"

You have all of the children asleep on their cots when the fire engine whizzes by, siren and all.

When a 5 year old refers to a Bird of Paradise blossom as a "Bird of Transylvania."

When a child cuts a piece out of her security blanket and gives it to you.

When you take a group to a local farm and one child says, "All this mooing is giving me a headache."

Bibliography

Adams, J. *Learning and Memory: an Introduction*, Homewood, Ill.: The Dorsey Press, 1976.

Ainsworth, M. D. S. "The development of infant-mother attachment." In B. M. Caldwell and H. N. Ricciuti (eds.) *Review of Child Development Research, Vol. 3*, Chicago: University of Chicago Press, 1973.

Ainsworth, M. D. S., Bell, S. M. J., and Stayton, D. "Individual differences in strange situation behavior of one-year-olds." In H. R. Schaffer (ed.) *The Origins of Human Social Relations*, London: Academic Press, 1971.

Ariés, P. *Centuries of Childhood*, New York: Knopf, 1962.

Allen, K. E., Henke, L. B., Harris, F. R., Baer, D. M., and Reynolds, N. J. "Control of hyperactivity by social reinforcement of attending behavior." *Journal of Educational Psychology*, 1967, 58, 231–237.

Almy, M. *The Early Childhood Educator at Work*, New York: McGraw-Hill, 1975.

Anastasiow, N. S., and Hanes, M. L. *Language Patterns of Poverty Children*, Springfield, Ill.: Charles C. Thomas, 1976.

Atkinson, K., MacWhinney, B., and Stoel, C. "An experiment on recognition of babbling." *Papers and Reports on Child Language Development*, Stanford, Ca.: Stanford U.P., 1970.

Bergman, J. "Are little girls being harmed by 'Sesame Street?'" In J. Stacey, S. Bereaud, and J. Daniels (eds.) *And Jill Came Tumbling After: Sexism in American Education*, New York: Dell, 1974.

Berman, L. M. *New Priorities in the Curriculum*, Columbus, Oh.: Charles E. Merrill, 1968.

Biber, B. *Challenges Ahead for Early Childhood Education*, Washington, D.C.: National Association for the Education of Young Children, 1969.

Biber, B. "A developmental-interaction approach: Bank Street College of Education." In M. C. Day, and R. K. Parker (eds.) *The Preschool in Action*, Boston: Allyn and Bacon, 1977.

Biber, B., Shapiro, E., Wickens, D., in collaboration with Gilkeson, E. *Promoting Cognitive Growth*, Washington, D.C.: National Association for the Education of Young Children, 1977.

Biehler, R. F. *Psychology Applied to Teaching*, Boston: Houghton Mifflin, 1974.

Bird, C., and Briller, S. W. *Born Female*, New York: Pocket Books, 1972.

Blank, M. *Teaching Learning in the Preschool: A Dialogue Approach*, Columbus, Oh.: Charles E. Merrill, 1973.

Boardman, E. L. "An investigation of the effect of preschool training on the developmental vocal accuracy in young children." *Council for Research in Music Education Bulletin*, 1967, 11, 46–49.

Braine, M. D. S. "Piaget on reasoning: a methodological critique and alternative proposals." In W. Kessen, and C. Kuhlmann (eds.) *Thought in the Young Child*. Monographs of the Society for Research in Child Development, 1962, 27, No. 2.

Braine, M. D. S. "The ontogeny of English phrase structure: the first phase." *Language*, 1963, 39, 1–13.

Braun, S. J., and Edwards, E. P. *History and Theory of Early Childhood Education*, Worthington, Oh.: Charles A. Jones, 1972.

Bronfenbrenner, U. *Two Worlds of Childhood*, New York: Russell Sage Foundation, 1970.

Bronfenbrenner, U. "Is early intervention effective?" In *A Report on Longitudinal Evaluations of Preschool Programs, Vol. 2*, Washington, D.C.: DHEW Publication No. (OHD) 76–30025, 1974.

Brown, C., and Seitz, J. " 'You've come a long way, baby.' Historical perspectives." In R. Mayan (ed.) *Sisterhood is Powerful*, New York: Random House, 1970.

Brown, R. *A First Language: the Early Stages*, Cambridge, Ma.: Harvard U.P., 1973.

Bruner, J., Jolly, A., and Sylva, K. *Play—Its Role in Development and Evolution*, New York: Basic Books, 1976.

Buckley, H. "The little boy." *School Arts*, vol. 61, no. 2, October 1961, pp. 24–25.

Bull, J. "High school women: oppression and liberation." In J. Stacey, S. Bereaud, and J. Daniels (eds.) *And Jill Came Tumbling After: Sexism in American Education*, New York: Dell, 1974.

Cazden, C. B. "Suggestions from studies of early language acquisition." In C. B. Cazden (ed.) *Language in Early Childhood Education*, Washington, D.C.: National Association for the Education of Young Children, 1972.

Cazden, C. B., Baratz, J. C., Labov, W., and Palmer, F. H. "Language development in day-care programs." In C. B. Cazden (ed.) *Language in Early Childhood Education*, Washington, D.C.: National Association for the Education of Young Children, 1972.

Chafetz, J. S. *Masculine/Feminine or Human?* Itasca, Ill.: F. E. Peacock, 1974.

The Child Development Associate Credential and Credential Award System, Washington, D.C.: The Child Development Consortium, 1976.

Chomsky, N. *Language and Mind*, New York: Harcourt Brace Jovanovich, 1968.

Clay, M. M. *What Did I Write?* London: Heinemann, 1975.

Cohen, D. J., and Zigler, E. "Federal day care standards: rationale and recommendations." *Young Children*, 1978, 33, 24–32.

Comer, J. P., and Poussaint, A. F. *Black Child Care*, New York: Simon and Schuster, 1975.

Davidoff, L. L. *Introduction to Psychology*, New York: McGraw-Hill, 1976.

Décarie, T. G. *Intelligence and Affectivity in Early Childhood*, (trans. E. P. Brandt and L. W. Brandt.) New York: International U.P., 1965.

Durant, W. *Our Oriental Heritage*, New York: Simon and Schuster, 1954.

Durkin, D. *Teaching Them To Read*, Boston: Allyn and Bacon, 1970.

Eliot, A. *Fundamental Principles* Nursery Training School of Boston, mimeograph, 1944.

Ellis, H. C. *Fundamentals of Human Learning and Cognition*, Dubuque, Ia.: Wm. C. Brown, 1972.

Ellis, M. J. *Why People Play*, Englewood Cliffs, N.J.: Prentice-Hall, 1973.

Engel, R. C. *Language Motivating Experiences for Young Children*, Sherman Oaks, Ca.: Rose C. Engel, 1968.

Evans, E. D. *Contemporary Influences in Early Childhood Education*, New York: Holt, Rinehart and Winston, 1971.

Fantz, R. L. "The origin of form perception." *Scientific American*, 1961, 204, 66–72.

Farrell, W. *The Liberated Man*, New York: Bantam, 1975.

Featherstone, H. "The use of settings in a heterogeneous preschool." *Young Children*, March 1974, 147–154.

Ferster, C. S., and Skinner, B. F. *Schedules of Reinforcement*, New York: Appleton, 1957.

Fisher, E. "Children's books: the second sex, junior division." In J. Stacey, S. Bereaud, and J. Daniels (eds.) *And Jill Came Tumbling After: Sexism in American Education*, New York: Dell, 1974.

Flavell, J. H. *The Developmental Psychology of Jean Piaget*, New York: Van Nostrand, 1963.

Fleischmann, B., Gilmore, S., and Ginsburg, H. "The strength of nonconservation." *Journal of Experimental Child Psychology*, 1966, 4, 353–368.

Friedan, B. *The Feminine Mystique*, New York: Dell, 1974.

Ginsburg, H., and Opper, S. *Piaget's Theory of Intellectual Development: an Introduction*, Englewood Cliffs, N.J.: Prentice-Hall, 1969.

Goldberg, P. "Are women prejudiced against women?" In J. Stacey, S. Bereaud, and J. Daniels (eds.) *And Jill Came Tumbling After: Sexism in American Education*. New York: Dell, 1974.

Goodlad, J. I., Klein, M. F., Novotney, J. M., and associates. *Early Schooling in the United States*, New York: McGraw-Hill, 1973.

Goodnow, J. J., and Bethon, G. "Piaget's tasks: the effects of schooling and intelligence." *Child Development*, 1966, 37, 573–582.

Greenberg, P. *The Devil Has Slippery Shoes*, Toronto: Macmillan, 1969.

Guthrie, E. R. *The Psychology of Learning*, New York: Harper, 1952.

Hall, J. F. *Classical Conditioning and Instrumental Learning: A Contemporary Approach*, Philadelphia: Lippincott, 1976.

Hamilton, M. L. *Father's Influence on Children*, Chicago: Nelson-Hall, 1977.

Harrison, D. S., and Trobasso, T. *Black English: a seminar*. New York: Wiley, 1976.

Hayes, D., and Grether, J. "The school year and vacation: when do students learn?" Paper presented at the Eastern Sociological Convention, New York, 1969.

Hergenhahn, B. R. *Theories of Learning,* Englewood Cliffs, N.J.: Prentice-Hall, 1976.

Hermanson, L. W. "An investigation of the effects of timbre on simultaneous vocal pitch acuity of young children." *Dissertation Abstracts International,* 1972, 3558-A.

Hewett, F. M., and Forness, S. R. *Education of Exceptional Learners,* Boston: Allyn and Bacon, 1974.

Hilgard, E. K., Atkinson, R. C., and Atkinson, R. L. *Introduction to Psychology,* New York: Harcourt Brace Jovanovich, 1975.

Hill, D. M. *Mud, Sand, and Water,* Washington, D.C.: National Association for the Education of Young Children, 1977.

Hirsch, E. S. (ed.) *The Block Book.* Washington, D.C.: National Association for the Education of Young Children, 1974.

Holmes, M. B. *Child Abuse and Neglect Programs: Practice and Theory,* Washington, D.C.: Public Health Service; Alcohol, Drug Abuse, and Mental Health Administration, DHEW Publication No. (ADM) 78-344, 1977.

Honig, A. *Parent Involvement in Early Childhood Education,* Washington, D.C.: National Association for the Education of Young Children, 1975.

Honig, A., and Carterette, E. C. "Evaluation by women of painters as a function of their sex and achievement and sex of the judges." *Bulletin of the Psychonomic Society,* 1978, 11, 356–358.

Houston, J. P. *Fundamentals of Learning,* New York: Academic Press, 1976.

Houston, J. P., Bee, H., Hatfield, E., and Rimm, D. *Invitation to Psychology,* New York: Academic Press, 1979.

Hulse, S. H., Deese, J., and Egeth, H. *The Psychology of Learning,* New York: McGraw-Hill, 1975.

Jenkins, G. G., and Shacter, H. S. *These Are Your Children,* Glenview, Ill.: Scott, Foresman, 1975.

Johnston, M. K., Kelley, C. S., Harris, F. R., and Wolf, M. M. "An application of reinforcement principles to development of motor skills of young children." *Child Development,* 1966, 37, 379–387.

Jones, E. "Teacher education: entertainment or interaction?" *Young Children,* 1978, 33, 15–23.

Kamii, C., and DeVries, R. *Piaget, Children, and Number,* Washington, D.C.: National Association for the Education of Young Children, 1976.

Kamii, C., and DeVries, R. "Piaget for early education." In M. C. Day and R. K. Parker (eds.) *The Preschool in Action,* Boston: Allyn and Bacon, 1977.

Kanowitz, L. *Women and the Law: the Unfinished Revolution,* Albuquerque: University of New Mexico Press, 1969.

Karnes, M. B. *Research and Development Program on Disadvantaged Children: Final Report,* Washington, D.C.: U.S. Office of Education, 1969.

Karnes, M. B., and Zehrbach, R. R. "Educational intervention at home." In M. C. Day and R. K. Parker (eds.) *The Preschool in Action,* Boston: Allyn and Bacon, 1977.

Karnes, M. B., Zehrbach, R. R., and Teska, J. A. "Conceptualization of the GOAL (Game-Oriented Activities for Learning) curriculum." In M. C. Day, and R. K. Parker (eds.) *The Preschool in Action,* Boston: Allyn and Bacon, 1977.

Katz, L. G. *Talks with Teachers*, Washington, D.C.: National Association for the Education of Young Children, 1977.

Kelber, M. "What Bella Knew." *Ms.* vol. 7 no. 10, April 1979, p. 98.

Kellogg, R. *Analyzing Children's Art*, Palo Alto, Ca.: National Press Books, 1969.

Kimble, G. A. *Hilgard and Marquis' Classical Conditioning and Learning*, New York: Appleton, 1961.

Kimble, G. A. *Foundations of Conditioning and Learning*, New York: Appleton, 1967.

Kneller, G. F. (ed.) *Foundations of Education*, New York: Wiley, 1971.

Knitzer, J. "Parental involvement: the elixir of change." In D. N. McFadden (ed.) *Early Childhood Development Programs and Services: Planning for Action*, Washington, D.C.: National Association for the Education of Young Children, 1972.

Kohl, H. R. *On Teaching*, New York: Schocken, 1976.

Kohl, H. R. *Reading, How To*, New York: Bantam, 1973.

Lally, J. R., and Honig, A. S. "The family development research program." In M. C. Day and R. K. Parker (eds.) *The Preschool in Action*, Boston: Allyn and Bacon, 1977.

Lamb, M. E. *The Role of the Father in Child Development*, New York: Wiley, 1976.

Lane, M. B. *Education for Parenting*, Washington, D.C.: National Association for the Education of Young Children, 1975.

Langenbach, M., and Neskora, T. W. *Day Care: Curriculum Considerations*, Columbus, Oh.: Charles E. Merrill, 1977.

Lansing, K. M. "The research of Jean Piaget and its implication for art education in elementary schools." *Studies in Art Education*, 1966, 7.

Lazar, I., Hubbell, V. R., Murray, H., Rosche, M., and Royce, J. *Summary: the Persistence of Preschool Effects*, Washington, D.C.: DHEW Publication No. (OHD) 78-30129, 1977.

Lenneberg, E. H. *Biological Foundations of Language*, New York: Wiley, 1967.

Levenstein, P. "The mother-child home project." In M. C. Day and R. K. Parker (eds.) *The Preschool in Action*, Boston: Allyn and Bacon, 1977.

Levine, J. A. *Who Will Raise the Children? New Options for Fathers (and Mothers)*, New York: J. B. Lippincott, 1976.

Lieberman, J. N. "Playfulness and divergent thinking: an investigation of their relationship at the kindergarten level." *Journal of Genetic Psychology*, 1965, 107, 219–224.

Lieberman, J. N. *Playfulness: An Attempt to Conceptualize a Quality of Play and the Player*, New York: Private publication from Brooklyn College of CUNY and presented in part at Eastern Psychological Association, April 1966.

Logan, F. A. *Fundamentals of Learning and Motivation*, Dubuque, Ia.: Wm. C. Brown, 1970.

Lovell, K. *The Growth of Basic Mathematical and Scientific Concepts in Children*, London: University of London Press, 1961.

Lundin, R. W. *Personality: A Behavioral Analysis*, New York: Macmillan, 1974.

Maccoby, E. E., and Jacklin, C. N. *The Psychology of Sex Differences*, Stanford, Ca.: Stanford U.P., 1974.

Maier, N. R. F. *Frustrations: the Study of Behavior Without a Goal*, New York: McGraw-Hill, 1949.

Maier, S. F. "Failure to escape traumatic electric shock: incompatible skeletal-motor responses or learned helplessness?" *Learning and Motivation*, 1970, 1, 157–169.

Maslow, A. H. *Motivation and Personality*, New York: Harper and Row, 1970.

McDonald, D. T., and Ramsey, J. H. "Awakening the artist: music for young children." *Young Children*, 1978, 33, 26–32.

McDonald, M. "Transitional tunes and musical development." *The Psychoanalytic Study of the Child*, 1970, 25, 503–520.

McNeil, D. *The Acquisition of Language: the Study of Developmental Psycholinguistics*, New York: Harper and Row, 1970.

Mead, M. *Sex and Temperament in Three Primitive Societies*, New York: Dell, 1969.

Merton, R. K. *Social Theory and Social Structure*, Glencoe, Ill.: Free Press, 1957.

Michel, P. "The optimum development of musical abilities in the first years of life." *Psychology of Music 1*, 1973, 2, 14–20.

Miller, G. A. *Language and Communication*, New York: McGraw-Hill, 1951.

Miller, W., and Ervin, S. "The development of grammar in child language." In U. Bellugi and R. Brown (eds.) *The Acquisition of Language*, Monograph of the Society for Research in Child Development, 1964, 29, 9–34.

Montessori, M. *Dr. Montessori's Own Handbook*, Cambridge, Ma.: Robert Bentley, Inc., 1914.

Montessori, M. *The Child*, Adyar Madias 20, India: The Theosophical Publishing House, 1961.

Montessori, M. *The Discovery of the Child*, Adyar Madias 20, India: Kalakshetra Publications, 1962.

Montessori, M. *The Montessori Method*, New York: Schocken, 1965.

Montessori, M. *The Child in the Family*, (trans. N. R. Cirillo.) Chicago: Henry Regnery Company, 1970.

Mowbray, J. K., and Salisbury, H. H. *Diagnosing Individual Needs for Early Childhood Education*, Columbus, Oh.: Charles E. Merrill, 1975.

Mowrer, O. H., and Lamoreaux, R. R. "Fear as an intervening variable in avoidance conditioning." *Journal of Comparative Psychology*, 1946, 39, 29–50.

Mussen, P. H., Conger, J. J., and Kagan, J. *Child Development and Personality*, New York: Harper and Row, 1974.

Neill, A. S. *Summerhill: a Radical Approach to Child Rearing*, New York: Hart, 1960.

Neumann, E. A. *The Elements of Play*, Urbana, Ill.: unpublished doctoral dissertation, University of Illinois, 1971.

Nichols, J. *Men's Liberation*, New York: Penguin, 1975.

Nimnicht, G. P., Arango, M., and Adcock, D. "The parent/child toy library program." In M. C. Day and R. K. Parker (eds.) *The Preschool in Action,* Boston: Allyn and Bacon, 1977.

Nimnicht, G. P., Arango, M., and Cheever, J. "The responsive educational program." In M. C. Day and R. K. Parker (eds.) *The Preschool in Action,* Boston: Allyn and Bacon, 1977.

Ostwald, P. F. "Musical behavior in early childhood." *Developmental Medicine and Child Neurology,* 1973, 15, 367–375.

Papalia, D. E., and Olds, S. W. *A Child's World: Infancy Through Adolescence,* New York: McGraw-Hill, 1975.

Pavlov, I. P. *Conditioned Reflexes,* (tran. G. V. Anrep.) London: Oxford U.P., 1927.

Piaget, J. *Le Développement de la Notion de Temps Chez l'Enfant,* Paris: Presses Universitaires de France, 1946 (*a*).

Piaget, J. *Les Notions de Mouvement et de Vitesse Chez l'Enfant,* Paris: Presses Universitaires de France, 1946 (*b*).

Piaget J. *The Origins of Intelligence in Children,* (trans. M. Cook.) New York: International U.P., 1952.

Piaget, J. *The Construction of Reality in the Child,* (trans. M. Cook.) New York: Basic Books, 1954.

Piaget, J. *The Language and Thought of the Child,* New York: World Publishing, 1955.

Piaget, J. *Play, Dreams and Imitations in Childhood,* (trans. G. Gattegno and F. M. Hodgson.) New York: Norton, 1962.

Piaget, J. *The Child's Conception of Number,* New York: Norton, 1965.

Piaget, J., and Inhelder, B. *The Psychology of the Child,* (trans. H. Weaver.) New York: Basic Books, 1969.

Premack, A. J., and Premack, D. "Teaching language to an ape." In R. C. Atkinson (ed.) *Psychology in Progress,* San Francisco: W. H. Freeman, 1975.

Prescott, E. "Is day care as good as a good home?" *Young Children,* 1978, 33, 13–19.

Rachlin, H. *Introduction to Modern Behaviorism,* San Francisco: W. H. Freeman, 1976.

Rekers, G. A., and Lovaas, O. I. "Behavioral treatment of deviant sex-role behaviors in a male child." *Journal of Applied Behavior Analysis,* 1974, 7, 173–190.

Responding to Individual Needs in Head Start: a Head Start Series on Needs Assessment, Washington, D.C.: DHEW, Office of Human Development, Office of Child Development, Bureau of Child Development Services, DHEW Publication No. (OHD), 75-1075, 1974.

Roche, R. L. *The Child and Science: Wondering, Exploring, Growing,* Washington, D.C.: Association for Childhood Education International, 1977.

Rogers, C. R. *On Becoming a Person,* Boston: Houghton Mifflin, 1961.

Rubin, K. "Play behaviors of young children." *Young Children,* 1977, 32, 16–24.

Schaefer, E. S., and Aaronson, M. "Infant education research project: implementation and implications of home tutoring program." In M. C. Day and R. K. Parker (eds.) *The Preschool in Action,* Boston: Allyn and Bacon, 1977.

Schickedanz, J. A. "Please read that story again!" *Young Children,* 1978, 33, 48–55.

Schwarz, J. C., and Wynn, R. "The effect of mother's presence and previsits on children's emotional reaction to starting nursery school." *Child Development,* 1971, 42, 871–881.

Seligman, M. E. P. "Reversing depression and learned helplessness." In P. G. Zimbardo and F. L. Ruch (eds.) *Psychology and Life,* Glenview, Ill.: Scott, Foresman, 1977.

Sexism in Education, Minneapolis: The Emma Willard Task Force on Education. Box #14229, Minneapolis, Mi. 55414, 1971.

Shulder, D. "Does the law oppress women?" In R. Morgan (ed.) *Sisterhood is Powerful,* New York: Vintage, 1970.

Shuter, R. *The Psychology of Musical Ability,* London: Methuen, 1968.

Siqueland, E. R., and Lipsitt, L. P. "Conditioned head-turning in newborns." *Journal of Experimental Child Psychology,* 1966, 3, 356–376.

Skinner, B. F. *Verbal Behavior,* New York: Appleton-Century-Crofts, 1957.

Smilanksy, S. *The Effects of Sociodramatic Play on Disadvantaged Preschool Children,* New York: Wiley, 1968.

Smith, F. "Making sense of reading—and of reading instruction." *Harvard Educational Review,* 1977, 47, 386–395.

Smith, R. B. *Music in the Child's Education,* New York: Ronald Press, 1970.

Solomon, R. L. "Punishment." *American Psychologist,* 1964, 19, 239–253.

Spelt, D. K. "The conditioning of the human fetus." *Journal of Experimental Psychology,* 1948, 38, 338–346.

Stone, J. G., and Janis, M. G. *Daily Program I for a Child Development Center: an Overview,* Washington, D.C.: DHEW, Office of Human Development, Office of Child Development, Bureau of Child Development Services, Project Head Start, Publication No. (OHD) 73-1016, 1974.

Strassman, H. D., Thaler, M. B., and Schein, E. H. "A prisoner of war syndrome: apathy as a reaction to severe stress." *American Journal of Psychiatry,* 1956, 112, 998–1003.

Strouse, J. (ed.) *Women and Analysis,* New York: Dell, 1974.

Tough, J. *Talking, Thinking, Growing,* New York: Schocken, 1974.

Trey, J. E. "Women in the war economy—World War II." *The Review of Radical Economics 4,* June 1972.

Ulich, R. *History of Educational Thought,* New York: American Book Company, 1968.

Von Frisch, K. "Decoding the language of the bee." *Science,* 1974, 185, 663–668.

Warner, D., and Quill, J. *Beautiful Junk,* Washington, D.C.: DHEW, Office of Human Development, Office of Child Development, Project Head Start, Publication No. (OHD) 76-31036, 1977.

Wasserman, S. "Key vocabulary: impact on beginning reading." *Young Children,* 1978, 33, 33–38.

Watson, J. B., and Rayner, R. "Conditioned emotional reactions." *Journal of Experimental Psychology*, 1920, 3, 1–14.

Webster's New Collegiate Dictionary, Springfield, Ma.: G. and C. Merriam, 1951.

Weikart, D. P. *Preschool Intervention: A Preliminary Report of the Perry Preschool Project*, Ann Arbor, Mi.: Campus Publishers, 1967.

Weikart, D. P., Rogers, L., Adcock, C., and McClelland, D. *The Cognitively Oriented Curriculum*, Washington, D.C.: ERIC-NAEYC, 1971.

White, B. L., and Watts, J. C. *Experience and Environment. Vol. 1*, Englewood Cliffs, N.J.: Prentice-Hall, 1973.

White House Conference on Children. *Report to the President*, Washington, D.C.: U.S. Government Printing Office, 1970.

Whorf, B. L. *Language, Thought, and Reality*, New York: Wiley, 1956.

Williams, C. D. "The elimination of tantrum behavior by extinction procedures." *Journal of Abnormal and Social Psychology*, 1959, 59, 269.

Williams, J. L. *Operant Learning: Procedures for Changing Behavior*, Monterey, Ca.: Brooks/Cole, 1973.

Wolpe, J. *Psychotherapy by Reciprocal Inhibition*, Stanford, Ca.: Stanford U.P., 1958.

Yerkes, R. M., and Morgulis, S. "The method of Pavlov in animal psychology." *Psychological Bulletin*, 1909, 6, 257–273.

Zigler, E. F. "America's Head Start program: an agenda for its second decade." *Young Children*, 1978, 33, 4–11.

Index